Minorities in Global History

Global History: European Perspectives and Approaches

In Association with the European Network in Universal and Global History (ENIUGH)

Series editors: Matthias Middell (Leipzig University) and Katja Castryck-Naumann (Centre for the Study of University of Leipzig, Germany)

Global history has become an increasingly common and successful way to study history over the last three decades. As this method increases in use, more attention has been paid to the historiography, theory and skills associated with doing global history. To date, research in global history is primarily visible when coming from the Anglo-American world. This series seeks to contribute also the many other European perspectives in order to highlight the diversity of global histories and its historiography.

Published in association with the European Network in Universal and Global History, this series provides an overview of current trends in global history research from across the European continent. Taking a non-Eurocentric approach and anchored in the variety of area and transregional studies, it publishes research on developments in and outside of Europe along with innovative historiographical studies critiquing the value and uses of global history and histories of globalization. Exploring 'globalization-critical movements' it will question who is doing what kind of globalization, and with what interests and goals? In doing so it seeks to demonstrate that there are many types of globalization being done in different ways. Contributing to the critical reflection of Eurocentrism in global history, it positions Europe within global processes, and critically assesses European approaches to extra-European developments.

Founded in 2002, The European Network in Universal and Global History brings together more than 600 European global historians and organizes a major conference every three years. With a steering committee of around twenty elected representatives from various European countries, it represents the best research in Europe on Global History.

Minorities in Global History

*Cultures of Integration and
Patterns of Exclusion*

Edited by
Holger Weiss

BLOOMSBURY ACADEMIC
LONDON • NEW YORK • OXFORD • NEW DELHI • SYDNEY

BLOOMSBURY ACADEMIC

Bloomsbury Publishing Plc, 50 Bedford Square, London, WC1B 3DP, UK
Bloomsbury Publishing Inc, 1359 Broadway, New York, NY 10018, USA
Bloomsbury Publishing Ireland, 29 Earlsfort Terrace, Dublin 2, D02 AY28, Ireland

BLOOMSBURY, BLOOMSBURY ACADEMIC and the Diana logo are trademarks of
Bloomsbury Publishing Plc

First published in Great Britain 2024
This paperback edition published in 2025

Copyright © Holger Weiss, 2024

Holger Weiss has asserted his right under the Copyright, Designs and Patents Act,
1988, to be identified as Editor of this work.

For legal purposes the Acknowledgments on p. 167 constitute an extension
of this copyright page.

Cover image © Gypsies camp in suburban area, Vaulx-en-Velin, France.
Serge Mouraret/Alamy Stock Photo

All rights reserved. No part of this publication may be: i) reproduced or transmitted in any form, electronic or mechanical, including photocopying, recording or by means of any information storage or retrieval system without prior permission in writing from the publishers; or ii) used or reproduced in any way for the training, development or operation of artificial intelligence (AI) technologies, including generative AI technologies. The rights holders expressly reserve this publication from the text and data mining exception as per Article 4(3) of the Digital Single Market Directive (EU) 2019/790.

Bloomsbury Publishing Plc does not have any control over, or responsibility for, any third-party websites referred to or in this book. All internet addresses given in this book were correct at the time of going to press. The author and publisher regret any inconvenience caused if addresses have changed or sites have ceased to exist, but can accept no responsibility for any such changes.

A catalogue record for this book is available from the British Library.

A catalog record for this book is available from the Library of Congress.

ISBN: HB: 978-1-3503-8221-3
PB: 978-1-3503-8224-4
ePDF: 978-1-3503-8222-0
eBook: 978-1-3503-8223-7

Typeset by Newgen KnowledgeWorks Pvt. Ltd., Chennai, India

For product safety related questions contact productsafety@bloomsbury.com.

To find out more about our authors and books visit www.bloomsbury.com
and sign up for our newsletters.

Contents

List of Illustrations   vii

1   Cultures of Integration and Patterns of Exclusion: An Introduction   1
Holger Weiss

Part I   Concepts and Contexts in Processes of Minoritization

2   The Majority as Other: The Township Courts of Imperial Russia   19
Jane Burbank

3   Chinese Citizenship and Land Rights in the Sino-Korean Borderland   37
Kwangmin Kim

4   The National Question in Finnish Communism: Leninist-Stalinist-Kuusinenist Theory and the Finland-Swedish Minority in the Interwar Period   51
Jonas Ahlskog and Mats Wickström

5   The Chagossian Diaspora: Deportation, Exile, and Resistance   67
Mohammad Shameem Chitbahal

Part II   Strategies and Activities of Minority Communities and Indigenous Peoples

6   Imperial In-Betweens: The Portuguese Communities in Hong Kong and Shanghai during the Second World War   85
Helena F. S. Lopes

7   Countering Economic Marginalization: Africanization Strategies in Tanzania's and Ghana's Insurance Markets during Decolonization   105
Eva Kocher and Francis Daudi

8   Copper, Colonialism, and Local Conflicts: The Expansion of Early Modern Global Industrial Economy in Northern Torne River Valley, and Its Local Repercussions   123
Jonas Monié Nordin

9   Kazakhstani Poles and Germans as Second-Class Citizens:
    "Underground" Catholicism in Soviet Kazakhstan   141
    Jerzy Rohoziński

10 A Forest Sámi Reindeer Herder's Diary during the Covid-19 Pandemic,
    Swedish Side of Sábme   153
    May-Britt Öhman and Henrik Andersson

Part III   Minority Rights and Their Politization

11 Staying in Contact: The Role of Minorities in Diplomatic Contacts
    between Western Europe and Southeast Asia after Decolonization   173
    Andreas Weiß

12 Universal Basic Income as a Tool against Minority Marginalization   187
    David P. Schweikard and Craig Willis

13 "A Woman without a Country"—Marriage, Derivative Citizenship, and
    the Consequences of Conflicting Nationality Laws in the Interwar Period   205
    Laura Frey

14 Defending the Rights of Women as "Mothers, Workers, and Citizens."
    WIDF's Practices of Cooperating with Female Activists in Latin America
    (1960s–70s)   221
    Yulia Gradskova

Part IV   Representations of Minorities in National History Curriculums

15 Reversal of Exclusion? Education and National Narratives amid
    Changing Majority/Minority Power Dynamics in Rwanda and Burundi   239
    Denise Bentrovato

List of Contributors   259
Index   265

Illustrations

Figures
2.1 Painting titled *At the Township Court*, showing whips   25
2.2 Township judges at Bun'kovo, Bogorodskii County,
    Moscow Province, 1906   30
6.1 Group photograph of the Portuguese Benevolent Association
    (*Associação de Beneficência de Shanghai*) Committee   89
10.1 Female reindeer right before calving   163

Tables
2.1 Categories of Misdemeanors Described in the *Statutes on Punishments
    Applicable by the Justices of the Peace* and Usable in the Township Courts   27
3.1 Jilin Provincial Authority's Bylaw (1910–11) and Korean Land Rights
    in Yanbian and Hunchun   44
3.2 Japanese Actions and the Restrictions of Korean Land Rights, 1915–27   45

1

Cultures of Integration and Patterns of Exclusion: An Introduction

Holger Weiss

The Sixth European Congress on Global History convened online in Åbo (Turku), Finland, in June 2021. Convening under the theme "Minorities, Cultures of Integration and Patterns of Exclusion," the aim of the Congress was to address the exposure to and challenges of historical and contemporary mechanisms and policies of minoritization, marginalization, and exclusion in its relation to past and present cultures of integration from a global perspective. Initially, the organizers proposed the theme as it reflected one of the core activities—minority research—of the host university. Already using the name Åbo instead of Turku articulates this perspective—Åbo is the Swedish name of Turku, and the host university Åbo Akademi University is the Swedish university in Finland. According to universities act of 2009, Åbo Akademi University is to serve the needs for higher education of the Swedish-speaking minority in Finland, currently about 5 percent of the population who mainly live in the southern and western coastal areas and on the Åland Islands.

However, the congress theme intended to challenge the participants for opening up and addressing patterns of inclusion and exclusion from a global historical perspective. Minorities exist of different types, some are visible with established rights, such as the Swedish-speaking population in Finland, and others—in light of Black Lives Matters and multiple other past and present movements addressing the rights of gender, sex, age, religious, ethnic minorities, and Indigenous people—are still invisible. They are not seen in mainstream (call it dominant, hegemonic, or majority) articulations of the past, present, and future, and are still fighting for their rights and their history to be addressed and respected. An attempt to put their voice on the table was made a few years ago in Finland when the association "Historians without Borders—Finland" (HWB-F) published its assessment, titled "Whose History? A Report on the State and Challenges of Historical Research, Teaching and Dialogue in Finland."[1] The report scrutinized and critically addressed the absence of the voices of old and new minorities in Finland other than the Swedish-speaking one (such as the Sámi, Romani, Tatars, and Jews alongside the Vietnamese, Somali, Estonian, Arabic, Kurdish, or Russian) in Finnish schoolbooks and university syllabuses. The question we then raised—and that our congress will do, too—was how to integrate their voices, experiences of exclusion, and feelings of invisibility. Our discussion sparked a critical dissemination and research by Finnish historians of the colonization of Sápmi—the land of the Sámi people—by the Finnish state,[2] encounters between majority and minority populations such as Russian and Jewish peddlers in Finland,[3] and of the Finnish involvement in colonization projects all over the world.[4]

The Finnish case illuminates the relationship between majority and minority populations, especially in the analysis of historical and contemporary conditions and processes of being and making a minority. Following the independence of Finland in 1917, the Finnish Parliament granted the Swedish-speaking population the position as a national linguistic minority and made Swedish as the second national language. However, before 1809, when Finland became part of the Russian Empire as a Grand Duchy, Swedish was the official language of the Kingdom of Sweden and the Finnish and Sami populations constituted the minority populations within the kingdom but the majority ones in the eastern and northern parts of the kingdom. Religious minorities, such as Roman Catholics or Jews, were outlawed in the Evangelical Lutheran kingdom until the late eighteenth century and remained so in Finland until the Russian period when Jewish and Tatar alongside Catholic and Russian Orthodox population settled in the Grand Duchy. After 1809, the Swedish-speaking population in Finland became a minority in the Grand Duchy but the Swedish-speaking aristocracy and burghers remained in their dominant political and cultural positions. This situation slowly changed during, as part of the national awakening, the latter part of the nineteenth century when Finnish gradually became the official language of the state, largely as an outcome of political and educational reforms that were initiated through the Diet of Finland and supported by the Russian imperial authorities. For the Sámi population, the only Indigenous population in Europe, the situation did not change. As late as 1995, the status of the Sámi was written into the constitution of Finland; since 1996, they have had constitutional self-government in the Sámi homelands in the spheres of language and culture.

The core issue not only in Finland but all over the world, as minority researchers underscore, is the role of the political entity and its position toward minority groups, be it a premodern empire or a modern nation-state, alongside various processes of territorialization and minoritization. The focus is on processes of marginalization and the creation of minority communities,[5] on attitudes toward languages and cultures of minority groups and Indigenous peoples,[6] and the exclusion of groups through processes of minoritization that render them marginal such as women, ethnic and religious minorities, migrants, or people in lower economic classes.[7] Others include politics of assimilation as a form of state-enforced "otherization" and marginalization of minority groups and Indigenous people.[8] These questions translate for global historians into scrutinizing the various concepts defining and describing minorities and minority positions as well as practices and narratives of inclusion, belonging, and protection or exclusion, discrimination, and segregation with a focus on transnational and transregional constellations as well as comparative perspectives.[9] At best, minority groups are tolerated, though most of them have been victims of subordination and marginalization.[10] Sociologist Louis Wirth already in 1945 remarked that discrimination marked a minority group, "... because of their physical or cultural characteristics are singled out from the others in society in which they live for differential and unequal treatment, and who therefore regard themselves as objects of collective discrimination."[11]

Critical reflections on stateless, poor, and marginalized nations' experiences of colonial and postcolonial atrocities alongside state and government policies to dominate them made George Manuel to describe them as the Fourth World.[12] In 1975, the World Council of Indigenous People adapted the term as the generalizing term for Indigenous people.[13] Since then, the concept as well as the so-called Fourth World Theory are used to designate both the poorest and most underdeveloped states of the world and to describe any oppressed or underprivileged victim of a state.[14] Some authors use it as a generic term to embrace "subpopulations existing in a First World country, but with the living standards of those in a third world, or developing country,"[15] or "the poorest of the poor."[16] Others, in turn, define the "Fourth World" as a generalization for thousands of self-identifying nations, regions, and even city-states with territorial aspirations.[17]

Moreover, a fundamental challenge for historical and contemporary research on minorities is how to define a minority. Historically and globally, religious communities and ethnic/ethnolinguistic minorities were the core targets of local dominant groups and territorial regimes.[18] The first attempt to define what constitutes a national minority was made in the draft version of the Supplement of European Convention on Human Rights in 1950 (European Convention for the Protection of Human Rights and Fundamental Freedoms, 1953). Subsequent documents embrace a wide spectrum as vulnerable groups, including children, teenagers, elderly, ethnic, religious, and linguistic minorities, Indigenous peoples, irregular migrants, persons with disabilities, LGBT persons, stateless persons, travelers, and women. Reflecting the genocidal atrocities and state-led violence against subordinate groups during the twentieth century, the 1992 UN Declaration on the Rights of Persons Belonging to National or Ethnic, Religious and Linguistic Minorities alongside the Permanent Court of International Justice combines territory and identity-markers (race, religion, language, cultural traditions) in its definition of a minority community. Such a narrow definition of a minority group, however, excludes age and gender groups, persons with disabilities, irregular migrants, and stateless persons as well as Indigenous peoples. Consequently, the Indigenous people, who earlier had been treated as a subcategory of minorities, were covered by the Indigenous and Tribal Peoples Convention of the ILO (1989) and the UN Declaration on the Rights of Indigenous Peoples (2007) whereas the rights of persons with disabilities are addressed by a UN convention adopted in 2006. However, the rights of LGBT people (the Yogyakarta Principles of 2006, supplemented in 2017) initially were launched as a global charter at the United Human Rights Council in Geneva in 2007 but were rejected by the UN General Assembly.[19]

The fourteen contributions in this volume, most of them being rewritten texts originally presented at the 2021 ENIUGH Congress,[20] further deepen our understanding of past and present processes of minoritization and experiences of minority and subordinated groups. Grouped into four thematic parts, the present volume opens up for global historians to address the unequal relationship between dominant and subordinated groups. Taken together, the various case studies are an answer to Angelika Epple's theoretical and methodological reflections on global history as relational history with a special focus on the temporal "relationing" and "making of" entities: "Entities come into existence through relations but both are in constant flux. However, relations are not abstract and 'out there' but are made by actors. Thus, global historians should bridge the gap between the micro-level of individual actors and the macro-level of global structures."[21]

The first part of the volume discusses concepts and contexts in processes of minoritization. Jane Burbank's chapter focuses on the making of the peasants as the "other" in the Russian Empire through the formulation of their distinctive legal treatment after 1861. Her case study is a distinct example of how the conceptualization of "otherness" is formulated by a dominant and hegemonic minority group and expressed and enacted in law. Kwangmin Kim's chapter analyzes how Chinese imperial authorities developed the concept of territorially based rule in response to (unauthorized) Korean settlers in the Sino-Korean borderlands in the late nineteenth and early twentieth centuries. Mats Wickström and Jonas Ahlskog address in their chapter the challenges of Finnish communists to come to terms with the Leninist-Stalinist concept of nationality and national self-determination and its application to the Finland-Swedish minority in the interwar period. Mohammad Shameem Chitbahal, in turn, highlights the fate of the Chagossians, the inhabitants of the Chagos Archipelago in the Indian Ocean, as an uprooted exile community in Mauritius after their deportation from Diego Garcia when the island was transformed into a US air base in the 1970s.

The second part focuses on strategies and activities of minority communities and Indigenous people under colonial and postcolonial conditions. This topic has a long historiography in anthropology, ethnography, and sociology, as well as imperial/colonial, business, economic, and social history, among others focusing on the experiences of entrepreneurial/trading minorities in Europe, the Middle East, Africa, Asia, and the Pacific.[22] Other studies have highlighted the complex relationship between comprador intermediaries, commercial brokers, local elites, and colonial authorities (who themselves could be defined as a minority or dominant/hegemonic subgroup in their respective colonial territory).[23] Helena F. S. Lopes's chapter sheds light on the transimperial encounters and global entanglements of the Portuguese communities in Hong Kong and Shanghai during the Second World War. The chapter by Eva Kocher and Francis Daudi, in turn, illuminates the strategies of African American entrepreneurs in West Africa on developing local financial markets in Ghana and contrasts them with state-led initiatives of Africanizing the insurance market in Tanzania.

For many minority communities and Indigenous peoples, however, modern processes of territorialization, not least in combination with their stigmatization, disempowerment, and exclusion,[24] in the modern nation-state emerged as a "lethal polity," although, as Mark Levene notes, "empires were racist, hierarchical and often practiced retributive genocide when challenged ... but were not inherently genocidal."[25] Various studies on the consequences of premodern/modern colonization projects, be it in the Americas, Asia, Australia, or Europe, have underscored their negative if not devastating effects on minority communities and Indigenous peoples.[26] Jonas Monié Nordin's chapter adds to the discussion by presenting a case study on early modern metal extraction in northern Fennoscandia and the conflicts it generated between private enterprises and the local Sámi population in the upper parts of the Torne River Valley. Jerzy Rohoziński, in turn, focuses on the deported Catholic underground minority in Soviet Kazakhstan and their struggle for legalization and official registration during the 1970s. May-Britt Öhman's and Henrik Andersson's chapter brings the discussion to the contemporary era as their case study sheds light on the experiences of a Sámi reindeer farmer in northern Sweden during the Covid-19 pandemic.

The third part addresses the emergence and articulation of minority rights and their politicization. The weakness of national and, from the nineteenth century, international protection of minority rights is, among others, highlighted by Javaid Rehman. The Final Act of the Congress of Vienna in 1814/15 included clauses for the protection of national as well as religious minorities. The final act of the Congress of Paris in 1856, in turn, included clauses on the status of Jews and Christians in the Ottoman Empire, and the final act of the Congress of Berlin in 1878 had clauses on the status of Jews in Romania, Serbia, and Bulgaria. However, these clauses did not protect the Jewish population in the Russian Empire and neither was there an international outcry against the Jim Crow Laws and discrimination of the Black population in the United States. Although US president Woodrow Wilson's ideals of self-determination contained clauses on minority rights, the final version in the Covenant of the League of Nations did not articulate his ideas. Instead, the League of Nations upheld a patchwork for the protection of minorities, including Minority Treaties with five Eastern European states between 1919 and 1920, special chapters on minorities in the Peace Treaties of 1919–23, as well as some subsequent treaties and unilateral declarations by various states in the early 1920s. However, many regions of the world remained under the shadow of legalized/legitimized racial oppression, and the League of Nations' rudimentary minority protection collapsed in the wake of the Second World War, the Holocaust, the European postwar refugee crisis, and exodus of minorities after the partition of India in 1947. On the other hand, the devastating consequences of state-led mass violence and genocidal policies against minorities paved the way for a new international order for protecting minorities, spearheaded by the United Nations, and the adoption in 1948 of both the Declaration on Human Rights and the Convention on the Prevention and Punishment of the Crime of Genocide.[27]

Minority and human rights have since then become integrated in the agenda of international organizations. Andreas Weiß's chapter highlights how the European Communities (ECs) and its associated European institutions that aimed to protect minorities extended its protection to groups in Southeast Asia, notably in Indonesian-occupied West Papua and East Timor, during the Cold War Era. In the post–Cold War Era, the Framework Convention for the Protection of National Minorities (FCNM), passed by the Council of Europe in 1995 and active since 1998, notes that "the upheavals in European history have shown that the protection of national minorities is essential to stability, democratic security and peace in this continent." The FCNM highlights that "a pluralist and genuinely democratic society should … respect the ethnic, cultural, linguistic and religious identity of each person belonging to a national minority." Finally, it stresses the necessity to create a climate of tolerance and dialogue "to enable cultural diversity to be a source and a factor, not of division, but of enrichment for each society."[28] Targeted national policies among EU member states address patterns of exclusion and marginalization but, as Craig Willis and David Schweikard note in this volume, have a limited effect and are often accompanied by an increase in stigmatization and the creation of welfare traps. As a potential remedy, Willis and Schweikard evaluate the potential of a Universal Basic Income as a tool to break recurring marginalization and exclusion in the EU.

Parallel to the emergence of minority rights was the fight for women's rights during the twentieth century. In some cases, minority and women's rights overlapped, as Laura Frey's case study on the experience of marital denaturalization by German and British women and the international campaign for equal nationality rights of married women, resulting in the 1957 UN Convention on the Nationality of Married Women. Yulia Gradskova's chapter highlights another aspect on the interlinkages between the fight for women's, human, and minority rights in countries outside Europe during the Cold War; her study scrutinizes the international mobilization through and transnational networks by the Women's International Democratic Federation.

The fourth and final part focuses on the representation of minorities in national history curriculums.[29] Several researchers have highlighted the need to embrace an inclusive and multiperspective history education as to counteract intolerance, racism, homophobia, and xenophobia and to promote dialogue, diversity, and multicultural education.[30] However, most school textbooks in European countries are silent on minorities,[31] although one could argue this to reflect the situation of any history curricula that used the framework of the nation-state and reflects the ideas and notions of the dominant and/or hegemonic group.[32] The Finnish history curriculum, for example, Tanja Kohvakka notes, builds on the idea of a homogenous Finnish nation and often lacks adequate representation of old and new minorities in Finland.[33] Similarly, Andrew Mansfield underscores the need to diversify the history subject curriculum in English secondary schools by including the multiple viewpoints of various ethnic minorities when teaching the history of the British Empire. In his mind, global history serves as a potential perspective to counteract the hitherto hegemonic White Anglocentric perspective.[34] Some national history curricula make room for minorities, though. In Egypt, for example, although the Christian (Coptic) minority figures in school textbooks, the Copts are largely portrayed as a persecuted and victimized group of people,[35] whereas Turkish school textbooks preserve an ethno-religious national identity.[36] This situation therefore poses a positive challenge for (global) historians, as there is a need for inclusive national history curricula. Of equal importance is the need for revision of the history curricula in postconflict settings, as Rosalie Metro underlines in her observation on interethnic reconciliation among Burmese migrants and refugees in Thailand.[37] Denise Bentrovato's chapter in this volume on competing memory politics and opposing historical truths around collective victimhood in postcolonial Rwanda and Burundi makes a similar plea. Her investigation draws attention to dissident discourses on intergroup history and social identities and the problematic mechanisms for their construction, preservation, and transmission especially in the history curriculum as part of concurrent government-sponsored reconciliation and nation-building projects.

Ultimately, the various case studies in the four parts open up for a theoretical and methodological discussion about the potentials and challenges of studying the history and experience of minorities from a global historical perspective. Among the forerunners in this field is Philip D. Curtin's *Cross-Cultural Trade in World History* that focused on trading relationships and ethnolinguistic diaspora (minority) or intermediary groups,[38] while Subaltern Studies opened up for a critical debate on the relationship between dominant and subordinated groups.[39] Since then, historical research on minorities has branched out into a myriad of subthemes, often in combination of, inspired by, or conducted within the fields of Minority Studies, Genocide Studies, Human Rights Studies, Migration Studies, Black/African American Studies, Indigenous Studies, and, not least, Women and Gender Studies as well as Postcolonial and Critical Race Studies. Researchers have scrutinized the challenges that processes of territorialization, modernization, and homogenization within both empires and nation-states have posed on cultural, linguistic, and religious minorities and Indigenous peoples ranging from the early premodern to the late modern/present era, in the Global North as well as in the Global South.[40] Research on the history of minorities has unearthed experiences and policies of not only discrimination, stigmatization, marginalization, and segregation alongside forced assimilation, racism, persecution, ethnic cleansing, resettlement, and physical, cultural, and ecological extermination but also protection, dialogue, and tolerance.[41] Homogeneity has proven to be an illusion,[42] whereas the categorization and classification of languages and populations was an integral part of minoritization of inhabitants in empires as well as nation-states.[43] State-enforced minority politics have generally had a negative, at best a tolerating, at worst a devastating, effect on minorities although, as Roy Bar Sardeh and Lotte Houwink ten Cate suggest, minority politics provided a framework for intellectuals in colonized Asia and Africa to question European powers' treatment of marginalized communities and became a rubric for sociopolitical emancipation.[44]

Notes

1. Emma Sofia Hakala, Hakola Iina, and Jenni Laakso, eds., "Whose History? A Report on the State and Challenge of Diverse Historical Research, Teaching and Dialogue in Finland," *HWB Report 4* (Helsinki: Historians without Borders in Finland, 2019), accessed November 6, 2023, https://historianswithoutborders.fi/wp-content/uploads/2019/01/Whose-History_final.pdf.
2. Rinna Kullaa, Janne Lahti, and Sami Lakomäki, eds., *Kolonialismi Suomen rajaseuduilla* (Helsinki: Gaudeamus, 2022).
3. Jutta Ahlbeck, Ann-Catrin Östman, and Eija Stark, eds., *Encounters and Practices of Petty Trade in Northern Europe, 1820–1960: Forgotten Livelihoods* (Cham: Palgrave Macmillan, 2022).
4. Raita Merivirta, Leila Koivunen, and Timo Särkkä, eds., *Finnish Colonial Encounters: From Anti-Imperialism to Cultural Colonialism and Complicity* (Cham: Palgrave Macmillan, 2021).
5. See, for example, Bridget Anderson, Sara Araújo, Laura Brito, Mehmet Ertan, Jing Hiah, Trudie Knijn, Isabella Meier, Julia Morris, and Maddalena Vivona, "Reference

Document on the Histories of Minoritisation in Austria, Hungary, Netherlands, Portugal, Turkey and the United Kingdom" (Ethos Working Paper, July 2018), accessed November 6, 2023, https://ethos-europe.eu/sites/default/files/5.2_minoritisation_histories_29-07-18.pdf; Heather Sharkey and Aline Schlaepfer, "Roundtable: Minoritization and Pluralism in the Modern Middle East," *International Journal of Middle East Studies* 50, no. 4 (2018): 757–85.

6. Isabelle Léglise and Sophie Alby, "Minorization and the Process of (de)Minoritization: The Case of Kali'na in French Guiana," *International Journal of the Sociology of Language*, no. 182 (2006): 67–85; Myat The-Thitsar, "Empowering or Endangering Minorities? Facebook, Language, and Identity in Myanmar," *Asian Ethnicity* 23, no. 4 (2022): 718–40.

7. Afsoun Afsahi, "Towards a Principle of Most-Deeply Affected," *Philosophy & Social Criticism* 48, no. 1 (2022): 40–61.

8. For example, Markus Dressler, "Historical Trajectories and Ambivalences of Turkish Minority Discourse," *New Diversities* 17, no. 1 (2015): 9–26; Krista A. Goff, *Nested Nationalism: Making and Unmaking Nations in the Soviet Caucasus* (Ithaca: Cornell University Press, 2020); Jonas Monié Nordin, Lotta Fernstål, and Charlotte Hyltén-Cavallius, "Living on the Margin: An Archaeology of a Swedish Roma Camp," *World Archaeology* 53, no. 3 (2021): 517–30.

9. See, for example, Carl H. Nightingale, *Segregation: A Global History of Divided Cities* (Chicago: University of Chicago Press, 2012).

10. See, for example, Sadia Saeed, *Politics of Desecularization: Law and the Minority Question in Pakistan* (Cambridge: Cambridge University Press, 2017); Ilyse R. Morgenstein Fuerst, "Minoritization, Racialization, and Islam in Asia," in *Routledge Handbook on Islam in Asia*, ed. Chiara Formichi (London: Routledge, 2021).

11. Louis Wirth, "The Problem of Minority Groups," in *The Science of Man in the World Crisis*, ed. Ralph Lindon (New York: Columbia University Press, 1945), 347.

12. George Manuel and Michael Posluns, *The Fourth World: An Indian Reality* (Minneapolis: University of Minnesota Press, [1974] 2018).

13. Chadwick Allen, "Blood as Narrative/Narrative as Blood: Declaring a Fourth World," *Narrative* 6, no. 3 (1998): 236–55.

14. Yvonne P. Sherwood, "Toward, with, and from a Fourth World," *The Fourth World Journal* 14, no. 2 (2016): 15–27.

15. Catherine Merri, "An Introduction to the Fourth World: Does 'Working Class' Mean the Same Thing for All Races?," *Medium* (blog), 2020, accessed November 6, 2023, https://medium.com/@merricatherine/an-introduction-to-the-fourth-world-1b054b680bb9; Annsilla Nyar, "Understanding the Place of Women Workers in the 'Fourth World,'" *Agenda* 21, no. 72 (2007): 111–22.

16. Quentin Wodon, ed., *Attacking Extreme Poverty: Learning from the Experience of the International Movement ATD Fourth World* (Washington, DC: The World Bank, 2001).

17. Richard Griggs and Peter R. Hocknell, "The Geography and Geopolitics of Europe's Fourth World," *IBRU Boundary and Security Bulletin* 3, no. 4 (1996): 59–67.

18. Huda Seif, "The Accursed Minority: The Ethno-Cultural Persecution of Al-Akhdam in the Republic of Yemen: A Documentary & Advocacy Project," *Muslim World Journal of Human Rights* 2, no. 1 (2005): 1–39; Rok Stergar and Tamara Scheer, "Ethnic Boxes: The Unintended Consequences of Habsburg Bureaucratic Classification," *Nationalities Papers* 46, no. 4 (2018): 575–91. For a broad, inclusive perspective on minorities in a national context, see, for example, Greg Fealy

and Ronit Ricci, eds., *Contentious Belonging: The Place of Minorities in Indonesia* (Singapore: ISEAS Publishing, 2019).
19. Further, see Ugo Caruso and Rainer Hofmann, eds., *The United Nations Declaration on Minorities: An Academic Account on the Occasion of Its 20th Anniversary (1992–2012* (Leiden: Brill Nijhoff, 2015).
20. The chapters by Nordin, Wickström and Ahlskog, as well as Öhman and Andersson include case studies from the Nordic countries, which were included on the editor's request.
21. Angelika Epple, "Calling for a Practice Turn in Global History: Practices as Drivers of Globalization/s," *History and Theory* 57, no. 3 (2018): 390–407.
22. Christine Dobbin, *Asian Entrepreneurial Minorities: Conjoint Communities in the Making of the World Economy, 1570–1940* (London: Routledge, 1996). Further, see the outline by Robin Cohen, "Diasporas, the Nation-State, and Globalisation," in *Global History And Migrations*, ed. Gungwu Wang (New York: Routledge, 1997); I. P. X. Malki, "Between Middlemen and Interlopers: History, Diaspora, and Writing on the Lebanese of West Africa," *Diaspora: A Journal of Transnational Studies* 20, no. 1 (2011): 87–116; Vernon D. Johnson, "Coloured South Africans: A Middleman Minority of Another Kind," *Social Identities* 23, no. 1 (2017): 4–28.
23. Colin Newbury, *Patrons, Clients, and Empire: Chieftaincy and Over-Rule in Asia, Africa, and the Pacific* (Oxford: Oxford University Press, 2003); Jason Oliver Chang, "Four Centuries of Imperial Succession in the Comprador Pacific," *Pacific Historical Review* 86, no. 2 (2017): 193–227.
24. Walter P. Zenner, "Middleman Minorities and Genocide," in *Genocide and the Modern Age: Etiology and Case Studies of Mass Death*, ed. Isidor Wallimann and Michael N. Dobkowski (Syracuse, NY: Syracuse University Press, 2000), 253–81. Further, see Irena Grosfeld, Seyhun Orcan Sakalli, and Ekaterina Zhuravskaya, "Middleman Minorities and Ethnic Violence: Anti-Jewish Pogroms in the Russian Empire," *Review of Economic Studies* 87, no. 1 (2020): 289–342.
25. Mark Levene, *Genocide in the Age of the Nation State, Vol. 2: The Rise of the West and the Coming of Genocide* (London: I.B. Tauris, 2005). Further, see Christian Gerlach, *Extremely Violent Societies: Mass Violence in the Twentieth-Century World* (Cambridge: Cambridge University Press, 2010).
26. Gunlög Fur, *Colonialism in the Margins: Cultural Encounters in New Sweden and Lapland* (Leiden: Brill, 2006).
27. Javaid Rehman, *The Weaknesses in the International Protection of Minority Rights* (The Hague: Kluwer Law International, 2000).
28. National Minorities (FCNM), "Framework Convention for the Protection of National Minorities," accessed March 30, 2023, https://www.coe.int/en/web/minorities.
29. Interestingly, there exists no global assessment on representations of minorities in school textbooks as compared to representations of the Holocaust; see Peter Carrier, Eckhardt Fuchs, and Torben Messinger, *The International Status of Education about the Holocaust: A Global Mapping of Textbooks and Curricula* (Paris: United Nations Educational, Scientific and Cultural Organization 2015).
30. Among others, Gita Steiner-Khamsi, "Minority-Inclusive History Curricula in Secondary Schools: Adopting Methods of Comparison and Multiperspectivity," *European Journal of Intercultural Studies* 7, no. 1 (1996): 29–43; Kevin Lowe and Tyson Yunkaporta, "The Inclusion of Aboriginal and Torres Strait Islander Content in the Australian National Curriculum: A Cultural, Cognitive and Socio-Political Evaluation," *Curriculum Perspectives Journal* 33, no. 1 (2013): 1–14; Brad M. Maguth

and Nathan Taylor, "Bringing LGBTQ Topics into the Social Studies Classroom," *The Social Studies* 105, no. 1 (2014): 23–8.
31. See, for example, Linn Normand, "From Blind Spot to Hotspot: Representations of the 'Immigrant Others' in Norwegian Curriculum/Schoolbooks (1905–2013)," *Journal of Curriculum Studies* 53, no. 1 (2021): 124–41.
32. Sirkka Ahonen, "Politics of Identity through History Curriculum: Narratives of the Past for Social Exclusion—or Inclusion?," *Journal of Curriculum Studies* 33, no. 2 (2001): 179–94; D. Kim Reid and Michelle G. Knight, "Disability Justifies Exclusion of Minority Students: A Critical History Grounded in Disability Studies," *Educational Researcher* 35, no. 6 (2006): 18–23. For the situation in multiethnic counties such as Canada and China, see Bing Wang, "A Comparison of the Portrayal of Visible Minorities in Textbooks in Canada and China," *Comparative and International Education* 35, no. 2 (2006): 76–94; Fei Yan and Edward Vickers, "Portraying 'Minorities' in Chinese History Textbooks of the 1990s and 2000s: The Advance and Retreat of Ethnocultural Inclusivity," *Asia Pacific Journal of Education* 39, no. 2 (2019): 190–208.
33. Tanja Kohvakka, "The Representation of Minorities in the Finnish National Core Curriculum for History," *Multicultural Education Review* 14, no. 2 (2022): 85–100.
34. Andrew Mansfield, "Increasing Inclusion for Ethnic Minority Students by Teaching the British Empire and Global History in the English History Curriculum," *Oxford Review of Education* (2022): 1–16, https://doi.org/10.1080/03054985.2022.2087618.
35. Ehaab D. Abdou, "Copts in Egyptian History Textbooks: Towards an Integrated Framework for Analyzing Minority Representations," *Journal of Curriculum Studies* 50, no. 4 (2018): 476–507.
36. Kenan Çayır, "Citizenship, Nationality and Minorities in Turkey's Textbooks: From Politics of Non-Recognition to 'Difference Multiculturalism,'" *Comparative Education* 51, no. 4 (2015): 519–36.
37. Rosalie Metro, "Postconflict History Curriculum Revision as an 'Intergroup Encounter' Promoting Interethnic Reconciliation among Burmese Migrants and Refugees in Thailand," *Comparative Education Review* 57, no. 1 (2013): 145–68.
38. Philip D. Curtin, *Cross-Cultural Trade in World History*, Studies in Comparative World History Series (Cambridge: Cambridge University Press, 1984). See also Walter P. Zenner, *Minorities in the Middle: A Cross-Cultural Analysis* (Albany: State University of New York Press, 1991).
39. For critical reflections, see Patricia Nelson Limerick, "Has 'Minority' History Transformed the Historical Discourse?," *Perspectives on History*, American Historical Association, November 1997, accessed November 6, 2023, https://www.historians.org/research-and-publications/perspectives-on-history/november-1997/has-minority-history-transformed-the-historical-discourse, and Dipesh Chakrabarty, "Minority Histories, Subaltern Pasts," *Perspectives on History*, American Historical Association, November 1997, accessed November 6, 2023, https://www.historians.org/research-and-publications/perspectives-on-history/november-1997/minority-histories-subaltern-pasts.
40. See, for example, the contributions of the research group The Myth of Homogeneity, "The Myth of Homogeneity: Minority Protection and Assimilation in Western Europe, 1919–1939," accessed March 30, 2023, https://themythofhomogeneity.org/. For global perspectives, see Ken S. Coates, *A Global History of Indigenous Peoples* (London: Palgrave Macmillan UK, 2004), https://doi.org/10.1057/9780230509078; Sophie Croisy, ed., *Globalization and "Minority" Cultures: The Role of "Minor"*

Cultural Groups in Shaping Our Global Future (Leiden: Brill, 2015). For non-Western experiences, for example, see Laura Robson, ed., *Minorities and the Modern Arab World: New Perspectives* (Syracuse, NY: Syracuse University Press, 2016); Farahnaz Ispahani, *Purifying the Land of the Pure: A History of Pakistan's Religious Minorities* (Oxford: Oxford University Press, 2017).

41. See, for example, Panikos Panayi, *Minorities in Wartime: National and Racial Groupings in Europe, North America and Australia during the Two World Wars* (London: Bloomsbury, 2016); Matthew Frank, *Making Minorities History: Population Transfer in Twentieth-Century Europe* (Oxford: Oxford University Press, 2017); Philipp Ther, *The Outsiders: Refugees in Europe since 1492* (Princeton, NJ: Princeton University Press, 2019).
42. Michael Weiner, ed., *Japan's Minorities: The Illusion of Homogeneity*, 2nd ed. (Abingdon, Oxon: Routledge, 2009).
43. See, for example, Fuat Dundar, "Empire of Taxonomy: Ethnic and Religious Identities in the Ottoman Surveys and Censuses," *Middle Eastern Studies* 51, no. 1 (2015): 136–58.
44. Roy Bar Sadeh and Lotte Houwink ten Cate, "Toward a Global Intellectual History of 'Minority,'" *Comparative Studies of South Asia, Africa and the Middle East* 41, no. 3 (2021): 319–24.

Bibliography

Abdou, Ehaab D. "Copts in Egyptian History Textbooks: Towards an Integrated Framework for Analyzing Minority Representations." *Journal of Curriculum Studies* 50, no. 4 (2018): 476–507.

Afsahi, Afsoun. "Towards a Principle of Most-Deeply Affected." *Philosophy & Social Criticism* 48, no. 1 (2022): 40–61.

Ahlbeck, Jutta, Ann-Catrin Östman, and Eija Stark, eds. *Encounters and Practices of Petty Trade in Northern Europe, 1820–1960: Forgotten Livelihoods*. Cham: Palgrave Macmillan, 2022.

Ahonen, Sirkka. "Politics of Identity through History Curriculum: Narratives of the Past for Social Exclusion—or Inclusion?" *Journal of Curriculum Studies* 33, no. 2 (2001): 179–94.

Allen, Chadwick. "Blood as Narrative/Narrative as Blood: Declaring a Fourth World." *Narrative* 6, no. 3 (1998): 236–55.

Anderson, Bridget, Sara Araújo, Laura Brito, Mehmet Ertan, Jing Hiah, Trudie Knijn, Isabella Meier, Julia Morris, and Maddalena Vivona. "Reference Document on the Histories of Minoritisation in Austria, Hungary, Netherlands, Portugal, Turkey and the United Kingdom." Ethos Working Paper, July 2018. Accessed November 6, 2023. https://ethos-europe.eu/sites/default/files/5.2_minoritisation_histories_29-07-18.pdf.

Bar Sadeh, Roy, and Lotte Houwink ten Cate. "Toward a Global Intellectual History of 'Minority.'" *Comparative Studies of South Asia, Africa and the Middle East* 41, no. 3 (2021): 319–24.

Carrier, Peter, Eckhardt Fuchs, and Torben Messinger. *The International Status of Education about the Holocaust: A Global Mapping of Textbooks and Curricula*. Paris: United Nations Educational, Scientific and Cultural Organization (UNESCO), 2015.

Caruso, Ugo, and Rainer Hofmann, eds. *The United Nations Declaration on Minorities: An Academic Account on the Occasion of Its 20th Anniversary (1992–2012)*. Leiden: Brill Nijhoff, 2015.

Çayır, Kenan. "Citizenship, Nationality and Minorities in Turkey's Textbooks: From Politics of Non-Recognition to 'Difference Multiculturalism.'" *Comparative Education* 51, no. 4 (2015): 519–36.

Chakrabarty, Dipesh. "Minority Histories, Subaltern Pasts." Accessed November 6, 2023. *Perspectives on History*, American Historical Association, November 1997. https://www.historians.org/research-and-publications/perspectives-on-history/november-1997/minority-histories-subaltern-pasts.

Chang, Jason Oliver. "Four Centuries of Imperial Succession in the Comprador Pacific." *Pacific Historical Review* 86, no. 2 (2017): 193–227.

Coates, Ken S. *A Global History of Indigenous Peoples*. London: Palgrave Macmillan UK, 2004. https://doi.org/10.1057/9780230509078.

Cohen, Robin. "Diasporas, the Nation-State, and Globalisation." In *Global History and Migrations*, edited by Gungwu Wang. New York: Routledge, 1997.

Croisy, Sophie, ed. *Globalization and "Minority" Cultures: The Role of "Minor" Cultural Groups in Shaping Our Global Future*. Leiden: Brill, 2015.

Curtin, Philip D. *Cross-Cultural Trade in World History*. Studies in Comparative World History Series. Cambridge: Cambridge University Press, 1984.

Dobbin, Christine. *Asian Entrepreneurial Minorities: Conjoint Communities in the Making of the World Economy, 1570–1940*. London: Routledge, 1996.

Dressler, Markus. "Historical Trajectories and Ambivalences of Turkish Minority Discourse." *New Diversities* 17, no. 1 (2015): 9–26.

Dundar, Fuat. "Empire of Taxonomy: Ethnic and Religious Identities in the Ottoman Surveys and Censuses." *Middle Eastern Studies* 51, no. 1 (2015): 136–58.

Epple, Angelika. "Calling for a Practice Turn in Global History: Practices as Drivers of Globalization/s." *History and Theory* 57, no. 3 (2018): 390–407.

Fealy, Greg, and Ronit Ricci, eds. *Contentious Belonging: The Place of Minorities in Indonesia*. Singapore: ISEAS Publishing, 2019.

Frank, Matthew. *Making Minorities History: Population Transfer in Twentieth-Century Europe*. Oxford: Oxford University Press, 2017.

Fur, Gunlög. *Colonialism in the Margins: Cultural Encounters in New Sweden and Lapland*. Leiden: Brill, 2006.

Gerlach, Christian. *Extremely Violent Societies: Mass Violence in the Twentieth-Century World*. Cambridge: Cambridge University Press, 2010.

Goff, Krista A. *Nested Nationalism: Making and Unmaking Nations in the Soviet Caucasus*. Ithaca: Cornell University Press, 2020.

Griggs, Richard, and Peter R. Hocknell. "The Geography and Geopolitics of Europe's Fourth World." *IBRU Boundary and Security Bulletin* 3, no. 4 (1996): 59–67.

Grosfeld, Irena, Seyhun Orcan Sakalli, and Ekaterina Zhuravskaya. "Middleman Minorities and Ethnic Violence: Anti-Jewish Pogroms in the Russian Empire." *Review of Economic Studies* 87, no. 1 (2020): 289–342.

Hakala, Emma Sofia, Hakola Iina, and Jenni Laakso, eds. "Whose History? A Report on the State and Challenge of Diverse Historical Research, Teaching and Dialogue in Finland." Accessed November 6, 2023. *HWB Report 4*. Helsinki: Historians without Borders in Finland, 2019. https://historianswithoutborders.fi/wp-content/uploads/2019/01/Whose-History_final.pdf.

Ispahani, Farahnaz. *Purifying the Land of the Pure: A History of Pakistan's Religious Minorities*. Oxford: Oxford University Press, 2017.

Johnson, Vernon D. "Coloured South Africans: A Middleman Minority of Another Kind." *Social Identities* 23, no. 1 (2017): 4–28.

Kohvakka, Tanja. "The Representation of Minorities in the Finnish National Core Curriculum for History." *Multicultural Education Review* 14, no. 2 (2022): 85–100.

Kullaa, Rinna, Janne Lahti, and Sami Lakomäki, eds. *Kolonialismi Suomen rajaseuduilla*. Helsinki: Gaudeamus, 2022.

Léglise, Isabelle, and Sophie Alby. "Minorization and the Process of (de)Minoritization: The Case of Kali'na in French Guiana." *International Journal of the Sociology of Language*, no. 182 (2006): 67–85.

Levene, Mark. *Genocide in the Age of the Nation State, Vol. 2: The Rise of the West and the Coming of Genocide*. London: I.B. Tauris, 2005.

Limerick, Patricia Nelson. "Has 'Minority' History Transformed the Historical Discourse?" Accessed November 6, 2023. *Perspectives on History*, American Historical Association, November 1997. https://www.historians.org/research-and-publications/perspectives-on-history/november-1997/has-minority-history-transformed-the-historical-discourse.

Lowe, Kevin, and Tyson Yunkaporta. "The Inclusion of Aboriginal and Torres Strait Islander Content in the Australian National Curriculum: A Cultural, Cognitive and Socio-Political Evaluation." *Curriculum Perspectives Journal* 33, no. 1 (2013): 1–14.

Maguth, Brad M., and Nathan Taylor. "Bringing LGBTQ Topics into the Social Studies Classroom." *The Social Studies* 105, no. 1 (2014): 23–28.

Malki, I. P. X. "Between Middlemen and Interlopers: History, Diaspora, and Writing on the Lebanese of West Africa." *Diaspora: A Journal of Transnational Studies* 20, no. 1 (2011): 87–116.

Mansfield, Andrew. "Increasing Inclusion for Ethnic Minority Students by Teaching the British Empire and Global History in the English History Curriculum." *Oxford Review of Education*, 2022, 1–16. https://doi.org/10.1080/03054985.2022.2087618.

Manuel, George, and Michael Posluns. *The Fourth World: An Indian Reality*. Minneapolis: University of Minnesota Press, 1974.

Merivirta, Raita, Leila Koivunen, and Timo Särkkä, eds. *Finnish Colonial Encounters: From Anti-Imperialism to Cultural Colonialism and Complicity*. Cham: Palgrave Macmillan, 2021.

Merri, Catherine. "An Introduction to the Fourth World: Does 'Working Class' Mean the Same Thing for All Races?" Accessed November 6, 2023. *Medium* (blog), 2020. https://medium.com/@merricatherine/an-introduction-to-the-fourth-world-1b054b680bb9.

Metro, Rosalie. "Postconflict History Curriculum Revision as an 'Intergroup Encounter' Promoting Interethnic Reconciliation among Burmese Migrants and Refugees in Thailand." *Comparative Education Review* 57, no. 1 (2013): 145–68.

Morgenstein Fuerst, Ilyse R. "Minoritization, Racialization, and Islam in Asia." In *Routledge Handbook on Islam in Asia*, edited by Chiara Formichi. London: Routledge, 2021.

National Minorities (FCNM). "Framework Convention for the Protection of National Minorities." Accessed March 30, 2023. https://www.coe.int/en/web/minorities.

Newbury, Colin. *Patrons, Clients, and Empire: Chieftaincy and Over-Rule in Asia, Africa, and the Pacific*. Oxford: Oxford University Press, 2003.

Nightingale, Carl H. *Segregation: A Global History of Divided Cities*. Chicago: University of Chicago Press, 2012.

Nordin, Jonas Monié, Lotta Fernstål, and Charlotte Hyltén-Cavallius. "Living on the Margin: An Archaeology of a Swedish Roma Camp." *World Archaeology* 53, no. 3 (2021): 517–30.

Normand, Linn. "From Blind Spot to Hotspot: Representations of the 'Immigrant Others' in Norwegian Curriculum/Schoolbooks (1905–2013)." *Journal of Curriculum Studies* 53, no. 1 (2021): 124–41.

Nyar, Annsilla. "Understanding the Place of Women Workers in the 'Fourth World.'" *Agenda* 21, no. 72 (2007): 111–22.

Panayi, Panikos. *Minorities in Wartime: National and Racial Groupings in Europe, North America and Australia during the Two World Wars.* London: Bloomsbury, 2016.

Rehman, Javaid. *The Weaknesses in the International Protection of Minority Rights.* The Hague/Boston: Kluwer Law International, 2000.

Reid, D. Kim, and Michelle G. Knight. "Disability Justifies Exclusion of Minority Students: A Critical History Grounded in Disability Studies." *Educational Researcher* 35, no. 6 (2006): 18–23.

Robson, Laura, ed. *Minorities and the Modern Arab World: New Perspectives.* Syracuse, NY: Syracuse University Press, 2016.

Saeed, Sadia. *Politics of Desecularization: Law and the Minority Question in Pakistan.* Cambridge: Cambridge University Press, 2017.

Seif, Huda. "The Accursed Minority: The Ethno-Cultural Persecution of Al-Akhdam in the Republic of Yemen: A Documentary & Advocacy Project." *Muslim World Journal of Human Rights* 2, no. 1 (2005): 1–39.

Sharkey, Heather, and Aline Schlaepfer. "Roundtable: Minoritization and Pluralism in the Modern Middle East." *International Journal of Middle East Studies* 50, no. 4 (2018): 757–85.

Sherwood, Yvonne P. "Toward, with, and from a Fourth World." *The Fourth World Journal* 14, no. 2 (2016): 15–27.

Steiner-Khamsi, Gita. "Minority-Inclusive History Curricula in Secondary Schools: Adopting Methods of Comparison and Multiperspectivity." *European Journal of Intercultural Studies* 7, no. 1 (1996): 29–43.

Stergar, Rok, and Tamara Scheer. "Ethnic Boxes: The Unintended Consequences of Habsburg Bureaucratic Classification." *Nationalities Papers* 46, no. 4 (2018): 575–91.

The Myth of Homogeneity. "The Myth of Homogeneity: Minority Protection and Assimilation in Western Europe, 1919–1939." Accessed March 30, 2023. https://themythofhomogeneity.org/.

Ther, Philipp. *The Outsiders: Refugees in Europe since 1492.* Princeton, NJ: Princeton University Press, 2019.

The-Thitsar, Myat. "Empowering or Endangering Minorities? Facebook, Language, and Identity in Myanmar." *Asian Ethnicity* 23, no. 4 (2022): 718–40.

Wang, Bing. "A Comparison of the Portrayal of Visible Minorities in Textbooks in Canada and China." *Comparative and International Education* 35, no. 2 (2006): 76–94.

Weiner, Michael, ed. *Japan's Minorities: The Illusion of Homogeneity*, 2nd ed. Abingdon, Oxon: Routledge, 2009.

Wirth, Louis. "The Problem of Minority Groups." In *The Science of Man in the World Crisis*, edited by Ralph Lindon, 347–72. New York: Columbia University Press, 1945.

Wodon, Quentin, ed. *Attacking Extreme Poverty: Learning from the Experience of the International Movement ATD Fourth World.* Washington, DC: The World Bank, 2001.

Yan, Fei, and Edward Vickers. "Portraying 'Minorities' in Chinese History Textbooks of the 1990s and 2000s: The Advance and Retreat of Ethnocultural Inclusivity." *Asia Pacific Journal of Education* 39, no. 2 (2019): 190–208.

Zenner, Walter P. "Middleman Minorities and Genocide." In *Genocide and the Modern Age: Etiology and Case Studies of Mass Death*, edited by Isidor Wallimann and Michael N. Dobkowski, 253–81. Syracuse, NY: Syracuse University Press, 2000.

Zenner, Walter P. *Minorities in the Middle: A Cross-Cultural Analysis*. Albany: State University of New York Press, 1991.

Part I

Concepts and Contexts in Processes of Minoritization

2

The Majority as Other: The Township Courts of Imperial Russia

Jane Burbank

Introduction

The establishment of the township court in 1861 created a separate judicial instance to be used by Russia's enormous peasant population. Subsequently most minor judicial matters involving peasants—misdemeanors and small property disputes—were decided in local courts by peasant judges. At these instances, decisions on property matters were not bound by the regulations of the empire's civil code; in criminal cases, judges were instructed to apply an array and degree of punitive sanctions that differed from those in the criminal code. After 1861 the judicial regime for peasants was reformed and adjusted more than once, but the township court with its distinctive practices remained in place until the collapse of the empire in 1917.

Viewed quantitatively, peasants were the majority—the vast majority—of the empire's population. Russia's elites were mostly of noble status and a tiny minority in the empire. Nonetheless, judicial authorities conceived of peasants as "others," who required distinctive legal treatment. The maintenance of a separate legal jurisdiction and distinctive regulations for peasants for over fifty years calls into question a neat alignment of majority/minority with inclusion/exclusion in the Russian Empire. This article explores the attitudes of Russian reformers and legal experts about the place of peasants in the empire's legal system. I look first at the goals expressed in the 1860s in connection with the abolition of serfdom and at the structural elements of the imperial legal system that impacted these conceptions. I then turn to the regulations established for the township courts and their peasant litigants, rules different from those of the reformed circuit courts accessible by all subjects. The issue of peasants' aberrant legal condition remained alive for legal reformers for decades, as the imperial regime attempted its own transformations of the township courts. My goal is to reveal the conceptualizations of likeness and difference both enacted in Russian imperial law and envisioned by critics of autocracy. I argue that Russia's reformers were more concerned to replace the state's overseers of peasant legal institutions with the expertise of legal professionals than with the inclusion of peasants—the vast majority of the population—as equal members of a political commons.

Emancipation Does Not Mean Equality

The determination of many, but not all, high-status officials and lay elites (jurists, ministers, deputized nobles, and others) to put an end to serfdom, combined with support from the highest levels of the autocracy, led to the emancipation of 1861.[1] Emperor Alexander II's Manifesto of February 19, 1861, concerned peasants "attached" to a landlord to whom they owed labor and other obligations. People of this dependent status constituted approximately half of the peasants in the empire at the time. The term that described their condition translates literally as "the right of attachment." Serfdom was expressed as this "right" and referred to the landlord's right to have such dependents.[2] Most of the other peasants in the empire were registered as "state peasants"; they were subject to taxation and labor obligations to various official institutions, including the imperial family. The decree of 1861 was aimed at extracting the dependent peasants from their landlords' control.

The first statute of the law of February 19, 1861, abolished "the right of attachment" over peasants inhabiting landlords' estates or working in landlords' households, "forever."[3] This statute was part of the emperor's introduction to a new "General Regulation on Peasants, Emerging from Enserfed Dependence." The rights of the emancipated peasants were to be defined by both this General Regulation and other legal codes; these compilations of laws addressed the rights, property arrangements, administrative and judicial institutions, and taxes and duties of the former serfs.[4]

A major goal of the reform, in the descriptions of Russian commentators, was equality, specifically, the "equality of Russian citizens before the law."[5] The end of serfdom signified a commitment to inclusionary justice: the "attached" peasants, released from obligations, both financial and legal, to their landlords, would join other subjects in their access to the judicial system, itself under revision during the restructuring that followed Russia's defeat in the Crimean War. Russian elites were acutely aware of their empire's image in international circles, including the opprobrium attached to Russian serfdom.[6] The predominant view from abroad was that serfdom was the equivalent of slavery, despite vast differences between the conditions of slaves in most areas of the world from those of Russian peasants. (Notable among such disparities were differences in residence, land usage, and personal autonomy. In Russia "attached" peasants mostly lived in their own villages and cultivated lands collectively; they were not subject to sale by their landlords.)[7] International critics of Russian serfdom also disregarded of Russia's 1805 commitment to the suppression of slavery and the slave trade and the subsequent efforts of the empire to stop the trade in the Black Sea.[8]

The commitment of Russian reformers to the abolition of serfdom cannot be doubted; their eloquence and actions were in large part responsible for the enactment in 1861 of this revolutionary change in Russian law and social relations. But were these advisors and advocates able to imagine a society of equals, one in which the people known as peasants would be the majority and they, educated professionals, mostly of "noble" status, if not origin, would be a minority? The vocabulary of majority/minority was not available to these reformers, but they surely were aware of their own small number in the empire. What does the history of the legislation on the peasants, and in particular on their courts, tell us about the possibilities for and constraints upon inclusionary, universally applicable law in the Russian Empire? And more generally, about elite conceptions of social body of their polity?

To begin to respond to these questions, we should note that Russia's reformers had to work within a particular legal system, an imperial regime that excelled at dealing with unlike populations. The Russian polity from its beginnings was multiethnic, as the rulers of Muscovy extended their power over dispersed settlements and nomadic peoples. Mongol overlords and other Eurasian contacts left their imprint on Russian administration and law. A defining quality of Russia's imperial way of rule was incorporation without assimilation of multiple ethnic, social, and religious groups, each allowed to pursue, under disciplined supervision, a variety of legal and confessional practices.[9] There was no single superior citizenship, as in Roman descent empires. Instead, the law was designed to address a variety of imperial subjects, each with differentiated rights.

This imperial situation did not foster the concept of a national "majority" nor the idea of "minorities."[10] Russians themselves were one of many peoples of the empire. They could distinguish themselves from other peoples of the empire, labeled inconsistently as *inorodtsy* (people of other origin).[11] But Russians did not enjoy uniform rights as an ethnic group. As for other subjects, their rights were defined by a variety of intersecting conditions—estate status, religion, work, location, and so on. What mattered for most legal situations was estate status, *soslovie*, and it was this category, rigidified in the eighteenth century, that defined the differentiated rights of the nobility, townspeople, clerics, and peasants.[12]

The structure of the Russian law—its incorporation of different regulations and rights for the vast array of populations, religions, territories of the empire—enabled flexible adjustments to specific and changing social circumstances.[13] Codification of the empire's laws in the nineteenth century preceded the emancipation decree by over two decades, but the enormous effort at coordinating centuries of accumulated rules had not produced a body of law that applied equally to all.[14] The Russian legal system enabled officials to address problems as they arose, through a well-developed system of proposal, discussion, editing, and revision, all of it dependent, ultimately, on the emperor's accord.[15]

The reformers of the mid-nineteenth century were well aware of the intricacies of the system. They understood that the end of serfdom would have ramifications for multiple aspects of Russia's social life. As one engaged historian put it, looking back on the period:

> The significance of serfdom [*krepostnoe pravo*, the right to attach] in Russian life was generally recognized as *universal*; this right, or rather denial of right "conditioned all sides of everyday life [*byt*], from the biggest to the very smallest. It was a brake, decisively preventing the development of Russia." (emphasis in original)[16]

This entanglement of serfdom with every element of social life meant that undoing serfdom would have to be linked to multiple changes in the law and Russian society.

Reformers saw the 1861 Regulation as part of a series of reforms designed to transform Russia, to bring it into a "new era of development."[17] The means to do this, though, would of necessity be piecemeal. The very title of the 1861 compendium—"The General Regulation on Peasants, Emerging from Enserfed Dependence"—indicated that it was addressed to a portion of the population, not the whole.

The 1861 *Regulation* was thus not "general." It was an element in the collected and codified laws of the Russian Empire, but its provisions were not part of the civil or criminal codes. Procedures and rules for the local administration of the peasantry were issued under this set of rules. The *Regulation* was subsequently modified, as were other codes and laws, but retained its separate status. In early twentieth-century editions of the *Collected Laws of the Russian Empire*, the *Regulation* appeared under a revised title—"The General Regulation on Peasants"—as a component of "The Regulation on the Rural Estate," all eight books of which constituted a "Special Appendix to the Ninth Volume" of the codification.[18] That the majority of the empire's population remained governed by a "Special Appendix" for the final half century of Romanov Russia signals the resilience of the profoundly undemocratic structures of the state.

Defining Peasants and their Rights after 1861

The reformers of the 1860s, as noted earlier, were convinced that the emancipation would entail a total reform of the autocratic system. The reformers' goals were extensive—"to weaken bureaucratic omnipotence and arbitrariness, guarantee the right of the individual, to give space for society's self-activism, extend the freedom of speech and scientific research, ... [to change] the whole "old system ... of guardianship or orders [*opeka ili komanda*]."[19] This all-out assault on the existing order had consequences for the legal situation of Russian peasants after 1861. Reformers' acute resentment of whole system, and especially of the insulting power of police and minor bureaucrats, put issues other than the peasantry on their minds after 1861. A whole series of reforms—of the entire court system, the military, and local self-governance (the zemstvo)—took precedence over the condition of the peasantry. Thoroughgoing attention to the consequences of the emancipation rules was put off for decades.[20]

A few adjustments and additions to laws affecting peasants were made in the aftermath of the 1861 reform, with enormous consequences for the lives of a large part of the empire's population. These laws dealt with several categories of peasants who had not been serfs at the time of the emancipation—"*udel'nye*" peasants who lived on the imperial family's properties, "*gornozavodskie*" peasants who worked in mines or other industries, and the huge population of "state [*gosudarstvennye*]" peasants who lived on state lands. It was in the state's interest to make provisions for how these groups were to pay taxes, what lands they could be allotted, and what kinds of obligations they would owe in the post-emancipation order. The result, in the acidic description of A. A. Leont'ev, an expert on peasant tradition, was the enlargement of the category of peasants: the state peasants, formerly considered to be the model for the new laws made for the emancipated, were turned into people subject to regulations designed for ex-serfs.[21] The vastly expanded "peasant" portion of the empire, ex-serfs and all the rest, would henceforth be an overwhelming majority, accounting for 77 percent of the population in the 1897 census.[22]

Consistent with the tradition of differentiated law, the rules for how these different groups of unenserfed peasants were to pay for allocations of land and whether they, like the ex-serfs, would receive any land at all and for how much "repayment" were not identical. In what might be seen as a window on official attitudes toward a huge segment of the population, "state" peasants received land allocations inferior to those of emancipated serfs. The issue of whether these peasants were already the holders of the lands where they resided was solved by the State Council's decision of 1862:

> The state peasants do not have either the right of ownership, nor of possession over the lands allotted to them, but have only the right of usage, ... it was essential to clearly indicate in the law that the right of ownership of these lands belongs to the state.[23]

This decision, affirmed by the sovereign, expressed the underlying condition of the largest group of Russia's peasants: they lived on the state's lands and the state would determine the conditions of their usage of these lands.

Township Courts: Rules for the Majority Made by the Minority

I now turn to the township courts, an institution established in connection with the emancipation's deep inroads into the social and administrative organization of the polity. As we have seen, the targets for Russia's liberal reformers in the 1860s were the bureaucracy and the police. Convinced that local administrations and courts were corrupt and arbitrary, reformers insisted that the emancipation would have to entail their replacement. The initial chair of the Editing Commission responsible for the emancipation rules, Ia. I. Rostovtsev, commenting on proposals from the nobility for reforms, observed that all deputies were convinced that the local administrations and courts are in terrible shape, that their actions are "arbitrary, corrupt (*zloupotrebitel'nye*), hidden, and invisible," and that with these courts and "this police order" no secure reform could be accomplished.[24] A major concern of advocates for reform was not to enhance the powers of the despised officials and policemen. If the emancipation meant handing over the supervision of peasants' legal and other matters from landlords to officials, this would be disastrous. The active group of nobles from Tver Province commented:

> It would mean the division of all estates in the state into two *hostile camps* [emphasis in original]: the camp of the fully empowered *chinovniki* [officials] and the camp of the rightless and voiceless inhabitants.[25]

The deep hostility to rule by officials on the part of Russia's nobles was a major argument in favor of an "independent" court and local self-government.[26] This antipathy may have been a factor in the judicial provisions for the rural township courts established in 1861. Reformers who so desperately wanted to escape the state's guardianship (*opeka*) and orders (*komanda*) provided peasants with a rural court system that allowed them to do a great of jurisprudence on their own.

Since I have written at length about this court,[27] here I consider only some indicators of how elite law writers were thinking about peasants (the majority of the population) in their creation and revision of the rules for the township courts. Some kind of judicial institution had been seen by all as an essential part of the emancipation. Before 1861, some 25 million people were dependent on their landlords for "justice."[28] The famous court reform of 1864, however, left the system of a separate township-level court for the peasant estate in place. Peasants were subject to jury duty in the circuit courts and could use this new adversarial court system for some matters,[29] but misdemeanors and minor civil matters in peasant villages would be adjudicated at the township court with its distinctive procedures. The idea of one court for all, a foundation of the judicial reform of 1864 that established the circuit court system and a bar association, somehow ignored the fact that the "majority" of the population was entitled to use a special court set up for "peasants," or as they were later labeled, "the rural population."

Let us look at some of the differences between the judicial provisions for the township courts and those of the other, "ordinary," reformed courts where criminal activity was concerned. A striking example is corporal punishment. Most forms of corporal punishment were abolished by imperial law in 1863, but the "rod" was kept at the township court.[30] Dzhanshiev, writing about this salient example of treating the majority as an inferior population, interpreted the outcome of debates on physical punishment as the result "of bureaucratic indecisiveness, and in part of routine and chancery conflicts [*nedorazumenie*]."[31]

The issue of corporal punishment had been explicitly discussed during the preparation of the emancipation laws. Members of the Editing Commission were divided on whether to keep the lash or not, but the view of Count Pahlin, an outspoken advocate for corporal punishment, carried the day. In 1862, the issue was revisited, and corporal punishment was outlawed in army barracks, military courts, and criminal courts but not the township courts. Some feared that abolition of bodily punishment would send a signal to the peasants that since a change had been made in the emancipation rules, they could expect more revisions in their favor. In 1864, the question came up in connection with the reform of the courts. Once again, the rod was retained for township courts.[32]

The State Council's opinion on the question of the lash for peasants expressed recurring arguments about "peasant" values. Peasants, "who were accustomed since childhood to crude forms of address" did not take a beating seriously; a lashing not only "does not arouse, generally, especially among the guilty, fear." Instead, peasants prefer it to "deprivation of freedom [arrest], the payment of a fine, or being sent to do public work."[33]

Lashing remained an option at the township courts until 1904,[34] and continued to be associated with the plight of peasants at the township courts even after that date: see the illustration from a 1911 publication in Figure 2.1. It is difficult to imagine a more vivid example of distinction within a society than this: peasants could, by law, be

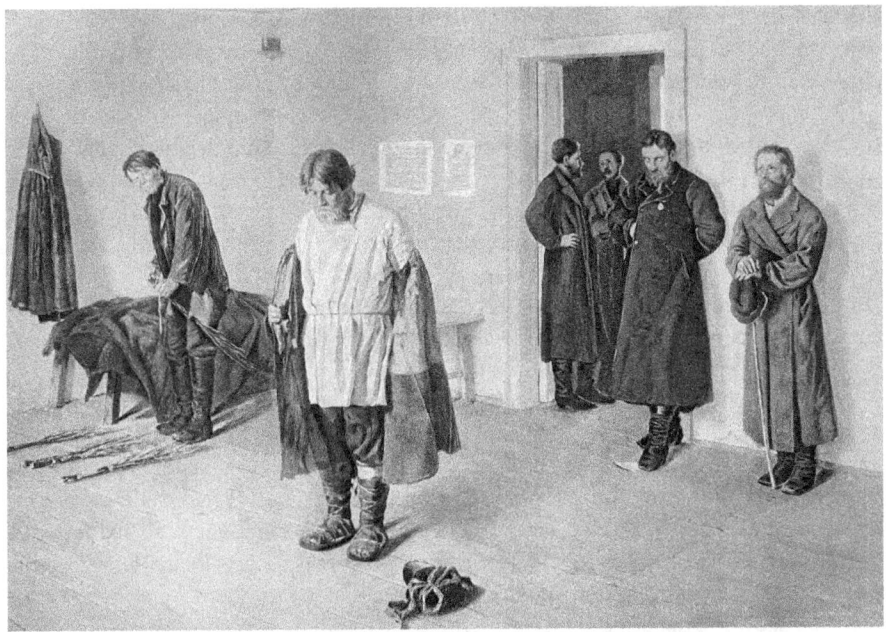

Figure 2.1 Painting titled *At the Township Court*, showing whips.

Source: A. K. Dzhivelegov, S. P. Mel'gunov, and V. I. Picheta eds., *Velikaia reforma*, vol. 6, 160–1. Moscow: Sytin, 1911.

sentenced to a beating, while others in the same society had been freed, gradually, and as usual by groups, from the degradation of legal bodily punishment.

The legal imagination of Russian elites can be scrutinized from another angle: the kinds of crimes that could be adjudicated at the rural courts. In 1859, an imperial commission was established to reform "our jurisprudence on small crimes and misdemeanors" in anticipation of the creation of a new criminal code. This endeavor involved high-ranking officials extracting "less important crimes" that could be adjudicated by a new institution, distinct from the policing apparatus of the Ministry of Internal Affairs. The outcome was the establishment in 1866 of a new institution—the Justices of the Peace. These courts were empowered to use a list of statutes and accompanying punishments.[35] The Justices of the Peace were eliminated in rural areas in 1889.[36] But in a move typical of Russia's piecemeal yet path-dependent way of making law, the township courts were empowered at that time to use a subset of the *Statutes on Punishments Applicable by the Justices of the Peace* to describe, decide, and punish misdemeanors for their peasant clientele.

The eighty-four statutes from the *Statutes on Punishments Applicable by the Justices of the Peace* that defined crimes punishable by township courts covered a multitude of activities. The statutes in the first chapter of this code addressed procedural issues; all remaining statutes were grouped according to the type of criminal activity to be punished. The chapter headings of the *Statutes on Punishments* allow us to enter the legal imaginary of officials through their definitions of minor crime. The largest component of statute law in the *Statutes on Punishments*—chapters three through ten—concerned the defense of public welfare; a second kind of misdemeanor was defined by statutes concerning individual dignity; a third category concerned violations of property rights; and one chapter addressed violations of family rights. In my study of township courts, I found that the rural courts considered all these kinds of cases, but did not use all the statutes available to them (see Table 2.1). What we can see from this survey is that peasant judges were empowered to work with only a subset of the misdemeanors thought by legislators to be punishable at an all-class court. Legal authorities thus made distinctions between actions that they agreed that peasants could adjudicate themselves and other minor crimes that they imagined to be out of the range of peasant litigators and judges.

Another telling distinction made by law writers as they constructed and revised peasant institutions was the regime of punishments that could be applied by rural legal authorities. Punishments at the township courts were established according to *The General Regulation on Peasants* rather than by the *Statutes on Punishments Applicable by the Justices of the Peace*. In place of the application of sanctions specified for each statutory misdemeanor in the *Statutes on Punishment Applicable by the Justices of the Peace*, township courts used a single set of punishments for all criminal cases. After the 1904 abolition of corporal punishment, township judges could sentence convicted people to a reprimand in the presence of the court, a fine ranging from 25 kopeks to 30 rubles, or arrest of up to fifteen days and in exceptional cases thirty days, under either simple or harsh circumstances. Harsh arrest meant being fed only bread and water.[37] The upper limits on terms of arrest and fines at township courts were generally much lower than those indicated in the *Statutes on Punishments*.

This softening of punishments could be explained in multiple ways. Did legislators not want peasant judges to be empowered to use harsh measures against other peasants? Were peasant violations not as important to society as those made by other people? Or do we see a paternalism at work, as elite law writers let peasant violators off more lightly than other people for violations against order and well-being in their villages?

The Local Court: A Second Chance?

In the decades after the "great reforms" of the 1860s, the township courts came under scrutiny and criticism, in large part from public figures who could not imagine peasant judges as competent to speak for the law.[38] In 1889, the imperial administration inaugurated a major change in the supervision of the township court and other peasant affairs: a new official, the *zemskii nachal'nik* (conventionally translated as land captain) was to oversee the functioning of the township courts, including the selection of judges and a regular review of the courts' decisions.[39] This "reform" outraged liberal critics of the autocracy. The land captain, who by law was to be of noble estate, represented precisely the two types of authority that liberal jurists detested most—the local landlord (potentially a former serf owner) and the bureaucrat.

Table 2.1 Categories of Misdemeanors Described in the *Statutes on Punishments Applicable by the Justices of the Peace* and Usable in the Township Courts

Type of violation	Chap. in UN	Statute nos.	No. of pages in UN	No. of statutes in UN	No. of statutes usable by TCs
Against Administrative Order	2	29–34	48	6	4
Against Decorum, Order, and Peace	3	35–51	40	17	12
Against Public Improvement	4	52–57	19	6	4
Of the Regulation on Passports	5	58–64	8	7	1
Of the Regulation on Construction and Means of Communication	6	65–87	31	23	6
Of the Rules on Caution with Fire	7	88–98	6	11	8
Of the Regulation on Post and Telegraph	8	99–101	2	3	0
Against Public Health	9	102–116	25	15	3
Against Personal Safety	10	117–129	9	13	12
Insults to Honor, Threats, and Violence	11	130–142	82	13	12
Against Family Rights	12	143–144	2	2	1
Against Others' Property	13	145–181	184	37	17

Sources: Ustav o nakazaniiakh nalagaemykh mirovymi sud"iami, ed. N. S. Taganster, 12th ed. St. Petersburg: Tipografia M. Markusheva, 1912, 576; *Obshchee polozhenie o krest'ianakh*, st. 127. Since three of the eighty-four statutes assigned to the township courts are sections of other statutes, the total number of the statutes listed here is fewer than eighty-four.

One response of legal experts to this major setback was to take up again the cause of including peasants in a court structure open to all, that is, ending peasants' status as legal minors (but not a minority) who had to be coddled with particular regulations and distinctive punishments. In the early years of the twentieth century, a new generation of reformers argued for the institution of a "local court" (*mestnyi sud*), in which all residents of a locality, not just peasants, would participate. The judges of this new court would be educated professionals, who could bring their expertise to judicial process in the countryside. The power of the hated land captain could thus be undone.

The proposal for a local court became entangled in the stormy politics of this time and connected to high-stakes controversies over transformations in landholding and property rights.[40] The imperial government initiated a review of peasant institutions, including the township court, in 1904.[41] Sergei Witte, the former minister of finance, commenting on proposals for reform of peasant institutions,[42] cited the view that "it was desirable to eliminate the isolation of the peasants in rights in general and particularly with regard to administration and courts."[43] In that year, the imperial administration took a major step toward aligning peasant rights with those of other estates: corporal punishment was abolished. Two years later, the law of October 5, 1906, ended many restrictions on peasants' movements and access to educational institutions and state service.[44] This significant change in peasants' rights did not satisfy legal reformers, particularly because the 1906 law left in place the township courts and the power of the land captains over peasants and these courts.[45]

The campaign for an all-estate local court gathered steam after the institution of an elected legislative body, the Duma, to advise the emperor, and a less censored press, both results of the revolution of 1905. Possibly the census of 1897 had also heightened attention to the proportion of the population whose legal affairs were for the most part litigated in the township courts. For reformers the peasants' overwhelming numbers provided evidence of the gravity of the case for an inclusive local court. Commenting bitterly in 1904 in a new legal journal on the government's proposed reorganization (rather than replacement) of the township courts, V. Efimov noted that the commission's work revealed that these rural courts were responsible for deciding "the huge majority of both misdemeanors and property disputes for at least 80 percent of the whole population of the empire."[46] A few years later, with the court reform still pending, leading lawyers had formed their own "peasant law" division. The report in a legal journal on this group's first conference in 1909 bemoaned the fact that most legal practitioners knew nothing about peasant law or peasant life, "although these subjects involve the interests of almost three-quarters of the population of Russia." Providing "legal aid" to this "most helpless, most poor, and most exploited" population was a most urgent "social task" of Russia's lawyers.[47]

The language of this commentary suggests the underlying tension in reformers' attitudes toward the people who indeed constituted the vast majority of the population of the empire. Legal experts could simultaneously advocate for including peasants with other subjects in an all-estate legal instance and attest the inferiority of peasants and their need for aid and assistance. Whatever their numbers, peasants were still represented as minors, who need the guidance of legal specialists.[48]

Coda

For many of Russia's elite reformers, the end of serfdom was a step toward the goal of "equality of all citizens before the law."[49] But could equality happen in Imperial Russia? Could even well-intentioned reformers imagine themselves and peasants as equals who possessed the same set of legal rights?

As reformers looked for ways out of serfdom in the 1850s and 1860s, at least some of them defended the ability of their co-citizens to participate with empathy and reason in a reformed legal system. Countering the objection that a jury trial system could not be introduced due to the "ignorance of the people," one committee had referred to the history of the jury trial in England:

> It's hardly the case that the English people of that time were more educated than ours. England introduced the jury trial everywhere where its dominion was achieved, and everywhere this institution brought about beneficial consequences. The jury trial exists even in New Zealand. *Is it possible that the savages of that island are more developed than our people?* To decide about the guilt of a criminal, you need only common sense and conscience—nothing more.[50]

This purported confidence in the reasoning and morals of "our people" was infused with assumptions about progress and development (*razvitie*) as well as savagery and civilization. The argument depended on imperial comparisons. Russian peasants who were in some fashion the equivalent of English commoners of four hundred years earlier and at the same time more advanced than New Zealanders of their own day would have the "common sense and conscience" to use the law for general good.

After the emancipation and the creation of the township courts, this belief in peasant legal wisdom gave way to other preoccupations, while reformers took on the tasks, as they saw them, of civilizing their country and its citizens.[51] The township courts, meanwhile, flourished for the next half century, enabling the peasant majority in the empire to use nearby legal instances for most of their judicial matters.[52] Under the "temporary" regulations of the imperial judicial system, decisions about a specific subset of misdemeanors was entrusted to peasant judges, who could assign a range of punishments that were less harsh than those to be used in courts for the general population. Minor civil disputes and matters of inheritance could be judged according to "local customs." Oversight was provided, after 1889, by a noble supervisor from the region. See the picture of the judges of a 1906 township court seated around a table, with the noble supervisor and possibly his son standing among them (Figure 2.2).

There was the rub. When legal specialists and other liberal reformers re-opened the question of these apparently aberrant, but massively used peasant courts, the dominant issue was not so much inclusionary justice but the extrusion of state officials from judicial process. As Ekaterina Pravilova points out, lawyers, historians, journalists, and other intellectuals in the Russian Empire shared a moralistic attitude toward the workings of the law. Lawyers insisted on their profession's "freedom" to interpret the criminality or not of violent or other actions charged as crimes.[53] A better justice for

Figure 2.2 Township judges at Bun'kovo, Bogorodskii County, Moscow Province, 1906. Used by permission from Indiana University Press/cover photo by Jane Burbank, *Russian Peasants Go to Court: Legal Culture in the Countryside, 1905–1017*.

peasants could not be that of state officials and the police. Interpretation should occur instead in courts informed by the expertise of lawyers and other specialists.

In the first decades of the twentieth century, liberal reformers sought to replace the township courts with a new "local" court that would no longer be exclusively a peasant institution, presided over by peasant judges chosen by their villages. After years of discussion, the state promulgated a "law on the local court" on June 15, 1912, with a reorganization to begin in January 1914. Legal reformers did not celebrate this endeavor. For one thing, the revised local courts retained the township court structure of special rules for peasants and an even more limited repertoire of permitted actions. In the matter of landed property—the most sensitive issue in this era of land reform—cases would be decided elsewhere. The court would still have an "estate character"; people not of peasant status were not required to appear before it. Judges would still be peasants, elected by their villages. Although literacy would now be a prerequisite for appointment, there was no requirement for any kind of legal education. The land captain was eliminated, but oversight was provided by an array of institutions designed to supervise these separate peasant jurisdictions. In the words of a leading authority on Russia's peasants and their legal practices, the reform created a "legal chaos" for peasants, a "great disaster for the people."[54]

In experts' heated discussions of the separate peasant courts in the early twentieth century, the dominant posture was that of helping peasants, rather than engaging them in the decisions of how they—or others—could be helped. In 1906, in connection with elections to the newly established imperial Duma, N. Druzhinin, a prominent legal expert, called for "ending the peasant question once and for all" on the basis of "wide participation of the population in legislation and administration … [and] the creation of popular representation on the basis of a general electoral right." This demand was the dramatic conclusion to an article on "how to overcome the juridical helplessness of the peasants" that called for expanded education and legal aid and "special measures to spread legal knowledge to the people [*narod*]."[55]

Fifty years after the institution of the township court, reformers appeared oblivious to the legal experience of their peasant co-subjects. "Common sense" and "conscience" dropped out of the picture, as reformers focused on the need to educate the peasantry about the law. For decades reformers had assaulted the inadequacies of the state's adjustments to the township courts, insisting on the need for legal expertise in the countryside. Despite or in ignorance of this political battle, the township courts were still functioning when the empire crashed in 1917, and peasants were still a majority in the state and an "other" in reformers' conceptions of the law.

Notes

1. Daniel Field, *Rebels in the Name of the Tsar* (Boston: Unwin Hyman, 1989); I. A. Khristoforov, *"Aristokratichecheskaia" oppositsiia velikim reformam (konets 1850–seredina 1870-kh gg.)* (Moscow: Russkoe slovo, 2002).
2. On the complex history of serfdom in Russia in relation to law and to other forms of enforced labor, see Alessandro Stanziani, "Serfs, Slaves, or Wage Earners? The Legal Status of Labour in Russia from a Comparative Perspective, from the Sixteenth to the Nineteenth Century," *Journal of Global History* 3, no. 2 (2008): 183–202.
3. *Polnoe sobranie zakonov Rossisskoi imperii*, Sobr. 2 [hereafter PSZRI2], t. XXXVI. ot. 1, 1861. (St.Petersburg, 1863), p. 141, no. 36657, st. 1.
4. *Obshchee polozhenie o krest'ianakh, vyshedshikh iz krepostnoi zavisimosti* [hereafter OPK], published as law no. 36657 in PSZRI2, t. XXXVI. ot. 1, 1861. (St. Petersburg, 1863), 141–69.
5. G. A. Dzhanshiev, *Epokha velikikh reform*, 10th rev. ed. (St. Petersburg: Tipo-litografiia V. M Vol'fa, 1907), 121.
6. Michel Tissier, "La puissance russe et la sortie du servage (XIXe-début du XXe siècle)," in *La Russie et l'URSS du milieu du XIXe siècle à 1991*, ed. Joëlle Alazard, Myriam Deniel-Ternant, Aline Fryszman, Marianne Guérin, and Philippe Prudent (Levallois-Perret: Bréal/Association des professeurs d'histoire et de géographie, 2022), 153–65.
7. On serfs' conditions in Russia, see Tracy Dennison, *The Institutional Framework of Russian Serfdom* (New York: Cambridge University Press, 2011). For comparison with American slavery, see the classic study by Peter Kolchin, *Unfree Labor: American Slavery and Russian Serfdom* (Cambridge, MA: Harvard University Press, 1987) and Stanziani's corrective: "Serfs, Slaves or Wage Earners?."
8. On Russia's actions and diplomacy concerning the slave trade, see Liubov Kurtynova-d'Herlugnan, *The Tsar's Abolitionists: The Slave Trade in the Caucasus and Its Suppression* (Leiden: Brill, 2010).
9. On Russia's imperial expansion and its significance for political culture, see Jane Burbank, "All Under the Tsar: Russia's Eurasian Trajectory," in *The Limits of Universal Rule: Eurasian Empires Compared*, ed. Yuri Pines, Michal Biran, and Jörg Rüpke (Cambridge, UK: Cambridge University Press, 2021), 342–75.
10. As Eric Weitz observed, "Minorities are an invention of the nation-state." Eric D. Weitz, *A World Divided: The Global Struggle of Human Rights in the Age of Nation-States* (Princeton, NJ: Princeton University Press, 2019), 162.

11. John W. Slocum, "Who, and When Were the Inorodtsy? The Evolution of the Category of 'Aliens' in Imperial Russia," *Russian Review* 57 (1998): 173–90.
12. On *soslovie* (estate), see Tomila V. Lankina, *The Estate Origins of Democracy in Russia: From Imperial Bourgeoisie to Post-Communist Middle Class* (Cambridge, UK: Cambridge University Press, 2022), 45–66. For a nineteenth-century legal scholar's perspective on the relation between estate-based rights and serfdom, see V. N. Latkin, *Leksii po istorii russkogo pravda* (St. Petersburg: Tipografiia S.Peterburgskoi odinochnoi tiur'my, 1912), 353–4.
13. Jane Burbank, "An Imperial Rights Regime: Law and Citizenship in the Russian Empire," *Kritika: Explorations in Russian and Eurasian History* 7, no. 3 (2006): 397–431.
14. On the codification process, see Tatiana Borisova, "The Digest of Laws of the Russian Empire: The Phenomenon of Autocratic Legality," *Law and History Review* 30, no. 3 (2012): 301–25.
15. Tatiana Borisova and Jane Burbank, "Russia's Legal Trajectories," *Kritika: Explorations in Russian and Eurasian History* 19, no. 3 (2018): 469–508.
16. Dzhanshiev, *Epokha velikikh reform*, 120–1. Source of the quoted material not indicated in Dzhanshiev's account, although he cites many opinions backing up this view.
17. Ibid., 121.
18. The General Regulation on Peasants (Obshchee polozhenie o krest'ianakh ([OPK])) was issued as Book One of The Regulation on the Rural Estate (Polozhenie o sel'skom sostoianii ([PSS])). All eight books of The Regulation on the Rural Estate constitute the "Special Appendix to the Ninth Volume" of the Collected Laws of the Russian Empire (Svod zakonov Rossiiskoi imperii, IX, Osoboe prilozhenie [SZ]). In this article, I use the following edition of the Collected Laws: *Svod zakonov Rossiiskoi imperii v piati knigakh*, edited by I. D. Mordukhai-Boltovskii (St. Petersburg: Deiatel, 1912).
19. Ibid., 125.
20. See A. A. Leont'ev's blistering attack on the failures of the reform: A. A. Leont'ev, "'Zakonodatel'tsvo o krest'ianakh posle reforma,'" in *Velikaia reforma*, eds., A. K. Dzhivelegov, S. P. Mel'gunov, and V. I. Picheta, vol. 6 (Moscow: Sytin, 1911), 159.
21. Ibid., 161–8.
22. *Rossiia 1913 god: Statistiko-dokumental'nyi sbornik* (St. Petersburg: Blits, 1995), 219.
23. Leont'ev, *Zakondatel'stvo o krest'ianakh*, 165.
24. Dzhanshiev, *Epokha velikikh reform*, 123.
25. Ibid., 122.
26. Ibid.
27. Jane Burbank, *Russian Peasants Go to Court: Legal Culture in the Countryside, 1905–1917* (Bloomington: Indiana University Press, 2004), https://pages.nyu.edu/russian-peasants-go-to-court/.
28. Dzhanshiev, *Epokha velikikh reform*, 124.
29. On peasants' use of the circuit courts, see Stefan Kirmse, *The Lawful Empire: Legal Change and Cultural Diversity in Late Tsarist Russia* (Cambridge, UK: Cambridge University Press, 2019).
30. On corporal punishment in Russian law, see Abby M. Schrader, *Languages of the Lash: Corporal Punishment and Identity in Imperial Russia* (DeKalb: Northern Illinois University Press, 2002).
31. Dzhanshiev, *Epokha velikikh reform*, 232.

32. Ibid., 232–42.
33. Ibid., 241.
34. Leont'ev, *Zakondatel'stvo o krest'ianakh*, 187–8.
35. For the opening of the first instances of this court and its subsequent fate, see Dzhanshiev, *Epokha velikikh reform*, 452–74; on the history of the reform, see N. S. Tagantsev's introduction in *Ustav o nakazaniakh, nalagaemykh mirovymi sud'iami*, N. S. Tagantsev, ed., 12th ed. exp. (St. Petersburg: Tip. M. Merkusheva, 1912), V–VIII.
36. On the Justices of the Peace and their courts, see V. L. Isachenko, *Mirovoi sud: Prakticheskii kommentarii po pervuiu knigu Ustava grazhdanskogo sudoproizvodstva* (St. Petersburg: Tipografiia M. Merkusheva, 1913). In rural areas, these courts were abolished in 1889 in connection with the reform of the township courts; see Joan Neuberger, "Popular Legal Cultures: The St. Petersburg Mirovoi Sud," in *Russia's Great Reforms, 1855–1881*, ed. Ben Eklof, John Bushnell, and Larissa Zakharova (Bloomington: Indiana University Press, 1994), 232. Neuberger's article explores the way the Justice of the Peace courts functioned in St. Petersburg.
37. OPK, sts. 143, 144. I use the term "arrest" to refer to a verdict sentencing a person to confinement in the local jail. Arrest meant confinement, rather than referring to detention before a case was heard.
38. On the township courts and peasant judges in public opinion, see Cathy A. Frierson, *Peasant Icons: Representations of Rural People in Late 19th Century Russia* (New York: Oxford University Press, 1993), 62–75.
39. On the land captains' performance of their duties, see Jane Burbank, "Supervising the Supervisors: Bureaucracy, Personality and Rule of Law in Kazan Province at the Start of the 20th Century," *Acta Slavica Japonica* 38 (2017): 1–21.
40. The most visible of these disputed reforms were the "Stolypin" laws designed to convert peasant communal lands into the property of individual households. See David A. J. Macey, *Government and Peasant in Russia, 1861–1906: The Prehistory of the Stolypin Reform* (DeKalb: Northern Illinois University Press, 1987).
41. See V. Efimov's report on the projected court reform, "O novoi organizatsii volostnogo suda," *Sudebnoe obozrenie* 2, no. 21 (May 23, 1904): 435–38.
42. Witte's report was connected to a controversial study of peasant conditions: Macey, *Government and Peasant in Russia, 1861–1906*, 103–11.
43. V. Efimov, "'Zapiska po krest'ianskomu delu stats-sekretaria S. Iu. Vitte,'" *Sudebnoe obozrenie* 2, no. 50 (December 12, 1904), 1009.
44. Burbank, *Russian Peasants Go to Court*, 29.
45. See the harsh response to the law of October 5, 1906, in a leading juridical journal: *Iuridicheskaia gazeta* 70 (October 26, 1906), 2050–4.
46. V. Efimov, *O novoi organizatsii volostnogo suda*, 435.
47. "V sektsii krest'ianskogo prava," *Sudebnaia letopis*, February 17, 1909, no. 4: 8.
48. For experts' campaigns for legal education of peasants, see Michel Tissier, "Malaise dans la culture juridique libérale en Russie après 1905: 'pédagogie des libertés' et éducation au droit,'" *Cahier du monde russe* 48, nos. 2–3 (2007): 185–208.
49. Dzhanshiev, *Epokha velikikh reform*, 121.
50. Ibid., 122–3; emphasis in original.
51. Yanni Kotsonis, *Making Peasants Backward: Agricultural Cooperatives and the Agrarian Question in Russia, 1861–1914* (New York: St. Martin's Press, 1999); Michel Tissier, "Le droit pour le peuple: vulgariser le droit en Russie au tournant du XXe siècle," *Bulletin de l'Institut Pierre Renouvin*, no. 18 (2004): 83–103.

52. On the widespread and growing use of the township courts from 1905 through 1914, see Burbank, *Russian Peasants Go to Court*, 74–7.
53. Ekaterina Pravilova, "Truth, Facts, and Authenticity in Russian Imperial Jurisprudence and Historiography," *Kritika: Explorations in Russian and Eurasian History* 21, no. 1 (Winter 2020): 7–39.
54. A. Leont'ev, "Volostnoi sud po novomu zakonu o mestnom sude," *Pravo* (January 12, 1914), no. 2, 103–19.
55. N. Druzhinin, "V chem zakliuchaetsia i kak mozhet byt' ustranena iuridicheskaia bezpomoshchnost' krest'ian?," *Iuridicheskaia gazeta* (March 2, 1906), no. 13, 229–35.

Bibliography

Sources

Druzhinin, N. "V chem zakliuchaetsia i kak mozhet byt' ustranena iuridicheskaia bezpomoshchnost' krest'ian?." *Iuridicheskaia gazeta*, March 2, no. 13 (1906): 229–35.
Dzhanshiev, G. A. *Epokha velikikh reform*, 10th rev. ed. St. Petersburg: Tipo-litografiia V.M. Vol'fa V. M, 1907.
Efimov, V. "O novoi organizatsii volostnogo suda." *Sudebnoe obozrenie* 2, no. 21 (May 23, 1904): 435–8.
Efimov, V. "Zapiska po krest'ianskomu delu stats-sekretaria S. Iu. Vitte." *Sudebnoe obozrenie* 2, no. 50 (December 12, 1904): 1009.
Isachenko, V. L. *Mirovoi sud: Prakticheskii kommentarii po pervuiu knigu Ustava grazhdanskogo sudoproizvodstva*. St. Petersburg: Tipografiia M. Merkusheva, 1913.
Iuridicheskaia gazeta, October 26, 1906: 70.
Leont'ev, A. "Zakonodatel'tsvo o krest'ianakh posle reforma." In *Velikaia reforma*, edited by A. K. Dzhivelegov, S. P. Mel'gunov, and V. I. Picheta, vol. 6, 159. Moscow: Sytin, 1911.
Leont'ev, A. "Volostnoi sud po novomu zakonu o mestnom sude." *Pravo*, no. 2 (January 12, 1914): 103–19.
Mordukhai-Boltovskii, I. D., ed. *Svod zakonov Rossiiskoi imperii v piati knigakh*. St. Petersburg: Deiatel, 1912.
Polnoe sobranie zakonov Rossisskoi imperii, Sobr. 2 [PSZRI2], t. XXXVI. ot. 1, 1861 (St. Petersburg, 1863).
Rossiia 1913 god: Statistiko-dokumental'nyi sbornik. St. Petersburg: Blits, 1995.
Tagantsev N. S., ed. *Ustav o nakazaniiakh, nalagaemykh mirovymi sud"iami*, 12th ed. exp. St. Petersburg: Tip. M. Merkusheva, 1912.
"V sektsii krest'ianskogo prava." *Sudebnaia letopis'*, no. 4 (February 17, 1909): 8.

Research Literature

Borisova, Tatiana. "The Digest of Laws of the Russian Empire: The Phenomenon of Autocratic Legality." *Law and History Review* 30, no. 3 (2012): 301–25.
Borisova, Tatiana, and Jane Burbank. "Russia's Legal Trajectories." *Kritika: Explorations in Russian and Eurasian History* 19, no. 3 (2018): 469–508.
Burbank, Jane. "All Under the Tsar: Russia's Eurasian Trajectory." In *The Limits of Universal Rule: Eurasian Empires Compared*, edited by Yuri Pines, Michal Biran, and Jörg Rüpke, 342–75. Cambridge, UK: Cambridge University Press, 2021.

Burbank, Jane. "An Imperial Rights Regime: Law and Citizenship in the Russian Empire." *Kritika: Explorations in Russian and Eurasian History* 7, no. 3 (2006): 397–431.
Burbank, Jane. *Russian Peasants Go to Court: Legal Culture in the Countryside, 1905–1917*. Bloomington: Indiana University Press, 2004.
Burbank, Jane. "Supervising the Supervisors: Bureaucracy, Personality and Rule of Law in Kazan Province at the Start of the 20th Century." *Acta Slavica Japonica* 38 (2017): 1–21.
Dennison, Tracy. *The Institutional Framework of Russian Serfdom*. New York: Cambridge University Press, 2011.
Field, Daniel. *Rebels in the Name of the Tsar*. Boston: Unwin Hyman, 1989.
Frierson, Cathy A. *Peasant Icons: Representations of Rural People in Late 19th Century Russia*. New York: Oxford University Press, 1993.
Khristoforov, I. A. *"Aristokraticheckeskaia" oppositsiia velikim reformam (konets 1850-seredina 1870-kh gg)*. Moscow: Russkoe slovo, 2002.
Kirmse, Stefan. *The Lawful Empire: Legal Change and Cultural Diversity in Late Tsarist Russia*. Cambridge, UK: Cambridge University Press, 2019.
Kolchin, Peter. *Unfree Labor: American Slavery and Russian Serfdom*. Cambridge, MA: Harvard University Press, 1987.
Kotsonis, Yanni. *Making Peasants Backward: Agricultural Cooperatives and the Agrarian Question in Russia, 1861–1914*. New York: St. Martin's Press, 1999.
Kurtynova-d'Herlugnan, Liubov. *The Tsar's Abolitionists: The Slave Trade in the Caucasus and Its Suppression*. Leiden: Brill, 2010.
Lankina, Tomila V. *The Estate Origins of Democracy in Russia: From Imperial Bourgeoisie to Post-Communist Middle Class*. Cambridge, UK: Cambridge University Press, 2022.
Latkin, V. N. *Leksii po istorii russkogo pravda*. St. Petersburg: Tipografiia S.Peterburgskoi odinochnoi tiur'my, 1912.
Macey, David A. J. *Government and Peasant in Russia, 1861–1906: The Prehistory of the Stolypin Reform*. DeKalb: Northern Illinois University Press, 1987.
Neuberger, Joan. "Popular Legal Cultures: The St. Petersburg Mirovoi Sud." In *Russia's Great Reforms, 1855–1881*, edited by Ben Eklof, John Bushnell, and Larissa Zakharova. Bloomington: Indiana University Press, 1994.
Pravilova, Ekaterina. "Truth, Facts, and Authenticity in Russian Imperial Jurisprudence and Historiography." *Kritika: Explorations in Russian and Eurasian History* 21, no. 1 (Winter 2020): 7–39.
Schrader, Abby M. *Languages of the Lash: Corporal Punishment and Identity in Imperial Russia*. DeKalb: Northern Illinois University Press, 2002.
Slocum, John W. "Who, and When Were the Inorodtsy? The Evolution of the Category of 'Aliens' in Imperial Russia." *Russian Review* 57 (1998): 173–90.
Stanziani, Alessandro. "Serfs, Slaves, or Wage Earners? The Legal Status of Labour in Russia from a Comparative Perspective, from the Sixteenth to the Nineteenth Century." *Journal of Global History* 3, no. 2 (2008): 183–202.
Tissier, Michel. "Le droit pour le peuple: vulgariser le droit en Russie au tournant du XXe siècle.'" *Bulletin de l'Institut Pierre Renouvin*, no. 18 (2004): 83–103.
Tissier, Michel. "La puissance russe et la sortie du servage (XIXe-début du XXe siècle)." In *La Russie et l'URSS du milieu du XIXe siècle à 1991*, edited by Joëlle Alazard, Myriam Deniel-Ternant, Aline Fryszman, Marianne Guérin, and Philippe Prudent, 153–65. Levallois-Perret: Bréal/Association des professeurs d'histoire et de géographie, 2022.

Tissier, Michel. "Malaise dans la culture juridique libérale en Russie après 1905: 'pédagogie des libertés' et éducation au droit.'" *Cahier du monde russe* 48, nos. 2–3 (2007): 185–208.

Weitz, Eric D. *A World Divided: The Global Struggle of Human Rights in the Age of Nation-State*. Princeton, NJ: Princeton University Press, 2019.

3

Chinese Citizenship and Land Rights in the Sino-Korean Borderland

Kwangmin Kim

Introduction

In 1881 the Qing government conducted the first systematic land survey of the southern Manchuria located north of Tumen and Yalu Rivers.¹ A long-standing military frontier between China and Korea, the government prohibited permanent settlement of any population—both Han Chinese and Manchu bannerman as well as Koreans—in this area since at least the late seventeenth century. However, in an effort to raise new revenue for military bases established along Sino-Russian border, whose situation had become increasingly intense after Russia's acquisition of present-day Russia's Maritime Province (*Primorsky Krai*) from the Qing in 1860, the Qing government decided to open the undeveloped mountain land to Han Chinese migrants and their agricultural development.

To their surprise, the Qing surveyors quickly discovered that a substantial number of ethnic Korean squatters from the adjoining Korean territory across the Tumen River had already been cultivating the land there. These Korean settlers received land certificates issued by and paid taxes to a Korean authority in Hamkyŏngdo, a northern province of Chosŏn Kingdom.² In response to this discovery the Qing court made a decision that represented a radical departure from the earlier practice. Instead of expelling and punishing the settlers, which had been a roughly two-century-long practice, the Qing court ordered them to be naturalized and pay taxes to the Qing government.

This decision turned out to be a pivotal moment in the history of the Sino-Korean borderland. Not only did it trigger a decades-long border dispute that eventually led to the demarcation of the modern boundary between China and Korea in 1909, but also the community of Koreans settlers registered under the Qing became the *Chaoxianzu*, a Korean ethnic minority within the modern Chinese nation. Reflecting this legacy, the *Chaoxianzu*, with a population of approximately 2,400,000 in 2020, is still largely concentrated in the border zone.

The decision signaled the rise of a distinctively modern form of statehood in China. The idea that anyone who farmed the land of China was or must become Chinese represented a territorial mode of sovereignty that exercises uniform and exclusive control over the territorially defined national community. According to French historian Peter Sahlins, this is emblematic of the modern nation-state in Europe gradually from the seventeenth to the late nineteenth century.[3] This chapter explores the entangled process of the rise of the territorial sovereignty and formation of Chaoxianzu within the local context of the Sino-Korean borderland. It also examines the long-lasting legacy of the decision to link citizenship and land rights, one that shaped patterns of political integration and economic exclusion of the Korean minority within the broader Chinese nation.[4]

Territorial Sovereignty and Jurisdictional Sovereignty in Qing Manchuria

Sahlins contrasts territorial sovereignty with French and other European states under the Old Regime, which envisioned its rule in terms of its jurisdiction over subjects rather than over a territory. Jurisdictional sovereignty can be defined as "relations between king and subjects (*regnicole* in France)," "symbolically affirmed in the oaths of loyalty and allegiance by individual or corporate groups."[5] In practical terms, what sovereignty based on personal relations meant is that the monarch's jurisdiction over his or her territory was always uneven and incomplete. There were always enclaves (i.e., fiefs, bailiwicks, counties) in which other sovereigns could exercise some or all aspects of jurisdiction (i.e., taxation, justice, military affairs, ecclesiastical policies) within the territorial boundary of the kingdom. In addition, individuals and groups residing within a kingdom were subject to different rules regarding various aspects of administration, depending on the nature and origin of relations they formed with the monarch.

Jurisdictional sovereignty fit well with the mode of the Qing state's sovereignty (1644–1911), one that consisted of interpersonal dependence between the Qing emperor and the various groups of people—Manchu, Han Chinese, Mongols, Tibetans, and Muslims.[6] Each constituent was administered differently. For instance, the Qing emperor collected rent ("banner rent," *qizu*) from the Manchu bannermen. Meanwhile, Chinese landowners paid tax (*fushui*), and the Mongols paid tribute (*gong*).

A corollary to the jurisdictional mode of sovereignty of the Qing Empire was the unevenness of the state's domination over its territory. Each group was supposed to live within each cultural or political zone within the empire, and they were prohibited from moving into other cultural zones. Take Manchuria or China's Northeast, with which this chapter is primarily concerned, for example. Considered as the homeland of Manchu, Han Chinese were not permitted to settle there as permanent residents. Except for the very early Qing period and some subsequent periods of famines and natural disasters in China, in general, the Qing government only allowed them to enter Manchuria on a temporary basis as merchants and laborers. They were ordered to return to their residence in China once their temporary businesses had ended.

Even the small number of Chinese who were allowed to settle in Manchuria under special circumstances were treated differently from Manchu residents. The Chinese belonged to Chinese administrative units specially established to govern them. The land owned by a Chinese settler was designated as "civilian land," as opposed to "banner land" that belonged to a Manchu bannerman. The Qing government collected taxes from the civilian land in silver, while it collected rent from the banner land in such forms as black beans. The tax on banner land was much lighter. In 1693, civilian land paid three *fen* of silver per mu of land as tax, while the banner land paid one *sheng* of black beans per land unit, which was the equivalent of six mu. Calculated on the basis of the price of black beans at the time, the banner land paid rent of less than 0.1 *fen* of sliver per mu. In terms of monetary value, the tax rate of civilian land was thirty times higher than that of the banner land.[7] In addition, bannermen could neither sell nor conditionally sell (*dian*) their land to Han Chinese civilians.[8] The former were permitted to rent their land out to civilians but for no more than three years, according to a 1737 government decision recorded in *Da Qing Huidian Shili* (Collected administrative statutes and precedents).[9]

Adding another layer to the unevenness of territorial rule, moreover, the Qing state enclosed the large swath of mountainous land in the Sino-Korean border area along the Tumen and Yalu Rivers, where the Qing officials discovered the Korean settlers in 1881, as a special frontier zone. The Qing prohibited any group, not only Koreans but also Manchu and Han Chinese, from settling in this area permanently due to the various symbolic, economic, and diplomatic considerations. Anyone who encroached on the space was immediately expelled and punished.[10]

Therefore, the Qing court's announcement in 1881 that ordered naturalization of and tax payment by the unauthorized Korean settlers in the enclosed military zone area was a radical departure from the earlier practice of the Qing state. The court announced that those who farmed the land of China (Middle Plain; *zhongyuan*) were Chinese (people of Middle Plain; *zhongyuan zhi min*). Thus, the Koreans farming within the Qing boundary (represented as *zhongyuan*) would be issued a land certificate from the Chinese government. They must register in the tax register of the Dunhuna County of the Qing, adopt Chinese (in fact, Manchu Qing) clothing and hairstyle, and become Chinese (*zhongyuan zhi min*).[11]

This statement is notable on a couple of accounts. One stunning aspect is that this statement came from the multicultural Manchu ruler, who would never have considered the Manchuria as "*zhongyuan*," nor considered the people farming the land as "*zhongyuan zhi min*." *Zhongyuan* was a geographical term that referred to north China specifically and China broadly, and was clearly distinguished from Manchuria during the Qing period. The designation of the border zone as *zhongyuan* thus indicated a significant conceptual transformation of Manchuria—the emperor's special domain—into a part of China.

Equally important is the emergence of the new territorial mode of defining Chinese nationhood that this statement signaled. According to this statement, being Chinese meant owning a revenue-producing land asset within the Chinese state's—that is, the Qing's—tax jurisdiction. Effectively requiring naturalization of Korean settlers, so to speak—adoption of Chinese clothing and hairstyle—based on the location of their residence and cultivation, this statement represented a clear departure from the jurisdictional sovereignty. This territorially defined sovereignty articulated in the statement was exclusive as well. There was no way for Korean settlers to remain Korean (maintaining Korean hairstyle and clothing) and still own land in China. They either had to become Chinese or abandon their ownership to Chinese land and leave.

In other words, the 1881 decision represented two simultaneous and equally radical changes with regard to the territoriality of Qing rule. Not only did the Sino-Korean border become a part of Chinese territory, but the Qing ruler also came to conceptualize its sovereignty not as rule over persons but over territory. Notably, this decision anticipated the systematic extension of the principle of uniform territorial sovereignty over jurisdictional sovereignty in terms of tax collection, which occurred in all of Manchuria roughly thirty years later. In the first decade of the twentieth century the Qing government eliminated the distinction between banner land and civilian land, and had civilian local officials manage tax collection in silver for both without distinction. The Qing government also allowed the people, including both bannermen and civilians, to claim "wasteland" by registering the land with the government regardless of its location in either the former banner or civilian jurisdiction. The people paid the same amount of tax in silver.[12]

Perhaps it was the changes of the international security environment that compelled the Qing court to make the decision in 1881. After all, the Qing decided to open the former military frontier to Chinese civilian migration and their agricultural development only a year prior in order to raise new revenue to support the new military reinforcements in the Qing military bases in the border area. These bases—Hunchun, Ningguta, and Sanxing—were established to defend against the growing Russian military presence in the Russian Far East since Russia acquired the territory due to the agreement in Peking Convention in 1860.[13] This necessitated the transformation of the former military zone into civilian territory in which the state exercised civilian administrative power including taxation, as a space that had equal status with other parts of China.[14]

However, at the same time, the decision to naturalize Koreans as Chinese rather than expelling and replacing them with Chinese settlers was also the result of the Qing's accommodation to the demographic reality of the borderland. The ethnic Koreans composed the majority of the settlers, outnumbering ethnic Chinese by a wide margin. While in broader Manchuria Chinese from northern China formed the major migrant group, Koreans were the dominant group in the border area primarily due to easier geographical access. At least since the 1860s they worked in the thriving ginseng plantations in the area that were funded primarily by Han Chinese investors, thus already turning the enclosed military frontier into revenue-producing territory.[15]

Therefore, in most likelihood, it was Korean settlers who provided labor and capital, needed for the development of the large portion of the "wasteland" that the Qing government opened for agricultural development in 1880. A record from the *Archive of Hunchun Lieutenant Commander* provides a good example. In 1891 three Koreans crossed the border accompanied by an interpreter. They approached a Chinese person who acquired the legal title to a plot of wasteland from the Qing government in the jurisdiction of Hunchun military command. The Koreans entered into an agreement with him to farm the wasteland and pay grain rent beginning in the third year.

Afterward they soon brought their families to the Qing side, and built grass huts where they temporarily resided. They farmed the land, and went back to the Korean side of the border only after the fall harvest. They returned in the spring next year. They did not change their hairstyle or clothing.[16]

Although the Korean farmers mentioned that they came from the Korean side because "they were poor and had no land to farm and thus could not make a living," close examination of the evidence reveals that they were profit-seeking land developers in most likelihood. Although the Han Chinese was a titleholder to the wasteland, he contributed neither capital nor labor to the farming. Not only did the Koreans provide their own labor, but they probably also had to build their houses and prepare the seed on their own. Indeed, it was the Korean tenants who sought the rental opportunity in the first place and proactively even hiring an interpreter to look for landlords. The Korean farmers may have sought to rent wasteland on the Qing side because of various economic advantages, including the ample fertile land, low rent, and lack of competition in the rental market, all due to the general scarcity of a farming population on the Qing side.

If the Qing state was going to produce revenue from the borderland effectively, it was imperative to claim Koreans as exclusively Chinese. For the Qing state was not the only state that had claim on the revenue produced from the Koreans. The Chosŏn government of Korea, from whose territory the Koreans originally came, also had equally legitimate claim over the revenue on the basis of the jurisdictional mode of the sovereignty. And indeed it had been exercising taxation power over the Koreans by issuing land certificates to them. In this context the imperative of exclusive inclusion—the inclusion of the Koreans for the purpose of excluding rival claims by another state—on the basis of residence emerged as the defining characteristic of the Qing state's relations with Korean settlers.

Chinese Citizenship and the Pattern of Inclusion and Exclusion of the Korean Minority

The linkage between Chaoxianzu's land rights and citizenship, forged from the very time of its formation, sets the patterns of political assimilation and socioeconomic exclusion of the Korean minority within the Chinese nation-state in the long run, rendering the land property rights of Koreans precarious in the early twentieth century. The naturalization requirement for ethnic Koreans' acquisition of land rights was first codified in law in 1909 when the Qing established the Great Qing Citizenship Law (*Daqing gouji tiaoli*), the first citizenship law enacted in China.[17] Subsequently the provincial authorities in Fengtian and Jilin—the two areas in which Korean settlers were concentrated—established bylaws to facilitate the implementation of the citizenship law in Manchuria.

A brief examination of the bylaws shows that the Qing government at the time began to enforce the naturalization requirement with a slightly different political purpose in mind, from that of the 1880s and 1890s. To say the conclusion first, in the 1880s and 1890s the Qing state required naturalization of Koreans to integrate them into the Chinese nation—the naturalization allowed the Qing government to claim the Koreans and the revenue that they produced in *exclusion* of the potential rival claim from the Korean state. By the time of the passage of the Great Qing Citizenship Law in 1909, however, the Qing state started to use the citizenship requirement for a subtly different purpose—*both* political assimilation and economic exclusion. The requirement enabled the state to forcefully assimilate the Koreans into the Chinese nation, while strictly restricting and even depriving Koreans of land rights.

The reason behind this change was the transformation of security environment in Manchuria. As Japanese Empire expanded its power over Manchuria and Korea in early twentieth century, Qing officials began to consider Korean settlers as a potential security threat to the Qing rule in Manchuria. The critical moment in the change came after the establishment of the Japanese protectorate in Korea in 1906. In 1908, the Japanese governor-general of Korea announced that Koreans in the border area—referred to as Yanbian by the Qing, and Kando (Kantō) by Koreans and Japanese—would be considered subjects of the Japanese Empire regardless of their naturalization status in China. The Japanese authority reasoned, "Koreans could not abandon their [Korean] citizenship under any kind of circumstances" because the Chosŏn government of Korea prior to the annexation never allowed their subjects to abandon its citizenship. Therefore, in the eyes of the Japanese authority, the Koreans still remained Koreans and thus Japanese imperial subjects even after their acquisition of Chinese citizenship.[18]

Under this circumstance, the Qing authority suspected, Koreans' acquisition of land rights in the Yanbian area would eventually lead to the expansion of the Japanese domain in Manchuria.[19] The signing of the Kando (Jiandao) Convention between the Qing and the Japanese Empires in 1909 deepened the Qing officials' suspicion. As an unstable compromise between the two governments to solve the decades-long Sino-Korean boundary dispute concerning the border area—a dispute the Japanese state inherited from the Chosŏn state—the two governments reached an agreement. On the conditions that the Koreans would follow Qing laws and the Japanese government would not exercise their extraterritorial jurisdiction over Koreans, the Qing government would allow Korean settlers to enjoy protection of their land property and buildings even without acquiring Chinese citizenship in Yanbian.[20]

The bylaws to the 1909 citizenship law installed by the Qing provincial authorities in Fengtian and Jilin constituted a direct response to this condition. The essence of the responses was to accelerate political assimilation of the Koreans as Chinese and to restrict the unnaturalized Koreans' land rights in the border area at the same time. In order to speed up their political assimilation the bylaws lowered the requirement for applying for Chinese citizenship to better facilitate its acquisition by Korean settlers. According to the 1909 citizenship law, foreigners were able to apply for Chinese citizenship only after having resided in China for ten years, provided that they also met other requirements. However, the Fengtian provincial government's bylaw allowed unnaturalized Koreans to apply for Chinese citizenship after two years of residence in the province.[21] Similarly, bylaw of the Jilin authority (the Southeast Circuit of military defense in Jilin to be specific; hereafter Southeast Circuit) effectively lowered the residence requirement to five years in the Yanbian area. The bylaw stipulated that

Koreans who wanted to be naturalized but had resided there less than five years were allowed to register provisionally with the local authorities first and enjoyed the right of the naturalized Koreans.[22]

Meanwhile, the Qing authorities also began to use the naturalization requirement to restrict the land rights of the Korean settlers. Table 3.1 lists the cases of restrictions of land rights stipulated in the Southeast Circuit's bylaw from 1910 to 1911. The bylaws divided the area of Korean residence in the border area into two categories. In the "mixed residence area" unnaturalized Koreans were allowed to reside with the Han Chinese population, thanks to the agreement of the Kando Convention. Yanji and Helong areas belonged to this category. Unnaturalized Koreans were, however, prohibited from residing in the "unmixed residence area." Hunchun and Wangqing areas belonged to this category.

In the unmixed residence zone, the 1910 bylaw denied not only the unnaturalized Koreans' land ownership but also their right to rent and work as agricultural laborers. The mixed residence zone did not provide a better situation for unnaturalized Korean settlers in spite of the agreement of the Kando Convention. The bylaw even denied their right to rent and cultivate government-controlled wasteland. The only exception to this rule was government-controlled wasteland originally developed by unnaturalized Koreans, and in all probability with their own capital. In this case, the Koreans were able to continue to cultivate the land.

Notably, by 1910–11 Koreans including the unnaturalized ones had resided in both the mixed residence zone and the unmixed residence zone for decades. Therefore, the Southeast Circuit's bylaw amounted to dispossession of Koreans' long-held land rights, including ownership, renting, and working as laborers, rather than preventive measures to stop incoming aliens from taking over Chinese land in the future.

The restrictions of Korean land rights in the Yanbian area became strengthened and also spread to other parts of Manchuria, especially Fengtian Province, as the Chinese authorities encountered a series of Japanese expansion in Manchuria in the 1910s and 1920s. Table 3.2 lists major cases of this Japanese expansion in Manchuria and the restrictions of Korean land rights that the Chinese government enacted in the 1910s and 1920s. Although this is not an exhaustive list of cases of land right restrictions, the list shows the correlation between the Japanese expansion and the expanding scope of the restriction of Korean land rights.

The Treaty of Southern Manchuria and Eastern Mongolia, signed by the Japanese Empire and the Chinese government under the leadership of Yuan Shikai in 1915, was a major step in Japanese colonial expansion in Manchuria. The most relevant part of the treaty for the purpose of this chapter is the Japanese acquisition of the right to *shangzu* in southern Manchuria and eastern Mongolia. Translated as "renting based on mutual understanding," the right of *shangzu* is a controversial concept on which the Chinese and the Japanese governments did not agree. In essence, this is a right of Japanese citizens to rent land property for industrial, commercial, and agricultural purposes in Manchuria for a certain period—maximum thirty years. And it could be renewed unconditionally. While the Japanese viewed the right essentially as a land ownership, the Chinese considered it a rental right. This disagreement had never been resolved prior to the establishment of the Japanese-controlled Manchukuo state.

Table 3.1 Jilin Provincial Authority's Bylaw (1910–11) and Korean Land Rights in Yanbian and Hunchun

Southeast Circuit's bylaw, 1910		Affected land rights
Hunchun and Wangqing (unmixed residence area)	Required Chinese landlords to expel unnaturalized Korean renters who cultivated their land by winter of 1910. (Those who applied for citizenship would not be expelled.)	Unnaturalized Koreans' right to rent and cultivate private land of Chinese landlords
	Expelled unnaturalized Korean renters who had reclaimed government-controlled wasteland after the autumn harvest in 1911, even if they built facilities and houses there and were still enjoying the rent holiday privilege due to their contribution. (Those who applied for citizenship would not be expelled.)	Unnaturalized Koreans' right to rent and cultivate government wasteland
	Immediately expelled Koreans who had developed wasteland on behalf of Han Chinese landlords after the announcement of the 1909 citizenship law.	Unnaturalized Koreans' right to rent/cultivate government wasteland newly acquired after 1909
Southeast Circuit's bylaw, 1911		
Yanji and Helong (mixed residence area)	Allowed unnaturalized Koreans to only cultivate the government-controlled wasteland, which they had originally reclaimed themselves.	Unnaturalized Koreans' right to rent and cultivate government wasteland, except for that land they had originally reclaimed.
	Prohibited Chinese landlords from using unnaturalized Koreans to cultivate the *wasteland* they rented from the government.	Unnaturalized Koreans' right to work as agricultural laborers
	Prohibited Chinese from selling their land to unnaturalized Koreans in Korean residential areas.	Unnaturalized Koreans' right to own land
Hunchun and Wangqing	Prohibited unnaturalized Koreans from obtaining land rights and from residing mixed with Chinese.	Unnaturalized Koreans' land rights and right of residence
	Prohibited Chinese from hiring unnaturalized Koreans for work.	Unnaturalized Koreans' right to work as agricultural laborers
	Prohibited unnaturalized Koreans from owning land. The government planned to buy back the land and expel the Koreans.	Unnaturalized Koreans' right to own land and reside there

Sources: Zhao Xingyuan, "Qing zhengfu dui Tumenjiangbei de Chaoxian yimin de guanli," *Dongbei Shidi* 3 (2009): 45–6; Longfan Jiang and Yongzhe Cui, "Ri Han hebing yu Jiandao Chaoxianren de guoji wenti: jianlun Zhong Ri liangguo zai Chaoxianren guoji wenti shang de zhengce fenzheng," *Dongjiang Xuekan* 16, no. 4 (1999): 12–13.

Table 3.2 Japanese Actions and the Restrictions of Korean Land Rights, 1915–27

Japanese action: Treaty of southern Manchuria and eastern Mongolia, 1915
Restriction of Korean land rights: Fengtian provincial government announced the "Regulations for investigating land, privately reclaimed, purchased, acquired through conditional sale and mortgage by unnaturalized Koreans," in 1915 (land ownership)
Japanese action: Mitsuya Agreement (*Mitsuya kyōtei*), 1925
Restriction of Korean land rights: Jilin Province established a regulation regarding the irrigated land, 1926 (Right of cultivation; land ownership for naturalized Koreans)
Restriction of Korean land rights: Chinese police in Fengtian Province announced that beginning in that year Koreans were not allowed to rent from Chinese landlords in Fengtian Province; the police ordered Chinese landlords to change their rental contracts to wage labor contract, April 1926 (Right to rent)
Restriction of Korean land rights: Tonghua County ordered Koreans to leave their residence immediately, January 1925 (Right of residence)
Restriction of Korean land rights: Linjiang County ordered Korean settlers in Mao'er'shan to leave immediately, April 1, 1927 (Right of residence)

Sources: Zhongguo bianjiang shidi yanjiu zhongxin and Liaoning Sheng dang'an guan, *Dongbei Bianjiang Dang'an Xuanji*, vol. 43, 263–75 (Guilin: Guangxi shifan daxue chubanshe, 2007); Shutian Li and others, eds., *Jilin nongye dangan* [Archival materials on agriculture in Jilin], 149 (Jilin: Jilin wenshi chubanshe, 1990); Manshū Iminshi Kenkyūkai, ed., *Nihon teikokushugi ka no Manshū imin* [Migration in Manchuria under Japanese imperialism], 507–15 (Tōkyō: Ryūkei Shosha, 1976).

Immediately after the signing of the treaty the Chinese warlord government based in Fengtian sought to remove the right to land ownership that unnaturalized Koreans had already acquired through various means, including private land reclamation, purchase, and conditional sale. The warlord government insisted that all land rights that Japanese citizens, including Koreans, acquired in Manchuria must be treated as *shangzu* according to the 1915 treaty. Because *shangzu* is not ownership but a rental right, it argued, all the landownership that the Koreans had enjoyed had to be nullified. Therefore, the Koreans must sell their land to the Chinese government within a certain designated time. The government allowed unnaturalized Koreans, who reclaimed wastelands on their own, to remain in the lands but only as renters.

In 1925 Japan and the warlord government in Manchuria signed the Mitsuya Agreement, which forced the warlord regime to suppress the anti-Japanese Korean resistance in Manchuria. Afterwards the Chinese government established another series of restrictions of Korean land rights. Notably, the government even restricted some of the land rights of naturalized Koreans during this time. In 1926, Jilin Province established a regulation on the management of paddy field, a special type of land property that Koreans had specialized in developing since the late nineteenth century.[23] The fourth article stipulated that the Koreans, who cultivated the paddy field as tenants, had to acquire Chinese citizenship, while the fifth article only allowed them to rent the land for cultivation. In other words, even naturalized Korean tenants would not have an opportunity to obtain ownership of irrigated land, even though they had probably developed it in the first place. The state implemented all dispossession and restriction of land rights in the name of the protection of state sovereignty.

These restrictions did not mean that unnaturalized Korean settlers were completely deprived of land rights on the ground. On the contrary, they devised many ways to own, rent, or work on the land. The measures included registering their land under the name of naturalized Koreans or Chinese and paying the latter a fee for the service, for instance. The unnaturalized Koreans owned almost as much land as Han Chinese in Yanji.[24] The demographic condition in which Koreans were still the main source of agricultural labor as tenants and wage laborers made the complete restriction of Korean land rights impractical. However, the deprivation of their legal land rights repressed the wages of Korean workers because they had to work illegally. This situation also enabled the Chinese landlords to ask for higher rents and shorter rental periods, systematically helping Chinese landlords to have the upper hand in their relations with Korean renters and wage laborers.[25]

In 1927 the Japanese governor-general of Korea published the report, titled "the condition of Koreans in Manchuria and Siberia." The report noted the sharp deterioration of conditions for the Korean renters in southern Manchuria. The turning point was roughly ten years prior to the report. The timing roughly corresponded to the signing of the 1915 treaty of southern Manchuria and eastern Mongolia. Chinese landlords became reluctant to sign the contract of conditional sale with Koreans, a practice that Koreans utilized to obtain the transfer of customary land ownership from Chinese in the local context.[26] The terms of the rental contract that Korean tenants signed with Chinese landlords worsened. The rental period was reduced to one to two years, a third of the norm in the earlier period. Rent payment in kind increased twice from one Chinese *shi* of unhulled rice per unit of land to two *shi*. Rent payment in cash increased from seven *yuan* to ten *yuan*, even reaching as high as sixty *yuan*. Sharecropping agreements gained popularity instead of the yearly rental contract. Korean tenants also lost ground in sharecropping agreements. The rental period reduced. The ratio of division of harvest between landlords and tenants, which used to ranged from 7:3 to 4:6, became became 5:5 division by 1927.[27]

Conclusion

Territorial sovereignty, state power exercised over a territorially defined national community, is a key to the understanding of the modern nation-state. This chapter explores the emergence of the territorial sovereignty in the specific context of the Sino-Korean borderland and the constitutive role played by the ethnic Korean settlers in the process. The late Qing state adopted territorially based citizenship and nationhood in an effort to put exclusive claim on the revenue produced by Korean settlers, who emerged as the leading source of labor in the military frontier in the late nineteenth century. While claiming the former military frontier as a revenue-producing territory of China, the Qing state forced the unauthorized Korean settlers to be naturalized as Chinese rather than expelling them, as it had done for over a century.

It turned out the close linkage between Chinese citizenship and land rights, forged from the very moment of the formation of Chaoxianzu, came to have a long-lasting legacy, setting in motion distinctive patterns of political assimilation and economic exclusion of the Korean minority with the broader Chinese nation in the long run. The late Qing state was inclusive in its intention, applying the naturalization requirement by focusing on securing Korean labor by granting Chinese citizenship to Korean settlers. In contrast, the twentieth-century Chinese state was exclusive, using the citizenship requirement to restrict if not outright deny Korean settlers' various land rights and in response to the growing expansion of the Japanese Empire in Manchuria. The Chinese state increasingly treated the Koreans as a potential tool of Japanese colonization and a threat to the security of state sovereignty in Manchuria.

Notes

This work was supported by the National Research Foundation of Korea Grant, funded by the Korean Government (2017S1A6A3A01079727).

1. Xianqian Wang, *Donghua xu lu* [Sequel to the record of Donghua [Gate]], vol. 44 (Shanghai: Shanghai guji chubanshe, 2002); Zhaoquan Yang and Yumei Sun, *Zhong Chao Bianjie Shi* [History of Sino-Korean border] (Changchun: Jilin wenshi chubanshe, 1993), 232–4.
2. Yang and Sun, *Zhong Chao Bianjie Shi* [History of Sino-Korean border], 232–4.
3. Peter Sahlins, *Boundaries: The Making of France and Spain in the Pyrenees*, reprint edition (Berkeley: University of California Press, 1991), 2–3.
4. By examining the rise of the formation of Chaoxianzu within the context of the structural changes in territorial practices of the Qing state, this work complements and complicates the previous scholarship that examines the issue within the contexts of the transnational, diplomatic, or traditional Chinese imperial practices. See Alyssa Park, *Sovereignty Experiments: Korean Migrants and the Building of Borders in Northeast Asia, 1860–1945* (Ithaca, NY: Cornell University Press, 2019); Seonmin Kim, *Ginseng and Borderland: Territorial Boundaries and Political Relations between Qing China and Chosŏn Korea, 1636–1912* (Berkeley: University of California Press, 2017); Nianshen Song, *Making Borders in Modern East Asia: The Tumen River Demarcation, 1881–1919* (Cambridge: Cambridge University Press, 2018).
5. Sahlins, *Boundaries*, 28.
6. Pamela Crossley calls the different groups that formed the jurisdictional sovereignty of the Qing "constituencies." Pamela Kyle Crossley, *A Translucent Mirror: History and Identity in Qing Imperial Ideology* (Berkeley: University of California Press, 2002).
7. Yoshiyuki Sudō, ed., *Shindai Manshū Tochi Seisaku no Kenkyū Toku Ni Kichi Seisaku o Chūshin to shite* [Qing land policy in Manchuria, especially on the banner land] (Tōkyō: Kawade Shobō, 1944), 150–1. At the time the price of one *sheng* of black bean was roughly 0.5 *fen* (5 *li* 3 *hao* to 6 *li* 5 *hao* to be exact).
8. According to the arrangement of conditional sale, a buyer acquired the temporary right to use the seller's land by loaning funds to the seller for a certain period of time. The seller had the right to repurchase the land by repaying the loans without interest.

9. Yi Zheng, ed., *Dongbei Nongye Jingji Shiliao Jicheng* [Collection of historical source on agricultural development in (China's) Northeast] (Changchun: Jilin wenshi chubanshe, 2005), 102; Kun'gang and Qiduan Liu, *Qinding Da Qing Huidian Shili* [Collected administrative statutes and precedents], vol. 607 (Shanghai: Shanghai guji chubanshe, 2002).
10. Kim, *Ginseng and Borderland*.
11. Taofu Wang, *Qingji Waijiao Shiliao: Guangxu Chao* [Primary source of the Late Qing foreign relations; Guangxu reign] (Beiping (Beijing): Waijiao shiliao bianzuan chu, 1932–5); Yang and Sun, *Zhong Chao Bianjie Shi* [History of Sino-Korean border], 236–8.
12. Zheng, *Dongbei Nongye Jingji Shiliao Jicheng* [Collection of historical source on agricultral development in (China's) Northeast], 352–3, 363; Shichang Xu, *Dongsansheng zhenglüe* [Political Strategy Regarding the Three Eastern Provinces] (Changchun: Jilin wenshi chubanshe, 1989), "Caizheng, Fentian," "Ji Qingfu."
13. Longfan Jiang, "Qing Zhengfu Yiminshibian Zhengce yu Zhongguo Chaoxianzu de Xingcheng [Qing Government's Policy of 'Moving People to Fill Border' and the Formation of Chaoxianzu of China]," *Shehuikexue Zhanxian* 4 (2000): 187.
14. It should also be noted that local Russian authorities started to naturalize Korean migrants who settled in their domain at almost the same time as the Qing. According to Alyssa Park, there was a record about the Russian naturalization of Koreans as early as 1865. The tsarist government incorporated Koreans into the state peasantry and provided them with land (Park, *Sovereignty Experiments*, 55).
15. For a detailed examination of this process, see Kwangmin Kim, "Korean Migration in Nineteenth-Century Manchuria: A Global Theme in Modern Asian History," in *Mobile Subjects: Boundaries and Identities in the Modern Korean Diaspora*, ed. Wen-hsin Yeh (Berkeley: Institute of East Asian Studies, University of California, 2013), 17–37.
16. Zhongguo di 1 lishi dang'an guan, *Hunchun Fudutong Yamen Dang* [The Hunchun Lieutenant-General's office archives], vol. 178 (Guilin: Guangxi shifan daxue chubanshe, 2006), 403; GX21/2/25 (1895), Hunchun fudutong yamen Zuosi's investigation report on Korean Kim Injŏn and others.
17. For a good introduction to the Great Qing Citizenship Law, see Song, *Making Borders in Modern East Asia*, 234–6.
18. Longfan Jiang and Yongzhe Cui, "Ri Han Hebing yu Jiandao Chaoxianren de Guoji Wenti: Jianlun Zhong Ri Liangguo zai Chaoxianren Guoji Wenti Shang de Zhengce Fenzheng [Japanese annexation of Korea and Kando Korean's citizenship: discussion of the policy struggle between Chinese and Japanese governments regarding the citizenship of Koreans]," *Dongjiang Xuekan* 16, no. 4 (1999): 9–10.
19. Manshū Iminshi Kenkyūkai, ed., *Nihon Teikokushugi Ka No Manshū Imin* [Migration in Manchuria under Japanese imperialism] (Tōkyō: Ryūkei Shosha, 1976), 500–1.
20. Longfan Jiang, *Jindai Zhong Ri Han Sanguo Dui Jiando Chaoxian Ren de Zhengce Yanjiu* [Chinese, Japanese and Korean governments' policy regarding Koreans in Yanbian during the modern period] (Mudanjiang: Heilongjiang Chaoxian minzu chubanshe, 2000), 125–6.
21. Jiang and Cui, "Ri Han Hebing yu Jiandao Chaoxianren de Guoji Wenti: Jianlun Zhong Ri Liangguo zai Chaoxianren Guoji Wenti Shang de Zhengce Fenzheng [Japanese annexation of Korea and Kando Korean's citizenship: discussion of the policy struggle between Chinese and Japanese governments regarding the citizenship

of Koreans]," 11. For more examples of flexible application see Song, *Making Borders in Modern East Asia*, 236, fn 38.
22. Jiang and Cui, "Ri Han Hebing yu Jiandao Chaoxianren de Guoji Wenti: Jianlun Zhong Ri Liangguo Zai Chaoxianren Guoji Wenti Shang de Zhengce Fenzheng [Japanese annexation of Korea and Kando Korean's citizenship: discussion of the policy struggle between Chinese and Japanese governments regarding the citizenship of Koreans]," 13; Xingyuan Zhao, "Qing Zhengfu dui Tumenjiangbei de Chaoxian Yimin de Guanli [Qing government's management of the Korean migrants in the north of Tumen River]," *Dongbei Shidi* 3 (2009): 44–5.
23. Shutian Li, Yuliang Ma, Yanyu Wang, Jilin shifan xueyuan guji yanjiusuo, and Jilin shi dang'an guan, eds., *Jilin Nongye Dangjuan* [Archival Materials on Agriculture in Jilin] (Jilin: Jilin wenshi chubanshe, 1990), 149. "The simplified regulation regarding the development of irrigated land revised by Jilin county's shiyeju (business bureau), MG15/9/26 (1926)."
24. Hyun Ok Park, *Two Dreams in One Bed: Empire, Social Life, and the Origins of the North Korean Revolution in Manchuria* (Durham, NC: Duke University Press, 2005), 118.
25. Manshū Iminshi Kenkyūkai, *Nihon Teikokushugi Ka no Manshū Imin* [Migration in Manchuria under Japanese imperialism], 551–6.
26. Ibid., 552.
27. Ibid., 554.

Bibliography

Published Sources

Kun'gang and Qiduan Liu. *Qinding Da Qing Huidian Shili* [Collected administrative statutes and precedents], vol. 607. Shanghai: Shanghai guji chubanshe. 2002.
Li, Shutian, Yuliang Ma, Yanyu Wang, Jilin shifan xueyuan guji yanjiusuo, and Jilin shi dang'an guan, eds. *Jilin Nongye Dangjuan* [Archival materials on agriculture in Jilin]. Jilin: Jilin wenshi chubanshe, 1990.
Wang, Taofu. *Qingji Waijiao Shiliao: Guangxu Chao* [Primary source of the Late Qing foreign relations; Guangxu reign]. Beiping (Beijing): Waijiao shiliao bianzuan chu, 1932–5.
Wang, Xianqian. *Donghua xu lu* [Sequel to the record of Donghua [Gate]], vol. 44. Shanghai: Shanghai guji chubanshe, 2002.
Xu, Shichang. *Dongsansheng zhenglüe* [Political strategy regarding the Three Eastern Provinces]. Changchun: Jilin wenshi chubanshe, 1989.
Zheng, Yi, ed. *Dongbei Nongye Jingji Shiliao Jicheng* [Collection of historical source on agricultural development in (China's) Northeast]. Changchun: Jilin wenshi chubanshe, 2005.
Zhongguo bianjiang shidi yanjiu zhongxin, and Liaoning Sheng dang'an guan, eds. *Dongbei Bianjiang Dang'an Xuanji: Qingdai, Mingguo* [Selected archival material regarding northeastern frontier (Manchuria): The Qing and the Republican period], vol. 43. Guilin: Guangxi shifan daxue chubanshe, 2007.
Zhongguo di 1 lishi dang'an guan. *Hunchun Fudutong Yamen Dang* [The Hunchun Lieutenant-General's office archives], vol. 178. Guilin: Guangxi shifan daxue chubanshe, 2006.

Research Literature

Crossley, Pamela Kyle. *A Translucent Mirror: History and Identity in Qing Imperial Ideology.* Berkeley: University of California Press, 2002.

Jiang, Longfan. *Jindai Zhong Ri Han Sanguo dui Jiando Chaoxian Ren de Zhengce Yanjiu* [Chinese, Japanese and Korean governments' policy regarding Koreans in Yanbian during the modern period]. Mudanjiang: Heilongjiang Chaoxian minzu chubanshe, 2000.

Jiang, Longfan. "Qing Zhengfu dui Chaoxian Yimin de Zhengce: Huairou yu Tonghua Zhengce Wei Zhongxin [Qing Government's policy toward Korean migrants: appeasement and assimilation]." *Yanbian Daxue Xuebao (Shehui Kexue Ban)* 2 (1998): 63–7.

Jiang, Longfan. "Qing Zhengfu Yiminshibian Zhengce yu Zhongguo Chaoxianzu de Xingcheng [Qing government's policy of 'moving people to fill border' and the formation of Chaoxianzu of China]." *Shehuikexue Zhanxian* 4 (2000): 187–93.

Jiang, Longfan, and Yongzhe Cui. "Ri Han Hebing yu Jiandao Chaoxianren de Guoji Wenti: Jianlun Zhong Ri Liangguo zai Chaoxianren Guoji Wenti Shang de Zhengce Fenzheng [Japanese annexation of Korea and Kando Korean's citizenship: discussion of the policy struggle between Chinese and Japanese governments regarding the citizenship of Koreans]." *Dongjiang Xuekan* 16, no. 4 (1999): 9–16.

Kim, Kwangmin. "Korean Migration in Nineteenth-Century Manchuria: A Global Theme in Modern Asian History." In *Mobile Subjects: Boundaries and Identities in the Modern Korean Diaspora*, edited by Wen-hsin Yeh, 17–37. Berkeley: Institute of East Asian Studies, University of California, 2013.

Kim, Seonmin. *Ginseng and Borderland: Territorial Boundaries and Political Relations between Qing China and Chosŏn Korea, 1636–1912.* Berkeley: University of California Press, 2017.

Manshū Iminshi Kenkyūkai, ed. *Nihon Teikokushugi Ka no Manshū Imin* [Migration in Manchuria under Japanese imperialism]. Tōkyō: Ryūkei Shosha, 1976.

Park, Alyssa. *Sovereignty Experiments: Korean Migrants and the Building of Borders in Northeast Asia, 1860–1945.* Ithaca, NY: Cornell University Press, 2019.

Park, Hyun Ok. *Two Dreams in One Bed: Empire, Social Life, and the Origins of the North Korean Revolution in Manchuria.* Durham, NC: Duke University Press, 2005.

Sahlins, Peter. *Boundaries: The Making of France and Spain in the Pyrenees.* Reprint edition. Berkeley: University of California Press, 1991.

Song, Nianshen. *Making Borders in Modern East Asia: The Tumen River Demarcation, 1881–1919.* Cambridge: Cambridge University Press, 2018.

Sudō, Yoshiyuki, ed. *Shindai Manshū Tochi Seisaku no Kenkyū Toku ni Kichi Seisaku o Chūshin to shite* [Qing land policy in Manchuria, especially on the banner land]. Tōkyō: Kawade Shobō, 1944.

Sun, Chunri. "Qingmo Zhong Chao 'Jiandao Wenti' Jiaoshe Zhi Yuanwei [Full Details of the negotiation regarding the Jiandao (Kando) problem during the Late Qing period]." *Zhongguo Bianjiang Shidi Yanjiu* 12, no. 4 (2002): 48–58.

Yang, Zhaoquan, and Yumei Sun. *Zhong Chao Bianjie Shi* [History of Sino-Korean border]. Changchun: Jilin wenshi chubanshe, 1993.

Zhao, Xingyuan. "Qing Zhengfu dui Tumenjiangbei de Chaoxian Yimin de Guanli [Qing government's management of the Korean migrants in the north of Tumen River]." *Dongbei Shidi* 3 (2009): 41–6.

4

The National Question in Finnish Communism: Leninist-Stalinist-Kuusinenist Theory and the Finland-Swedish Minority in the Interwar Period

Jonas Ahlskog and Mats Wickström

> *Everything changes … . Social life changes, and with it the "national question" changes, too. At different periods different classes enter the arena, and each class has its own view of the "national question." Consequently, in different periods the "national question" serves different interests and assumes different shades, according to which class raises it, and when.*[1]
>
> –J. V. Stalin, 1904

The contradiction between socialism and nationalism is arguably the most studied ideological opposition in the history of modern European political thought. Ever since the inception of the socialist labor movement in the mid-nineteenth century, enormous amounts of ink have been spilled on attempts to either transcend or reinforce the apparent contradiction between international working-class solidarity and nationalist sentiment. Every classical socialist thinker has wrestled with the question—from Marx, Engels, and Kautsky to Luxemburg, Bauer, Lenin, and Stalin—and all self-respecting communist parties during the twentieth century had a specific policy on the so-called national question. After the collapse of communism, a great number of studies have aimed to describe and explain the ways in which ruling European communist parties in general, and Soviet international organizations in particular, tried to harness the power of nationalism for communist causes in Europe and liberation movements in the colonies. As a result, contemporary scholarship agrees that nationalism was a central, yet historically variant, ingredient in the policies of communist movements throughout the twentieth century. Consequently, the supposed incompatibility of the opposing ideologies of nationalism and internationalist communism is a myth decidedly busted by post–Cold War scholarship.[2]

Despite the wide-ranging political and scholarly interest in the topic, the role of nationalism for communist movements in Western liberal-democratic states, especially states with significant ethno-national minorities, remains neglected by scholars. The main aim of this chapter is to investigate this historical phenomenon by way of a particular empirical case study, namely, the communist movement in the binational state of Finland in the interwar period. Here Leninist-Stalinist nationality theory was put to work both in relation to the bourgeois-dominated Finland-Swedish minority and in relation to the rise of fascism in Finland.

We argue that contemporary research has been dominated by a depersonalized "clash of discourses" paradigm in which the main task for the historian is to describe how the agents managed to combine two contradictory political ideologies. This perspective tends to reduce the role of nationalism in communist political movements to instances of deviation, while, simultaneously, equating the question of nationalism with loyalty to the state, an issue that, albeit important, only partially elucidates the relationship between communism and nationalism. In contrast, we use a contextualist perspective for understanding the ways in which national questions were an integral element in the communist movement that went beyond issues of state loyalty.

The Leninist-Stalinist Theory of the Nation

Lenin and Stalin considered the national question to be absolutely crucial for communist revolutions both at home and abroad. Consequently, both Lenin and Stalin wrote several articles explicitly on the national question, and the position they developed was subsequently adopted as the official policy of the Soviet Union and the international communist organizations under its control. The most significant ideological innovation of Lenin and Stalin was, undoubtedly, their fruitful incorporation of nationalism in the Marxist view of the development of capitalism. National claims were no longer derided as merely false consciousness, but supported as a legitimate stage in the historical development toward communism. This was based on the supposition that consciousness of nationhood and consciousness of class traveled together. After all, nationalism, they believed, must rely on the identification and construction of an Indigenous people (the nation) in opposition to the largely cosmopolitan ruling classes of Europe. Accordingly, Lenin proclaimed that "the struggle [of the masses] against all oppression, for the sovereignty of the people, or the nation [is] progressive."[3]

The question resonated deeply within the Marxist tradition; Marx himself had stated, on the topic of the conflict between Irish and English workers, that any nation that oppressed another forged its own chains.[4] The idea was that the bourgeois hegemony in each nation would be strengthened when workers from different nations were agitated to act against one another. In other words, the question of national self-determination was a decisive part in the global communist revolution, even if Marx, and particularly Engels, made a sharp distinction between progressive historical nations and reactionary peoples without history; only the former had the necessary conditions for—and a right to—sovereignty.[5]

However, Lenin's and Stalin's ideological innovation translated in principle into support for the right of every nation to self-determination, even up to the point of separation and the formation of independent states. In the early years of the Bolshevik regime, this right was also exercised by former members of the Russian Empire, such as Finland and Ukraine among others. Nonetheless, the period in which succession from Bolshevik-ruled Russia was a practical possibility was very short, and most minority areas had been brought back under Soviet control within a few years, with the exception of Finland, the Baltic States, and parts of Poland. The *de facto* right of national self-determination ended with the establishment of the Soviet Union in 1922. However, more significant for Western European communism is the fact that the right to self-determination remained central to the Soviet constitution, even if devoid of meaning within the union. The constitutions of 1924, 1936, and 1977 all declared that the republics of the federation were sovereign and possessed the right to secede at will from the Soviet Union. As Walker Connor has argued, this symbolic paragraph played a very important role in Comintern propaganda about the Soviet Union as the supporter of oppressed peoples both in the colonies and in multinational states.[6]

Until Khrushchev's so-called secret speech about the cult of personality surrounding Stalin and the deplorable consequences thereof at the Twentieth Congress of the Communist Party of the Soviet Union in 1956, Stalin was an unassailable ideological authority, both within Finnish and international communism. Stalin's specialty as a Marxist theoretician was the question of nationality, within which he made a name for himself in 1913 with one of his most important works, *Marxism and the National Question*, originally published under the title "The National Question and Social-Democracy" in issues 3–5 of the Bolshevik journal *Prosveshchenye* (Enlightenment).[7] After the October Revolution of 1917, Stalin was named People's Commissar for Nationalities in the first Soviet government, a seat he held until 1923. Even before he emerged victorious from the struggle for power following Lenin's death in 1924, Stalin was an expert in questions of nationality—both in his own eyes and in those of others.[8]

Stalin wrote *Marxism and the National Question* primarily as an indictment of the Austrian Social Democrat Otto Bauer. Bauer was a leading Austro-Marxist ideologue and social democratic politician whose first work, *Die Nationalitätenfrage und die Sozialdemokratie* (1907), elevated him as a theoretician within the international workers' movement.[9] In addition to having his sights set on Austrian social democracy and its national program, which he considered flawed, the General Jewish Workers' Union in Lithuania, Poland, and Russia (the Bund) was also in Stalin's ideological aim. The combination of socialism and Jewish minority nationalism within the Bund was heavily influenced by the Austro-Marxist idea of national cultural autonomy as a non-territorial principle of governance for a multinational democratic state.[10]

According to Stalin, policies of cultural autonomy relied on a faulty theoretical footing. The most egregious false conclusion was that the idea of cultural autonomy spiritualized the concept of the nation by differentiating the national character of a people and the material conditions for their life in a way that Stalin considered un-Marxist. What Bauer called national character was, for Stalin, merely "a reflection of the conditions of life, a coagulation of impressions derived from [the] environment."[11] According to Stalin, it was the soil, the territory, that was the basis of the nation and, therefore, also the starting point for a Marxist policy of nationality: "How can one [like Bauer] limit the matter to national character alone, isolating and divorcing it from the soil that gave rise to it?"[12] Stalin accused Bauer of mystification and brought up the Jews as an example of how the Bauerian principle of national character failed to correspond to material and political realities:

> Bauer's point of view, which identifies a nation with its national character, divorces the nation from its soil and converts it into an invisible, self-contained force. The result is not a living and active nation, but something mystical, intangible and supernatural. For, I repeat, what sort of nation, for instance, is a Jewish nation that consists of Georgian, Daghestanian, Russian, American and other Jews, the members of which do not understand each other (since they speak different languages), inhabit different parts of the globe, will never see each other, will never act together, whether in time of peace or in time of war?[13]

In Stalin's view, Bauer had misunderstood the very idea of a nation. In order to correct this both unscientific and politically detrimental misapprehension, Stalin presented his own definition of a nation, a definition of a concept that, three decades later, would have a great ideological importance for Finnish communism in general and Finland-Swedish communism in particular:

> *A nation is a historically evolved, stable community of language, territory, economic life, and psychological make-up manifested in a community of culture.*
> It goes without saying that a nation, like every other historical phenomenon, is subject to the law of change, has its history, its beginning and end.
> It must be emphasized that none of the above characteristics is by itself sufficient to define a nation. On the other hand, it is sufficient for a single one of these characteristics to be absent and the nation ceases to be a nation.[14]

Even if Stalin considered the four criteria constituting a nation (a common language, territory, economic life, and mentality) to be equal parts, he was of the opinion that the basis of nationhood was, primarily, a "large and stable stratum connected with the land" that serves to "naturally rivet the nation together," that is, a resident agrarian population.[15]

Importantly, Stalin had a clear answer to the question: "What must be our attitude towards [minority] nations which for one reason or another will prefer to remain within the general frame-work [i.e. a democratized state]?"[16]—an issue that would later be relevant for the Finland-Swedes. According to Stalin, in a state with "complete democracy,"[17] there was no longer a need for the majority nationality to oppress national minorities (i.e., minority groups that constituted a nationality in accordance with the four prerequisites), nor for the national minorities to create culturally autonomous alliances over state borders, since their demands would be met:

> A minority is discontented not because there is no national union but because it does not enjoy the right to use its native language. Permit it to use its native language and the discontent will pass of itself.
> A minority is discontented not because there is no artificial union but because it does not possess its own schools. Give it its own schools and all ground for discontent will disappear.

> A minority is discontented not because there is no national union, but because it does not enjoy liberty of conscience, liberty of movement, etc. Give it these liberties and it will cease to be discontented.
>
> Thus, *national equality in all forms (language, schools, etc.) is an essential element* in the solution of the national question. A state law based on complete democracy in the country is required, prohibiting all national privileges without exception and all kinds of disabilities and restrictions on the rights of national minorities.[18]

Stalin's four prerequisites for nationality became a Leninist-Stalinist guideline to determine which groups could legitimately claim to constitute a nation, with the associated right to self-determination. These Bolshevik tenets of national self-determination legitimized, among other things, its recognition of Finland's independence on December 31, 1917[19], and the Bolshevik solution to the national question became a matter of practical policy in the Soviet Union, which was formally a federation. According to Russian-American historian Yuri Slezkine, the first five-year period (1928–32) of the Soviet Union was "the most extravagant celebration of ethnic diversity that any state had ever financed."[20] Until 1936, all nationalities had, in principle, a right to secede from the state.[21] Nations were recognized on both a personal basis and a territorial basis, despite the fact that the former could be interpreted as an expression of Austro-Marxist cultural autonomy.[22]

The Binational Setting of Finnish Communism

Swedish was until the turn of the twentieth century the main educational and administrative language in the Grand Duchy of Finland, which had been an autonomous part of the Russian Empire since the Kingdom of Sweden lost its eastern part to Russia in 1809. The elite of Finland spoke Swedish, but Swedish was also the language of peasants, fishers, and workers in the coastal regions of southern and western Finland. The large majority of Swedish-speakers in Finland belonged to the latter social groups. Many municipalities were monolingually Swedish as around 14 percent of the population of Finland was Swedish speaking in 1880. As a response to the rise of majoritarian Finnish ethno-nationalism in the latter part of the nineteenth century, the Swedish speakers consolidated and mobilized as a minority nation on the ideological basis that the Swedes in Finland were not Finns nor Swedish-speaking Finns but rather a Swedish nationality in Finland. According to this minority nationalist theory, the Swedish nationality of Finland was distinctly separate from but equal to the Finnish nationality of Finland, that is, the ethnic Finns. Together these two main nationalities (ethnoses) of Finland formed the (political) binational people of Finland, Finland's demos. Finland-Swede, a self-descriptive ethnonym for the Swedish speakers, was introduced in the early twentieth century to emphasize ethnic distinctiveness and domicile in Finland.[23]

In 1906, a minority nationalist party called the Swedish People's Party (SPP) was formed due to democratization in Finland in the wake of the Russian Revolution of 1905. Although the SPP was basically a bourgeois party, it managed to gather the majority of the Swedish-speaking vote in the first democratic parliamentary elections of Finland in 1907 with 12.6 percent of the total vote. The Social Democratic Party of Finland (SDP) received 37 percent of the vote and won the election.[24]

The downfall of the Russian Empire due to the upheavals of the First World War pawed the way for Finland's independence, which was declared on December 6, 1917. At the beginning of 1918, Finland fell into civil war between revolutionary Reds and bourgeois Whites. The war ended in victory for the Whites in the spring of 1918. Most of the leaders of the Reds escaped to Soviet Russia, where they founded the Communist Party of Finland (CPF) in August 1918. The CPF was illegal in Finland and until 1944 its leadership and key organizations operated out of the Soviet Union. The SDP quickly reformed after the war, but the new nonrevolutionary line of the party prompted many members to leave the Social Democrats and turn to communism. In May 1920, the Socialist Workers' Party of Finland was formed as a domestic branch of what historian Tauno Saarela for simplicity's sake has called Finnish communism.[25] Finnish communism was, however, neither a monolingual nor a mononational phenomenon as the Republic of Finland was both officially bilingual and de facto binational.

The question of nationality was of ideological and strategic importance for the Finnish communists, particularly the Finland-Swedish communists. The socialist Finnish society they were working toward would liberate the working majority of Finland-Swedes from capitalist exploitation and bourgeois oppression. The oppression directed toward Finland-Swedish workers was also considered more severe, since the kind of workers' education that had been practiced among the Finnish-speaking working class rarely reached Swedish-speaking workers. In the minds of the Finland-Swedish communists, it was also crucial that the workers should participate in class struggle *without* compromising their Finland-Swedish national identity. In fact, the transition to socialism was intended to strengthen the vital necessities of the Finland-Swedish *nationality* and secure its future in Finland. As we will show, this communist vision of a future for the Finland-Swedes was grounded in Marxist-Leninist theory, and particularly in Stalin's premier contribution to this theoretical construct prior to the Russian revolution: *Marxism and the National Question* (1913).[26]

The Finland-Swedish communists were active in a political field that was constituted along minority nationalist lines. It was therefore of utmost strategic importance for the communists to develop a unique minority nationalist standpoint and to communicate it to the Finland-Swedish people whom they considered to be oppressed. Simultaneously, leading Finland-Swedish communists believed that the party's future success among the voting public hinged on a believable policy for protecting Swedishness in Finland. The democratization of Finland that they were talking about, establishing a socialist society under communist rule, was therefore to be combined with the liberation of the Finland-Swedish minority.

Finnish Communism and the Nationality Question until the Crackdown on Communism in 1930

The CPF was constituted in Moscow in August 1918 and had two native countries—the Soviet Union and Finland. The party leadership resided in the Soviet Union and the party's policies were drafted there in accordance with the Soviet model.[27] For the Swedish-speaking population of Finland this meant that the CPF, following an orthodox interpretation of Soviet doctrine, took a clear stand with regard to Finland-Swedish self-determination in the 1920s:

> Even the most far-reaching goals of autonomy of the Swedish population and the complete independence of the Ålanders [the people of the Åland Islands in the Baltic Sea], their secession from the Finnish state, must be courageously and consistently supported. It must be understood that the basis of the national question is the question of the farmers, and thus that the farmers and fishermen are the driving force of the Swedish national movement. It must be brought to their attention that the communists of Finland unwaveringly support their right to national self-determination, not just in words but also in deeds, up to secession from the state.[28]

The peasant question as a basis for the question of nationality followed one of Stalin's primary claims in *Marxism and the National Question*: that nationhood was bound to the soil and to those who tilled it. The Finland-Swedish farmers and fishermen were nationally minded and thus supported the bourgeois Swedish National Movement, which in terms of party politics was the SPP, in the belief that it was the only entity that could safeguard their national interests. In contrast to the SPP, the Finnish communists argued that the Swedish population of Finland had a right not only to autonomy within the Finnish state, but also to secede entirely from that state. By outdoing the SPP in the nationality question, the CPF tried to gain a breakthrough among the Finland-Swedes. If the Finland-Swedes truly gained national self-determination, their opportunities for democratization would also increase, thanks to a class-bound normalization of the political realities within the group. According to Stalin's theory, national autonomy moved the focus of the workers from struggles between nations to their own class struggle within the nation.[29] In an autonomous or independent ethno-territory, the Finland-Swedish bourgeoisie would lose its entrenched position as the self-evident defenders of the Swedish nation against Finnish ethno-nationalism (*aitosuomalaisuus*, True Finnishness), and the true class dynamics of the group would turn the matter in favor of the working class.

Nya Folkbladet (1926–30), the only Finland-Swedish communist newspaper, featured articles on the nationality question and unsurprisingly propagated for the right to self-determination of Finland-Swedes. The main thrust of *Nya Folkbladet* in the nationality question were attacks on the capitalist SPP and the SDP. The SPP was accused of deceiving the Finland-Swedish majority with phony minority nationalism and of always prioritizing the interest of the Swedish-speaking upper class over the interests of the Swedish nationality, that is, the mass of Swedish-speakers in Finland, even if it meant allying with Finnish fascists. The SDP, in turn, was said to be infested with True Finnish chauvinism and had turned away from the principles of Marxist and international socialism in the nationality question (as well as most other questions).[30] Neither the SPP nor the SDP cared if Swedish-Finland was fennicized and the Finland-Swedes robbed of their rights as long as the bourgeois masters in both parties could continue to "bathe in sunlight" and to be well fed at the top of a Finnish Finland.[31]

The communist message of national self-determination for the Swedish nationality in Finland was also featured in the 1927 parliamentary election campaign of the Socialist Workers' and Smallholders' Electoral Organization (STPV), a public branch of Finnish communism. The STPV connected fascism with the nationality question and warned of "extreme fascist elements" inspired by international examples (i.e., Italy) that strived to enact a coup d'état in Finland and establish a complete fascist dictatorship. According to the STPV, one of the forms of Finnish fascism was True Finnishness, which at the moment primarily pursued the oppression of the rights of the Swedish minority nationality in Finland. The STPV took an opposite position: the calls for an expansion of self-determination by the Swedish "common people" should be settled in accordance with the will of the "common people." The STPV's eighteen-point list of demands also included a point on the Swedish minority: the principle of national self-determination should be applied to the Swedish minority nationality and "the Swedish people [in Finland]" must be allowed to govern over the regions in which they lived.[32] Importantly, this demand was premised on the fundamental territorial condition of the Leninist-Stalinist theory of nationhood, namely, that the Swedish nationality was not merely a specific cultural identity, but a people in possession of their own territory for implementing national self-government.

The STPV's unconditional support for Finland-Swedish self-determination was continued in the 1929 parliamentary elections, where it also opposed the oppression of Finland's "minority nationalities" in general.[33] Which minority nationalities the STPV referred to in addition to the named Swedish minority is unclear and falls outside the scope of the study, but presumably at least the Saami minority as it could be defined as a nation according to Stalin's conditions.

The STPV was outlawed in the summer of 1930 as a part of a general crackdown on communism brought about by the fascistoid and flourishing Lapua Movement. Even though the Lapua Movement imploded in a disastrous coup attempt in 1932, hardline anti-communism continued as state policy. In the mid-1930s, the accelerating growth of fascist power and the (belated) response of the Comintern in the form of the anti-fascist Popular Front called new attention to the national question in Finland.

Otto Ville Kuusinen's Stalinist Defense of the Swedish Nationality in Finland and the National Question in the CPF's Popular Front Strategy

In May of 1935, the Sweden-based communist newspaper *Ny Dag*[34] published a four-part series of articles[35] by Otto Ville Kuusinen, a prominent figure in the Comintern and the undeniable leader of the CPF.[36] The article series was a translation of Kuusinen's manuscript "Kansallisuuskysymyksestä Suomessa" (On the National Question in Finland), in which he theoretically developed the stance of the CPF regarding the Finnish national question.

Kuusinen criticized the "Finnish chauvinist theory of nationality" for its faulty and confused use of concepts. According to Kuusinen, the Finnish chauvinist theory of nationality—which the Finnish bourgeoisie had adopted—defined the Swedes in Finland as belonging to "the Finnish nationality." Kuusinen was of the opinion that the Finnish bourgeoisie thereby denied the national existence of the Finland-Swedes and forced a foreign nationality upon them. This denial of the Finland-Swedish claim to a nationality was grounded in an intentional mixing of the concepts of a people and a homeland with the concept of nationality. Kuusinen stated that a people was the population of a state and that a homeland was the same as a state. However, the fact that Finland-Swedes were a part of the population (people) and the state (homeland) of Finland did not mean "that there is not more than one nationality or nation in Finland." According to Kuusinen, a "ruling majority nation" was, of course, not "the only existing nation" in a multinational state such as Finland. He remarked that not even the Polish majority nationalists claimed that the people of Poland consisted solely of Poles, since a significant number of the population of the country consisted of other nationalities. Kuusinen also brought up Switzerland—a people that was primarily made up of three nationalities—as an example.[37]

In Kuusinen's view, "Finnish chauvinism" used the invalid theoretical conclusion mentioned earlier as a basis for claiming that there was only a Swedish "'language group' within the Finnish nation" and that there was no national question in Finland, but merely "a 'question of language.'" To claim otherwise was also, in the minds of these chauvinists, "nothing less than 'treason against the homeland,'" as Kuusinen puts it. Kuusinen admonished those Finland-Swedes who, lacking "inner clarity" in the national question, did not completely reject the Finnish chauvinist theory of nationality, but instead teetered "hither and yon," which played into the hands of Finnish chauvinism.[38]

According to Kuusinen, "comrade Stalin" had answered the question of what a nation or a nationality was "already in 1913," that is, in *Marxism and the National Question*. Based on Stalin's definition, Kuusinen answered the question of whether the Swedish population of Finland constituted a nationality or a nation, which he claimed to be "one and the same thing in this context"[39]:

> First, the community of language is indubitably a clear fact; second, excepting Åland, the territorial community of the Swedes is a reality in two areas of the country, in the coastal regions of southern Finland and Ostrobothnia, even if both of these Swedish areas of settlement are separated from one another; additionally, Swedish-speaking groups are found here and there, interspersed in the cities of the interior of the country (these are, as a matter of fact, merely "language groups"); third, economic community is also a fact in the Swedish area, even though the economic life of the Swedish and Finnish populations is naturally intertwined in many ways; fourth, the Swedish culture in Finland presents its own national character, separate from the Finnish national character, although both of these national cultures have influenced each other greatly. Therefore, the Swedish population of southern Finland and Ostrobothnia should self-evidently be considered a separate nationality, nationally related to the people of Sweden, but not of the same nationality. The Swedes of Finland, the Ålanders excepted, share only a community of language and a closeness of culture with the people

of Sweden, but not enduring cultural community, not to mention territorial or economic community.[40]

Considering the modest number of the Swedish-speaking minority (around 10 percent) in relation to the Finnish-speaking majority (around 90 percent) at the time, it is relevant to ask why the position and status of the Finland-Swedish minority was at all relevant for the communist leader Kuusinen. The explanation lies mainly in the Leninist-Stalinist theory of revolution. Accordingly, Kuusinen argued that the social democrats underestimated the importance of the question of nationality for the question of revolution.[41] The question of nationality was not only a question of the fate and well-being of Finland-Swedes—it was decisive for Finnish class struggle as a whole. For Kuusinen, the national question in Finland was one of the primary tools that Finnish fascism used to agitate the nationalities of Finland against one another and thus splinter the working class.[42] According to Kuusinen, the Finland-Swedes fulfilled the same purpose in the agitation of the Finnish fascists as the Jews did for their German counterparts.[43]

Kuusinen claimed that it was a duty and an honor for the class-conscious Finnish worker to fight in the forefront for the position of the Swedish nationality in Finland. For him, the defense of the Finland-Swedish nation was even a prerequisite for the Finnish class struggle itself; if the Finnish working class did not defend the Finland-Swedes, it would also not be able to free itself from the class oppression of the bourgeoisie, an oppression that misled it into attacking its brothers in the working class. In addition to this external relation, that is, that national conflicts tend to overshadow class struggle, Kuusinen was also of the opinion that there was an internal link between class consciousness and an understanding of the interests of one's own nationality. Kuusinen claimed that the Finland-Swedish worker who had yet to awaken their proletarian class consciousness was also indifferent to the struggle to defend their own nationality against foreign oppression.[44] Class consciousness and consciousness of the question of nationality were two sides of the same coin: the worker who understood their class position understood simultaneously that they belonged to a nationality that was being oppressed by the owning class, and that the latter only spoke of the interests of the nationality when these coincided with its own interests.

Kuusinen's tenets on the intertwinement of the class struggle and the national question in Finland were also incorporated in the Popular Front strategy that the CPF adopted in the wake of the strategical turn of the Comintern in 1935. According to the CPF, chauvinism was the most dangerous weapon of the fascists, and in Finland it was used to turn the Finnish population against "the Swedes," that is, the Finland-Swedes. This state of affairs had to be made clear to the Swedish population of Finland: if they wanted to defend themselves effectively, then they had to join the Popular Front together with the other opponents of fascism. They also had sharply to separate themselves from "the Swedish fascists," that is, Finland-Swedish fascists (many high-profile fascists in Finland were Swedish-speaking). The Finnish working class was, in turn, duty-bound to defend the equality and right to self-determination of the Swedish minority nationality in Finland.[45] The Finnish communists had, however, neither the means nor the manpower to carry out their Popular Front strategy in Finland, and in 1937–38, Finnish communism in the Soviet Union was severely decimated in Stalin's

Great Terror. The wily Otto Ville Kuusinen survived the purges, but the puppet regime (the Terijoki government), which Kuusinen headed during the Soviet invasion of Finland in 1939–40 (the Winter War), was rejected by many communists in Finland, several of which also fought against the Red Army in the war.[46] Nationalism trumped Stalinist imperialism.

The Legacy of the Leninist-Stalinist-Kuusinenist Conception of the National Question in Finland

After the legalization of communism in Finland in 1944, the Terijoki government was basically memory-holed by the party and both Stalin and Kuusinen, who outlived the former by many years, functioned as grand ideological authorities and idols in Finnish communism.[47] This state of affairs suited the Finland-Swedish communists, who in the early postwar period could lean on the prewar writings on the national question of both leaders to champion their brand of communist minority nationalism, which in many aspects was much more radical than the policies of the SPP.[48] The latest hurrah of Leninist-Stalinist-Kuusinenist nationality theory among Finland-Swedes occurred in the 1970s, when the so-called Hurrare movement in Ostrobothnia drew on both communist tradition and the black movements in the United States and the so-called ethnic revival in Europe. The name of the movement was an attempt to reclaim "hurri," a Finnish ethnic slur for Finland-Swedes.[49] Many of the international sources of inspiration for the Hurrare movement were also influenced by communist thought in their combination of nationalism and socialism. Today the Finland-Swedish minority, which has shrunk to 5 percent of the population, would no longer meet Stalin's criterion for constituting a nation (perhaps with the exception of parts of Ostrobothnia) and almost no one would today remember that the communists were once the champions of Finland-Swedish national self-determination.

Despite the collapse of communism, the historical dynamics of the national question is still very much part of the European political landscape. Arguably, the complex issue of what constitutes a nation, and especially what kinds of political rights nationhood involves, is one of the most pressing social concerns in relation to the rise of new nationalisms, identity politics, and reparation movements in post–Cold War Europe. The enduring relevance of the national question—although very few would use that title today—stems from a feature of nationalism that has been exemplified and explained in the present study, namely, the capability of nationalist ideology to seamlessly intermix with political movements that, at least at a doctrinal level, appear to be its very opposite. However, as our study shows, the apparent contradiction between nationalism and socialism was in no way an impediment on the endorsement of nationalist policies among Finnish communist agents and institutions during the interwar period. On the contrary, the recognition of nationhood for the Finland-Swedes was considered an integral part of the class struggle. This historically revealed, fluid, and shape-shifting dimension of nationalism will be an interesting element for future historians to explore among self-confessedly non-nationalist social and political movements in the present.

Notes

1. Joseph V. Stalin, "The Social-Democratic View on the National Question," Marxists Internet Archive, accessed March 23, 2023, https://www.marxists.org/reference/archive/stalin/works/1904/09/01.htm. Emphasis in original.
2. John Schwarzmantel, "Nationalism and Socialist Internationalism," in *The Oxford Handbook of the History of Nationalism*, ed. John Breuilly (Oxford: Oxford University Press, 2013), 635–55.
3. Quoted in Andrea Graziosi, "Communism, Nations and Nationalism," in *The Cambridge History of Communism: Volume 1: World Revolution and Socialism in One Country 1917–1941*, ed. Silvio Pons and Stephen A. Smith, vol. 1 (Cambridge: Cambridge University Press, 2017), 456.
4. Karl Marx in a confidential communication to German socialist leaders that was later to become famous, regarding the British rule in Ireland. See Ian Fraser and Lawrence Wilde, *The Marx Dictionary* (New York: Continuum, 2011), 147.
5. Walker Connor, *The National Question in Marxist-Leninist Theory and Strategy* (Princeton, NJ: Princeton University Press, 1984), 12.
6. Connor, *The National Question*, 52–9.
7. Erik van Ree, *The Political Thought of Joseph Stalin: A Study in Twentieth Century Revolutionary Patriotism* (London: Routledge Curzon, 2002), 64.
8. Timothy Snyder, *Sketches from a Secret War: A Polish Artist's Mission to Liberate Soviet Ukraine* (New Haven: Yale University Press, 2005), 35.
9. Michael Forman, *Nationalism and the International Labor Movement: The Idea of the Nation in Socialist and Anarchist Theory* (University Park, PA: Pennsylvania State University Press, 1998), 95–6.
10. Hélène Carrère D'Encausse, *The Great Challenge: Nationalities and the Bolshevik State, 1917–1930* (New York: Holmes & Meier Publishers, 1992), 28.
11. Joseph V. Stalin, *Marxism and the National Question* (Moscow: Foreign Languages Publishing House, 1945), 14.
12. Ibid., 14.
13. Ibid., 15.
14. Ibid., 11; emphasis in original.
15. Ibid., 45.
16. Ibid., 71.
17. Ibid., 70.
18. Ibid., 72–3; emphasis in original.
19. Not only Lenin, but also Stalin and Trotsky were signatories for the recognition of Finland's independence by the Council of People's Commissars.
20. Yuri Slezkine, "The USSR as a Communal Apartment, or How a Socialist State Promoted Ethnic Particularism," *Slavic Review* 53, no. 2 (1994): 414.
21. Ree, *The Political Thought of Joseph Stalin*, 192.
22. According to the Austro-Marxist principle of personality, a nation consists of individuals who share a national character, regardless of where they are.
23. Max Engman, *Språkfrågan: Finlandssvenskhetens uppkomst 1812–1922* (Helsingfors: SLS, 2016).
24. Engman, *Språkfrågan*.
25. Tauno Saarela, *Suomalaisen Kommunismin Synty 1918–1923* (Helsinki: Kansan sivistystyön liitto, 1996), 16–17.

26. Theodore R. Weeks, "Separatist Nationalism in the Romanov and Soviet Empires," in *The Oxford Handbook of the History of Nationalism*, ed. John Breuilly (Oxford: Oxford University Press, 2013), 207.
27. Tauno Saarela, *Finnish Communism Visited*, Papers on Labour History VII (Helsinki: The Finnish Society for Labour History, 2015).
28. Suomen Kommunistinen Puolue, *Puoluekokousten, konferenssien ja Keskuskomitean plenumien päätöksiä. Ensimmäinen kokoelma* (Leningrad: Valtion Kustannusliike Kirja, 1935), 96, 201–2, 261–2, 361.
29. Stalin, *Marxism and the National Question*, 73–4.
30. See, for example, *Nya Folkbladet*, February 18, 1927; May 27, 1927; May 3, 1929.
31. Ibid., June 24, 1927.
32. *Työväenjärjestöjen Tiedonantaja*, May 25, 1927.
33. *Työväenjärjestöjen Tiedonantaja*, June 7, 1929.
34. The so-called Communist Laws of 1930 banned communist press in Finland, a ban that the CPF tried to circumvent through its office in Stockholm, among other means.
35. *Ny Dag*, May 9, 1935; May 14, 1935; May 15, 1935; May 17, 1935.
36. Kimmo Rentola, *Kenen joukoissa seisot? Suomalainen kommunismi ja sota 1937–1945* (Porvoo: WSOY, 1994), 25–30.
37. *Ny Dag*, May 9, 1935; May 14, 1935; May 15, 1935; May 17, 1935.
38. Otto Ville Kuusinen, "Kansallisuuskysymys Suomessa." Unpublished manuscript, 1935.
39. Ibid.
40. Ibid.
41. Ibid.
42. That struggles of nationality distracted the workers from class struggle is also a central theme in Stalin's *Marxism and the National Question*, see, for example, pages 73 and 74.
43. Kuusinen, "Kansallisuuskysymys Suomessa."
44. Ibid.
45. Suomen Kommunistinen Puolue, *Yhteiseen taisteluun pääoman hyökkäystä vastaan: SKP:n VI puoluekokouksen päätökset*, 25–6.
46. Rentola, *Kenen joukoissa seisot?*
47. Saarela, *Finnish Communism Visited*.
48. Mats Wickström and Jonas Ahlskog, "Stalin och det svenska i Finland: Kommunistisk nationalitetsteori och den tidiga finlandssvenska folkdemokratin," *Historiska och litteraturhistoriska studier* 93 (2018): 135–59, https://doi.org/10.30667/hls.66419; Mats Wickström and Jonas Ahlskog, "'Vi lever och kommer att leva': Kommunisten och bildningsborgaren Harri Edgrens kulturkamp för finlandssvenskarnas fortlevnad," *Historiska och litteraturhistoriska studier* 94 (2019): 103–33, https://doi.org/10.30667/hls.76270.
49. Victor Wilson and Mats Wickström, "I minoritetsnationens tjänst: John Gardberg och det lokalt förankrade försvaret av Svenskfinland i Karis, ca 1930–1970," *Historisk Tidskrift för Finland* 105, no. 1 (2020): 33.

Bibliography

Carrère D'Encausse, Hélène. *The Great Challenge: Nationalities and the Bolshevik State, 1917–1930*. New York: Holmes & Meier Publishers, 1992.

Connor, Walker. *The National Question in Marxist-Leninist Theory and Strategy.* Princeton, NJ: Princeton University Press, 1984.
Engman, Max. *Språkfrågan: Finlandssvenskhetens uppkomst 1812–1922.* Helsingfors: SLS, 2016.
Forman, Michael. *Nationalism and the International Labor Movement: The Idea of the Nation in Socialist and Anarchist Theory.* University Park, PA: Pennsylvania State University Press, 1998.
Fraser, Ian, and Lawrence Wilde. *The Marx Dictionary.* New York: Continuum, 2011.
Graziosi, Andrea. "Communism, Nations and Nationalism." In *The Cambridge History of Communism: Volume 1: World Revolution and Socialism in One Country 1917–1941*, edited by Silvio Pons and Stephen A. Smith, vol. 1, 449–74. Cambridge: Cambridge University Press, 2017.
Kuusinen, Otto Ville. "Kansallisuuskysymys Suomessa." Unpublished manuscript, 1935.
Ree, Erik van. *The Political Thought of Joseph Stalin: A Study in Twentieth Century Revolutionary Patriotism.* London: Routledge Curzon, 2002.
Rentola, Kimmo. *Kenen joukoissa seisot? Suomalainen kommunismi ja sota 1937–1945.* Porvoo: WSOY, 1994.
Saarela, Tauno. *Finnish Communism Visited.* Papers on Labour History VII. Helsinki: The Finnish Society for Labour History, 2015.
Saarela, Tauno. *Suomalaisen kommunismin synty 1918–1923.* Helsinki: Kansan sivistystyön liitto, 1996.
Schwarzmantel, John. "Nationalism and Socialist Internationalism." In *The Oxford Handbook of the History of Nationalism*, edited by John Breuilly, 635–55. Oxford: Oxford University Press, 2013.
Slezkine, Yuri. "The USSR as a Communal Apartment, or How a Socialist State Promoted Ethnic Particularism." *Slavic Review* 53, no. 2 (1994): 414–52.
Snyder, Timothy. *Sketches from a Secret War: A Polish Artist's Mission to Liberate Soviet Ukraine.* New Haven: Yale University Press, 2005.
Stalin, Joseph V. *Marxism and the National Question.* Moscow: Foreign Languages Publishing House, 1945.
Stalin, Joseph V. "The Social-Democratic View on the National Question." Marxists Internet Archive. Accessed March 23, 2023. https://www.marxists.org/reference/archive/stalin/works/1904/09/01.htm.
Suomen Kommunistinen Puolue. *Puoluekokousten, konferenssien ja Keskuskomitean plenumien päätöksiä. Ensimmäinen kokoelma.* Leningrad: Valtion Kustannusliike Kirja, 1935.
Suomen Kommunistinen Puolue. *Yhteiseen taisteluun pääoman hyökkäystä vastaan: SKP:n VI puoluekokouksen päätökset.* Suomen kommunistinen puolue, 1935. Accessed March 23, 2023. https://helda.helsinki.fi/handle/10138/175702.
Weeks, Theodore R. "Separatist Nationalism in the Romanov and Soviet Empires." In *The Oxford Handbook of the History of Nationalism*, edited by John Breuilly, 199–219. Oxford: Oxford University Press, 2013.
Wickström, Mats, and Jonas Ahlskog. "Stalin och det svenska i Finland: Kommunistisk nationalitetsteori och den tidiga finlandssvenska folkdemokratin." *Historiska och litteraturhistoriska studier* 93 (2018): 135–59. https://doi.org/10.30667/hls.66419.
Wickström, Mats, and Jonas Ahlskog. "'Vi lever och kommer att leva': Kommunisten och bildningsborgaren Harri Edgrens kulturkamp för finlandssvenskarnas fortlevnad." *Historiska och litteraturhistoriska studier* 94 (2019): 103–33. https://doi.org/10.30667/hls.76270.

Wilson, Victor, and Mats Wickström. "I minoritetsnationens tjänst: John Gardberg och det lokalt förankrade försvaret av Svenskfinland i Karis, ca 1930–1970." *Historisk Tidskrift för Finland* 105, no. 1 (2020): 1–35.

Newspapers

Ny Dag
Nya Folkbladet
Työväenjärjestöjen Tiedonantaja

5

The Chagossian Diaspora: Deportation, Exile, and Resistance

Mohammad Shameem Chitbahal

Exile is a form of uprootedness that compels one to move from one place to another as either transient migration or endless wandering provoking homesickness, nostalgia, or melancholia toward homeland, family members, mother tongue, or anything one has left behind. The host country is not considered as a "new home" but as a place of exile with the hope and expectation of a potential return. If forced exile for political and economic circumstances differs from voluntary exile both lead to break up with the past and start a new life. The Chagossians endured forced exile as a consequence of secret negotiations between the UK and the United States and the Mauritian government. Once they arrived in Mauritius, they resisted as they never recognized it as their country or their new home, longing for a possible return.

Without any plans to integrate them into the Mauritian society, the Chagossians felt abandoned. They never considered themselves as Mauritians and struggled to return to their homeland. The term "diaspora" initially referred to the Jews and other dispersed religious groups living as minorities among other people. Since the 1950s, the term emancipated from its religious and negative connotation relating today to the high number of migratory realities that are sometimes profoundly distinct from the initial Jewish diaspora. The Chagossian diaspora has been living in exile as minorities among Mauritians since the early 1970s.

The clash of Eastern and Western ideologies is primarily assigned to the American presence in the Indian Ocean. It was only after the Second World War that the United States became interested in the region with the prerogative of assuring security in Europe and East Asia. The unforeseeable nature of geopolitics in the region and the US and Soviet encounters and the access to oil supply at a reasonable price drove the Americans to reconsider their interest in that part of the globe. According to Neetika Verma, the Americans believed, in the 1950s, that their arrival in the Indian Ocean would restrict the Soviet influence, deemed harmful for peace and stability for the countries of the region as they challenged each other.[1] Rene Rémond considers that the Cold War between the United States and the Soviets did not end between 1963 and 1989 but was only the *status quo* period that saw the birth of an agreement.[2] Both powers agreed to put an end to nuclear experiments everywhere on the planet and not to use the nuclear bomb they both possessed against each other. Last but not least, the British withdrawal from the Suez Canal and other colonies during the 1950s changed the American perspective toward the Indian Ocean as the United States wished to "replace" the British in the region. Undoubtedly, both decolonization and the Cold War were the result of accentuated interest of the United States in the Indian Ocean region.

In this chapter, we shall see how the Cold War and decolonization affected the Chagossians' fate as the Americans militarized the Indian Ocean, emphasizing on the goals set behind the detachment of the Chagos Archipelago from the Mauritian territory that forced the Chagossians to exile in atrocious circumstances. We shall see how the Chagossians went from an indigenous population to a minority in diaspora as Diego Garcia now hosts a very important American base.

According to John Bowen, the word "indigenous" includes people transferred from their homeland to places they do not belong and find difficult to adapt.[3] Everyone has the right to self-determination with regard to international law but it does not automatically confer the indigenous status to all people.[4] People who are expelled from their homeland lose not only their land on which they worked and lived but their very self. The act of confiscating land from people is the process that Gilles Deleuze names "deterritorialization." On the other hand, reterritorialization occurs when people who are expelled from their homeland are forced to exile, thus transforming their culture on the economic and social aspects.[5] Hence, deterritorialization and reterritorialization are indivisible.

The First Settlers of the Chagos Archipelago—an Outcome of Slavery

The Chagos Archipelago is a group of sixty-four small islands in the middle of the Indian Ocean, halfway between Africa and Indonesia, 1,000 miles south of India. It was uninhabited when discovered in 1512 by the Portuguese navigators sailing from the Cape of Good Hope to Goa. The eighteenth century was a period of great rivalry between the Dutch, the French, and the British East India companies for dominance over the spice trade in the Indian Ocean. In 1721, France (which had already colonized Réunion in 1649) claimed Mauritius (Isle de France). France also took possession of the Seychelles group and the Chagos Islands.[6]

The first inhabitants of the Chagos Archipelago settled there by the end of the eighteenth century, living mostly on the main islands of the atoll—Diego Garcia,[7] Peros Banhos, and Salomon. They were descendants of slaves coming from Madagascar and Mozambique, brought to the archipelago on behalf of French Mauritian companies that harvested coconut groves.[8] Coconut trees were the natural wealth of the archipelago for they were used to produce coconut oil to be exported.

Records in the archives indicate that the first Chagossians were from Mauritius and the Seychelles. Others came from continental Africa as part of an illegal slave trade taking advantage of Chagos's isolation from colonial authority. By 1783, twenty-two enslaved Africans first settled there, brought there by Pierre Marie le Normand, a French plantation owner in Mauritius.[9] He owned many slaves in Mauritius (Ile de France) among which the number of lepers grew at a fast rate. In 1783, Le Normand presented to the governor, Vicomte de Souillac, a request to create a settlement in Diego Garcia. Le Normand received a favorable reply the same year and took twenty-two slaves to Diego Garcia where they set up the first coconut plantations. Once isolated in Diego Garcia, Le Normand believed its climate and some special soup (made up of turtle, fish, and coconut) would purge the blood of lepers from all impurities. A leprosy facility was set up in Diego Garcia to be used as a quarantine station for the lepers of Ile-de-France.[10] The government encouraged the lepers to create fisheries and to develop the coconut plantations so that the island would become self-sufficient. In the meantime, landholders became active in Diego Garcia. These were Lapotaire, Cayeux, and Didier.

The Anglo-French Rivalry Leading to the Settlement of the Chagos Archipelago and Its Development

By the middle of the eighteenth century, the Indian Ocean went through the English and French colonial experience. At first, there seemed to be an interest for exotic items (spices, tea),[11] on both sides, which later turned into political interest in view of territorial expansion. While the Anglo-French rivalry increased in Europe, their struggle to gain naval and economic control in the Indian Ocean mounted. Thus, the strategic position of the Chagos Islands became a major target for the French as they claimed Peros Banhos for the first time in 1744.[12]

On May 4, 1786, the British took full possession of Diego Garcia. Le Normand protested against the arrival of the British, and Vicomte de Souillac sent a letter to Bombay, hoping to get back Diego Garcia. To avoid diplomatic conflicts, the British Council of Bombay ordered the British committee to leave Diego Garcia.[13] In 1815, after a military defeat, the French surrendered all the Indian Ocean islands to the British (except for Réunion Islands). The strategic position of the Indian Ocean islands attracted mostly the British as they could be used to control sea routes toward India where respective companies were struggling for supremacy over spice trade. As historian Auguste Toussaint asserts, the unique features representing a real unity of the insular territories attracted Western powers.[14] During the eighteenth and nineteenth centuries, the British and the French challenged one another to secure their influence on the western Indian Ocean islands. The British dominated and finally took possession of Cape Town, Mauritius, the Seychelles, the Chagos Islands, the Maldives, Tasmania, Australia, Malaysia, Singapore, and part of India. After the Portuguese, the Dutch, and the French Empires' domination in the region, the British made the Indian Ocean the "British lake" for about 150 years. Thus, after defeating the French, in the words of Philippe Leymarie, the British became the uncontested master of the Indian Ocean for a century.[15]

Under the terms of the 1814 Peace Treaty of Paris, France ceded the Chagos Archipelago to Britain as part of the "lesser dependencies of Mauritius."[16] Until 1913, all the dependencies were administered by Mauritius[17] and in order to form a separate crown, the Seychelles was detached from Mauritius. However, the Chagos Archipelago continued to be administered by Mauritius until it was detached to become the British Indian Ocean Territory (BIOT) in 1965, to make way for a military base.

Island Bases Became a Necessity for Americans in the Indian Ocean

As assessed earlier, the 1,500 Chagossians were forced to exile to Mauritius for mainly defense purposes initiated by both the United States and the UK. It was only after thirty years of struggle while in exile that the Chagossians' plight to return home was acknowledged by the Royal High Court of Justice in London on November 3, 2000. The court identified the forced exile of the Chagossians to Mauritius as illegal. However, the decision of the Chagossians' right to return could not be implemented as the growing hostility pursued by the American government increased even more after the 9/11 attacks in New York. The military base at Diego Garcia gained importance and became more useful against the organizers and sponsors of the 2001 terrorist attacks as they were believed to settle in Afghanistan. Furthermore, the military intervention against Saddam Hussein regime in April 2003 was another argument to render Diego Garcia base more meaningful and thus compromising the return of the Chagossians to their homeland. The Americans have been refraining from leaving Diego Garcia despite the court's ruling as it has several characteristics. Diego Garcia is isolated and "ideally located" in the middle of the Indian Ocean. It is unapproachable for the average citizen as until now we are unaware of anybody who has been able to see the military installations.[18] There is no doubt that the strategic position of the Chagos Archipelago makes it particularly suitable for different military tasks. Diego Garcia is thus crucial for the US military arsenal and this is the main reason why the Chagossians cannot go back to their homeland. Moreover, the United States wanted to make the Indian Ocean region a "zone of peace." Diego Garcia, while hosting the US military base, was intended to meet this objective. However, as Alexander Cooley observes, American overseas bases do not only serve for "security measures" but are embodiments of the US power, identity, and diplomacy.[19]

Installing insular bases in the Indian Ocean became necessary for several reasons. Alfred Thayer Mahan was known as the most famous expansionist theorist whose works inspired and influenced Theodore Roosevelt (*Preparedness*[20]). Prior to the First World War, Mahan considered British history as a good example to follow since it showed to what extent maritime power contributed to national greatness and pride. Therefore, it was essential for the United States to rebuild its navy and acquire "colonies in order to make refueling stations" in different regions of the world. In line with it, after the Second World War, Stuart Barber, the initiator of the *Strategic Island Concept*,[21] had experienced a taste of island life as a naval intelligence officer in Hawai'i during the Second World War. In the late 1950s, as a civilian working for the navy at the Pentagon, he believed the navy should construct small airstrips, oil storage, and logistical facilities "to support minor peacetime deployments and "major war-time operations." Barber believed island naval bases would become essential, by the 1960s, to maintain military dominance in the Indian Ocean. In a letter sent to Horacio Rivero, the then director of the Long-Range Objectives Group at the navy, Stuart Barber wrote: "Virtually all of Africa, and certain Middle Eastern and Far Eastern territories presently under Western control will gain either complete independence or a high degree of autonomy."[22] Barber thus spotted Diego Garcia as a perfect location and advised the navy to consider it. Apart from decolonization and the arrival of the Soviets in the Indian Ocean, a vacuum in the navy's telecommunication scheme in the region was another good reason for the United States to consider Diego Garcia as an ideal spot for a communications facility. In order to implement the project, the United States wanted Britain to detach the Chagos Archipelago from Mauritius.

Decolonization and the Cold War Affect the Chagossians' Destiny

After long and secret negotiations between the United States and the UK regarding construction expenditures and compensation to be allotted to the Mauritian government and the Chagossians, both powers signed the first agreement on December 30, 1966.[23] Article 1 stipulated that the Chagos territory would remain under British sovereignty. Article 11 specified that the UK government had planned to keep the islands available for an unlimited time in order to respond to the potential needs of both governments in terms of defense requirements. The Anglo-American future secret plan was to expel the Chagossians from their homeland for "security measures." The priority, however, was to negotiate the excision of the Chagos Archipelago from the Mauritian territory with their local government. While the Chagos Archipelago was retained as the new BIOT, an Anglo-American agreement was signed to make the largest island, Diego Garcia, available for a major US military base.[24]

Mauritius gained its independence on March 12, 1968. However, the British government imposed that the Chagos Archipelago be detached from the Mauritian territory. In return, they would accelerate the decolonization process of Mauritius. Formal secret documents, now available at the National Archives in London, reveal how the United States negotiated with the British to keep the Chagos Islands for defense purposes. Those secret documents also reveal the conversations between the British and Mauritian politicians. For instance, on September 23, 1965, at the Lancaster House in London, the Mauritian delegation agreed to the detachment of the Chagos Archipelago in exchange of £3 million. It was also agreed that the archipelago would be returned to Mauritius when they would no more be needed for defense purposes.

The remarkably close relationship between the United States and the UK after the Second World War period regarding defense issues played an important part in the negotiation. Peter Harris describes it as a "purported transatlantic bridge that binds the UK and the US together in close cooperation."[25] As the United States placed the greatest importance in using Diego Garcia for defense purposes, the British authorities were determined to meet their demands at all costs. Despite the hesitation of the Mauritian authorities, the British government did its utmost to convince their counterparts for the excision of the Chagos Archipelago. Mauritius wanted independence and the excision of the Mauritian territory was nonnegotiable.

On November 8, 1965, three years before Mauritius was granted independence, the British government created the BIOT.[26] To facilitate the process by avoiding any parliamentary debate, the Chagos Archipelago was separated from Mauritius in 1965 by an order in council. In 1971, an "immigration ordinance" issued by the commissioner of the BIOT required the compulsory removal of all the islanders and to be transferred to Mauritius. Section 4 of the ordinance reads as follows:

> No person shall enter the Territory or, being in the Territory, shall be present or remain in the Territory, unless he is in possession of a permit or his name is endorsed on a permit in accordance with the provisions of section 5 and section 7 of this Ordinance respectively.[27]

Obviously, the Chagossians have never been consulted about their removal from their homeland as the British considered them only as foreign contract workers. Subsequent to their removal, a treaty was concluded between the UK and the United States by which the island of Diego Garcia was leased for fifty years (renewed in 2016 for another twenty years). Thus, the Chagos Archipelago was kept under British administration to make way for a joint UK–US military base on its largest island, Diego Garcia.

On February 25, 2019, the International Court of Justice at The Hague gave its advisory opinion on the legal consequences of the separation of the Chagos Archipelago from Mauritius:

> By thirteen votes to one, is of the opinion that, having regard to international law, the process of decolonization of Mauritius was not lawfully completed when that country acceded to independence in 1965, following the separation of the Chagos Archipelago.[28]

The 1514 (XV) Resolution of December 14, 1960, states that "any attempt aiming at the partial or total disruption of the national unity and territorial integrity of a country is incompatible with the purposes and principles of the United Nations Charter." With regard to this resolution, on a legal basis, the detachment of the Chagos Archipelago from the Mauritian territory jeopardizes its territorial integrity and thus makes the process of decolonization incomplete, leading to the Chagossians' loss of homeland.

The Exclusion of the Chagossians from Their Homeland

The exclusion of the Chagossians from their homeland occurred in several stages between 1965 and 1973. First, islanders who had gone on trips to Mauritius were told they could not go home as their islands had been sold. Charlesia Alexis from Diego Garcia who went for her father's medical treatment was told so when she went to fetch her return ticket at an agency in Mauritius.[29] Gradually, supplies sent from Mauritius to the Chagos Islands were restricted to force them to obey and leave. Coconut plantations were closed and the remaining islanders were put on ships and taken to Mauritius and Seychelles. In total, about 1,500 Chagossians were sent to Mauritius and another 500 to Seychelles. According to testimonies from Chagossians, on January 24, 1971, all islanders were instructed to gather at East Point.[30] The shutting down of the plantations was announced and every islander would be sent to Mauritius.[31] The Chagossians felt hopeless. Some were ready to go but most of them wanted to stay there. Diego Garcia was first evacuated and some months later, all islands of the archipelago were in the same state. In August 1971, the *Nordvear*[32] embarked the last Chagossian families who had resisted. Sir Bruce Greatbach, the then commissioner of the BIOT, ordered to kill the pets of the islanders and the stray dogs of the island to force those who resisted to obey. Marcel Moulinié had the responsibility to exterminate the animals and he gave details in an interview to David Vine about how he proceeded:

> He first tried to shoot the dogs with the help of Seabees armed with M16 rifles. When this failed as an expeditious extermination method, he attempted to poison the dogs with strychnine. This too failed. He finally used raw meat to lure the dogs into a sealed copra-dying shed. He locked them inside and gassed the howling dogs with exhaust piped in from the U.S. military vehicle. He burnt the dog's carcasses in the shed and the Chagossians were left to watch and ponder their fate.[33]

The objective behind the above mentioned methods was clearly to upset and destabilize the Chagossians who resisted. Thus, by 1971, Diego Garcia was completely evacuated to make way for the Anglo-American base. Thirty years later, the United States used the base for its attacks on Iraq and Afghanistan between 2001 and 2003.[34]

From Indigenous to Minority

The 1976 Prosser Report mentions the 1,500 people from 426 families living in the Chagos Archipelago before their deportation lead a peaceful life, in an almost self-sufficient system since four to five generations, devoted to food-crop growing, vegetable gardening, artisanal inshore fishing, animal farming, and collecting coconut fruit. Most islanders worked in the coconut plantations that were used for producing coconut oil intended for exportation. Others were fishermen or domestic servants at the landowners' or colonial administrators' house.[35]

Following their deportation in 1971, Chagossians living in Mauritius have been leading a miserable life, trying hard to rebuild their lives in the slums of Mauritius, mostly next to Port Louis in Cassis, Roche-Bois, Pointe-aux-Sables, and Baie du Tombeau. Upon their arrival, Mauritius was independent but an impoverished and overpopulated nation where unemployment was constantly growing and the arrival of the Chagossians increased the amount of unemployment. Moreover, Chagossians could hardly find proper accommodation. In some cases, they were nine in a single living room and were unable to feed themselves properly. Their bad living conditions lead to homesickness and death short after. A year following the arrival of the Chagossians in Mauritius, a survey showed how sorrow, poverty, and lack of medical care led to forty-four deaths. In 1975, the Minority Rights Group (based in London) conducted a survey that concluded that at least one Chagossian in forty from Mauritius died from starvation. Diseases, extreme poverty, unemployment, family dispersion, distress, and difficulties in adapting to the Mauritian society were the main causes of numerous deaths. In addition, the Chagossians vainly struggled to fit in the fast-going and stressful life of Port Louis.

More than fifty years after their forced exile, the Chagossians still cannot totally fit in the Mauritian society. In a secret telegram, now available at the National Archives in Kew, the Chagossians are described as nonindigenous in the following terms by the British officials:

> There will be no indigenous population except seagulls who have not yet got a committee. Unfortunately, along with the birds go some few Tarzans or Men Fridays whose origins are obscure and who are being hopefully wished on to Mauritius etc.[36]

Stating that the Chagossians were not indigenous was easier for the British and the Americans to justify their deportation for a military base as it prevented them to face severe criticism from other governments. The displacement of Indigenous peoples during the decolonization era was a sensitive issue. The British and the American officials took all the precautions to avoid any information leak regarding their project at Diego Garcia and the fate of its local population.

In Mauritius, in their struggle for survival, most Chagossians relied on welfare assistance and support and mercy from relatives and friends. Some of them worked episodically for meager wages as dockworkers, domestic servants, or lorry helpers. The absence of host structures and the disregard of the Mauritian government toward the Chagossians made their integration almost impossible. Their expertise acquired from the oil industry in the archipelago was of no use in Mauritius. Furthermore, the Chagossians suffered discrimination and prejudice just like the Afro-Mauritians with whom they were confused. Afro-Mauritians form the minority and usually get access only to jobs that are at the bottom of the ladder with the lowest income. The Chagossians, once transferred to Mauritius, far from their homeland had difficulties in coping their own culture with the local one. Due to the abovementioned factors, they inevitably formed part of the minority in Mauritius. Their peaceful life henceforth belonged to the past and the present one was a nightmare for most of them. Testimonies from Chagossians show the high degree of nostalgia, homesickness that lingered in their story when they compare their past and present life.[37]

The Chagossians' Strong Link with Land, Landscape, and Places

Like most other indigenes around the world, the Chagossians affirm a special relationship to their ancestral lands and territories. Land is not only valued as a daily livelihood but it also carries spiritual, social, cultural, and intergenerational value and meaning. People derive much of their identity and cultural vitality from a deep sense of attachment to the land, landscape, and places when they have been living there for long. On the other hand, as Julian Burger notes when Indigenous communities lose their land, they undergo a cycle of poverty and anguish that strikes at the very essence of who they are.[38]. Landscape is imbued with cultural value and meaning. Chagossians have been making claims to their land on grounds that extend beyond formal rules and regulations. The claims are essentially linked with the ecological relationships they have maintained with nature (trees, land, sea), which are often reflected in songs, stories, or even memory. While the Chagossians live in exile, the songs and stories relate specific experiences that took place on their homeland. For instance, songs composed in exile by the members of the Chagos Tambour Group and other Chagossian singers idealize the Chagos Archipelago as a simple and idyllic island paradise, highlighting the positive characteristics of life there by making stark contrasts with their negative life experience in Mauritius.[39] In 2002, the professional musician, *Ton Vié*, who left Chagos in 1967, released an album *Peros Vert* (Green Peros) in which he describes how Green Peros is surrounded by white sand and recalls how he used to spend all day by the sea. To quote his song:

> We gathered water in cans; we had our straw houses, we slept on coconut husk mattresses; we lived the African way, We Chagossians inhabitants had no problems on the islands, On our islands, we had plenty of food, On our islands, we shared what we had.[40]

The song describes clearly an idealized African lifestyle. A contrast is made with the life in Mauritius that is characterized by suffering and hardship. Nevertheless, since their deportations Chagossians do not compose songs that relate to the negative aspects of life in Chagos. They instead portray an idyllic island paradise belonging to their past. References were yet made to racial hierarchies, employment hardships, and sexual exploitation in those composed and performed in Chagos before exile.[41]

The Struggles of the Chagossians Continue

In the 1980s, the Chagossians made hunger strikes and protested, facing police intimidations violence and arrests. While claiming to go back to their homeland the Chagossians requested for more compensation from the British and the Mauritian governments. Prominent Chagossians leaders and former hunger strikers such as Aurélie, Charlesia, and Alexis created the first support organization, the Chagos Refugees Group (CRG), which is today presided by Olivier Bancoult.

Thanks to the struggle, between 1982 and 1985, many but not all Chagossians in Mauritius received land and cash payments totaling around $4,620.[42] In 2000, the Royal High Court of Justice in London invalidated the Immigration Ordinance concerning the BIOT that prevented the Chagossians to go home. Thus, the jurisdiction observed on November 3, 2000, that the "transfer" of the islanders was illegal. The UK government did not appeal the decision but made a new ordinance that authorized the islanders to return to all the islands of the Chagos Archipelago except for Diego Garcia.

In 2004, the UK government reintroduced immigration control in BIOT by declaring that "no person had the right of abode in BIOT nor the right without authorization to enter and remain there."[43] The Chagossians were thus not allowed to go back home and were forced to remain in exile.

Despite the 2000 court's judgment in favor of the Chagossians, the right to return could not be accomplished due to the growing hostility of the American government after 9/11. Diego Garcia military base became one of the most important foreign bases for the United States. The successful military operations from Diego Garcia seems to have jeopardized the return of the Chagossians to their homeland despite the court's ruling. André Oraison reminds the importance of the Chagos Islands, in terms of geopolitics and geostrategy, allowing the United States as from the 1970s to operate promptly all around the Indian Ocean region.[44] It leads us to believe the military base would continue to exist in the Indian Ocean, despite the marginalization of the Chagossians' sufferings. In the words of the Chagossian Diaspora in Mauritius, they are neither fighting against the military base nor security, but they "only want to go back home."

Notes

1. Neetika Verma, "Geopolitics of Indian Ocean in the Post Cold War Period Its Implications for India's Maritime Security." (Jammu, University of Jammu, 2017), accessed July 13, 2019, https://shodhganga.inflibnet.ac.in:8443/jspui/handle/10603/189730.
2. René Rémond, *Introduction À l'Histoire de Notre Temps. 3: Le Xxe Siècle de 1914 À Nos Jours*, enlarged édition (Paris: Points, 2014), 82.
3. John R. Bowen, "Should We Have a Universal Concept of 'Indigenous Peoples' Rights'?: Ethnicity and Essentialism in the Twenty-First Century," *Anthropology Today* 16, no. 4 (2000): 14.
4. Ibid.
5. *Capitalism and Schizophrenia*, a project between 1970 and 1980; see Gilles Deleuze and Félix Guattari, *Anti-Oedipus: Capitalism and Schizophrenia* (Minneapolis: University of Minnesota Press, 1983).
6. Auguste Toussaint, *Histoire de l'Ile Maurice* (Paris: Presses Universitaires De France, 1974), 23.
7. Diego Garcia is the main and the biggest island of the Chagos Archipelago.
8. Madeleine Ly-Tio-Fane and S. Rajabally, "An Account of Diego Garcia and Its People," *Journal of Mauritian Studies* 1, no. 1 (1986): 92.
9. "Permits to Slave Holders to Transport Slaves between Islands, 1830." This document is located in the Mauritius Archives with the reference MA: IA 32.
10. Robert Scott, *Limuria: The Lesser Dependencies of Mauritius* (Westport, CT: Greenwood Press, 1976), 20.
11. In 1813, when the East India Company lost its monopoly, manufacturers in Great Britain started the conquest of the Indian market. Progressively, the Westerners had great demands for spices, silk, tea, coffee, and sugar. These were produced in Mauritius, Ceylon, and India.
12. Scott, *Limuria*, 63–9.

13. Ibid.
14. Toussaint, *Histoire de l'Ile Maurice*, 16.
15. Philippe Leymarie, *Ocean Indien: Le Nouveau Coeur Du Monde* (Paris: Karthala, 1981), 23.
16. It included the Seychelles, the Chagos Archipelagos, and other various islands of the Indian Ocean.
17. Robert Louis Stein, *The French Slave Trade in the Eighteenth Century: An Old Regime Business* (Madison: University of Wisconsin Press, 1979), 9.
18. The only journalist who has been there is Massimo Calabressi. See https://content.time.com/time/subscriber/article/0,33009,1661696,00.html.
19. Alexander Cooley, *Base Politics: Democratic Change and the U.S. Military Overseas* (Ithaca: Cornell University Press, 2008), Preface XI.
20. The Preparedness Movement was a campaign that began prior to US entry into the First World War in April 1917 to increase its military capabilities and to convince the US citizenry of the need for American involvement in the conflict and ongoing military preparedness. Former president Theodore Roosevelt was among those who sought to persuade the administration of President Woodrow Wilson and the population at large that the country must prepare itself for war. Roosevelt wrote two books on the subject, *America and the World War* (1915) and *Fear God and Take Your Own Part* (1916) that helped popularized the Preparedness Movement.
21. The concept on which the construction of island bases is thought to be an effective strategy.
22. Information about Stuart Barber is part of several letters that have remained unpublished. He wrote these to Captain Paul B. Ryan in the 1980s to explain about how and why he gave these ideas to the navy several decades earlier.
23. See "Exchange of Notes Constituting an Agreement Concerning the Availability for Defense Purposes of the British Indian Ocean Territory" (with annexes). London, December 30, 1966, available at https://treaties.un.org/doc/Publication/UNTS/Volume%20603/volume-603-I-8737-English.pdf.
24. From documents in The National Archives (London), "Defence Facilities in the Indian Ocean: Record of a Meeting with an American Delegation Headed by J.C. Kitchen." September 25, 1965. FO 371/184528 Z4/171/G.
25. Peter Harris, "Decolonising the Special Relationship: Diego Garcia, the Chagossians, and Anglo-American Relations," *Review of International Studies* 39, no. 3 (2013): 708, https://doi.org/10.1017/S0260210512000319.
26. The name British Indian Ocean Territory given to the Chagos Archipelago as per the agreement of the lease.
27. BIOT (British Indian Ocean Territory), *The Immigration Ordinance 1971*, no. 1 (1971): 3.
28. "Legal Consequences of the Separation of the Chagos Archipelago from Mauritius in 1965," Advisory Opinion, I.C.J. Reports (2019), 95.
29. Shenaz Patel, *Le Silence des Chagos* (Paris: Editions de l'Olivier, 2005), 26–7.
30. The location of the manager's house on the eastern part of Diego Garcia. This part included fields of coconut palms.
31. David Vine, *Empire's Footprint: Expulsion and the United States Military Base on Diego Garcia* (New York: City University of New York, 2006), 191.
32. Vessel transporting cargo and people between Mauritius and the Chagos Archipelago.
33. David Vine, *Island of Shame: The Secret History of the U.S. Military Base on Diego Garcia* (Princeton, NJ: Princeton University Press, 2011), 113–14.

34. Rémy Herrera and Joelle Cicchini explain how the base at Diego Garcia was developed with a rise of personnel between 2001 and 2003.
35. See "Resettlement in Mauritius of islanders of Chagos Archipelago: Prosser Report," TNA FCO 31/2071.
36. As the Permanent Under-Secretary of State at the Foreign Office, Sir Paul Gore-Booth described the Chagossians in these words in a telegram sent to the US authorities on August 24, 1966.
37. For testimonies from Chagossians, see https://www.chagossupport.org.uk/in-their-own-words.
38. Julian Burger, *The Gaia Atlas of First Peoples: A Future for the Indigenous World* (New York: Doubleday, 1990), 122.
39. Laura Jeffery, "How a Plantation Became Paradise: Changing Representations of the Homeland among Displaced Chagos Islanders," *Journal of the Royal Anthropological Institute* 13, no. 4 (2007): 958–9.
40. Ibid.
41. Ibid.
42. Vine, *Island of Shame*, 146.
43. BIOT, *Orders in Council*.
44. André Oraison, "Diego Garcia: Enjeux de La Présence Américaine Dans L'océan Indien," *Afrique Contemporaine* 207, no. 3 (2003): 122.

Bibliography

Primary Sources

Ackroyd, J. H. *Report of the Police and Stipendiary Magistrate for the Smaller Dependencies 1880*. Magistrate for Lesser Dependencies, March 22, 1880. Mauritius Archives: RA 2568.

Bancoult, Olivier. Interview with Olivier Bancoult, spokesperson for the Chagossians in Mauritius. September 3, 2019. Pointe aux Sables, Mauritius.

Barber, Stuart. "Letter to Paul B. Ryan (United States Navy Captain)." Received by Paul B. Ryan, April 26, 1982.

BIOT (British Indian Ocean Territory). *The Immigration Ordinance 1971*, no. 1, 1971.

—The British Indian Ocean Territory. *Orders in Council*, Court at Buckingham Palace, June 10, 2004.

Defence Facilities in the Indian Ocean: Meeting between United States and United Kingdom Officials. May 14, 1965. FO 371/184524 Z4/62/G.

Defence Facilities in the Indian Ocean: Record of a Meeting with an American Delegation Headed by J.C. Kitchen. September 25, 1965. FO 371/184528 Z4/171/G.

Defence Interests in Indian Ocean (Draft Telegram) from Commonwealth Relations Office. W. Circular 114. May 15, 1965. FO 371/184524 Z4/70/G.

Defence Interests in the Indian Ocean—Memorandum by the Foreign Secretary, Defence Secretary and the Commonwealth Secretary. February 24, 1965. FO 371/184522 Z4/12/G.

Exchange of Notes Constituting an Agreement Concerning the Availability for Defense Purposes of the British Indian Ocean Territory (with annexes). London, December 30,

1966, accessed January 10, 2021, available at https://treaties.un.org/doc/Publication/UNTS/Volume%20603/volume-603-I-8737-English.pdf.
Extract from COS Committee. "Mauritius" (65) 25th Meeting. May 18, 1965. FO 371/184524 Z4/85.
Letter from E. H. Peck, Foreign Office, to N.C.C. Trench, British Embassy, Washington. April 21, 1965. FO 371/184523 Z4/35.
Legal Consequences of the Separation of the Chagos Archipelago from Mauritius in 1965, Advisory Opinion, I.C.J. Reports, 2019.
Mauritius Defence Issues—Record of a Meeting in the Colonial Office. September 20, 1965. FO 371/184528 Z4/165/G.
Mauritius Defence Issues—Record of a Meeting in the Colonial Office. September 20, 1965. FO 371/184528 Z4/169.
MAURITIUS. Visits of Sir S. Ramgoolam, Prime Minister of Mauritius, to UK: Records of Meeting with Prime Minister. September 20, 1965. PREM 13/3320.
Permits to Slave Holders to Transport Slaves between Islands, 1830. (Mauritius Archives), MA: IA 32.
Record of a Conversation between the Prime Minister (Harold Wilson) and the Premier of Mauritius, Sir Seewoosagur Ramgoolam, at Downing Street. September 23, 1965. FO 371/184528 Z4/172.
Prosser Report—Resettlement in Mauritius of islanders of Chagos Archipelago. TNA FCO 31/ 2071.
Telegram from Sir John Shaw Rennie (Mauritius) to the Secretary of State for the Colonies. November 5, 1965. FO 371/184529 Z4/181 (C)/G.
United States. Diego Garcia, 1975: The Debate over the Base and the Island's Former Inhabitants: Hearings before the Special Subcommittee on Investigations of the Committee on International Relations, House of Representatives, Ninety-Fourth Congress, First Session, June 5 and November 4, 1975. Washington, U.S. Govt. Print. Off, 1975.

Research Literature

Bandjunis, Vytautas B. *Diego Garcia: Creation of the Indian Ocean Base*. San Jose, CA: Writer's Showcase, 2001.
Bezboruah, Manoranjan. *U.S. Strategies in the Indian Ocean: The International Response*. New York: Praeger, 1977.
Bowen, John R. "Should We Have a Universal Concept of 'Indigenous Peoples' Rights'?: Ethnicity and Essentialism in the Twenty-First Century." *Anthropology Today* 16, no. 4 (2000): 12–16.
Burger, Julian. *The Gaia Atlas of First Peoples: A Future for the Indigenous World*. London: Robertson McCarta, 1990.
Cooley, Alexander. *Base Politics: Democratic Change and the U.S. Military Overseas*. Ithaca: Cornell University Press, 2008.
Deleuze, Gilles, and Félix Guattari. *Anti-Oedipus: Capitalism and Schizophrenia*. Minneapolis: University of Minnesota Press, 1983.
Dumbrell, John. *A Special Relationship: Anglo-American Relations in the Cold War and after*. Houndmills, Hampshire: Macmillan, 2001.
Dumbrell, John. "The US–UK Special Relationship: Taking the 21st-Century Temperature." *British Journal of Politics & International Relations* 11, no. 1

(2009): 64–78. https://doi.org/10.1111/j.1467-856X.2008.00352.x (accessed November 15, 2019).

Dussercle, Roger. *Archipel De Chagos: En Mission, Diégo, Six Iles, Péros, Septembre-Novembre, 1934*. Port-Louis, Ile Maurice: General Printing & Stationery Cy, 1935.

Edis, Richard. *Peak of Limuria: The Story of Diego Garcia and the Chagos Archipelago*. London: Chagos Conservation Trust, 2004.

Harris, Peter. "Decolonising the Special Relationship: Diego Garcia, the Chagossians, and Anglo-American Relations." *Review of International Studies* 39, no. 3 (2013): 707–27. https://doi.org/10.1017/S0260210512000319.

Herrera, Rémy, and Joëlle Cicchini. "Some Notes about the U.S. Military Bases and Personnel Abroad." *Journal of Innovation Economics & Management* 12, no. 2 (2013): 127–49. https://doi.org/10.3917/jie.012.0127.

Ho, Engseng. "Empire through Diasporic Eyes: A View from the Other Boat." *Comparative Studies in Society and History* 46, no. 2 (2004): 210–46. https://doi.org/10.1017/S00104 1750400012X.

Jeffery, Laura. *Chagos Islanders in Mauritius and the UK: Forced Displacement and Onward Migration*. Manchester: Manchester University Press, 2016. Accessed January 29, 2018. https://www.jstor.org/stable/j.ctt155jcj0.

Jeffery, Laura. "How a Plantation Became Paradise: Changing Representations of the Homeland among Displaced Chagos Islanders." *Journal of the Royal Anthropological Institute* 13, no. 4 (2007): 951–68.

L'Estrac de, Jean Claude. *L'an Prochain à Diego Garcia…* Vacoas, Maurice: Editions le Printemps, 2011.

Leymarie, Philippe. *Ocean Indien: Le Nouveau Coeur Du Monde*. Paris: Karthala, 1981.

Ly-Tio-Fane, Madeleine, and S. Rajabally. "An Account of Diego Garcia and Its People." *Journal of Mauritian Studies* 1, no. 1 (1986): 90–107.

Madeley, John. *Diego Garcia: A Contrast to the Falklands*. London: Minority Rights Group, 1985.

Mahan, A. T. *The Influence of Sea Power upon History, 1660–1783*. First published 1890. London: Forgotten Books, 2017.

Oraison, André. "Diego Garcia: Enjeux de La Présence Américaine Dans L'océan Indien." *Afrique Contemporaine* 207, no. 3 (2003): 115–32.

Patel, Shenaz. *Le Silence des Chagos*. Paris: Editions de l'Olivier, 2005.

Rémond, René. *Introduction À l'Histoire de Notre Temps. 3: Le Xxe Siècle de 1914 À Nos Jours*. Enlarged édition. Paris: Points, 2014.

Sand, Peter H. *United States and Britain in Diego Garcia: Military Presence, Rendition, and Global Climate Change*. Basingstoke: Palgrave Macmillan, 2009.

Scott, Robert. *Limuria: The Lesser Dependencies of Mauritius*. Westport, CT: Greenwood Press, 1976.

Stein, Robert Louis. *The French Slave Trade in the Eighteenth Century: An Old Regime Business*. Madison: University of Wisconsin Press, 1979.

Toussaint, Auguste. *Histoire de l'Ile Maurice*. Paris: Presses Universitaires De France, 1974.

Verma, Neetika. "Geopolitics of Indian Ocean in the Post Cold War Period Its Implications for India's Maritime Security." University of Jammu, 2017. Accessed July 7, 2019. https://shodhganga.inflibnet.ac.in:8443/jspui/handle/10603/189730.

Vine, David. *Empire's Footprint: Expulsion and the United States Military Base on Diego Garcia*. New York: City University of New York, 2006.

Vine, David. *Island of Shame: The Secret History of the U.S. Military Base on Diego Garcia.* Princeton, NJ: Princeton University Press, 2011.

Links

https://www.chagossupport.org.uk/in-their-own-words.
Chagos Refugees Group. https://www.thechagosrefugeesgroup.com/.
Calabresi, Paradise in Concrete, 6.9.2007. https://content.time.com/time/world/article/0,8599,1659588,00.html.

Part II

Strategies and Activities of Minority Communities and Indigenous Peoples

6

Imperial In-Betweens: The Portuguese Communities in Hong Kong and Shanghai during the Second World War

Helena F. S. Lopes

Despite remaining mostly absent from studies on Hong Kong and Shanghai, the Portuguese constituted one of the largest communities in the two cities from the 1840s until the 1940s. Today, members of these communities are often identified (and self-identify) as Macanese, stressing their ancestral links to Macau, the South China enclave that was under Portuguese rule from the sixteenth century until 1999. "Portuguese" was the predominant term used in sources of the 1930s and 1940s and will be the one deployed here. The Portuguese in East Asia straddled different imperial spheres. Many epitomized the experiences of "global citizenship" that Margret Frenz has observed in the case of South Asians who moved across the British, French, and Portuguese imperial realms, or of "transimperial drifting," in Catherine Chan's description of the Hong Kong Portuguese.[1] During the Second World War, these communities were connected to different imperial powers, in particular Portugal (that was officially neutral), the UK (neutral in the war in Asia until 1941, but fighting against Japan as a member of the Allies afterwards), and Japan. They experienced occupation as prisoners of war (POWs), civilian internees, or "third nationals" with relative freedom of movement in the wartime Japanese Empire. They were also connected to different Chinese spheres, as the country was split between areas under occupation and "Free China" resisting Japan.

Centered on two minority communities who occupied a fluid space at the crossroads of different imperial spheres, this article sheds light on the history of the Portuguese diaspora in China in the 1930s and 1940, the ambiguities of wartime neutrality in East Asia, and regional and global connections involving Hong Kong, Shanghai, and Macau. It argues that the position of the Portuguese as imperial "in-betweens" was complicated during the war, and that despite an apparent strengthening of their ties to Portugal, due to the advantages of neutrality, they continued to be connected to other spheres and those multiple socioeconomic connections were key to the two communities' everyday survival under occupation.

The Portuguese nationals in East Asia were mostly Eurasian, usually born into families in which at least one of their ancestors had come from Macau.² They were diverse in origins and language. The Portuguese had familial ties to other communities, including the Chinese, Indians, Japanese, British, French, and Russians. A few Portuguese families in China did not have explicit connections to Macau, though they were linked to other parts of the Portuguese Empire, such as Goa.³ The Portuguese were almost invariably associated to Roman Catholicism, being active members of Catholic institutions and parishes in Hong Kong and Shanghai, such as the Sacred Heart Church in the latter.⁴ Religion also brought them closer to a French milieu. For instance, the chaplain of the Catholic members of the Shanghai Volunteer Corps (SVC) was Father Jacquinot de Besange, a French Jesuit who played a leading role in refugee relief during the war.⁵ Although most Portuguese in Hong Kong and Shanghai spoke English as the first language, multilingualism was common. The cases of two women born in Shanghai who later wrote memoirs of growing up in the city in the 1930s illustrate this: Margaret Gaan (née Margarida Oliveira), whose family had Portuguese, Swedish, and Chinese ancestry, spoke English and Chinese and attended a French Catholic school, while Renée Azevedo Logan, of Russian and Hong Kong Portuguese parentage, described a household where English was the main language of communication but Russian, French, Cantonese, and Shanghainese were also heard.⁶ Multilingualism was an important survival skill during the war years, allowing the Portuguese to continue to interact with a wide pool of people.

Studies of "in-between" communities or individuals in different temporal and geographic settings emphasize fluency in different languages as a hallmark of their position as mediators.⁷ In Hong Kong, Shanghai, and other Chinese treaty ports, professional groups such as the Chinese businessmen known as "compradors" (*maiban*) are prime examples of elite actors who mediated between communities and interests.⁸ Less is known, however, of non-elite intermediaries who, like many of their wealthier counterparts, also "evoked a world of mobility and fluid boundaries" that attracted some suspicion on different sides.⁹ This was linked to anxieties around race (as many intermediaries were mixed race) as well as to perceptions of their position as agents of empire. In the case of the Portuguese in East Asia, this situation was further complicated by the overlap of different imperial spheres. The territories covered in this chapter have also been regarded, explicitly or implicitly, as "in-between places" through which ideas and commodities of different origins and with different destinations circulated, where different communities interacted, and where new hybrid practices emerged.¹⁰ Homi K. Bhabha has argued that "'in-between' spaces provide the terrain for elaborating strategies of selfhood—singular or communal—that include new signs of contestation, in the act of defining the idea of society itself."¹¹ Bhabha's idea of a "cosmopolitan community envisioned in marginality" speaks to notions of "cosmopolitanism from below" patent in the cases of shared struggles among migrants and refugees.¹² While we lack elements to assess the extent to which the Hong Kong and Shanghai Portuguese engaged with more radical strands of political activism in the 1930s and 1940s, their contestation of forms of racial discrimination, the actions of many of them in supporting Allied resistance alongside non-Portuguese, and their constant personal and professional engagement with other communities evidence cosmopolitan practices springing, if not wholly from below, at least from the fluid in-betweenness of their position.

The Portuguese in Hong Kong and Shanghai were linked in various ways; nevertheless, they also operated under different administrative settings. Although many Portuguese in Shanghai had moved to the city from Hong Kong[13], in the latter, they lived in a British Crown Colony where, as has been noted, assuming a British identity offered specific opportunities for personal and professional fulfillment.[14] From the 1840s and until the 1940s, Shanghai was a divided city, consisting of the Chinese Municipality, the—nominally international but de facto British-dominated—International Settlement, and the French Concession. Portugal had a consular presence in Shanghai and the Portuguese also benefitted from extraterritoriality. This was a legal prerogative imposed on China in treaties signed in the late Qing period and that, in practice, protected foreign citizens from facing trial in Chinese courts, often allowing them to be treated with leniency in their consular court (or, in the case of the Portuguese, when they stood trial in Macau or elsewhere in the Portuguese Empire).[15] However, the self-identification of Portuguese communities in China with Portugal was flexible. The two women mentioned earlier, for example, underplayed their "Portugueseness" in their memoirs. During the Japanese occupation, there was a peak in assuming a Portuguese identity as links to a neutral country enhanced one's freedom of movement and offered a higher degree of protection.

At the start of an all-out war between China and Japan in 1937, the Portuguese communities in Shanghai and Hong Kong comprised many thousands. The 1931 census in Hong Kong listed 1,089 Portuguese, who were distinguished from other Europeans and also not officially counted as Eurasians, while other sources mention around 3,000 Portuguese in Hong Kong when the war began.[16] More than a thousand Portuguese remained in Hong Kong during the occupation—they were the second largest group of "third nationals"—but thousands of others chose to leave for neutral Macau.[17] In Shanghai, the Portuguese consul counted around 2,000 residents in 1937.[18] One estimate for 1939 placed them as the fifth largest community of foreign nationals, while other statistics for 1939–40 registered 2,381 in the French Concession alone.[19] There was a relative reduction in Portuguese residents by 1942—possibly due to departures for Macau—although the number of registered citizens rose again by 1945, likely due to an increase in registrations at the consulate during the occupation of the foreign settlements.[20]

The Portuguese were prominent as lower and mid-level staff in a range of commercial, banking, publishing, and other sectors in which racial discrimination was often a barrier to career progression. There was also an elite of middle-class professionals who played a crucial mediating role in relief activities during the Second World War, working with officials of different states for communal welfare. In the local administration, the Portuguese were either underrepresented or not represented at all. If in Hong Kong, the interwar years saw an increased participation of some in public affairs,[21] in Shanghai they never served in the Shanghai Municipal Council (SMC) that ran the International Settlement. Although it has been stated that in Hong Kong the British establishment did not discriminate against the Portuguese as what they did to the Chinese or other Eurasians,[22] several sources allude to different forms of bias.[23] In

Shanghai, notions of national, racial, and religious superiority were central to the self-conception of the influential British settler community known as "Shanghailanders."[24] While some individuals of different nationalities managed to live personal and professional lives that overcame such barriers, Jeffrey Wasserstrom suggested that these were a privileged minority of "bordercrossers."[25] This article rethinks the Portuguese as non-elite "bordercrossers" in Shanghai and Hong Kong. Although differences between these two urban communities have been observed, with the Hong Kong one seemingly closer to a British identity,[26] the experience of the two was similar during the war: displacement, professional disruption, economic instability, participation in resistance activities, and an increased importance of their Portuguese nationality and family connections to Macau.

Evacuation and Relief

Evacuation and relief efforts during the Second World War highlight the opportunities and challenges of the "in-between" position of Portuguese communities in China. On the one hand, they lacked the level of military cover that Britons and Americans enjoyed in Shanghai at the start of the war, or of explicit privilege that white Europeans benefitted in Hong Kong during the 1940 evacuation. On the other hand, Portugal's neutrality—and the extension of that status to its colonial territories—meant that Portuguese nationality offered possibilities for relative free movement even after the globalization of the conflict in late 1941. This included movement within occupied territories and between occupied and unoccupied areas, and to seek refuge in Macau.

The first plans to evacuate members of the Portuguese communities unfolded during the battle of Shanghai that started in August 1937. The Portuguese consul in the city, António Alves, nominated an emergency committee in charge of registering the number and addresses of the community members, and ensuring transport, accommodation, and food supplies to those displaced by the fighting.[27] Local volunteers were involved in relief initiatives from the start. Many Portuguese lived in Hongkou, a relatively poor part of the city where several industries were located and that was heavily hit.[28] Hongkou was also a main residential area for the Japanese community and Jewish refugees. In his memoir, Anatole Maher, whose parents were Portuguese and Japanese, recalls that his neighbors in Hongkou were often Eurasians of diverse origins (Chinese, German, Russian, Jewish, Filipino, American). Many Portuguese were fully integrated in this cosmopolitan urban environment.[29]

Working with the community, and mirroring evacuation plans put together for other foreign nationals in Shanghai, the consulate organized the departure of hundreds of destitute residents to Macau, as maintenance costs were believed to be lower there and could be passed on to the colonial authorities. Still, many Portuguese remained in Shanghai, where the consulate rented residences to accommodate refugees and women in the community gathered donated clothes (see Figure 6.1).[30] Those who departed for Macau stopped first in Hong Kong, a key destination for many of the Shanghai refugees irrespective of nationality.[31] There, a similar commission was set up by Hong Kong Portuguese in cooperation with the consulate, the Relief Commission for the

Figure 6.1 Group photograph of the Portuguese Benevolent Association (*Associação de Beneficência de Shanghai*) Committee. This association provided relief to poor members of the Shanghai Portuguese community.

Source: *Pela Pátria*, June 1940.

Portuguese Refugees from Shanghai (*Comissão de Socorros aos Portugueses Refugiados de Shanghai*).[32] Its role included receiving those who arrived from Shanghai, helping them find accommodation with relatives in Hong Kong, or facilitate their transport to Macau, where they were lodged by family members or in one of the facilities (hotels, schools, etc.) designated by the Macau government. A prominent figure in the Relief Commission was Oxford-educated barrister Leonardo (Leo) d'Almada e Castro, of a renown Hong Kong Portuguese family. That commission prepared the ground for a later institution, the Executive Commission for Refugees, set up in Macau by Portuguese refugees, the British consulate, and Macau officials after the occupation of Hong Kong.[33]

Leo d'Almada e Castro's involvement in relief efforts and his active role in criticizing discriminatory practices in evacuation procedures exemplify the complexity of the Portuguese experiences during the war as well as their flexible connections to different states. As a member of the Hong Kong Legislative Council, he vocally contested the racist criteria underpinning the 1940 evacuation of women and children.[34] Members of the Hong Kong Volunteer Defence Corps (HKVDC), where many local Portuguese men served, were initially told that their families would be treated the same as the dependents of regular troops and sent to Australia but only those deemed of "'pure' European descent"—that is, those considered white—were.[35] However, this and other discriminatory practices did not weaken the Portuguese Hong Kongers' loyalty to a British Hong Kong.

Relief initiatives by and for the Portuguese communities in 1937 were an important precedent to later waves of displacement in the wake of the Japanese invasion of Hong

Kong in December 1941 and the takeover of the Shanghai International Settlement in 1941–2. Plans for the evacuation of the Portuguese from Hong Kong were less systematic than in 1937 but also benefitted from a combination of ad hoc actions involving state and non-state actors. In late 1941, Portugal's acting consul in Hong Kong was not a "career diplomat" dispatched from Lisbon but an aged member of the local Portuguese community, Frank Soares, who had several family members among the HKVDC taken as POWs.[36] Soares opened his house in Kowloon to refugees and registered many British subjects as Portuguese so they could escape.[37]

When Hong Kong was occupied, thousands left for Macau. Their departure benefitted from arrangements between Portuguese and Japanese authorities, the latter keen to reduce the population of the occupied British colony. By the summer of 1942, it was reported that the Japanese were aiming to concentrate all Portuguese in Macau, with the Shanghai Portuguese also being "induced to go" there.[38] The first groups of refugees from Hong Kong, 1,900 people, arrived in Macau in February 1942.[39] Many came with nothing more than the clothes on their bodies, while those who stayed behind faced looting of their properties and widespread unemployment.[40] The initial estimates were largely surpassed, and the number of refugees in Macau from 1937 to 1945 rose to around 300,000, most of whom were Chinese but a significant number being Portuguese (including thousands who were British subjects). Portuguese authorities in Macau did not shut the door on Hong Kong refugees, and, in fact, they prioritized Portuguese refugees over any others. Employment was offered in public services like policing and firefighting.[41] A plethora of charitable initiatives, where other refugees were highly involved, ensured basic food provision, health care, and schooling.[42] Relief provision was a topic of intense discussion among government officials, with the Macau government, the Portuguese ministry of foreign affairs, the British consulate, and British authorities in London disputing who had funding responsibilities.[43]

The occupation years also saw the emergence of other relief initiatives that operated under highly ambivalent circumstances. During the war years, Portugal kept a consulate in Shanghai and the country's minister to China was also based there, even though Portugal did not recognize the collaborationist Reorganized National Government (RNG) in charge of the city. In Hong Kong, Portugal had no formal diplomatic representation during the occupation years, but Macau's proximity to Hong Kong ensured a degree of regular communication. The Portuguese Residents Association was set up in the latter with support from the Macau government and enabled by the Japanese authorities. Edgar and Chan see the institution as allowing a "favorable treatment" of the Macanese vis-à-vis other Eurasians in Hong Kong, as it provided easier access to rationed products.[44] It had an equivalent in Shanghai, where a Central Portuguese Association was formed in response to an appeal by the Portuguese minister to existing associations to join efforts to assist destitute members of the community.[45] In Hong Kong, the International Committee of the Red Cross delegate extended his services to some Portuguese residents but his Shanghai counterpart refused to do so due to the functioning of a Portuguese consulate.[46] Yet, the existence of a consulate in Shanghai did not shield the community from the occupation's effects in terms of loss of employment and food shortages.[47] Even memoirs from members of middle-class families note the gloom of life under occupation and the discomfort caused by forms of Japanese control.⁴⁸ Constant appeals in the Macau press to raise funds for compatriots in Shanghai are a testament to the community's ordeal.⁴⁹

"Passivity, Resistance, and Collaboration"

In his study of the experiences of Chinese intellectuals in Japanese-occupied Shanghai, Poshek Fu analyzed their responses as complex forms of passivity, resistance, or collaboration.⁵⁰ The Portuguese in Hong Kong and Shanghai adopted iterations of these responses, similar to other foreign nationals in relatively marginal positions in the cities' colonial hierarchies.⁵¹

After the battle of Shanghai ended, many Portuguese who had fled to Macau returned to the city. Associative efforts continued, and everyday activities resumed in the nominally neutral concessions as if the war in China had nothing to do with foreign nationals. A few months before Pearl Harbor, Shanghai newspapers were reporting on Clube Lusitano's lawn bowls victories, and star Portuguese jockey Charlie Encarnação was one of the protagonists of Champions Day at the Race Course.⁵² Even though some sportsmen, like Encarnação, continued to play during the occupation years, these illusions of carefree continuity did not last. The Japanese attack on American-, British-, and Dutch-controlled areas in Asia from December 1941, and subsequent internment of Allied nationals and the closure of their firms meant the loss of jobs and livelihood for many Portuguese. The disruption was less drastic for those working for Chinese companies still in operation. Margaret Gaan recalled in her memoir: "In a way, the Japanese occupation [after 1941] didn't matter. By then we were so familiar with restraints and restrictions that it was just something else to learn how to handle. In a short while we became accustomed to the external manifestations of the occupation."⁵³ Interaction with RNG municipal authorities was a reality even before December 1941 and was even celebrated in upper-class circles, as attested by photographs of a charitable "fun fair" organized by the Portuguese community showing happy confraternization with the RNG mayor of Shanghai, Chen Gongbo.⁵⁴

The war years in Shanghai, especially after the start of the Second World War in Europe saw the Portuguese community become involved in nationalist initiatives aligned with the Estado Novo (New State), Portugal's right-wing dictatorship that had a number of ideological affinities with the Axis. In October 1939, a national organization of the Portuguese Colony of Shanghai was set up.⁵⁵ In 1940, the Portuguese consul António Ribeiro de Melo started a Shanghai branch of Mocidade Portuguesa, a boys' organization that drew on fascist models, as well as the publication of a bilingual propaganda magazine, *Pela Pátria* (For the Fatherland). Engagement with Portuguese propaganda was seemingly a form of personal affirmation and, especially during the height of the occupation, survival, as closeness to the Portuguese consulate could ensure one's needs were brought forth to relevant authorities, such as to allow access to remittances from relatives in non-occupied areas.⁵⁶ The pages of *Pela Pátria* are illustrative of the community's ambiguous position. While some articles display events in which Portuguese engaged with Japanese and Chinese collaborators, others betray a sense of attachment to "old Shanghai," including nostalgia and dismay for the disbandment of the SVC imposed by Japan.[57] The effects of the Estado Novo wartime propaganda on the Shanghai Portuguese also appears to have had relatively superficial effects. Anatole Maher notes candidly in his memoir: "Although I had taken a night class sponsored by the Portuguese Consulate in 1942 during a brief patriotic spell among the Macanese community, I didn't learn much."[58]

Several Portuguese in Hong Kong and Shanghai continued to work under the Japanese occupation. Some of them played important roles in reducing the disruption caused to British companies. It was the case of the Hong Kong and Shanghai Bank employees in Hong Kong who are credited with assisting colleagues in need and ensuring the survival of the bank into the postwar, including by transferring banking records to London via Macau and Chongqing.[59] In Shanghai, some worked along the blurred lines between resistance and collaboration by engaging with smuggling operations, especially in the late 1930s. Gaan's uncle, who had connections with the Shanghai Green Gang, got rich in such schemes, and when the Japanese invaded the Settlement, fled to unoccupied China where he worked as an interpreter for the US forces in Kunming.[60]

Others did not shy away from working with the occupiers. In his study of occupied Hong Kong, Phillip Snow observed how "hundreds of Eurasians and Portuguese managed to recreate their traditional intermediary role by setting themselves up as 'brokers' to traffic between the conquerors on the one hand and the Hong Kong Chinese population on the other," some specializing in "meeting the needs of the Japanese forces for scrap metals and other strategic materials."[61] In Shanghai, wartime trading was also common. Adverts for several Portuguese companies that continued or started operating in the 1940s are a case in point.[62] According to Jim Silva, many lived through the occupation "fairly comfortably" by engaging in "buying and selling" and "living on one's wits" while "waiting for the war to end."[63] In his autobiography, Felipe Nery noted how foreign citizens in the city "traded in almost anything they could lay their hands on," with "the trading arena" being a Russian bakery in the French Concession, where he himself had tried his luck after being laid off from his SMC job when the RNG took over the administration.[64] Nery also sold piroshkis (Russian pies) made by his future Russian mother-in-law to eke out a living.[65] The "White Russians" were another marginalized community in Shanghai with numerous interactions with the Portuguese, including through marriage ties.[66] Wartime dealings were to haunt some in the postwar. When Chinese authorities liberated the city, and with the end of extraterritoriality, several Portuguese (and Russians) were arrested for collaboration with the enemy.[67]

Was there genuine support for the Japanese occupation? Surveying sources from the war period and memoirs written afterwards, it seems clear that few Portuguese in China manifested any genuine support for the Japanese wartime empire and its project of a "Greater East-Asia Co-Prosperity Sphere." In Hong Kong, attempts to co-opt the Portuguese by exposing the discrimination experienced under the British drew no enthusiastic endorsement.[68] As with other communities in Japanese-occupied Asia, the reality of the occupation exposed the contradictions of Japan's wartime empire: justified with a discourse of anti-colonial liberation but, in practice, an even more brutal colonial domination. Most of those who stayed in occupied cities had no means to leave or no means to live elsewhere. Different forms of survival, including personal, familial, and family businesses have been observed as important drivers for Chinese who continued to work under Japanese occupation,[69] and some of these are applicable to these Portuguese communities.

Some, however, openly resisted. This was more evident in Hong Kong than in Shanghai and, I argue, this is partly explained by the proximity of neutral Macau as an escape route. As British subjects, hundreds of Portuguese Hong Kongers were directly involved in military operations when Japanese forces invaded in 1941. Around 200 Portuguese members of the HKVDC were taken as POWs, spending the occupation years either incarcerated in one of the Hong Kong camps or being taken to camps in Japan. Some left accounts of their difficult captivity and forced labor experiences while others did not survive to see the end of the war.[70] Zinho Gosano and Cicero Rozario were two of the Portuguese POWs from Hong Kong sent to Sendai, in Japan in 1944. Their accounts describe their dramatic living conditions: 125 men per hut and forced to work in a mine 1,200 feet deep, 10–12 hours a day nonstop or in night shifts with a free day at each 10–13 days.[71] But even in this harrowing environment, the language skills of another Portuguese POW ameliorated their ordeal slightly as he managed to act as an intermediary with the mine's civilian boss, deemed less cruel than the military.[72]

In Shanghai, the Portuguese formed two companies of the International Settlement's SVC and were directly involved in rescue operations during the 1937 battle, assisting the evacuation of fellow community members.[73] Nevertheless, they were never involved in fighting against Japan, and the SVC was disbanded in 1942 after the takeover of the settlement. But some Portuguese in Shanghai suffered interment too. Privileging a British identity, they preferred not to capitalize on their connections to Portugal and endured the occupation as British nationals.[74]

Direct engagement with Allied resistance was evident among the Portuguese who sought refuge in Macau. Many were crucial actors in the British consulate's official and unofficial activities, from relief distribution to intelligence gathering. Some, such as Leo d'Almada e Castro, took on public intermediary roles, mediating between the consulate, the Portuguese authorities, and other refugees. Others, like Bernard Felix Xavier (former member of the Shanghai Municipal Police), or Eddie Gosano (a medical officer in the Hong Kong Medical Department), worked in underground intelligence, the former for the Office of Strategic Studies, the latter heading the Macau branch of the British Army Aid Group (BAAG) during a period of the occupation.[75] Others moved across worlds. José Maria (Jack) Braga, son of a renowned member of the Hong Kong Portuguese community, was involved in a variety of activities in Macau: teaching, journalism, business, liaising between the British consul, the governor, and refugees, and also in underground intelligence for the Allies, as well as assisting escapes to unoccupied China.[76] Other Portuguese staffed the BAAG working in and around occupied Hong Kong,[77] and others deserted their posts in the Macau garrison and escaped to "Free China" to fight for the Allies.[78]

Those who stayed in occupied Shanghai and Hong Kong were of paramount importance to assist, when possible, their relatives confined to POW and internment camps. Many used their freedom as "third nationals" to deliver them food or clothes.[79] Visits could also be used to transmit information, sometimes at great personal risk. Gloria Barretto, Leo d'Almada's sister, would send messages to the camps—where another brother was a POW—hidden in jam jars.[80] Assisting the resistance was a dangerous affair, and mere suspicion of Allied sympathies could generate violent reprisals. In Hong Kong, several Portuguese were arrested and even killed by the occupation forces.[81]

Remembrance of the role played by the Portuguese in Allied resistance in South China has been largely confined to the Macanese diaspora and is not widely known in either Britain or Portugal, the two countries of which most were citizens. It is also left out of Chinese accounts that, understandably, put Chinese resistance efforts at the center of analysis. Precisely because of their "in-betweenness," the Portuguese have been relegated to marginal positions in different national narratives of the war in Asia.

Conclusion: Postwar Challenges

For the refugees who found themselves in Macau, the enclave offered a temporary haven in a time of disruption, but it did not represent a final destination.[82] Indeed, the end of the Second World War and the Chinese Civil War that erupted soon after propelled new migratory waves of these Portuguese communities.

While scholars have posited that the war was a decisive turning point in the complete disintegration of the Hong Kong Portuguese community,[83] in fact, most refugees in Macau sought to return to the neighboring territory, reoccupied by the British after the Japanese defeat. Even though many had actively supported Allied resistance, returning to Hong Kong was subjected to restrictive border controls.[84] In December 1945 there were still 5,650 people drawing relief from the British consulate in Macau, including Portuguese.[85] British officials were more favorable toward the return of the Hong Kong Portuguese than of destitute Chinese and Indians, praising their "exemplary" behavior during the occupation, although they, too, were understood as part of a racialized hierarchy. As one official remarked: "It is generally recognized that such people fill positions in the community which would otherwise be filled by Chinese clerks and that they are therefore not lowering the standards of living of the European population."[86] If discriminatory discourses on postwar migration to Hong Kong suggest that there were limits to the social transformation propelled by the war, certain practices would showcase that different treatment in even more striking terms. In 1950, the British authorities asked for repayment to the maintenance grants given to Hong Kong refugees in Macau during the war, prompting an angry response in the press. Members of the Portuguese community lamented being discriminated when "as loyal British subjects" they had "refused to stay behind in Hong Kong and work for the enemy," and contrasted their treatment with that given to "European British persons," noting the different position of the Macau government that never raised the issue of "repayment" for the relief it had given to Portuguese citizens.[87] While wartime service was left unacknowledged for several Portuguese, a few went on to prominent roles in postwar Hong Kong. For example, Leo d'Almada e Castro was appointed president of the General Military Court and was the first Portuguese nominated to the King's Counsel in 1947.[88]

The Portuguese state continued to have a complex relationship with these communities. There were some postwar attempts to strengthen Portugal's influence in Hong Kong through initiatives such as the Portuguese Institute of Hong Kong, where figures like d'Almada had leading positions.[89] Yet, like the wartime effort to involve the local Portuguese in Estado Novo propaganda, these had little lasting impact. For some Portuguese officials, the Portuguese in Asia were uncomfortably "foreign." They decried their lack of fluency in Portuguese language, their Eurasian origins, and their relative poverty.[90]

In Shanghai, the war marked the end of an era of colonial privileges. The foreign concessions were formally dismantled in 1943, incorporated in the Chinese Municipality. For some Portuguese, the early postwar years under Nationalist rule initially brought work opportunities in reconstruction activities. Maher, for instance, worked as a field mechanic for the US army, as an apprentice at the Shanghai Dockyards, and as a building superintendent with Standard Vacuum Oil and China Water Transport, while Nery had different jobs for the American forces.[91] However, the spread of the Chinese Civil War and its devastating economic impact on Shanghai led to a massive, and ultimately final, exodus of the Portuguese. The closure of most foreign firms after the Communist victory in 1949 was the decisive catalyst. That year, the community was reduced to 1,402 people and only six Portuguese businesses remained.[92] Some reprised the Second World War escape routes, moving to Hong Kong and Macau. Several others migrated to the United States, Japan, Britain, Australia, and elsewhere—a few went to Portugal, too. Suggestions that poorer members would be relocated to other Portuguese colonies did not materialize, with the exception of those evacuated to Macau.[93] These attracted support from the Hong Kong Portuguese, as the 1937 refugees before them.[94]

The wartime experiences of the Portuguese in Hong Kong and Shanghai showcase the different ways in which "in-between" communities navigated wartime occupation and displacement in Asia. In their particular case, wartime survival was shaped by the opportunities offered by Portugal's neutrality and by multiple and, at times, ambiguous connections to different imperial and national(ist) spheres. Among those who made creative uses of Portuguese neutrality to either continue to work under occupation or to seek shelter in Macau, were many who contributed in different ways to support Allied resistance, even if that wartime service was left largely unrecognized.

Notes

1. Research for this article was funded by a Leverhulme Trust Early Career Fellowship. Margret Frenz, "To Be or Not to Be … a Global Citizen: Three Doctors, Three Empires, and One Subcontinent," *Modern Asian Studies* 55, no. 4 (2021): 1185–226; Catherine S. Chan, *The Macanese Diaspora in British Hong Kong: A Century of Transimperial Drifting* (Amsterdam: Amsterdam University Press, 2021).

2. The origins of the Macanese have merited some scholarly debate. See, for example, the special issue "The Macanese: Anthropology, History, Ethnology," *Review of Culture* 20, Second Series (Macau: Instituto Cultural de Macau, 1994).
3. For example, the Sam Lazaro family in Shanghai (Helena F. S. Lopes, "A Name, a Photograph, and a History of Global Connections," *Visualising China*, September 30, 2022, accessed September 30, 2022, https://visualisingchina.net/blog/2022/09/30/a-name-a-photograph-and-a-history-of-global-connections/.
4. Cindy Yik-yi Chu, "Catholic Church between Two World Wars," in *Foreign Communities in Hong Kong, 1840s–1950s*, ed. Cindy Yik-yi Chu (New York: Palgrave Macmillan, 2005), 85–109; António M. Pacheco Jorge da Silva, *The Portuguese Community in Hong Kong: A Pictorial History* (Macau: Conselho das Comunidades Macaenses, 2007), 38–41; F. A. (Jim) Silva, *"All Our Yesterdays…" The Sons of Macao- Their History and Heritage* (San Francisco, CA: UMA Inc. of California, 1979), 28–9, 37.
5. "Portuguese Community Observe [sic.] Mesquita Day," *North China Herald*, August 31, 1938; Marcia R. Ristaino, *The Jacquinot Safe Zone: Wartime Refugees in Shanghai* (Stanford: Stanford University Press, 2008).
6. Margaret Gaan, *Last Moments of a World* (New York: W.W. Norton & Company, 1978), 134; Renée Azevedo Logan, *Shanghai Times* (San Diego, CA: AMC Publications, 1998), 9–10, 20, 33, 52.
7. Yanna Yannakakis, *The Art of Being In-Between: Native Intermediaries, Indian Identity, and Local Rule in Colonial Oaxaca* (Durham, NC: Duke University Press, 2008); Henrietta Harrison, *The Perils of Interpreting: The Extraordinary Lives of Two Translators between Qing China and the British Empire* (Princeton, NJ: Princeton University Press, 2021).
8. Kaori Abe, *Chinese Middlemen in Hong Kong's Colonial Economy, 1830–1890* (London: Routledge, 2018).
9. Yannakakis, *The Art of Being In-Between*, 4.
10. Elizabeth Sinn, "Hong Kong as an In-Between Place in the Chinese Diaspora, 1849–1949," in *Connecting Seas and Connected Ocean Rims: Indian, Atlantic, and Pacific Oceans and China Seas Migrations from the 1830s to the 1930s*, ed. Donna R. Gabaccía and Dirk Hoerder (Leiden: Brill, 2011), 225–47; Robert Bickers, "Incubator City: Shanghai and the Crises of Empires," *Journal of Urban History* 38, no. 5 (2012): 862–78.
11. Homi K. Bhabha, *The Location of Culture* (London: Routledge, 2004), 2.
12. Pnina Webner, "Vernacular Cosmopolitanism," *Theory, Culture & Society* 23, nos. 2–3 (2006): 498; Francisco Bethencourt, "Cosmopolitanism: The Fortunes of a Word," in *Cosmopolitanism in the Portuguese-Speaking World*, ed. Francisco Bethencourt (Leiden: Brill, 2017), 19.
13. Alfredo Gomes Dias, "The Origins of Macao's Community in Shanghai. Hong Kong's Emigration (1850–1909)," *Bulletin of Portuguese-Japanese Studies* 17 (2008): 213.
14. Catherine S Chan, "Macau Martyr or Portuguese Traitor? The Macanese Communities of Macau, Hong Kong and Shanghai and the Portuguese Nation," *Historical Research* 93, no. 262 (2020): 756.
15. Catherine S. Chan and José Luís de Sales Marques, "Extradition, Extraterritoriality, and Murder: Managing Portuguese Criminals in Chinese Port Cities," *e-Journal of Portuguese History* 19, no. 1 (2021): 128–46.

16. Frank Welsh, *A History of Hong Kong* (London: HarperCollins, 1997), 437; Jean Gittins, *Stanley: Behind Barbed Wire* (Hong Kong: Hong Kong University Press, 1982), 8.
17. In April 1942, the Portuguese vice-consul in Guangzhou estimated that 1,500 Portuguese remained in Hong Kong, while more than 2,000 had moved to Macau (Vice-consul in Guangzhou to minister to China, April 28, 1942, 2P, A49, M114, Arquivo Histórico-Diplomático, Lisbon; hereafter AHD). The International Committee of the Red Cross Delegate in Hong Kong estimated that of the almost 7,000 "Third Nationals" in Hong Kong at the end of January 1943, 1,203 were Portuguese ("Rapport de Mr. Zindel sur l'activité de la Délégation du CICR à Hong Kong au 28 février 1943," 8-9, B G 017 07-060, International Committee of the Red Cross Archives, Geneva; hereafter ICRC).
18. António Alves, "Relatório sobre o conflicto Sino-Japonês em Shanghai," October 1937, 96, 2P, A48, M175, AHD. It is unclear whether these figures refer only to the International Settlement and the French Concession or whether they also include residents in the Chinese Municipality.
19. Christian Henriot, Lu Shi, and Charlotte Aubrun, eds., *The Population of Shanghai (1865–1953): A Sourcebook* (Leiden: Brill, 2019), 178; Virtual Shanghai, *Country of Origin of the Foreign Population in the Foreign Settlements (1939–1940)* (Virtual Shanghai, n.d.), accessed February 24, 2020, https://www.virtualshanghai.net/Data/Tables?ID=141.
20. Zhicheng Wang, *Portuguese in Shanghai* (Macau: Fundação Macau, 2000), accessed March 31, 2021 https://www.macaudata.mo/macaubook/ebook001/index.html.
21. Chan, *Macanese Diaspora*.
22. Felicia Yap, "Portuguese Communities in East and Southeast Asia during the Japanese Occupation," in *The Making of the Luso-Asian World: Intricacies of Engagement*, ed. Laura Jarnagin (Singapore: Institute of Southeast Asian Studies, 2011), 208.
23. For example, Eddie Gosano, *Hong Kong Farewell*, LBY K.00/965, Imperial War Museum, London (hereafter IWM).
24. Robert Bickers, "Shanghailanders: The Formation and Identity of the British Settler Community in Shanghai 1843–1937," *Past & Present*, no. 159 (1998): 170, 175.
25. Jeffrey N. Wasserstrom, "Cosmopolitan Connections and Transnational Networks," in *At the Crossroads of Empires: Middlemen, Social Networks, and State-Building in Republican Shanghai*, ed. Nara Dillon and Jean C. Oi (Stanford: Stanford University Press, 2008), 206–24.
26. Chan, "Macau Martyr."
27. Alves, "Relatório," 87–93; "Portuguese Form Committee," *North China Herald*, August 18, 1937.
28. Edward Denison and Guang Yu Ren, *Building Shanghai: The Story of China's Gateway* (Chichester: John Wiley & Sons, 2013), 69–72.
29. Tani Maher and Anatole Maher, *Memoirs: From Old Shanghai to the New World* (Bloomington: Xlibris, 2008), 37–8.
30. Alves, "Relatório," 107–9.
31. "Additional Refugees," *South China Morning Post*, August 25, 1937.
32. "Refugiados Portugueses de Shanghai: Relatorio do Consul de Portugal em Hong Kong Alvaro Brilhante Laborinho," November 1937, 9–23, 2P, A48, M175, AHD.
33. John Pownall Reeves, *The Lone Flag: Memoir of the British Consul in Macao during World War II* (Hong Kong: Hong Kong University Press, 2014), 49–50.

34. Luís Andrade de Sá, *The Boys from Macau: Portugueses em Hong Kong* (Macao: Fundação Oriente, 1999), 114–18.
35. Sá, *The Boys from Macau*, 114–18; Gittins, *Stanley*, 8.
36. Alfredo Gomes Dias, "Os Refugiados de Hong Kong (1942)," *Revista de Cultura* 34 (2010): 125.
37. Dias, "Os Refugiados," 122; Barnabas H. M. Koo, *The Portuguese in Hong Kong and China: Their Beginning, Settlement and Progress to 1949, Volume 2* (Macau: Instituto Internacional de Macau, 2013), 128.
38. "Extract from China News Week No. 2 dated 12.9.42," WO 208/378A, The National Archives, Kew (hereafter TNA).
39. Governor of Macau to Ministry of the Colonies, February 6, 1942, AOS, UL-10A1, cx. 767, Arquivo Nacional Torre do Tombo, Lisbon (hereafter ANTT).
40. Governor to Ministry of the Colonies, June 15, 1942, AOS, UL-10A1, cx. 767, ANTT.
41. Governor to Ministry of the Colonies, February 18, 1942, AOS, UL-10A1, cx. 767, ANTT.
42. For example, "As Crianças Portuguesas, Refugiadas de Hongkong," *A Voz de Macau*, April 2, 1942; "Recita de Beneficio," *A Voz de Macau*, May 1, 1943; Reeves, *The Lone Flag*, 61–4, 109–10; Stuart Braga, "Nossa Gente (Our People): The Portuguese Refugee Community in Wartime Macau," in *Wartime Macau: Under the Japanese Shadow*, ed. Geoffrey C. Gunn (Hong Kong: Hong Kong University Press, 2016), 126–35.
43. For example, Files in 2P, A49, M115, AHD; AOS, UL-10A1, cx. 767, ANTT; CO 825/30/12, TNA.
44. Brian Edgar and Catherine S. Chan, "Contested Allegiance: The Response of Hong Kong's Macanese Community to the Challenges of the Japanese Occupation," *Journal of the Royal Asiatic Society Hong Kong Branch* 61 (2021): 108.
45. António M. Pacheco Jorge da Silva, *The Portuguese Community in Shanghai: A Pictorial History* (Conselho das Comunidades Macaenses, 2012), 91–2; "Putaoya qiaomin zuzhi—Puqiao zhongyang xiehui," *Shenbao*, March 16, 1942.
46. Edouard Egle, ICRC delegate in Shanghai to ICRC, December 3, 1942, B G 017 07-015, ICRC.
47. Wang, *Portuguese in Shanghai*, 54.
48. Gaan, *Last Moments of a World*, chapters 21–22; Logan, *Shanghai Times*, chapters 7 and 8.
49. For example, "Os Portugueses em Shanghai," *Jornal de Notícias*, July 8, 1945.
50. Poshek Fu, *Passivity, Resistance, and Collaboration: Intellectual Choices in Occupied Shanghai, 1937–1945* (Stanford: Stanford University Press, 1993).
51. Bernard Wasserstein, "Ambiguities of Occupation: Foreign Resisters and Collaborators in Wartime Shanghai," in *Wartime Shanghai*, ed. Wen-hsin Yeh (New York: Routledge, 1998), 23–38; Felicia Yap, "At the Edge of Empire: The Eurasian, Portuguese, and Baghdadi Jewish Communities in British Hong Kong," in *From a British to a Chinese Colony: Hong Kong before and after the 1997 Handover*, ed. Gary Chi-hung Luk (Berkeley: Institute of East Asian Studies, University of California, 2017), 217–35.
52. "Lusitano Retains Mercury Cup," *North China Herald*, September 24, 1941; "Lusitano Captures Hongkew Park Championship," *North China Herald*, October 29, 1941; James Carter, *Champions Day: The End of Old Shanghai* (New York: W.W. Norton & Company, 2020), 182–4.
53. Gaan, *Last Moments of a World*, 206.
54. "A Nossa Fun Fair," *Pela Pátria*, July 1941, 10–11.

55. "Local Portuguese Organize," *North China Herald*, November 15, 1939.
56. For example, files in Consulado de Portugal em Xangai, M26, AHD.
57. "Shanghai Volunteers Disbanded" and "Companhia Portuguesa 'Coronel Mesquita' S.V.C.," *Pela Pátria*, July, August, and September 1942, 39–45.
58. Maher and Maher, *Memoirs*, 104–5.
59. Frank H. H. King, *The History of the Hong Kong and Shanghai Banking Corporation, Volume III—the Hong Kong Bank between the Wars and the Bank Interned, 1919–1945: Return from Grandeur* (Cambridge: Cambridge University Press, 1988), 573–4, 615.
60. Gaan, *Last Moments of a World*, 62–6, 187, 210–15.
61. Philip Snow, *The Fall of Hong Kong: Britain, China and the Japanese Occupation* (New Haven: Yale University Press, 2003), 121.
62. For example, *Pela Pátria*, October 1942, 15–20; Silva, *The Portuguese Community in Shanghai*, 94.
63. Silva, *All Our Yesterdays*, 44.
64. Felipe B. Nery, *Filho de Macau (A Son of Macao): An Autobiography* (New York: Vantage Press, 1988), 49–50.
65. Nery, *Filho de Macau*, 51.
66. Alfredo Gomes Dias, *Diáspora Macaense: Macau, Hong Kong, Xangai (1850–1952)* (Lisbon: CCCM, 2014), 343–7.
67. Moisés Silva Fernandes, *Confluência de Interesses: Macau Nas Relações Luso-Chinesas Contemporâneas 1945–2005* (Lisbon: Instituto Diplomático, 2008), 46–7; Yun Xia, "Traitors in Limbo: Chinese Trials of White Russian Spies, 1937–1948," *Nationalities Papers* 49, no. 6 (2021): 1096–112; Helena F. S. Lopes, "Ghosts of War: China's Relations with Portugal in the Post-War Period, 1945–49," *Historical Research* 94, no. 265 (2021): 617–19.
68. Edgar and Chan, "Contested Allegiance," 115.
69. For example, Jiu-Jung Lo, "Survival as Justification for Collaboration, 1937–1945," in *Chinese Collaboration with Japan, 1932–1945: The Limits of Accommodation*, ed. David P. Barrett and Larry N. Shyu (Stanford: Stanford University Press, 2001), 116–32; Parks M. Coble, *Chinese Capitalists in Japan's New Order: The Occupied Lower Yangzi, 1937–1945* (Berkeley: University of California Press, 2003).
70. Helena F. S. Lopes, "Entre Impérios: Prisioneiros Portugueses na Segunda Guerra Mundial na Ásia de Leste," in *Prisioneiros de Guerras: Experiências de Cativeiro no Século XX*, ed. Pedro Aires Oliveira (Lisbon: Tinta-da-China, 2019), 201–2.
71. Cicero Rozario, "Cicero Rozario's P.O.W. Memoirs: Experiences at Sendai Camp, Kyushu, Japan, Part 2 (Conclusion)," *Lustiano Bulletin* 16, no. 1 (2006): 23–6; José 'Zinho' Gosano, "The Life and Times of Father José 'Zinho' Gosano," *UMA News Bulletin* 34, no. 2 (2011): 13–14.
72. Rozario, "Cicero Rozario's P.O.W. Memoirs," 26.
73. Alves, "Relatório," 92–3, 114–15.
74. For example, Logan, *Shanghai Times*, 77.
75. Interview with Bernard Felix Xavier (1999), catalogue no. 19926, IWM; Gosano, *Hong Kong Farewell*, 26–9. On the BAAG see Edwin Ride, *BAAG, Hong Kong Resistance, 1942–1945* (Hong Kong: Oxford University Press, 1981).
76. Helena F. S. Lopes, *Neutrality and Collaboration in South China: Macau during the Second World War* (Cambridge: Cambridge University Press, 2023), 27, 225–6.
77. For example, Roy Eric Xavier, "The Macanese at War: Survival and Identity among Portuguese Eurasians during World War II," in *Wartime Macau: Under the Japanese*

Shadow, ed. Geoffrey C. Gunn (Hong Kong: Hong Kong University Press, 2016), 111–13.
78. Helena F. S. Lopes, "Questioning Neutrality: Sino-Portuguese Relations during the War and the Post-War Periods, 1937–1949" (Dissertation, University of Oxford, 2018), 237–9.
79. Koo, *The Portuguese in Hong Kong and China*, 133.
80. Ruy Barretto, "Barretto, Gloria d'Almada," in *Dictionary of Hong Kong Biography*, ed. May Holdsworth and Christopher Munn, illustrated edition (Hong Kong: Hong Kong University Press, 2012), 20.
81. António M. Pacheco Jorge da Silva, *The Portuguese Community in Hong Kong: A Pictorial History*, Volume II (Macau: Conselho das Comunidades Macaenses, 2010), 30–3; Yap, "Portuguese Communities," 217; Edgar and Chan, "Contested Allegiance," 114–15.
82. For example, "Reflections of a Refugee," *Macau Tribune*, January 30, 1944.
83. Yap, "At the Edge of Empire," 218, 231.
84. Sá, *The Boys from Macau*, 118–19.
85. Hong Kong Civil Affairs Administration, "Refugee Relief in Macau," December 19, 1945, HKRS170-1-333, Hong Kong Public Records Office (hereafter HKPRO).
86. C. G. M. Morrison, August 8, 1946, HKRS41-1-1168, HKPRO.
87. For example, "Macao Refugees," *South China Morning Post*, February 14, 1950; "Fairplay For Macao Refugees," *South China Morning Post*, February 15, 1950; "Macao Refugees," *South China Morning Post*, February 28, 1950.
88. Sá, *The Boys from Macau*, 53; Jason Wordie, "D'Almada e Castro Jr., Leonardo Horátio," in *Dictionary of Hong Kong Biography*, ed. May Holdsworth and Christopher Munn (Hong Kong: Hong Kong University Press, 2012), 116.
89. Eduardo Brazão, *O Instituto Português de Hong Kong* (Macau: Imprensa Nacional, 1947), 148–9.
90. For example, Eduardo Brazão, Relatório "Os Portugueses em Hong Kong," 1948, AHD; António Caeiro, *Os Retornados de Xangai: Histórias de Portugueses do Oriente* (Lisbon: Tinta-da-China, 2022), 148–9.
91. Maher and Maher, *Memoirs*, 71–5; Nery, *Filho de Macau*, 54.
92. Yuezhi Xiong, Xueqiang Ma, and Kejia An, eds., *Shanghai de waiguoren, 1842–1949* (Shanghai: Shanghai gu ji chu ban she, 2003), 219, 234.
93. Consul in Shanghai to Ministry of Foreign Affairs, July 2, August 22, and October 1, 1949, Consulado de Portugal em Xangai, M45, AHD.
94. "Portuguese Refugees from S'hai," *South China Morning Post*, November 15, 1950.

Bibliography

Archives

Arquivo Histórico-Diplomático, Lisbon (AHD)

2P, A48, M175
2P, A49, M114
2P, A49, M115
Consulado de Portugal em Xangai, M26
Consulado de Portugal em Xangai, M45
Eduardo Brazão, Relatório "Os Portugueses em Hong Kong," 1948

Arquivo Nacional Torre do Tombo, Lisbon (ANTT)

AOS, UL-10A1, cx. 767

Hong Kong Public Records Office (hereafter HKPRO)

HKRS41-1-1168
HKRS170-1-333

Imperial War Museum, London (IWM)

Eddie Gosano, *Hong Kong Farewell*, LBY K.00/965
Interview with Bernard Felix Xavier (1999), catalogue no. 19926

International Committee of the Red Cross Archives, Geneva (ICRC)

B G 017 07–015
B G 017 07–060

The National Archives, Kew (TNA)

CO 825/30/12
WO 208/378A

Newspapers

A Voz de Macau (Macau)
Jornal de Notícias (Macau)
Macau Tribune (Macau)
North China Herald (Shanghai)
Pela Pátria (Shanghai)
Shenbao 申報 (Shanghai)
South China Morning Post (Hong Kong)

Research Literature

Abe, Kaori. *Chinese Middlemen in Hong Kong's Colonial Economy, 1830–1890*. London: Routledge, 2018.

Barretto, Ruy. "Barretto, Gloria d'Almada." In *Dictionary of Hong Kong Biography*, edited by May Holdsworth and Christopher Munn, 20–1. Hong Kong: Hong Kong University Press, 2012.

Bethencourt, Francisco. "Cosmopolitanism: The Fortunes of a Word." In *Cosmopolitanism in the Portuguese-Speaking World*, edited by Francisco Bethencourt, 1–19. Leiden: Brill, 2017.

Bhabha, Homi K. *The Location of Culture*. London: Routledge, 2004.

Bickers, Robert. "Incubator City: Shanghai and the Crises of Empires." *Journal of Urban History* 38, no. 5 (2012): 862–78.
Bickers, Robert. "Shanghailanders: The Formation and Identity of the British Settler Community in Shanghai 1843–1937." *Past & Present*, no. 159 (1998): 161–211.
Braga, Stuart. "Nossa Gente (Our People): The Portuguese Refugee Community in Wartime Macau." In *Wartime Macau: Under the Japanese Shadow*, edited by Geoffrey C. Gunn, 116–40. Hong Kong: Hong Kong University Press, 2016.
Brazão, Eduardo. *O Instituto Português de Hong Kong*. Macau: Imprensa Nacional, 1947.
Caeiro, António. *Os Retornados de Xangai: Histórias de Portugueses do Oriente*. Lisbon: Tinta-da-China, 2022.
Carter, James. *Champions Day: The End of Old Shanghai*. New York: W.W. Norton & Company, 2020.
Chan, Catherine S. *The Macanese Diaspora in British Hong Kong: A Century of Transimperial Drifting*. Amsterdam: Amsterdam University Press, 2021.
Chan, Catherine S. "Macau Martyr or Portuguese Traitor? The Macanese Communities of Macau, Hong Kong and Shanghai and the Portuguese Nation." *Historical Research* 93, no. 262 (2020): 754–68.
Chan, Catherine S., and José Luís de Sales Marques. "Extradition, Extraterritoriality, and Murder: Managing Portuguese Criminals in Chinese Port Cities." *e-Journal of Portuguese History* 19, no. 1 (2021): 128–46.
Chu, Cindy Yik-yi. "Catholic Church between Two World Wars." In *Foreign Communities in Hong Kong, 1840s–1950s*, edited by Cindy Yik-yi Chu, 85–109. New York: Palgrave Macmillan, 2005.
Coble, Parks M. *Chinese Capitalists in Japan's New Order: The Occupied Lower Yangzi, 1937–1945*. Berkeley: University of California Press, 2003.
Denison, Edward, and Guang Yu Ren. *Building Shanghai: The Story of China's Gateway*. Chichester: John Wiley & Sons, 2013.
Dias, Alfredo Gomes. *Diáspora Macaense: Macau, Hong Kong, Xangai (1850–1952)*. Lisbon: CCCM and Fundação Macau, 2014.
Dias, Alfredo Gomes. "The Origins of Macao's Community in Shanghai. Hong Kong's Emigration (1850–1909)." *Bulletin of Portuguese-Japanese Studies* 17 (2008): 197–224.
Dias, Alfredo Gomes. "Os Refugiados de Hong Kong (1942)." *Revista de Cultura* 34 (2010): 117–28.
Edgar, Brian, and Catherine S. Chan. "Contested Allegiance: The Response of Hong Kong's Macanese Community to the Challenges of the Japanese Occupation." *Journal of the Royal Asiatic Society Hong Kong Branch* 61 (2021): 100–21.
Fernandes, Moisés Silva. *Confluência de Interesses: Macau Nas Relações Luso-Chinesas Contemporâneas 1945–2005*. Lisbon: Instituto Diplomático, 2008.
Frenz, Margret. "To Be or Not to Be ... a Global Citizen: Three Doctors, Three Empires, and One Subcontinent." *Modern Asian Studies* 55, no. 4 (2021): 1185–226.
Fu, Poshek. *Passivity, Resistance, and Collaboration: Intellectual Choices in Occupied Shanghai, 1937–1945*. Stanford: Stanford University Press, 1993.
Gaan, Margaret. *Last Moments of a World*. New York: W.W. Norton & Company, 1978.
Gittins, Jean. *Stanley: Behind Barbed Wire*. Hong Kong: Hong Kong University Press, 1982.
Gosano, José. 'Zinho.' "The Life and Times of Father José 'Zinho' Gosano." *UMA News Bulletin* 34, no. 2 (2011): 3–19.
Harrison, Henrietta. *The Perils of Interpreting: The Extraordinary Lives of Two Translators between Qing China and the British Empire*. Princeton, NJ: Princeton University Press, 2021.

Henriot, Christian, Lu Shi, and Charlotte Aubrun, eds. *The Population of Shanghai (1865–1953): A Sourcebook*. Leiden: Brill, 2019.

King, Frank H. H. *The History of the Hong Kong and Shanghai Banking Corporation, Volume III—the Hong Kong Bank between the Wars and the Bank Interned, 1919–1945: Return from Grandeur*. Cambridge: Cambridge University Press, 1988.

Koo, Barnabas H. M. *The Portuguese in Hong Kong and China: Their Beginning, Settlement and Progress to 1949, Volume 2*. Macau: Instituto Internacional de Macau, 2013.

Lo, Jiu-Jung. "Survival as Justification for Collaboration, 1937–1945." In *Chinese Collaboration with Japan, 1932–1945: The Limits of Accommodation*, edited by David P. Barrett and Larry N. Shyu, 116–32. Stanford: Stanford University Press, 2001.

Logan, Renée Azevedo. *Shanghai Times*. San Diego, CA: AMC Publications, 1998.

Lopes, Helena F. S. "Entre Impérios: Prisioneiros Portugueses na Segunda Guerra Mundial na Ásia de Leste." In *Prisioneiros de Guerras: Experiências de Cativeiro no Século XX*, edited by Pedro Aires Oliveira, 201–22. Lisbon: Tinta-da-China, 2019.

Lopes, Helena F. S. "Ghosts of War: China's Relations with Portugal in the Post-War Period, 1945–49." *Historical Research* 94, no. 265 (2021): 601–28.

Lopes, Helena F. S. "A Name, a Photograph, and a History of Global Connections." *Visualising China*, September 30, 2022. Accessed September 30, 2022. https://visualisingchina.net/blog/2022/09/30/a-name-a-photograph-and-a-history-of-global-connections/.

Lopes, Helena F. S., *Neutrality and Collaboration in South China: Macau during the Second World War*. Cambridge: Cambridge University Press, 2023.

Lopes, Helena F. S. "Questioning Neutrality: Sino-Portuguese Relations during the War and the Post-War Periods, 1937–1949." Dissertation, University of Oxford, 2018.

"The Macanese: Antropology, History, Ethnology." *Review of Culture* 20, Second Series. Macau: Instituto Cultural de Macau, 1994.

Maher, Tani, and Anatole Maher. *Memoirs: From Old Shanghai to the New World*. Bloomington: Xlibris, 2008.

Nery, Felipe B. *Filho de Macau, (A Son of Macao): An Autobiography*. New York: Vantage Press, 1988.

Reeves, John Pownall. *The Lone Flag: Memoir of the British Consul in Macao during World War II*. Hong Kong: Hong Kong University Press, 2014.

Ride, Edwin. *BAAG, Hong Kong Resistance, 1942–1945*. Hong Kong: Oxford University Press, 1981.

Ristaino, Marcia R. *The Jacquinot Safe Zone: Wartime Refugees in Shanghai*. Stanford: Stanford University Press, 2008.

Rozario, Cicero. "Cicero Rozario's P.O.W. Memoirs: Experiences at Sendai Camp, Kyushu, Japan, Part 2 (Conclusion)." *Lustiano Bulletin* 16, no. 1 (2006): 20–33.

Sá, Luís Andrade de. *The Boys from Macau: Portugueses em Hong Kong*. Macao: Fundação Oriente, 1999.

Silva, António M. Pacheco Jorge da. *The Portuguese Community in Hong Kong: A Pictorial History*. Macau: Conselho das Comunidades Macaenses, 2007.

Silva, António M. Pacheco Jorge da. *The Portuguese Community in Hong Kong: A Pictorial History*, Volume II. Macau: Conselho das Comunidades Macaenses, 2010.

Silva, António M. Pacheco Jorge da. *The Portuguese Community in Shanghai: A Pictorial History*. Macau: Conselho das Comunidades Macaenses, 2012.

Silva, F. A. (Jim). *"All Our Yesterdays…" The Sons of Macao—Their History and Heritage*. San Francisco, CA: UMA Inc. of California, 1979.

Sinn, Elizabeth. "Hong Kong as an In-Between Place in the Chinese Diaspora, 1849–1949." In *Connecting Seas and Connected Ocean Rims: Indian, Atlantic, and Pacific Oceans and China Seas Migrations from the 1830s to the 1930s*, edited by Donna R. Gabaccía and Dirk Hoerder, 225–47. Leiden: Brill, 2011.

Snow, Philip. *The Fall of Hong Kong: Britain, China and the Japanese Occupation*. New Haven: Yale University Press, 2003.

Virtual Shanghai. *Country of Origin of the Foreign Population in the Foreign Settlements (1939–1940)*. Virtual Shanghai, n.d. Accessed February 24, 2020. https://www.virtualshanghai.net/Data/Tables?ID=141.

Wang, Zhicheng. *Portuguese in Shanghai*. Macau: Fundação Macau, 2000. Accessed March 31, 2021. https://www.macaudata.mo/macaubook/ebook001/index.html.

Wasserstein, Bernard. "Ambiguities of Occupation: Foreign Resisters and Collaborators in Wartime Shanghai." In *Wartime Shanghai*, edited by Wen-hsin Yeh, 23–38. New York: Routledge, 1998.

Wasserstrom, Jeffrey N. "Cosmopolitan Connections and Transnational Networks." In *At the Crossroads of Empires: Middlemen, Social Networks, and State-Building in Republican Shanghai*, edited by Nara Dillon and Jean C. Oi, 206–24. Stanford: Stanford University Press, 2008.

Webner, Pnina. "Vernacular Cosmopolitanism." *Theory, Culture & Society* 23, nos. 2–3 (2006): 496–8.

Welsh, Frank. *A History of Hong Kong*. London: HarperCollins, 1997.

Wordie, Jason. "D'Almada e Castro Jr., Leonardo Horátio." In *Dictionary of Hong Kong Biography*, edited by May Holdsworth and Christopher Munn, 116. Hong Kong: Hong Kong University Press, 2012.

Xavier, Roy Eric. "The Macanese at War: Survival and Identity among Portuguese Eurasians during World War II." In *Wartime Macau: Under the Japanese Shadow*, edited by Geoffrey C. Gunn, 94–115. Hong Kong: Hong Kong University Press, 2016.

Xia, Yun. "Traitors in Limbo: Chinese Trials of White Russian Spies, 1937–1948." *Nationalities Papers* 49, no. 6 (2021): 1096–112.

Xiong, Yuezhi, Xueqiang Ma, and Kejia An, eds. *Shanghai de waiguoren, 1842–1949*. Shanghai: Shanghai gu ji chu ban she, 2003.

Yannakakis, Yanna. *The Art of Being In-Between: Native Intermediaries, Indian Identity, and Local Rule in Colonial Oaxaca*. Durham, NC: Duke University Press, 2008.

Yap, Felicia. "At the Edge of Empire: The Eurasian, Portuguese, and Baghdadi Jewish Communities in British Hong Kong." In *From a British to a Chinese Colony: Hong Kong before and after the 1997 Handover*, edited by Gary Chi-hung Luk, 217–35. Berkeley: Institute of East Asian Studies, University of California, 2017.

Yap, Felicia. "Portuguese Communities in East and Southeast Asia during the Japanese Occupation." In *The Making of the Luso-Asian World: Intricacies of Engagement*, edited by Laura Jarnagin, 205–28. Singapore: Institute of Southeast Asian Studies, 2011.

7

Countering Economic Marginalization: Africanization Strategies in Tanzania's and Ghana's Insurance Markets during Decolonization

Eva Kocher and Francis Daudi

Introduction

The history of insurance and reinsurance in West and East Africa is relatively understudied, yet the most important works on global reinsurance history address the African regions with a few pages, such as Niels Viggo-Haueter and Geoffrey Jones in 2017 or Borscheid in 2012.[1] However, the most substantial writings on reinsurance and insurance history in Africa mostly cover specific insurance branches (life insurance legislation, motor insurance, etc.)[2] and tackle the topic from a legal and often national perspective, to the detriment of a more global one, which would mostly better reflect the market situation. It is little astonishing that the industry itself played a substantial role in the production of central knowledge, with writings of prominent practitioners such as J. O. Irukwu.[3] Recent economic studies also attempt to cover the historical background of insurance in Africa to explain the continuing low rate of insurance inclusion.[4] Therefore, there is an important gap to fill for African and international economic historians, to learn more about the development insurance and reinsurance markets in British East and West Africa and throughout decolonization.

Insights from writings on African economic history as well as historical studies of multinational business in West Africa are a crucial point of reference for this research, also in terms of the methodology and conceptual framework. For instance, Austin and Uche have extensively published research on the history of financial institutions and their functioning in British West Africa, which provides decisive context for this research.[5]

Insurance was introduced to West Africa through colonialism and until for most of the twentieth century, it addressed the colonial classes' needs to cover risk. Therefore insurance models in Africa largely followed European standards. These were to some extent adapted to local contexts but usually resulted in higher pricing for the local populations, for example, via additional expense factor into premium calculation called, for example, "tropical loading," which, for instance, Okediji described in the case of Nigerian life insurance.[6] The larger local West African population had traditionally not been the target group of most of the European insurance firms that continued to dominate most of these insurance markets even decades after independence.[7]

However, by the 1940s British insurers had found an interest to offer insurance services to African elites.[8] The colonial administrative staff was especially identified as a growing segment of insurance clients. Sources from the British National Archives show that British insurers and brokers were interested in African mortality tables since 1947. Willington Eldred and Son Ltd. from London asked for so-called "experience cards" informing about the number of Africans in government service and their life expectancy applied in widows and orphans pension schemes, as a basis for computing life insurance premiums. However, a problem to this undertaking posed the lack of statistical and demographic information to calculate policies together with the view that only European ways of life were acceptable risks. Even the Eldred representative wrote, "I wish I could find some company who would do Endowment Assurance for Africans. It has got to be done sometime as every day I have to turn down cases and with the national feeling growing up over here I find it very difficult." However, he added on the next page, "I would not dream of asking you to take on the average African in a commercial … There are hundreds here who live and behave just like Europeans, have stacks of money and are Knights, O.B.E.s and What-nots."[9]

The living standard of a minority was thus the reference for the conditions under which insurance was to be disseminated in both British West and East Africa throughout decolonization. In both British and French West Africa, euro-centric, racist, and elitist bias resulted in significantly higher pricing of products for African clients and a continuing lack of insurance products for the broad population in West Africa by the dawn of independence in the mid-twentieth century. Insurance products were not tailored to the African majority population but targeted a small elite. This is also the case for other regions: Similarly, Tapen Sinha has described how Indian lives were treated as "substandard" during the colonial period, for which "Indians had to pay an ad-hoc premium of 20 percent or more," compared to a British person living in India.[10]

Consequently, African policymakers as well as the private sector developed postcolonial strategies to make insurance products more accessible to the broader local population, both in West Africa and in East Africa. This chapter will refer to such strategies as "Africanization" efforts, which is, however, also used in other contexts, for example, Stephanie Decker has already extensively described the strategy of Africanizing referring to employment strategies and efforts of multinational companies to increase especially lower- and middle-level staff in face of decolonization to ensure local goodwill.[11]

The intention to make insurance available and affordable to the African majority was certainly a key motivation behind a postindependence wave of the creation of national insurance companies in East and West Africa, for example, the establishment of the *Ghana State Insurance Corporation* in 1962 or the National Insurance Corporation (NIC) of Tanzania established in 1963.[12] However, before such state-led projects, entrepreneurial efforts aimed to provide West Africans with affordable insurance products via indigenous insurance companies. The first case study looks at the example of a group of insurance entrepreneurs, who established the local company "The Gold Coast Insurance" already in 1955, which introduced new insurance schemes based on African American mortality tables. The company group expanded even to Nigeria and played an important role in the later state insurance company, which took over these firms.

The second case study focuses on Tanzania: during decolonization, the government also set up state-owned companies and replaced non-African positions with Africans as part of the Africanization of the insurance industry. The National Insurance Corporation Ltd. (NIC) was given a monopoly of transacting insurance business in Tanzania from February 1967. Similarly, it became the center of Africanization when the government embarked on the strategy immediately after nationalization of the insurance sector. Africanization, however, cost NIC more than 54 percent of gross premiums between 1967 and 1968. Present studies ignored the significant roles played by state-owned insurance companies in non-Western regions during the decolonization process. Therefore, the second part of this chapter examines the process of Africanization "from within" with special reference to the NIC. Furthermore, this chapter shall evaluate the Africanization of the insurance market in Tanzania and the regulatory measures taken to back up this movement.

African American Insurance Entrepreneurship

While there exists extensive research on the topic of African American entrepreneurship in postindependence Ghana and its role for the national economy, the impact of American insurers and especially American life insurance has been widely ignored so far, by financial history in general as well as insurance history in particular.[13] As Steven Taylor has pointed out, African Americans expatriates in Ghana were often inspired not only by optimistic outlooks on the development of the country but also by personal and intellectual ties to Kwame Nkrumah and his Pan-Africanist ideas.[14]

To a certain extent, this is also true for the group of African Americans and their Ghanaian partners, who played a key role in advancing domestic insurance business in West Africa: the first documented commercial domestic insurance company established in West Africa was the Gold Coast Insurance Company, which started operations in 1956. While this company and its successor, the Ghana Insurance together with the Ghana General Insurance are generally acknowledged to be the first and only domestic companies in Ghana,[15] before culminating in the Ghanaian State Insurance in 1962, fewer were familiar with the circumstances of their establishment and business operations.

The Gold Coast Insurance was chartered in 1955 by two African American insurance experts: Robert Turner Freeman, Vertner W. Tandy, and their British colleague David Jones, together with their local partners and shareholders Henry P. Nyemitei, Kofi Johnson, and Anthony Kobina Woode. The company started operations in 1956. Both Freeman and Tandy were lawyers. Johnson and Nyemitei had worked for the British insurance industry before. Robert Turner Freeman had entered the life insurance industry in 1945 with the United Mutual Life Insurance Company of New York.

In a letter to Kwame Nkrumah from 1954 Robert Turner Freeman explained that a group from the Gold Coast had consulted him in 1948, seeking his expertise to formulate a plan of life insurance for the general population. "Unfortunately, and perhaps because of the lack of technical knowledge among those who conferred with me, the plan, while evolved, was not put into operation."[16] Freeman knew Nkrumah personally from his time at Lincoln University, and also, he was an experienced actuary and vice president of the United Mutual Life, a company that mainly insured Black lives in New York, Washington, Connecticut, New Jersey, as well as Puerto Rico and the Virgin Islands. Moreover, Robert Freeman had been successfully fighting higher premium rates for African Americans and submitted a study to the New York State Insurance Department that challenged reinsurance companies' higher premiums for Black lives. The consequence was the passing of legislation prohibiting discrimination in premium rates.[17]

With the same letter, Freeman also sent Nkrumah the project outline and prospectus, which he had written together with his two colleagues Tandy and Jones: "Prospectus of a life insurance program for the Gold Coast."[18] Despite the fact that they presented essentially a business plan, the undertaking was always referred to as a project or program by Freeman and his partners, focused on the aim to make insurance products in general and life insurance in particular available to the broader Ghanaian public, stressing also the macroeconomic benefits for the country and its contribution to economic independence.[19]

This document that was preserved together with the letter to Nkrumah states that "the program outlined herein proposes the formation of a new corporate institution ... permanently located within the Gold Coast"[20] while stressing economic advantages on both the individual level for the policy holders and the national level. The authors clearly used a rhetoric that drew on the discourse of national economic development by emphasizing the public benefit and the term of project when referring to their economic enterprise: the list of social and economic advantages stressed in the documentation covers the creation of employment, training possibilities, systematic saving, and funds for local investment, "which will make a contribution to the economic welfare of the nation."[21] The language of the document can be clearly placed within the development paradigm of the 1940s and 1950s, as described by Cooper and Packard.[22]

The entrepreneurs were supported in their venture not only by the local government from the very beginning but also by development agencies and experts, which played a crucial role in connecting them with local partners. In 1955 Dr. Robert Gardiner, the by then Head of Social Welfare and UN representative in Ghana, learned about the interest of Freeman and his colleagues and invited them to the Gold Coast, where they met Henry Nyemetei, Kofi Johnson, and Anthony Kobina Woode and chartered the Gold Coast Insurance Company. The local partners took care of paperwork on immigration and registration while the Americans returned home to the United States. Freeman sold his home and his belongings in New York and sent his wife with their kids to her family in Washington, DC. He and his colleagues collected USD 25,000 from personal friends as shareholders and returned to the Gold Coast in 1956. By that time, no insurance laws existed and the only requirement to start a business was the starting capital of USD 14,000.[23] In November 1955, the Gold Coast Insurance was registered and in March, 1956, the company started operations in a building now known as Koala Shopping Center, at Osu, Accra.[24] Robert Freeman Jr. acted as managing director and Mr. Vertner Tandy Jr. as his deputy, Henry Nyemitei held the position of agency director, Samuel Cofie Johnson, registrar, David D. Jones as secretary, and Antony Kobina-Woode the general agent for the western region. The group had analyzed the market and had insightful knowledge of the local industry and their products, especially thanks to their local partners, who were trained by British insurers operating in the Gold Coast and therefore familiar with their operations and products.[25] In a letter to Johnson from November 16, 1955, Vertner Tandy wrote: "Our company definitely will be able to write educational policies at a rate lower than those offered by Gresham even without the extra premium which they charge for covering African lives."[26] The company sold policy contracts for ten-, fifteen-, and twenty-year endowment policies, endowment at ages fifty-five and sixty and a children's educational endowment at age eighteen. Freeman used mortality tables of African Americans to calculate premium rates.[27]

While British insurers had mostly through other financial intermediaries such as banks and trade, the Gold Coast Insurance Company also pioneered in training local life insurance agents. Freeman built a 150-person strong agency force with local branches in the major cities, which grew substantially in the first years of operation. After Ghana gained independence in 1957, the company's name was changed to "Ghana Insurance Company."[28] However, the case of the Gold Coast Insurance also confirms that access to private capital to fund the formation of new businesses was heavily dependent on political patronage and connections to the elites in West Africa during decolonization.

Partnerships and Growth

The company flourished significantly after its establishment and the entrepreneurs expanded: in 1960, Freeman and Tandy founded their second company, the Ghana General Insurance together with the British Provincial to insure automobile, fire, and accident risks (property and casualty risks). Reinsurance treaties were signed with Mercantile & General Reinsurance and SwissRe. Especially with the latter, Freeman and Tandy had close ties, as they even received a personal loan in 1960 to invest in local real estate.[29]

In 1960, the success of the firms expanded further: the Western Region Finance Corporation of Nigeria asked Freeman to go into partnership with the western region government to establish an all-purpose insurance company in Lagos. As a result, the Great Nigeria Insurance Company was founded and chaired by J. O. B. Omotosho, with Tandy and Freeman as managing directors. Vertner Tandy was seconded to Lagos as general manager.

In 1962, the Ghanaian State acquired both companies, merging it via Executive Instrument EI 17 together with the Cooperatives Insurance Company to form the State Insurance Corporation (SIC). Robert Freeman managed the SIC until 1965. The SIC heavily relied on the experience and networks of the Ghana General and Ghana Life, as SIC also received assistance in the form of training and scholarships by SwissRe, the Provincial Insurance, the Albion Insurance, as well as the Mercantile & General Reinsurance.[30] Freeman left the SIC in 1965. In a letter to Nkrumah he explained that the main reason for his departure was his moral obligation to join the civil rights movement in the United States.[31]

The SIC premium income grew significantly until the 1980s: from 1962 until 1967 it built up to 7.9 million Cedi (7.7 million USD)[32], grew further to 19.5 million Cedi by 1972 to 55.5 million Cedi by 1977 and to 132.4 million Cedi by 1982.[33] Starting with six branch offices in 1963, it had expanded its network to several dozen by 1986.[34] According to the documentation at the Schomburg Center, Robert Freeman remained in close contact with African insurance markets and his professional and private network in West Africa all his life. He consulted several African states on insurance law, state insurance, and social security projects, for example, Lesotho, Ethiopia, and Guyana. His local partners Henry Nyemetei and Anthony Kobina Woode remained key figures for the Ghanaian and African insurance industry as cadre of the SIC, and Woode, for example, later became manager and also as promoter and cofounder of the African Insurance Organisation in 1972.[35]

Africanization from Abroad?

The case of the Gold Coast Insurance (Ghana Life) and the Ghana General is of particular interest for a number of aspects. First of all, it shows the unique position in which its founders were ideologically and professionally: The Ghana Life's success based largely on an innovative approach to provide cheaper products to the broader local population than the British firms, basing their premium calculation on American mortality tables and on the readiness to invest in local staff trained as agents. Moreover, the Ghana General combined the Africanized image and products with the collaboration and the expertise of a British insurance company, the Provincial. Freeman had the credibility of advancing the Ghanaian national cause, much in contrast to other foreigners associated with the colonial past, who met political and public opposition in civil service. This was the case for a British and an Indian employee of the SIC: their appointment was criticized in a parliamentary debate on October 21, 1963, where a member expressed that

> the Englishman in the State Insurance Corporation should not only be dismissed but should be deported together with the Indian because they have virtually and terribly become redundant. They do not give any assistance in the promotion of our State Insurance Corporation; they are there for their own personal interest ... the Managing Director himself is not a Ghanaian, but I have not brought him into the picture because I know that under him many more Ghanaians will be trained to become really qualified for the job in the State Insurance Corporation.[36]

This shows to what high degree this economic branch was politicized and the difficulties resulting for know-how transfer and international expertise. While local expertise existed and reflected in the local shareholders of the company Gold Coast insurance, the US entrepreneurs played a crucial role in the company history, with their network, their resources, and their innovative transfer of insurance schemes. Moreover, the documentation of the establishment of these companies shows the importance of the support of both the governmental institutions and international corporations such as SwissRe and a number of British insurers, which also played a crucial role in capacity building and training. Finally, the case points out the consequences of state intervention in this business branch: while the Ghana Life and the Ghana General were young and flourishing businesses, their absorption in the State Insurance Corporation meant to a certain extent a setback for local market development. Finally, the SIC as a state insurer was less flexible in the development of its portfolio and it had to take on much larger risks, for state corporations and critical infrastructures, and it had to cover all classes of risks, also, for instance, marine, in which the prior companies had no prior experience.

Africanizing the Whole Insurance Sector in Tanzania

This second case study focuses on Tanzania and it cross-examines the Africanization of insurance business in Tanzania. The first section of this part offers historical analysis of an attempt made by the government of Tanzania to restructure insurance markets of Tanzania through nationalization of the sector in 1967 as part of commanding heights of the economy. The second section of this part evaluates the Africanization of insurance business under the NIC that had hitherto given to transact insurance products as solely insurer in the country.

Africanization in postcolonial Tanzania was a product of decolonization, which continued and became more popular in the late 1960s.[37] While it started as only a program of replacing non-Africans with Africans and later more specifically Tanzanians in the civil services,[38] it adopted a different direction when the political elite within the then ruling party, TANU, demanded the Africanization of the economy. The decision to undertake Africanization of the insurance sector revealed at least two important steps. First was the creation of a state-owned insurance company. On October 16, 1963, the government announced the incorporation of NIC, famously known as *Shirika la Bima la Taifa la Tanganyika*.[39] The professional insurers such as Swiss Re, Colin Hood Insurance Brokers Limited, and Munich Re owned 49 percent of all shares while the then government of Tanzania took 51 percent of the remaining shares.[40] However, their role in the establishment of NIC was overshadowed with Africanization campaigns in the 1960s. Unlike Ghana, when Tanganyika attained her independence on December 9, 1961, there was no insurance owned by indigenous in the country. Indeed, NIC organized campaigns to raise awareness among Africans on the importance of insurance from November 1964.[41] The then president Julius Nyerere and vice president Abeid Karume took up their life insurance policies as first customers of this category of business on November 1, 1964. The second step was the nationalization of the insurance business in 1967. When NIC started underwriting both life and nonlife insurance in 1964, TANU activists vehemently demanded for state intervention into the business. Ruling party's activists in the parliament were convinced that if the government of Tanganyika and later Tanzania wanted to regain control of the insurance business and economy as a whole, the main strategy would have been taking over the business and transacting insurance by state-owned insurer, NIC. In parliamentary debate, Ali Mtaki noted that

> the expropriation of large amount [sic] of money abroad is dangerous because it removes the economy from our control and usually the cure is only one, that is, to close down all insurance companies and to remain with only one, which belongs to the state of Tanganyika.[42]

The debate entailed widening Africa's participation in the economy through nationalization of all key sectors of the economy.[43] Therefore, the insurance sector became one of the first key economic sectors to be nationalized in 1967. Moreover, it was argued that Africans were generally excluded and even after independence, international insurance companies dominated the market through their agencies.[44] The parliamentarians expressed hostility against dominance of foreign-based insurers amid the spread of socialist ideas in Tanzania. As Mtaki expressed, "In a country like this, aspiring for socialism, such foreign insurance, many times are against socialism."[45]

It should be made clear that only 5 percent of Tanzanians were in the formal sector between 1961 and 1965 and thus lacked disposable income.[46] This might have been the reason that excluded them from the markets as customers. Furthermore, according to the Tanganyika Development Plan for 1961–4, 99 percent of Tanzanians were rural dwellers and basically adopted risk-managing methods relevant to their environment, in particular clan- and community-based self-help schemes.[47] Consequently, international insurance companies attracted predominantly urban dwellers employed in formal sectors.[48]

The Africanization of the insurance sector in Tanzania was implemented in a dramatic way. Political leaders wanted to win people's confidence and show their commitment toward economic independence. Julius Nyerere, the then president of Tanzania noted,

> The agency of this Africanization policy arose out of the need to build up self-confidence of the people of Tanganyika-(Tanzania).[49]

While some scholars argued that the whole program of Africanization polarized the country between Africans and Africans of Asian descent,[50] that was not the case in the insurance sector. Tanzanians of Asian descent continued playing important roles as managers within the NIC and authorized agencies. An example was Gajenda Hiralal Thakore who led the corporation as the managing director between 1967 and 1970.[51] Indeed, this was a time when the government restructured insurance sector and established its monopoly over market through NIC.

From its establishment, NIC focused on the African population, which was generally "ignored" by agencies of international insurance companies. For instance, NIC introduced group insurance plans through which workers in their unions achieved what was defined as "personal monetary security."[52] Official records indicate that, under the Africanization strategy, NIC planned to reach people who lived in rural areas. However, there is no record of either any newly opened branches in the rural areas or rural insurance schemes. The corporation used well-established networks of cooperative unions to transact Africanized insurance products. By 1974, there were roughly 400 cooperative unions across the country. In addition to that, cooperative societies insured their members and properties such as tractors and warehouses.[53] Thus, they had to spread insurance services and at the same time remained important customers in rural Tanzania.

In addition, NIC embarked on social insurance schemes by targeting members of marketing boards and *Ujamaa*[54] villages. These villages, which were based on precolonial African social structures, had been created during an attempt to build an African socialist state after the Arusha Declaration in 1967. Peter Borscheid argues that the whole process of reviving African village communities had risk mitigation strategies. This had implications to the spread of commercial insurance in Tanzania.[55] Nonetheless, the industry in general showed development in terms of increased premiums. For instance, in his ten years' report, Nyerere noted,

> Since then [the Africanization of economy] great efforts have been made to expand insurance facilities to those sections of the population which were previously denied them.[56]

A closer look at rural insurance products transacted during Africanization, for example, savings-related schemes and farmers' assurance plans reveals strategies employed to spearhead financial inclusions through attracting peasants who had annual income patterns to make direct investments. A noticeable strategy employed to attract members of Ujamaa villages who were generally from low-income households was lowering the minimum insurable amount of life assurance in 1967.[57] However, the policy decision was taken six years later in 1973, when the government embarked on the provision of microinsurance products to peasants in rural Tanzania.[58] If the measure was business-sounding or not, seemingly, NIC was not for profit rather than extending life insurance benefits to small farmers and wage earners in rural areas. The corporation appealed to all Tanzanians, regardless of their places of living, to take up life assurance policies provided that they had certain income patterns. As Mr. Amon Nsekela, the then NIC chairman, insisted that "it is felt that with this relaxation in the minimum sum assured, every earning person in the country should be able to take out a life assurance policy."[59] He aptly added that "the monthly premium for a 'with profits' endowment assurance policy for Shs.2,500/- for a period of 30 years will be Shs.7/75 for a person taking out the policy at the age of 25 years, and Shs. 8/-if he takes it at 30."

Nsekela appealed to all wage earners to take life assurance policies. He said that when the minimum sum assured stood at Tsh 5,000/- (USD 648) it was very difficult for people in the low-income group to take life assurance policies as monthly premiums were high. While lowering the minimum sum life assured from Tsh 5,000 to Tsh 2,500(USD 324) was welcomed with praises among rural dwellers, five years later the measure was badly affected by high inflation and official devaluation of currency in 1978 and the Kagera war.[60] To sum up, the Africanization strategy in Tanzania was supported by the nationalization of insurance business in Tanzania, which placed the industry under a public-owned insurance corporation.

Africanizing the National Insurance Corporation of Tanzania

From the beginning, the state-owned insurance company lacked qualified personnel to fully achieve the Africanization strategy. Nevertheless, the government of Tanzania gave the NIC a mandate to Africanize the sector through the Act No. 4 of 1967.[61] The process of Africanization of the insurance market started by placing all the insurance transactions under NIC that became the sole insurer in Tanzania from February 1967. Indeed, State Insurance Corporation began with Africanization of the staff positions and then embarked into Africanization of insurance products in the market. NIC had only sixty employees who were handling small businesses of the corporation across the country, which had a population of over 12.8 million. Apparently, the corporation could not transact its businesses effectively owing to a shortage of staff; hence, it authorized private agencies to take over its activities in some areas. This had financial implications as NIC spent about 54 percent of its gross premiums for paying management expenses and commissions within the first eight months of 1967.[62] Moreover, this had fallen to 38 percent after one year.[63]

To Africanize staff within NIC, the Tanzanian government employed more than eight expatriates and 580 trained Africans by 1971.[64] It also established the Institute of Finance Management (IFM) in 1972 that offered short and long training courses to NIC employees. However, in the late 1970s, NIC expanded insurance activities that required more skilled human resources. It hatched the idea of establishing a training school that would stand as a center of "Africanized" courses.[65] For a decade, the NIC conducted on-job-training and seminars in collaboration with IFM and Chartered Insurance Institute of London.[66] Yet, socioeconomic changes in transition to neoliberal markets in the 1980s made the NIC to revisit the idea of setting up a specialized institute in Tanzania. In the late period of Africanization of the sector, the corporation established the insurance training institute in 1996.[67] It was a period when the whole agenda of Africanization had been gradually left by the corporation and political elite, which focused on restructuring insurance markets in a liberalized trajectory of the economy.

Like the Africanization of insurance in Ghana, NIC had extended the insurance services to the public largely through authorized agencies. A good example of these agencies was Sykes Insurance Consultants Ltd. and Syrub Singh Esq. The expansion of insurance facilities to Africans who were minority customers had led to the remarkable development witnessed through the increase of premiums income and national surpluses. For instance, between 1970 and 1977, the general fund of NIC including technical reserves had increased from Tanzanian shillings 2.6 million (USD 13,660)[68] to Tsh 11 million (USD 1.3 million) in 1977.[69] Additionally, the premium income had increased by six times from Tsh 5.4 million (USD 756,000) in 1970 to Tsh 29.6 million (USD 3.5 million) in 1977.[70]

Similarly, NIC Africanized fire insurance products in the state-owned companies. For instance, the corporation insured projects that had been implemented by the National Development Corporation and trade unions. This had positively impacted the growth of nonlife insurance categories. For instance, fire premiums rose more than any other nonlife insurance products in the market between 1970 and 1977.[71] This can be reflected through the rising of premiums since by 1970, fire premiums stood at Tsh 11.3 million (USD 1.6 million) but rose to Tsh 41 million (USD 4.9 million) in 1977. In the same period, fire reinsurance commissions amounted to Tsh 27.5 million (USD 3.3 million). It should be acknowledged that the rise of fire premiums in the 1970s was due to Ujamaa Projects that contributed largely to the growth of local industries and reduced dependence on foreign manufacturing goods.[72]

Though the drought that occurred in Tanzania between 1973 and 1974[73] had a tremendous impact on the Africanization of the economy, the "Africanized" NIC enjoyed the monopoly of the insurance market. The National Development Corporation imported grains to mitigate the short supply of the commodity that occurred in the 1970s. Thus, higher food imports contributed to the rise of premium income of marine insurance between 1973 and 1977.[74] For instance, between 1973 and 1974, income from premiums dramatically increased from Tsh 3.7 million (USD 527,036) in 1973 to Tsh 12 million (USD 1.6 million) in 1974.[75] Marine insurance was a dominant product in Tanzania's insurance market between 1976 and 1977 as it recorded an exceptionally high rate of growth. Its premium income had increased from Tsh 17 million (USD 2 million) in 1976 to Tsh 33.4 million (USD 4 million) in 1977 while the total surplus in that period was Tsh 6.5 million (USD 784,152).[76] This was also a time when the world experienced a great economic recession; however, this insurance class showed steady growth to the 1990s.

Conclusion

Africanization efforts in the immediate postcolonial period faced several challenges in both West Africa and East Africa. The majority of Africans lived in rural areas and were based in the informal sector. The formal sector in the commercial centers and especially the financial sector remained dominated by Europeans throughout decolonization: at independence, new governments were faced with the familiar problems of this financial dualism, notably lack of cheap credit from the formal sector for informal enterprises, which left both the African clientele and entrepreneurs disadvantaged in view of asymmetric competition.[77]

Both examples of state insurers in Ghana and Tanzania show close ties with national development agencies and followed a logic of a by-then uncontested idea of national economic development. These national companies failed to address the needs of this clientele but rather focused on worker schemes for a target group with formal employment and thereby a minority. The opportunity for insurance companies to engage in schemes designed for the needs of a local clientele such as microinsurance or agriculture insurance was only seized much later. Nationalization efforts in the insurance sector served to scale but they lacked flexibility when it comes to their products. Internal Africanization efforts from decolonization until the 1980s failed to revolutionize insurance products according to the local needs and purchasing power. The African Insurance Organisation (AIO) records noted: "The basic insurance product in Africa has not changed significantly in the last 25 years [1972-1997]. We have neither attempted to improve on them and address local needs nor employed modern insurance marketing techniques in serving our markets."[78] In addition to that, governments in both Ghana and Tanzania attempted to open the markets for African entrepreneurs who were previously excluded through regulatory measures: their entrance was impeded by lack of capital and skills needed to run insurance businesses. The postcolonial politicization of insurance and its integration in a national, macroeconomic development framework conflicted with the continuing dependency of international capital, networks, and technical expertise. Whereas nationalization programs differed in the degree to monopolize insurance, they still hampered market competition and did not offer a beneficial environment for the development of an indigenous insurance industry, in addition to other factors such as gaps in legislation and the lack of capital.

Africanization strategies targeting the insurance industry aimed at expanding ownerships of businesses and increasing their participation as customers through regulatory measures. The available sources show that insurance, as foreign-based insurance companies, wielded the greatest power in this economic sector and nationalization programs stifled entrepreneurial initiatives. Average Africans remained a minority in the market and their entrance was dwindled. The global economic recession between the 1970s and 1990s led to inflation and devaluation of currencies in Africa. This resulted in low disposable income and the capacity to purchase basic insurance needs among Africans who had become the majority in the markets during the postcolonial period. Ghana and Tanzania opted for deregulation of their insurance markets in the 1990s as an important step toward liberalization of the sector. However, the establishment of state insurers such as the SIC and the NIS in the 1960s had hindered or even entirely prevented the development of a domestic insurance industry and free market competition, which led to poor conditions for the subsequent deregulation of the insurance markets.

Notes

1. Niels Viggo Haueter and Peter Borscheid, eds., *World Insurance: The Evolution of a Global Risk Network* (Oxford: Oxford University Press, 2012), 311-23.
2. J. O. Irukwu, *Accident and Motor Insurance in West Africa* (Ibadan: Caxton Press West Africa, 1974); J. O. Irukwu, *Insurance Management in Africa* (Ibadan: Caxton Press West Africa, 1977); Olubunmi Okediji, "The Regulation of the Nigerian Life Insurance Industry 1960-1988," Doctoral Thesis, University of Warwick, 1992.
3. J. O. Irukwu, *Reinsurance in the Third World* (London: Witherby, 1982).
4. Adedokun Lateef Adetunji, E. Chuke Nwude, and Sergius N. Udeh, "Interface of Insurance and Economic Growth: Nigerian Experience," *International Journal of Economics and Financial Issues* 8, no. 4 (July 4, 2018): 16-26.

5. Chibuike U. Uche and B.E. Chikeleze, "Reinsurance in Nigeria: The Issue of Compulsory Legal Cession," *The Geneva Papers on Risk and Insurance. Issues and Practice* 26, no. 3 (2001): 490–504.
6. Okediji, "The Regulation of the Nigerian Life Insurance Industry 1960–1988," 107.
7. "By 1976 the number of indigenous companies had far surpassed that of the foreign … In real terms however, the impacts of these indigenous firms remained minimal" (Uche and Chikeleze, "Reinsurance in Nigeria," 492–3).
8. Exchange of letters between W. Elders & Sons Ltd. and the Secretariat of State for the Colonies 1947/1948, Kew National Archives CO 554/160/4.
9. Ibid., October 23, 1947, 3–4.
10. Tapen Sinha, "An Analysis of the Evolution of Insurance in India," in *Handbook of International Insurance: Between Global Dynamics and Local Contingencies*, ed. J. David Cummins and Bertrand Venard (New York: Springer US, 2007), 642.
11. Stephanie Decker, "How to Gain Local Goodwill and Influence Politicians' Building up Goodwill: British Business, Development and Economic Nationalism in Ghana and Nigeria, 1945–1977," Doctoral Thesis, University of Liverpool, 2006.
12. Cf., for example, the Parliamentary Debates Official Report, October 19, 1962, Bill for the State Insurance Corporation and Statement by Minister of Finance and Trade F.K.D. Goka, 571–4. NYPL Schomburg Center, Sc MG 795 Robert Freeman Papers: "… it was the Government's intention, to expand the operations of the newly established State Insurance Corporation to enable it to engage in all manner of insurance business and to cater for individual requirements of the people of this country." Also, see, NIC, "Mchango wa Shirika la Bima la Taifa katika Utekelezaji wa Azimio la Arusha," Kongamano la Chama Juu ya Utekelezaji wa Azimio la Arusha, Siasa ya Ujamaa na Kujitegemea, Uwasilisho wa Ndugu Gibbos Mwaikambo, Machi 15, 1987.
13. Cf., for example, Mary Dillard, *The Afro-American Community in Kwame Nkrumah's Ghana, 1951 to 1966* (Stanford: Stanford University Press, 1990).
14. Steven J. L. Taylor, *Exiles, Entrepreneurs, and Educators: African Americans in Ghana* (Albany: State University of New York Press, 2019).
15. For example, the Ghana Insurer's Association mentions only American shareholders of the Ghana General in their historical overview: www.ghanainsurers.org.gh/history-of-gia/, accessed July 2, 2020.
16. Letter by Robert T. Freeman to Kwame Nkrumah, July 12, 1954, NYPL Schomburg Center, Sc MG 795 Robert Freeman Papers, 2.
17. Biographical Material, Box 1, Folder 1, NYPL Schomburg Center, Sc MG 795 Robert Freeman Papers.
18. Letter by Robert T. Freeman to Kwam Nkrumah, July 12, 1954, NYPL Schomburg Center, Sc MG 795 Robert Freeman Papers.
19. "Prospectus of a life insurance program for the Gold Coast," submitted by Robert T. Freeman Jr., David D. Jones Jr., and Vertner W. Tandy Jr., New York City, July 26, 1955, 1. NYPL Schomburg Center, Sc MG 795 Robert Freeman Papers.
20. Ibid., 2.
21. Ibid., 4.
22. Frederick Cooper and Randall M. Packard, "The History and Politics of Development Knowledge," in *International Development and the Social Sciences: Essays on the History and Politics of Knowledge*, ed. Frederick Cooper and Randall M. Packard (Berkeley: University of California Press, 1997), 126–39.
23. Biographical Material, Box 1, Folder 1, NYPL Schomburg Center, Sc MG 795 Robert Freeman Papers.

24. Gold Coast Insurance Records Box 1, Folders 12–14, NYPL Schomburg Center, Sc MG 795 Robert Freeman Papers.
25. Correspondence Box 1, Folder 3, NYPL Schomburg Center, Sc MG 795 Robert Freeman Papers.
26. Letter by Vertner W. Tandy to Samuel C. Johnson, November 19, 1955, NYPL Schomburg Center, Sc MG 795 Robert Freeman Papers.
27. Gold Coast Insurance Records Box 1, Folders 12–14, NYPL Schomburg Center, Sc MG 795 Robert Freeman Papers.
28. Ghana Insurance Company Financial Records Box 2, Folders 1–4, NYPL Schomburg Center, Sc MG 795 Robert Freeman Papers.
29. Letter by Vertner Tandy to C. E. Geiser, March 23, 1960; NYPL Schomburg Center, Sc MG 795 Robert Freeman Papers, Box 2, Folder 13, Swiss Reinsurance Cp. Personal Loan, 1960–2.
30. State Insurance Corporation: First Report and Accounts 1963. NYPL Schomburg Center, Sc MG 795 Robert Freeman Papers.
31. Letter by Robert T. Freeman to Kwam Nkrumah, January 29, 1965, NYPL Schomburg Center, Sc MG 795 Robert Freeman Papers.
32. Official currency of Ghana since the abandonment of the British monetary system in 1965; for historical exchange rates to the USD, see Dzodzi Tsikata, *Changes in Ghanaian Currency 1958-2002* (Leiden: Brill, 2006).
33. NYPL Schomburg Center Sc MG 795 Box, Folder 7, State Insurance—25th Anniversary 1987.
34. Ibid.
35. African Insurance Organisation, *The AIO 1972-1997. 25 Years of Service to the African Insurance Industry* (Douala, 1997).
36. Parliamentary Debates Official Report Monday, October 21, 1963, Private Members Motion by Mr. S. I. Iddrissu, p. 13/114. NYPL Schomburg Center, Sc MG 795 Robert Freeman Papers.
37. Chambi Seithy Chachage, "A Capitalizing City: Dar Es Salaam and the Emergence of an African Entrepreneurial Elite (c. 1862–2015)," Doctoral Thesis, Cambridge, MA, Harvard University, 2018, https://dash.harvard.edu/handle/1/39947205.
38. For more discussion on Africanization of Civil Servants, cf. Andreas Eckert, "'We Must Run While Others Walk': African Civil Servants, State Ideologies and Bureaucratic Practices in Tanzania, from the 1950s to the 1970s," in *States at Work*, ed. Thomas Bierschenk and Jean-Pierre Olivier de Sardan (Leiden: Brill, 2014), 205–19.
39. Shirika la Bima la Taifa, *Insurance in Tanzania: NIC's 20 years* (Dar es Salaam: National Insurance Corp. of Tanzania, 1983).
40. Ibid., 2.
41. NIC, "Mchango wa Shirika la Bima la Taifa katika Utekelezaji wa Azimio la Arusha," Kongamano la Chama Juu ya Utekelezaji wa Azimio la Arusha, Siasa ya Ujamaa na Kujitegemea, Uwasilisho wa Ndugu Gibbos Mwaikambo, Machi 15, 1987.
42. Tanzania National Assembly Record (Hansard), January 1964: 210–11, Private Members Motion by Mr. C. I. Mtaki.
43. Samuel Mushi, "Tanzania," in *Indigenization of African Economies: Historical and Theoretical Background*, ed. A. Adedeji (New York: African Publishing Company, 1981), 204–5.
44. Mirghani Mohmed El Hassan, "The Role of Insurance and Its Regulation in Development: Sudan and Tanzania," Doctoral Thesis, University of Warwick, 1981.

45. Tanzania National Assembly Record (Hansard), January 1964, 210–11, Private Members Motion by Mr. C. I. Mtaki.
46. Tanzania Government, *The First Five-Year Plan for Economic and Social Development (1964–1969)* (Dar es Salam: Government Printer, 1964).
47. Sir Ernest Vasey, the then Minister of Finance in Tanganyika (since February 1960) was a brainchild of this plan. See "Tanganyika's Three-Year Plan," IMW-12, published on January 20, 1962.
48. Shirika la Bima la Taifa, *Insurance in Tanzania*.
49. Tanzania mainland formerly was known as Tanganyika. The country formed a union with Zanzibar in April 1964 to form the United Republic of Tanzania.
50. See, for example, detailed discussion in Dharam P. Ghai and Yash P. Ghai, "Asians in East Africa: Problems and Prospects," *The Journal of Modern African Studies* 3, no. 1 (1965): 35–51.
51. TNA, Acc. 589/BM 35/03.
52. Julius K. Nyerere, "Tanzania Ten Years after Independence," *The African Review: A Journal of African Politics, Development and International Affairs* 2, no. 1 (1972): 1–54.
53. Jimmy Nhende, "Umuhimu wa Kueneza Bima Kwa Wanakijiji," *Uhuru*, March 31, 1981. This was an article with title, "Importance of Expanding Insurance Benefits to Villagers," published on ruling party owned newspaper, *Uhuru* on March 31, 1981.
54. *Ujamaa* literally means "Familyhood" or "brotherhood." In the context of Tanzania, Ujamaa was ambitious projects in the postcolonial period, which consisted of rural development strategy, state-controlled economy, and redefining the role of political leaders. As a whole, *Ujamaa* was an attempt to build a typically African socialist country between 1967 and 1985. See further Andrew Coulson, *Tanzania, A Political Economy* (Oxford: Oxford University Press, 2013), 280–309.
55. Haueter and Borscheid, *World Insurance*, 318.
56. Nyerere, "Tanzania Ten Years after Independence."
57. Briefing by the Chairman of the NIC, Mr. Amon Nsekela, published in "The Nationalist" (a ruling party newspaper) on February 24, 1970.
58. Josephat Kanywanyi, "The Effects of Nationalization and Ujamaa-Socialism on Insurance Law and Practice," Doctoral Thesis, University of Dar es salaam, 1987.
59. Briefing by the Chairman of the NIC, Mr. Amon Nsekela, published in "The Nationalist" (a ruling party newspaper) on February 24, 1970.
60. The Kagera War, also known as the Uganda–Tanzania War, was fought between Tanzania and Uganda. It started as a border clash, which turned into a full-fledged war in 1978–9. The war ended when Tanzania People's Defence Force (TPDF) ousted Idi Amin Dada Oumee from power on April 11, 1979. For economic impacts of the Kagera War on Tanzania, see, David B. Ottaway, "Tanzanian Economy Hurt By Conflict with Uganda," *The Washington Post*, January 16, 1979. Also Dastan Kweka, "How Kagera War Ended Tanzania's Activist Foreign Policy," *The Chanzo Initiative*, December 14, 2021.
61. *Tanzania Nationalisation Laws*, in the International Legal Materials, vol. 6, no. 6, November 1967, 1194–228.
62. John Loxley, "The Monetary System of Tanzania since 1967: Progress, Problems and Prospects," in *Papers on the Political Economy of Tanzania*, ed. K. S. Kim (London: Heinemann, 1979), 128–31.
63. Ibid., 129.
64. Nyerere, "Tanzania Ten Years after Independence."
65. NIC/CS/MGT/98, "Notice of Meeting," March 11, 1998.

66. Ibid., 3.
67. NIC, "Board Meeting Report 2001," January 12, 2001.
68. The rates in American dollars are based on exchange rates of given years. For example, by December 1, 1977, 1 USD was equivalent to 8.2 Tanzanian shillings. For historical conversion of exchange rates, see, "Official Exchange Rate(LCU per US$, Period Average)-Tanzania," in *World Bank Open Data*, accessed from https://data.worldbank.org/ on March 11, 2023.
69. Shirika la Bima la Taifa, *Insurance in Tanzania*.
70. Ibid.
71. NIC, Annual Report 1970–1979, National Insurance Corporation (Record Office, Tabata).
72. Several studies has associated Ujamaa and development of Internal Industries. For example, see Jamal Msami and Samuel Wangwe, "Industrial Development in Tanzania," in *Manufacturing Transformation: Comparative Studies of Industrial Development in Africa and Emerging Asia*, ed. Carol Newman, John Rand, Abebe Shimeles, Måns Söderbom, Finn Tarp, and John Page, online edition (Oxford: Oxford Academic, 2016); M. B. K. Darkoh, "Tanzania's Industrial Development and Planning Experience," *Journal of Eastern African Research & Development* 14 (1984): 47–80.
73. John Shao, "Politics and the Food Production Crisis in Tanzania," *Issue: A Journal of Opinion* 14 (1985): 10–24, https://doi.org/10.1017/S0047160700505897.
74. NIC, Annual Report 1977, National Insurance Corporation (Record Office, Tabata).
75. Shirika la Bima la Taifa, *Insurance in Tanzania: NIC's 20 years*.
76. NIC, Annual Report, 1970–1979, National Insurance Corporation (Record Office, Tabata).
77. Cf. Gareth Austin, "African Economic Development and Colonial Legacies," *Revue Internationale de Politique de Développement*, no. 1 (March 1, 2010): 11–32.
78. See African Insurance Organisation, *The AIO 1972–1997*.

Bibliography

Archival Sources

Kew National Archives CO 554/160/4.
NIC, "Notice of Meeting," March 11, 1998, NIC/CS/MGT/98.
NIC, "Board Meeting Report 2001," January 12, 2001(Record Office, Tabata).
NIC, Annual Report, 1970–1979, National Insurance Corporation (Record Office, Tabata).
NIC, *Insurance in Tanzania: NIC's 20 years (1983)*. Dar es Salaam: National Insurance Corp. of Tanzania, (Record Office, Tabata).
NIC, "Mchango wa Shirika la Bima la Taifa katika Utekelezaji wa Azimio la Arusha," Kongamano la Chama Juu ya Utekelezaji wa Azimio la Arusha, Siasa ya Ujamaa na Kujitegemea, Uwasilisho wa Ndugu Gibbos Mwaikambo, Machi 15, 1987 (CCM Archive, Dodoma).
NYPL Schomburg Center, Sc MG 795 Robert Freeman Papers.
Tanzania National Archive, Acc. 589/BM 35/03.

Magazines and Newspapers

African Insurance Organisation, *The AIO 1972-1997. 25 Years of Service to the African Insurance Industry*. Douala, 1997.
"Briefing by the Chairman of the NIC, Mr. Amon Nsekela." *The Nationalist*, February 24, 1970.
Jimmy Nhende. "Umuhimu wa Kueneza Bima Kwa Wanakijiji." *Uhuru*, March 31, 1981.
Kweka, Dastan. "How Kagera War Ended Tanzania's Activist Foreign Policy." *The Chanzo Initiative*, December 14, 2021.
Ottaway, David B. "Tanzanian Economy Hurt by Conflict with Uganda." *The Washington Post*, January 16, 1979.

Government Reports

Ghana Parliamentary Debates Official Report, October 19, 1962.
Ghana Parliamentary Debates Official Report, October 21, 1963.
Tanzania Government. "The First Five-Year Plan for Economic and Social Development (1964-1969)," Government Printer, Dar es Salaam, 1964.
Tanzania Nationalisation Laws, in the International Legal Materials, November 1967, vol. 6, no. 6, 1194-228.
Tanzania Ten Years after Independence, Report by the President of TANU, Mwalimu Julius K. Nyerere on December 9, 1971.
United Republic of Tanzania. "Tanganyika's Three-year Plan." IMW-12, published on January 20, 1962.

Research Literature

Adetunji, Adedokun Lateef, E. Chuke Nwude, and Sergius N. Udeh. "Interface of Insurance and Economic Growth: Nigerian Experience." *International Journal of Economics and Financial Issues* 8, no. 4 (July 4, 2018): 16-26.
Austin, Gareth. "African Economic Development and Colonial Legacies." *Revue Internationale de Politique de Développement*, no. 1 (March 1, 2010): 11-32.
Chachage, Chambi Seithy. "A Capitalizing City: Dar Es Salaam and the Emergence of an African Entrepreneurial Elite (c. 1862-2015)." Doctoral Thesis, Harvard University, 2018. Accessed May 22, 2022. https://dash.harvard.edu/handle/1/39947205.
Cooper, Frederick, and Randall M. Packard. "The History and Politics of Development Knowledge." In *International Development and the Social Sciences: Essays on the History and Politics of Knowledge*, edited by Frederick Cooper and Randall M. Packard, 126-39. Berkeley: University of California Press, 1997.
Coulson, Andrew. *Tanzania, A Political Economy*. Oxford: Oxford University Press, 2013.
Decker, Stephanie. "'How to Gain Local Goodwill and Influence Politicians' Building up Goodwill: British Business, Development and Economic Nationalism in Ghana and Nigeria, 1945-1977." Doctoral Thesis, University of Liverpool, 2006.
Dillard, Mary. *The Afro-American Community in Kwame Nkrumah's Ghana, 1951 to 1966*. Stanford: Stanford University Press, 1990.
Eckert, Andreas. "'We Must Run While Others Walk': African Civil Servants, State Ideologies and Bureaucratic Practices in Tanzania, from the 1950s to the 1970s." In

States at Work, edited by Thomas Bierschenk and Jean-Pierre Olivier de Sardan, 205–19. Leiden: Brill, 2014.

El Hassan, Mirghani Mohmed. "The Role of Insurance and Its Regulation in Development: Sudan and Tanzania." Doctoral Thesis, University of Warwick, 1981.

Ghai, Dharam P., and Yash P. Ghai. "Asians in East Africa: Problems and Prospects." *The Journal of Modern African Studies* 3, no. 1 (1965): 35–51.

Haueter, Niels Viggo, and Peter Borscheid, eds. *World Insurance: The Evolution of a Global Risk Network*. Oxford: Oxford University Press, 2012.

Irukwu, J. O. *Accident and Motor Insurance in West Africa*. Ibadan: Caxton Press West Africa, 1974.

Irukwu, J. O. *Insurance Management in Africa*. Ibadan: Caxton Press West Africa, 1977.

Irukwu, J. O. *Reinsurance in the Third World*. London: Witherby, 1982.

Kanywanyi, Josephat. "The Effects of Nationalization and Ujamaa-Socialism on Insurance Law and Practice." Doctoral Thesis, University of Dar es Salaam, 1987.

Loxley, John. "The Monetary System of Tanzania since 1967: Progress, Problems and Prospects." In *Papers on the Political Economy of Tanzania*, edited by K. S. Kim, 128–31. London: Heinemann, 1979.

Msami, Jamal, and Samuel Wangwe. "Industrial Development in Tanzania." In *Manufacturing Transformation: Comparative Studies of Industrial Development in Africa and Emerging Asia*, edited by Carol Newman, John Rand, Abebe Shimeles, Måns Söderbom, Finn Tarp, and John Page, online edition. Oxford: Oxford Academic, 2016.

Mushi, Samuel. "Tanzania." In *Indigenization of African Economies: Historical and Theoretical Background*, edited by A. Adedeji, 204–37. New York: African Publishing Company, 1981.

Nyerere, Julius K. "Tanzania Ten Years after Independence." *The African Review: A Journal of African Politics, Development and International Affairs* 2, no. 1 (1972): 1–54.

Okediji, Olubunmi. "The Regulation of the Nigerian Life Insurance Industry 1960–1988." Doctoral Thesis, University of Warwick, 1992.

Shao, John. "Politics and the Food Production Crisis in Tanzania." *Issue: A Journal of Opinion* 14 (1985): 10–24. https://doi.org/10.1017/S0047160700505897.

Sinha, Tapen. "An Analysis of the Evolution of Insurance in India." In *Handbook of International Insurance: Between Global Dynamics and Local Contingencies*, edited by J. David Cummins and Bertrand Venard, 641–78. New York: Springer US, 2007.

Taylor, Steven J. L. *Exiles, Entrepreneurs, and Educators: African Americans in Ghana*. Albany: State University of New York Press, 2019.

Uche, Chibuike U., and B. E. Chikeleze. "Reinsurance in Nigeria: The Issue of Compulsory Legal Cession." *The Geneva Papers on Risk and Insurance. Issues and Practice* 26, no. 3 (2001): 490–504.

8

Copper, Colonialism, and Local Conflicts: The Expansion of Early Modern Global Industrial Economy in Northern Torne River Valley, and Its Local Repercussions

Jonas Monié Nordin

Then it was thoroughly investigated, if any member of the congregation, in the past had practiced or still practice ungodly superstition, such as offerings at [sacred] mountains, lakes, or playing the kåbdes *or drums and play them along with the joik or laula foul medlodies.*[1]

This is one of several inquiries concerning the use of drums, a traditional religious activity, and the practice of *joik*, traditional Sámi singing (*laula* in Finnish), in the court records of Torne lappmark, the northernmost of the traditional Sámi districts in Sweden, between 1639 and 1690.

In this chapter I examine the extractive industry in the Torne River Valley during the mid- and second half of the seventeenth century and its local repercussions. Moreover, the chapter outlines how this process was connected to the rise of global economy. I propose that not only the industrial localities and the extractive landscape, but also the church places and marketplaces and the local courts can be understood as a set of contact zones, as intersections of intellectual and material practices constructing identity and culture.

The concept of contact zones was coined by Mary Louise Pratt in 1992 but has been further developed by Kapil Raj, who uses the concept in contexts of more fundamental change, such as industrial installations, or the production of knowledge in colonial settings in Asia during the early modern period.[2] The seventeenth-century contact zones of Torne River Valley were depending upon the extraction industries, which changed and developed throughout the examined period of time. Active in this contact zone were Sámi workers and Sámi traders, Dutch workers, Swedish and German burghers, Finnish famers, and Dutch investors. Agents that shaped the courts, the production sites, and the marketplaces into localities where people met and power were negotiated.

Furthermore, in this chapter, I propose that an early path toward modernity was laid out as a collaborative yet contested industrial and global economy in the Torne River Valley in the second half of the seventeenth century. This development should be seen in tandem with the early and concurrent industrial development in the Caribbean, India, and Western Europe, and included not only economic exploitation but also more subtle changes.[3] This early modernity process was created by the cooperation between the various groups living in the Torne River Valley in collaboration and conflict with external groups, such as the Dutch and Swedish officials, clergymen, workers, and foreign visitors.

Torne lappmark and Swedish Colonialism

In the early modern period, the Torne River Valley was a multicultural and multiethnic area, inhabited by Finnish- (Kven and Lantalaiset), Swedish-, and Sámi-speaking groups together with other groups of people arriving in connection to the colonial and industrial movements. During the sixteenth century, Finnish-speaking people from southeastern Finland spread farming settlements in the Torne River Valley.[4] The territorial expansion of the Swedish realm, the Crowns' urge for stronger control in tandem with a growing population, led the integration of Torne River Valley and Torne lappmark into the Swedish legislative and judicial system. The court proceedings in Torne lappmark were held at the yearly market in late January or early February and consisted of a majority of Sámi men under the chair of the bailiff (*kronobefallningsman*). This year, when the court examined for Sámi ritual activities, in 1687, Jakob Grape (1660–1720) was acting as chair.

This blend of Sámi, Finnish, and Swedish members of court might seem as a conflict of interest—a court dominated by Sámi that was investigating what was locally regarded as traditional customs—but by the court and the laws of the realm it was considered as witchcraft. The court itself exemplifies this latent conflict, consisting as it was of Sámi court members from Siggevaara and Tingevaara Sámi villages, but chaired by the bailiff, the industrialist Jakob Grape. Jakob Grape was the son of the German-born industrialist Arendt Grape (1612–1687), one of the regions' most powerful men during the seventeenth century, and named after his father's foremost companion, the Dutch-born nobleman Jakob Momma Reenstierna (1625–1678).

During the period from 1639 to 1690 the court cases in Torne lappmark were dominated by ordinary cases such as adultery and conflict over land and fishing waters, just like in any local court of the Swedish realm. The number of cases concerning traditional Sámi religious and ritual practices were few, but they grew during the period of study, and during the 1680s every other year the use of drums, performance of *joik*, or the practice of what was perceived as witchcraft were addressed by the court.[5] Sámi themselves reported the use of drums and surrendered them to the court in several cases in 1680, 1681, 1687, and 1688.[6]

The term *lappmark* (i.e., Sámi territory) and the territorial denomination Lapland are exonyms, parallel to the term "lapp," nowadays generally considered a derogatory word and here only used in quotes. Swedish and Finnish Sápmi (the land of the Sámi) was from the early seventeenth century divided into a set of *lappmarker*, functioning as administrative and geographical instruments for the advancement of the Crowns' control of the Sámi subjects, the inland territories, and its resources. From the early seventeenth century the territorial control through the lappmark instrument expanded and the Crowns' and the Church's presence grew.

The lappmark division is today only of historic relevance but the names of the counties Swedish and Finnish Lappland are still in use. Each lappmark was furnished with one, or in some cases two church places and marketplaces. In Torne lappmark, Enontekiö/Enontekis (present day Markkina, meaning "the market") was founded as the marketplace of the region in the early seventeenth century. For the convenience of the Sámi of Siggesvaara and Tingevaara villages, and due to the expanding metal industry, an additional marketplace was founded in Čohkkiras/Jukkasjärvi about 1649. The church/chapel was, however, erected already in 1607.[7] Jukkasjärvi was together with Enontekis/Markkina the Crowns' church places and marketplaces in Torne lappmark, a region covering the Torne, Vittangi, and Mounio River valleys, from the Bothnian Gulf in the south to the mountains in the north and northwest.

The court cases concerning the use of drums and other Sámi ritual activities mirror a change in attitude toward Sámi traditional religion and religious practices in Scandinavia. The sixteenth and early seventeenth centuries were featured by a relative tolerant and inclusive view on religious practices. The Thirty Years' War and the expansion of Lutheran orthodoxy during the second half of the seventeenth century meant a growing intolerance toward Sámi traditional religious/magic practices. Locally this process was featured by the development in Torne River Valley and the founding of the Torne extraction industries. In 1642 copper and iron were discovered in Čunusavvon/Junosuando/Junosuanto leading to the opening of mines and establishment of a works site in Masugsnbyn/Masuni. Geavŋŋis/Kengis/Köngänen, in Pajala, by the Torne River became the center of the expanding Torne industries complex.

After ten years of modest success and changes in administration, the copper production expanded rapidly through the exploration of copper in Veaikevárri/Svappavaara/Vaskivuori. This finding meant entry of global investment through the arrival of the Dutch-born brothers, Abraham and Jakob Momma, in 1669 ennobled Reenstierna. No doubt it was the precious metals that drove the Mommas into investing in the Torne River Valley extraction industries, just like the Crown had done, when silver was found twenty years earlier in Násavarri/Nasafjäll, in the Arjeplog mountains, by the Norwegian–Swedish border.[8] Precious metals, copper, and silver had strong leverage in the establishment of metal industries in remote areas of the Swedish realm. A similar and related situation is visible today with a hunt for metal ores and rare earth metals in northern Scandinavia.[9]

As an outcome of the combined efforts of the activities of the Swedish Crown and private entrepreneurs, the upper part of Torne River Valley was included in the spheres of metal extraction, and industrial production aimed at global markets during the 1650s to early 1680s. Everyday life among the local inhabitants, the Sámi and the Kvens/Lantalainen, and Finns living in the region were rapidly changed. Mines were opened. Works with new and modern ways of organizing space and socioeconomic relations were established, and the region was rapidly included in the global economy. The latter meant an influx of global consumer goods, such as tobacco and the export of copper, iron, furs, and handicraft. This development also meant the expanding presence of Church and Crown authorities, exemplified by a growing tension at the yearly courts. In the footsteps of this development came the introduction of early tourism, including foreign travelers wanting to meet Sámi and collect Sámi objects, such as the abovementioned drums.

Copper, Colonialism, and Globalization

As a contact zone within the larger Sámi settlement area, identities and traditions were changed and developed during this period of great social and economic transformation. Torne River Valley became a region of contact on several levels during the early modern period, yet featured by contact between people, traditions, and economies. Here sedentary and nomadic lifestyles and economies met and mingled with extraction industries. Fishing, hunting, and reindeer pastoralism mingled with copper extraction and trade between the Arctic Ocean and the Bothnian Gulf. Lutheranism, orthodoxy, and Sámi traditional religions met and mingled. At least a handful of languages were spoken in the river valley.

The industrial development in northern Sápmi was closely related to the colonial expansion led by the Danish, Russian, and the Swedish Crowns, the Lutheran and Orthodox churches, and individual trade companies.[10] The wider colonial context in seventeenth-century Sápmi and Torne River Valley therefore needs to be considered in an analysis of the industrial development. The colonial processes included Christian mission and forced conversion, destruction of religious sites and ritual objects, confiscation and collecting of Sámi material culture, and changes in languages and traditions. Subsequently loss of land, water, and self-determination prevailed among the Sámi people of northern Fennoscandia, as a consequence of the expanding extraction industry.[11] These processes affected several levels of society, both drastic and slow, and unassuming. The court cases mentioned initially can be seen as an intersection of these two paces of change.

Industrialization in a Periphery

In 1643, copper and magnetite iron ores were found in Saivijokk (Junosuando) close to the Torne River Valley, some 350 kilometers north of Bothnian town Torneå (present-day Tornio). The county governor Frans Crusebjörn persuaded a group of burghers in Torneå to form a company and start processing the find, while the governor provided privileges, including exemption from taxes to the company. Iron production proved complicated, however, and the company was taken over by the German-born Torneå burgher Arendt Grape in 1646. Grape, who was well connected in the Bothnian trade networks, invested in a modern French type furnace by the Saivijokk River in 1647.[12] Two years later, a metalwork with a Walloon forge was founded in Geavŋŋis by the Torne River, later Swedified into Kengis (Finnish: Köngänen).

Profit was not immediate, and Grape soon needed more capital. In 1653, he sold two-thirds of the company to Abraham and Jacob Momma. The Mommas, including their older half-brother Willem Momma, who came from an old copper-making family in Jülich close to Aachen in the Rhine lands, were dominant agents in the global copper trade.[13] A new company, with renewed royal privileges, was founded in Torne River Valley.[14] Copper had recently been discovered in the Svappavaara mountain, northwest of Junosuando, attracting the interest of the Momma brothers. From this period of time industrial expansion in the Torne River Valley was rather swift. Svappavaara soon developed into the core mine of the consortium, with Kengis as not only the administrative center but also the center of the refinement of copper.

The involvement of the Momma brothers entailed at least four main supplements to the industry. First, swift and direct access to the global market through the brothers' trade networks, including the half-brother and other family members living in England. Second, access to knowledge and technology through the brothers' collective experience in brass and copper making.[15] Third, access to skilled laborers through tapping into the Dutch wave of migration to Scandinavia. Fourth, contacts with the power circles in Stockholm and the Swedish Board of Mines (Sw. Bergskollegium).

Global (i.e., the Americas, Africa, Arctic, and Europe) demand for brass and copper was a decisive motor in this development and so was the industrial and technical knowledge and skill of the Dutch workers and investors.[16] Copper and brass were pivotal for the Atlantic trade. The plantation industry of the Caribbean, the fur and tobacco trade in North America, and the gold trade in West Africa all rested on the access to copper and brass objects originating from Scandinavia.

Another pillar propelling the first wave of industrial development—or the very beginning of the Industrial Revolution—was made possible by the Indigenous knowledge of the Sámi and the Finnish inhabitants of the Torne River Valley. Most of the copper veins were found and reported to the authorities by Sámi and several of the veins were related to a sacred Sámi geography.[17] The discovery of silver in Násavarre in 1634 and Gierggevárre/Kedkevare, c. 1660, were both made by Sámi metal finders.[18] Other finds were made by local Finnish-speaking farmers, and most of the workforce in the mines and at the works consisted of Finns. The payrolls of the consortium, from Svappavaara mines and furnace, from the 1650s through to the 1670s, show a clearly multiethnic environment, which includes the Dutch/Walloon, southern Swedish, Finnish, Kven/Lantalaiset, and Sámi workers.[19]

Examining all these sources supports an understanding of the metalworks and mining sites as contact zones where people from different ethnic, linguistic, and social backgrounds met and influenced each other.[20] These zones also developed into localities of intersection between cultural and religious traditions and served as sites of introduction of new perspectives on land, nature, and magic, hence in practice laying a foundation of modernity.[21] In the long run these changes also meant the systematic hiding of and repression against Sámi religious practices and use of ritual objects.

The making of contact zones was also based on modern traits connected with a drive to shape and change social and extractive space. The works founded in Torne River Valley in the second half of the seventeenth century were all built on the principles of geometrical ordering of space, the physical distinctions of hierarchy, and the separation of people according to ethnic identity.[22] An overarching purpose with the activities was the accumulation of capital emphasized by the works one-purpose focus, the production of refined metals. Another modern trait in the layout of space, applied at the works, in central Sweden, as well as in the Torne River Valley, is the implementation of a modern conception of time, through the installation of time devices at several of the works.[23] Notably this is earlier than in other industrial conglomerates where centralized time was established in the early eighteenth century.[24]

Industrialization before Industrialism—Modernization before Modernity

What can be identified at the copper works of the Torne River Valley is not a local isolated path to industrial society based on global demands, but an entangled passage to modernity through the blend of local, Indigenous, regional, and global traits in the making of the modern world. The Industrial Revolution of England in the second half of the eighteenth century had, it might be argued, one of its predecessors in the dramatic changes in the production of metals in Scandinavia, including parts of Sápmi and the Torne River Valley. The metals and alloys that propelled early industrialization to a vast extent came from Scandinavia.[25] A part of that came from Sápmi.

The Industrial Revolution in Britain in the eighteenth century is one of the more decisive processes of change in the Western and global world.[26] Every aspect of the modern society has been affected in some way by the experience of industrialism. Pivotal factors such as a wide set of agrarian reforms, the emergence of global markets, technical innovation, and accumulation of capital made industrialization possible.

There are, however, other factors that to a growing degree are acknowledged as decisive for the industrial breakthrough. Two factors of importance for the industrial development in Britain concern global entanglement. First, the influx of capital through the slave economy from the second half of the seventeenth century, but with a radical increase during the eighteenth century, enabling industrial development in Europe.[27] Second, the raw material from the Baltic trade that was essential for British and continental European industrial development: the high-quality iron.[28] Copper and brass should be added to the repertoire of globally essential metals and alloys.[29]

It is here the Torne River Valley and its main export commodities in the seventeenth century, copper alongside furs, come into the picture. The growth of the plantation economy in the Americas created a drastic growth in the demand of metal tools, trade objects, and necessities for the shipping industry. In this global context, iron, brass, and copper from Scandinavia played an important role. Copper was needed for making of pans, vats, roofing, and sheathing of ships.[30] Brass, an alloy consisting of copper, tin, and zinc, or more often during the early modern period, calamine, was essential for the making of not only cauldrons, kettles, vats, and candlesticks but also more ephemeral objects such as needles, hooks, and pins. From both North America and the Torne River Valley, furs and hides together with leather products were important export products. Sámi handicraft such as boots, gloves, and caps were, as stated earlier, of the outmost importance during the cold seventeenth century.[31]

Copper and brass were essential for the manufacture of boiling furnaces for the whaling stations and the sugar plantations. The making of cooking vats for the distilling of whiskey or the brewing of ales were also founded on access to copper. In Indigenous communities in North America copper and brass were highly coveted, and among the Sámi, objects of copper alloy were held in high esteem.[32] In this context, one can claim that the copper from Falun in central Sweden, Røros in central Norway, and also from Svappavaara and Masugnsbyn in Torne River Valley functioned as one of the material bases for spurring globalization in the early modern world.

This industrial expansion brought about the innovation of a new form of industrial production, the metalworks, that is, the *bruk* in the Kingdom of Sweden, through the fusion of Dutch and Swedish conditions and considerations together with global market demand. Historian Göran Rydén has pointed to not only the particularity of the *bruk*, but also how they were consanguine to the plantations of the New World.[33] The Swedish verb *bruka* means literally "to cultivate" and "to use." It is related to the words "to plant" and "plantation." The two forms of production are also related. A *bruk* is a single-purpose, concentrated production unit, just like the plantation, with the aim of extracting and refining natural resource, usually metals. The *bruk* is run by an intense concentration of labor force, living on the production site, often in an orderly form. At the Swedish early modern *bruk* (in the following called "works"), a certain kind of culture or habitus developed, inspired by reformed Christian ethics, Dutch aesthetics, and early capitalist modes of production.[34]

The Mommas and the Global Trade

The Momma industry group's power grew not only through the metal production in central Sweden and in Torne River Valley, but also through the trade in Sámi products. Metal extraction was the raison d'être for the Momma's investments in Torne River Valley, but trade in Sámi products contributed to their business. The severe climate during the seventeenth century marking the peak of the "Little Ice Age" meant a drastic growing demand for fur products including boots, gloves, caps, and jackets, goods that were provided by Sámi producers and exported to continental Europe.[35]

The Momma brothers expanded the industrial conglomerate in the Torne River Valley during the 1650s and 1660s.[36] Maps, written records, and material evidence give testimony to a substantial expansion during this period. The well-preserved physical remains at most of the sites give a good picture of the size, form, and layout of the various works- and mining sites. The Momma brothers' business in northwestern Europe, including the Netherlands and England, expanded at the same time, with more brass works,[37] but also through the pursuing of other business opportunities such as investments in shipping, agriculture, and banking. In addition, their half-brother Willem traded copper kettles to the New World.[38]

Along with many other traders and entrepreneurs, several with Dutch extraction, the Momma brothers formed a class of "nouveau riche" in the Swedish realm.[39] When ennobled in 1669, the Momma brothers took the fitting name Reenstierna, meaning *Star of the Reindeer*—the reindeer being a key factor for their economic success and an important trade goods in the form of the boots, gloves, and hides, made of reindeer skin, and traded by the brothers. In fact, the investments in Sápmi played an important role for the brothers' brand making and as a symbol.[40]

In the early 1670s, the Momma Reenstierna brothers' expanding business consortium was, however, challenged. The Third Dutch–English Naval War in 1672–4 and the war between Denmark and Sweden in 1676–9, with the subsequent closing of borders and of the Sound, proved fatal for their business. In the court records of Torne lappmark, from the court held in Jukkasjärvi in January 1677, the successes on the battlefield of Lund were announced to the public.[41] The closing of the Sound had a severe impact on the copper production and trade and eventually led to the bankruptcy of the company. The death of the brothers in 1678 and 1690, respectively, meant the end of the Momma Reenstierna family as influential industrialists in Sweden.[42]

Minor efforts to continue the metal production in the Kengis consortium were attempted in the late seventeenth century and again in the eighteenth century. With the opening of Sjangeli copper mines in the mountains southeast of Lake Torne träsk/Duortnosjávri, in 1699, ignited hope that production would resurface. Sjangeli mine and its furnace in Vuolosjoki were never as successful as the Kengis consortium of the seventeenth century.

It would take until the late nineteenth century and the founding of the Kirunavaara-Luossavaara mines, in Kiruna/Giron, for metal production in the Torne River Valley to supersede that of the Momma Reenstierna brothers. This time it was iron instead of copper that manifested the coveted value. A local saying in the Torne River Valley goes: *Se oli Mommaan aikaista* (Fi.), meaning "it was at the time of the Mommas," alluding to events that took place a long time ago and in a time of prosperity.

Local Repercussions

From 1639 there is an almost complete set of court proceedings from Torne lappmark. Here disputes, settlements, and verdicts of the area are meticulously presented. The court records also give insights into the general political situation in the realm, as exemplified with the victory of the Battle of Lund in 1676, which was presented to the audience of the court. The Crowns' announcements were a recurrent section of the court proceedings, and they were read out loud to the audience, spreading the voice of the monarch and the government.

An example of societal currents and tensions presented in both Jukkasjärvi and Enontekis is the 1671 law forbidding Sámi nomadism in the southern and central parts of the realm.[43] This law was presented by the chair, several times during the 1670s and 1680s. The law was not directed to the Sámi of Torne lappmark, but it was part of a general change in attitude of the Crown toward the Sámi in central and southern Sweden, exemplified by reindeer nomadism outside the borders of the lappmarker. In 1673 the pressure grew in the north through the *Lappmarksplakatet*, the Lappmark law, aiming at the expansion of permanent settlement and farming in the Sámi lands.

The law of 1673 was not all successful from the Crowns' point of view, and a new law, supporting agricultural colonization in the Sámi lands, was published in 1695, promoting colonization.[44] The last years of the seventeenth century and the eighteenth century are featured by a growing tension between settlers and Sámi communities in the aftermath of the 1695 law. Now the systematic transfer of land and water from Sámi to Swedish settlers together with religious prosecution featured the colonial praxis.

In 1649 a servant of Arent Grape, Hans Akselsson, addressed the court in Jukkasjärvi and presented a copy of the royal decree demanding assistance in the transportation at Kengis works. The work effort would be paid, but presence was mandatory for the Sámi.[45] A year later Grape himself appeared at court, readdressing the transportation of iron and "other things" for proper payment. Grape emphasized that the work was voluntary.[46] Members of the Sámi villages had probably neglected to contribute and perhaps their absence can be understood as acts of resistance against the claims expressed by Akselsson. Grape tried to persuade the potential workforce rather than threaten them. In 1655 Grape appeared again, this time presenting the royal privilege, ordering the Sámi to assist in the ore transportation.[47] Neither demands nor persuasion seemed to work.

In the following years, from 1655 to 1663 the industrialists did not address the issue of transportation at court, but in 1663 Jakob Momma appeared and presented the royal privilege and demanded the Sámi attendance at the mines and the works. Momma also proposed that not only money could be gained, but also coveted commodities such as woolen cloth and flour could be obtained as payment.[48] The issue of transportation was not brought up again, indicating that the whole matter was solved.

From 1664 Grape was present at all the yearly courts held in Jukkasjärvi and in most of the proceedings held in Enontekis. This presence indicates the rise in situation and standing of Grape and the growing importance of the Torne industry. It also indicates that the board of the company saw the importance of being present at the courts to monitor their interests. The year 1686 marks the last time Arendt Grape attended court (he died by the end of that year), and in 1687, his son Jakob took over the position as chair of the assembly.

The court records inform of the importance of the metal extraction industry during the examined period and the importance of access to laborers by the works. At the same period of time the court records reveal an abating tolerance toward Sámi cultural and religious practices. The first court case against traditional Sámi religious practice appeared in Torne lappmark in 1671 when two Sámi, Jon Nilsson and Olof Larsson, were accused for having practiced *joik* "laula and trullsångh."[49] In 1675, the Sámi Nils Pedersen was brought to court accused of thievery, adultery, and the burying of his child in the forest (not in the church yard)—among many other things—disobeying the rules of the Sabbath. Nils Pedersen was also accused of witchcraft through the use of a drum. Moreover, he was accused of owning and using a (sacred) drum, a Goavddis in North Sámi. Both Nils Pedersen and his spouse Elin Pedersdotter were sentenced to death.[50]

The same year, in a court proceeding under the chair of Arent Grape in Enare/Inari/Aanaar, one Nils Henriksson was questioned concerning his drum practice.[51] In 1681, Kristoffer Amundsson was summoned to court for the use of a drum,[52] and in 1687 and 1688 the court actively inquired after the practice of so-called witchcraft and the use of drums as mentioned initially in this chapter.

What is evident from the court record of Torne lappmark during the period from 1639 to 1690 is the growing importance of Arent Grape as a person, his family, and his position through the metalworks of Torne River Valley. What is also evident is the growing pressure against Sámi ritual- and religious practice during the same period. The latter is not unique for Torne lappmark, however. A growing intolerance toward magical practices and activities that were labeled as witchcraft is visible across the realm, but in particular concerning the Sámi ritual/religious practice. In Lule lappmark tensions grew by the end of the century and in Pite lappmark, a Sámi man, Lars Nillsson, was burned at the stake for the use of his drum, trying to save the life of his drowned grandchild in 1693.[53]

Since the Thirty Years' War, the Swedish Crown had experienced rumors and propaganda flourishing in the European continent about the "ungodliness" of some of the subjects of the Swedish realm.[54] These rumors were seen as embarrassing and threatening to the Swedish realm and its pretentions to power over the north. In 1670, Johannes Schefferus, professor of law and rhetoric at Uppsala University, was commissioned to examine the whereabouts of Sámi religious practice. Three years later he published *Lapponia*, the first scientific examination of the Sámi culture and traditions.[55] The book became a veritable intellectual success, translated into Dutch, French, German, and English, and printed in many editions throughout the seventeenth and eighteenth centuries. This intriguing oeuvre was made possible through Schefferus's comprehensive correspondence with local Sámi and non-Sámi priests in Sápmi, Arendt Grape, and the Momma-Reenstierna brothers. Despite Schefferus's and his commissioner's intent, the idea of Sámi sorcery spread and was emphasized in every new edition.

One who had read *Lapponia* thoroughly was the French playwright and adventurer Jean-François Regnard who in 1681 traveled up the Torne River Valley passing Kengis, Svappavaara, and Jukkasjärvi. He spoke French to some of the workers in Kengis, and he exclaimed fascination of the far north, he stole Sámi sacred objects (drums), and desecrated a sacred Sámi offering site. Regnard was one of the first tourists to the far north and through his *Voyage de Laponie* (1681) he paved the road for many more tourists and visitors passing Kengis works on their way to Jukkasjärvi and Lake Torne träsk.[56]

Conclusions

This chapter has discussed the founding and development of the Torne River Valley's industrial consortium during the mid- and second half of the seventeenth century. In the 1640s, copper and iron were found by the rivulet Saivijock, in Junosuando, and soon furnaces and forges were established near the ore and through the foundation of the works in Kengis by the Torne River. The finding of a more substantial copper ore in Svappavaara and the financial problem of the company led to an ample investment by the Dutch brothers Abraham and Jakob Momma in 1653. From this time the extraction industry developed quickly with new works and mines and a substantial growth in work force.

Copper and brass were highly coveted materials in the Atlantic and global trade during the seventeenth century. Cauldrons, canons, candlestick, coins, hooks, kettles, pins, and ships' sheathings were among the objects made of copper and brass, of which a substantial part originated from Sweden. The Torne river industries existed solely out of the premises of producing valuable commodities for this global market.

The early modern industrialization process in the Torne River Valley created and developed contact zones featuring local adaptation through the role of local and Indigenous participation, and collaboration, including Sámi and Finnish knowledge, agency, and traditions. Concurrently, the layout, style, and architecture, within the industrial complexes, show that an overarching architectural program or idea was implemented in Torne River Valley, just as in many other worksites in Sweden at the same time, and in parallel to the expanding plantation industry in the Americas.

The records from the local court reveals the regional importance of the industrialists. Both Jakob Momma Reenstierna and Arendt Grape, two of the owners, appeared at court and appealed for workforce. During the consortiums' heydays in 1650s to the 1670s, Arendt Grape was chairing a majority of the court assemblies. Through the court records the authorities' view on Sámi traditional religion and ritual practices is clearly visible. The persecution of Sámi rituals, such as the use of the sacred drums, or the practice of *joik*, grew in amplitude throughout the examined period. The tension between the local traditional and ritual practice and the demand from the industrial corporation, the Crown, and other authorities grew.

The introduction of early extraction industry in the Torne River Valley meant a growing tension between the local Sámi communities, the Crown, and the Church. No doubt did the establishment of mines and works along Torne River mean not only growing demands and growing markets for Sámi products but also growing hostility toward Sámi traditional, religious, and magical practices.

Notes

1. "Sådant wardt noga ransakat, inqvirerat och Skiärskådat, om några i denne Församblingh, förr detta brukat och ännu bruka, några afgudiska widskeppelser, medelst offrande widh bärgh och stoora träsk. Sampt kåbdes eller Trummor; the pläga speela uppå medh Jåik eller särdeles Laula och stygg Melodie?," *Dombok Torneå lappmark: Jukkasjärvi og Enontekis tinglag. 1639–1699* [Court Records from Torneå lappmark, Jukkasjärvi and Enontekis Court Circuits], published by Dag A. Larsen and Kåre Rauø (Lenvik bygdemuseum, Finnsnes, 1997), January 31, 1687, 156.
2. M. L. Pratt, *Imperial Eyes: Travel Writing and Transculturation* (London: Routledge, 1992); K. Raj, *Relocating Modern Science: Circulation and the Construction of Knowledge in South Asia and Europe, 1650–1900* (Basingstoke: Palgrave Macmillan, 2007), 225.
3. G. Bhambra, *Rethinking Modernity: Postcolonialism and the Sociological Imagination* (Basingstoke: Palgrave Macmillan, 2007), 103–4.

4. J. Vahtola, "Folkens mångfald," in *Tornedalens historia I: Från istid till 1600-talet*, eds., O. Hederyd, Y. Alamäki, and M. Kenttä (Haparanda: Tornedalskommunernas historiebokskommitté, 1991), 176–208; T. Wallerström, *Norrbotten, Sverige och medeltiden: problem kring makt och bosättning i en europeisk periferi* (Stockholm: Almqvist & Wiksell, 1995); L. Elenius, "The Dissolution of Ancient Kvenland and the Transformation of the Kvens as an Ethnic Group of People. On Changing Ethnic Categorizations in Communicative and Collective Memories," *Acta Borealia* 36, no. 2 (2019): 117–48.
5. *Dombok Torneå lappmark*; see also E. Axelsson, "Samerna och statsmakten. Vardagligt motstånd och kulturell hybriditet i Torne lappmark under perioden 1639–1732," Master Thesis in History, Dept. of History, University of Umeå, 2015.
6. *Dombok Torneå lappmark*, 105, 114, 156, 162.
7. T. Wallerström, *Kunglig makt och samiska bosättningsmönster: studier kring Väinö Tanners vinterbyteori* (Oslo: Novus, 2017).
8. J. M. Nordin, *The Scandinavian Early Modern World: A Global Historical Archaeology* (London: Routledge, 2020), 115–21.
9. See, for instance, S. Persson, D. Harnesk, and M. Islar, "What Local People? Examining the Gállok Mining Conflict and the Rights of the Sámi Population in Terms of Justice and Power," *Geoforum* 86 (2017): 20–9.
10. L.-I. Hansen and B. Olsen, *Hunters in Transition: An Outline of Early Sámi History* (Leiden: Brill, 2014), 232–7; Nordin, *The Scandinavian Early Modern World*, 100–42.
11. Rydving, *The End of Drum-Time*; D. Lindmark and O. Sundström, *De historiska relationerna mellan Svenska kyrkan och samerna: en vetenskaplig antologi* (Skellefteå: Artos & Norma, 2016). H. Rydving, "The Christianization of the Sámi," in *The Pre-Christian Religions of the North: History and Structures*, vol. IV, ed., J. P Schjødt, J. Lindow, and A. Andrén (Turnhout: Brepols, 2020), 1745–59.
12. P. Norberg, *Forna tiders järnbruk i Norr- och Västerbotten* (Stockholm: Almqvist & Wiksell, 1958), 7–14; K. Awebro, "Kring bruksrörelsen i Tornedalen," in *Tornedalens historia II: Från 1600-talet till 1809*, ed., O. Hederyd and Y. Alamäki (Haparanda: Tornedalskommunernas historiebokskommitté, 1993), 365–6.
13. J. Day, "The Continental Origins of Bristol Brass," *Industrial Archaeology Review* 7, no. 1 (1984): 32–56; J. Morton, "The Rise of the Modern Copper and Brass Industry in Britain 1690–1750," PhD Thesis, University of Birmingham, 1985.
14. Norberg, *Forna tiders järnbruk i Norr- och Västerbotten*, 17–18.
15. After the death of Louis De Geer in 1652, the brothers came into control of a majority of the shares of the copper mine in Falun, which was the dominant source of copper in the whole world at that time. The brothers also ensured a close to monopoly situation through their control of all major brass works in Sweden.
16. N. Zaihde, "Colonies, Copper, and the Market for Inventive Activity in England and Wales, 1680–1730," *The Economic History Review* 66, no. 3 (2013): 805–25; see also L. Müller, *The Merchant Houses of Stockholm, c. 1640–1800: A Comparative Study of Early-Modern Entrepreneurial Behaviour* (Uppsala: Uppsala University, 1998).
17. See, for instance, the abovementioned Saivijokk in Masuni/Masugnsbyn, which probably was a sacred site. L. Bäckman, *Sájva: föreställningar om hjälp- och skyddsväsen i heliga fjäll bland samerna* (Stockholm: Almqvist & Wiksell International, 1975).
18. Cf. K. Awebro, *Luleå silververk: ett norrländskt silververks historia* (Luleå: Norrbottens museum, 1983).

19. A. Lindmark, *Torneå Lappmarks Kopparbruk anno 1655–1780* (Svappavaara: Albin Lindmark, 1963).
20. H. Weiss, "Introduction: Portals of Early Modern Globalisation and Creolisation in the Atlantic World during the Era of the Slave Trade," in *Ports of Globalisation, Ports of Creolisation. Nordic Possessions in the Atlantic World during the Era of the Slave Trade*, ed. H. Weiss (Leiden: Brill, 2016), 2–12.
21. Raj, *Relocating Modern Science*.
22. Nordin, *The Scandinavian Early Modern World*; J. M. Nordin and C.-G. Ojala, "An Industrial Revolution in an Indigenous Landscape: The Copper Extraction of the Early Modern Torne River Valley in Its Global Context," *Fennoscandia Archaeologica* XXXVII (2020): 61–81.
23. Nordin and Ojala, "An Industrial Revolution in an Indigenous Landscape," 77.
24. G. Rydén, *Hushållningens praktiker: arbete och boende i Dannemora bergslag under Charles de Geers tid*, forthcoming.
25. C. Evans and G. Rydén, *Baltic Iron in the Atlantic World in the Eighteenth Century* (Leiden: Brill, 2007).
26. Robert C. Allen, *The British Industrial Revolution in Global Perspective* (Cambridge: Cambridge University Press, 2009).
27. For example, J. Inikori, *Africans and the Industrial Revolution in England. A Study in International Trade and Economic Development* (Cambridge: Cambridge University Press, 2002).
28. Evans and Rydén, *Baltic Iron in the Atlantic World*; C. Evans and G. Rydén, "Voyage Iron. An Atlantic Slave Trade Currency, Its European Origins and West African Impact," *Past and Present* 239 (2018): 41–70.
29. S. Olofsson, "Copper on the Move: A Commodity Chain Between Sweden and France, 1720–1790," in *Locating the Global: Spaces, Networks and Interactions from the Seventeenth to the Twentieth Century*, ed. Holger Weiss (Berlin: De Gruyter Oldenbourg, 2020), 147–74.
30. N. Zahediah, "Colonies, Copper, and the Market for Inventive Activity in England and Wales."
31. J. M. Nordin and C.-G. Ojala, "Copper Worlds: A Historical Archaeology of Abraham and Jakob Momma-Reenstierna and Their Industrial Enterprise in the Torne River Valley, c. 1650–1680," *Acta Borealia* 34, no. 2 (2017): 103–33; cf. Day, "The Continental Origins of Bristol Brass"; M. Beaudry, *Findings: The Material Culture of Needlework and Sewing* (New Haven: Yale University Press, 2007); see also L. Lundmark, *Uppbörd, utarmning, utveckling: det samiska fångstsamhällets övergång till rennomadism i Lule lappmark* (Lund: Arkiv, 1982), 114–24.
32. See V. Immonen, "Intercontinental Flows of Desire: Brass Kettles in Lapland and in the Colony of New Sweden," in *Archaeologies of Mobility and Movement*, ed., M. C. Beaudry and T. G. Parno (New York: Springer, 2013), 17–30; Nordin, *The Scandinavian Early Modern World*.
33. G. Rydén, "Provincial Cosmopolitanism: An Introduction," in *Sweden in the Eighteenth-Century World: Provincial Cosmopolitans*, ed. G. Rydén (Farnham: Ashgate, 2013), 1–31.
34. See further F. Bedoire, *Hugenotternas värld: Från religionskrigens Frankrike till skeppsbroadelns Stockholm* (Stockholm: Bonnier, 2009).
35. D. Degroot, *The Frigid Golden Age: Climate Change, the Little Ice Age, and the Dutch Republic, 1560–1720* (Cambridge: Cambridge University Press, 2018); see also J. M. Nordin, "Center of Diversity: Sámi in Early Modern Stockholm in the Light of

European Colonial Expansion. A Historical Archaeological Approach," *International Journal of Historical Archaeology* 22 (2018): 663–85; Nordin, *The Scandinavian Early Modern World*.
36. Awebro, "Kring bruksrörelsen i Tornedalen"; Nordin and Ojala, "Copper Worlds."
37. The major brass works in Sweden owned by the Momma Reenstierna brothers were Gusum, Nyköping, Norrköping, and Skultuna.
38. Nordin, *The Scandinavian Early Modern World*, 113.
39. Bedoire, *Hugenotternas värld*, 188–91.
40. See G. Hoppe, *Vägarna inom Norrbottens län, från 1500-talet till våra dagar* (Uppsala: Uppsala universitet, 1945); Nordin and Ojala, "Copper Worlds."
41. *Dombok Torne lappmark*, February 5, 1677, 96.
42. P. Sondén, "Bröderna Momma-Reenstierna: Ett bidrag till den svenska handelns och industriens historia på 1600-talet," *Historisk tidskrift* 3 (1911): 143–80.
43. See J. M. Nordin, "Spaces of Resilience and Resistance: Sámi Habitation in Southern and Central Sweden During the Late Medieval and the Early Modern Period," *International Journal of Historical Archaeology* (2022): 1–26.
44. N. Arell, *Kolonisationen i lappmarken* (Stockholm: Esselte studium, 1979).
45. *Dombok Torne lappmark*, January 31, 1649, 6.
46. Ibid., January 29, 1650, 8.
47. Ibid., January 29, 1655, 11.
48. Ibid., January 28, 1663, 31.
49. Ibid., January 28, 1671, 54.
50. Ibid., February 5, 81–6, 89–90.
51. Ibid., February 5, 1675, 89–90.
52. Ibid., February 5, 1681, 114–15.
53. Rydving, *The End of Drum-Time*; Granqvist, K. "Till vem ger du din själ? Berättelsen om Lars Nillsson på liv och död," in *Fordom då alla djur kunde tala*, ed. Åsa Virdi Kroik (Stockholm: Rosima förlag, 2001), 50–9.
54. B. Löw, "Schefferus och hans Lapponia," in *Lapponia*, ed. J. Schefferus (Gebers: Stockholm, 1956 [1673]), 9–23.
55. J. Schefferus, *Lapponia* (Gebers: Stockholm, 1956 [1673]).
56. J-F. Regnard, *Voyage de Laponie/de Regnard. Œvres. T. 4*, 194–365 (Paris: Stereotype d'Herhan, 1805 [1881]).

Bibliography

Published Sources

Dombok Torneå lappmark: Jukkasjärvi og Enontekis tinglag. 1639–1699 [Court Records from Torneå lappmark, Jukkasjärvi and Enontekis Court Circuits], published by Dag A. Larsen, Dag A., and Kåre Rauø. Finnsnes: Lenvik bygdemuseum, 1997.

Research Literature

Allen, Robert C. *The British Industrial Revolution in Global Perspective*. Cambridge: Cambridge University Press, 2009.
Arell, N. *Kolonisationen i lappmarken*. Stockholm: Esselte studium, 1979.

Awebro, K. *Luleå silververk: ett norrländskt silververks historia.* Luleå: Norrbottens museum, 1983.
Awebro, K. "Kring bruksrörelsen i Tornedalen." In *Tornedalens historia II: Från 1600-talet till 1809*, eds. O. Hederyd and Y. Alamäki, 361–80. Haparanda: Tornedalskommunernas historiebokskommitté, 1993.
Axelsson, E. "Samerna och statsmakten. Vardagligt motstånd och kulturell hybriditet i Torne lappmark under perioden 1639-1732." Master Thesis in History, Dept. of History, University of Umeå, 2015.
Bäckman, L. *Sájva: föreställningar om hjälp- och skyddsväsen i heliga fjäll bland samerna.* Stockholm: Almqvist & Wiksell International, 1975.
Bhambra G. *Rethinking Modernity: Postcolonialism and the Sociological Imagination.* Basingstoke: Palgrave Macmillan, 2007.
Bedoire, F. *Hugenotternas värld: Från religionskrigens Frankrike till skeppsbroadelns Stockholm.* Stockholm: Bonnier, 2009.
Beaudry, M. *Findings: The Material Culture of Needlework and Sewing.* New Haven: Yale University Press, 2007.
Day, J. "The Continental Origins of Bristol Brass." *Industrial Archaeology Review* 7, no. 1 (1984): 32–56.
Degroot, D. *The Frigid Golden Age: Climate Change, the Little Ice Age, and the Dutch Republic, 1560-1720.* Cambridge: Cambridge University Press, 2018.
Elenius, L. "The Dissolution of Ancient Kvenland and the Transformation of the Kvens as an Ethnic Group of People. On Changing Ethnic Categorizations in Communicative and Collective Memories." *Acta Borealia* 36, no. 2 (2019): 117–48.
Evans, C., and G. Rydén, *Baltic Iron in the Atlantic World in the Eighteenth Century.* Leiden: Brill, 2007.
Evans, C., and G. Rydén, "Voyage Iron. An Atlantic Slave Trade Currency, Its European Origins and West African Impact." *Past and Present* 239 (2018): 41–70.
Granqvist, K. "Till vem ger du din själ? Berättelsen om Lars Nilsson på liv och död." In *Fordom då alla djur kunde tala*, edited by Åsa Virdi Kroik, 50–9. Stockholm: Rosima förlag, 2001.
Hansen, L.-I., and Olsen, B. *Hunters in Transition: An Outline of Early Sámi History.* Leiden: Brill, 2014.
Hoppe, G. *Vägarna inom Norrbottens län, från 1500-talet till våra dagar.* Uppsala: Uppsala universitet, 1945.
Immonen, V. "Intercontinental Flows of Desire: Brass Kettles in Lapland and in the Colony of New Sweden." In *Archaeologies of Mobility and Movement*, eds. M. C. Beaudry and T. G. Parno, 17–30. New York: Springer, 2013.
Inikori, J. *Africans and the Industrial Revolution in England. A Study in International Trade and Economic Development.* Cambridge: Cambridge University Press, 2002.
Lindmark, A. *Torneå Lappmarks Kopparbruk anno 1655-1780.* Svappavaara: Albin Lindmark, 1963.
Lindmark, D., and Sundström, O. *De historiska relationerna mellan Svenska kyrkan och samerna: en vetenskaplig antologi.* Skellefteå: Artos & Norma, 2016.
Löw, B. "Schefferus och hans Lapponia." In *Lapponia*, edited by J. Schefferus, 9–23. Gebers: Stockholm, 1956 [1673].
Lundmark, L. *Uppbörd, utarmning, utveckling: det samiska fångstsamhällets övergång till rennomadism i Lule lappmark.* Lund: Arkiv, 1982.

Morton, J. "The Rise of the Modern Copper and Brass Industry in Britain 1690–1750." PhD Thesis, University of Birmingham, 1985.
Müller, L. *The Merchant Houses of Stockholm, c. 1640–1800: A Comparative Study of Early-Modern Entrepreneurial Behaviour*. Uppsala: Uppsala University, 1998.
Norberg, P. *Forna tiders järnbruk i Norr- och Västerbotten*. Stockholm: Almqvist & Wiksell, 1958.
Nordin, J. M. "Center of Diversity: Sámi in Early Modern Stockholm in the Light of European Colonial Expansion. A Historical Archaeological Approach." *International Journal of Historical Archaeology* 22 (2018): 663–85.
Nordin, J. M. *The Scandinavian Early Modern World*.
Nordin, J. M. "Spaces of Resilience and Resistance: Sámi Habitation in Southern and Central Sweden during the Late Medieval and the Early Modern Period." *International Journal of Historical Archaeology* (2022): 1–26.
Nordin, J. M., and Ojala, C.-G. "Copper Worlds: A Historical Archaeology of Abraham and Jakob Momma-Reenstierna and Their Industrial Enterprise in the Torne River Valley, c. 1650–1680." *Acta Borealia* 34, no. 2 (2017): 103–33.
Nordin, J. M., and Ojala, C-G. "An Industrial Revolution in an Indigenous Landscape: The Copper Extraction of the Early Modern Torne River Valley in Its Global Context." *Fennoscandia Archaeologica* XXXVII (2020): 61–81.
Olofsson, S. "Copper on the Move: A Commodity Chain between Sweden and France, 1720–1790." In *Locating the Global: Spaces, Networks and Interactions from the Seventeenth to the Twentieth Century*, edited by Holger Weiss, 147–74. Berlin: De Gruyter Oldenbourg, 2020.
Persson, S. Harnesk, D., and Islar, M. "What Local People? Examining the Gállok Mining Conflict and the Rights of the Sámi Population in Terms of Justice and Power." *Geoforum* 86 (2017): 20–9.
Pratt, M. L. *Imperial Eyes: Travel Writing and Transculturation*. London: Routledge, 1992.
Raj, K. *Relocating Modern Science: Circulation and the Construction of Knowledge in South Asia and Europe, 1650–1900*. Basingstoke: Palgrave Macmillan, 2007.
Regnard, J-F. *Voyage de Laponie/de Regnard. Œvres. T. 4*, 194–365. Paris: Stereotype d'Herhan, 1805 [1881].
Rydén, G. "Provincial Cosmopolitanism: An Introduction." In *Sweden in the Eighteenth-Century World: Provincial Cosmopolitans*, edited by G. Rydén, 1–31. Farnham: Ashgate, 2013.
Rydén, G. *Hushållningens praktiker: arbete och boende i Dannemora bergslag under Charles de Geers tid*. Forthcoming.
Rydving, H. *The End of Drum-Time: Religious Change among the Lule Saami, 1670s–1740s*. Uppsala: Uppsala University, 1993.
Rydving, H. "The Christianization of the Sámi." In *The Pre-Christian Religions of the North: History and Structures*, vol. IV, eds. J. P. Schjødt, J. Lindow, and A. Andrén, 1745–59. Turnhout: Brepols, 2020.
Schefferus, J. *Lappland*. Uppsala: Gebers, 1956 [1673].
Sondén, P. "Bröderna Momma-Reenstierna: Ett bidrag till den svenska handelns och industriens historia på 1600-talet." *Historisk tidskrift* 3 (1911): 143–80.
Vahtola, J. "Folkens mångfald." In *Tornedalens historia I: Från istid till 1600-talet*, eds. O. Hederyd, Y. Alamäki, and M. Kenttä, 176–208. Haparanda: Tornedalskommunernas historiebokskommitté, 1991.

Wallerström, T. *Norrbotten, Sverige och medeltiden: problem kring makt och bosättning i en europeisk periferi*. Stockholm: Almqvist & Wiksell, 1995.
Wallerström, T. *Kunglig makt och samiska bosättningsmönster: studier kring Väinö Tanners vinterbyteori*. Oslo: Novus, 2017.
Weiss, H. "Introduction: Portals of Early Modern Globalisation and Creolisation in the Atlantic World during the Era of the Slave Trade." In *Ports of Globalisation, Ports of Creolisation. Nordic Possessions in the Atlantic World during the Era of the Slave Trade*, edited by H. Weiss, 1–21. Leiden: Brill, 2016.
Zahedieh, N. "Colonies, Copper, and the Market for Inventive Activity in England and Wales, 1680–1730." *The Economic History Review* 66, no. 3 (2013): 805–25.

9

Kazakhstani Poles and Germans as Second-Class Citizens: "Underground" Catholicism in Soviet Kazakhstan

Jerzy Rohoziński

The State Archive of Akmola Oblast (Kokchetav/Kokshetau) in Kazakhstan contains a number of documents recording the efforts made toward the end of the 1970s by two Catholic communities in order to achieve official registration. Although both petitions were successful, one was examined and endorsed fairly rapidly, while the other took nearly a decade to process. It is difficult to explain this difference, although the stance of the local administration must have played an important role. Unfortunately, the records do not tell us whether there was any ethnic or religious discrimination involved, if attempts were made at bribery, or indeed, if any other factors played a part. I, however, will try to answer the question as to what could be the reasons why one community obtains the approval faster, while the other takes longer. I will also show what religious practices were like in the underground when the community was not registered.

Religious "Underground" in Postwar Soviet Kazakhstan

According to data from 1962 by the Plenipotentiary of the Council for Religious Cults for Tselinnyi Krai[1] in Soviet Kazakhstan, of the twenty religious communities registered at the time, twelve are at Orthodox churches, four are at mosques, three are at houses of prayer of Evangelical Christians–Baptists, and one is at a Lutheran church. The remaining communities, and there are almost 300 of them, operate in the religious underground, remaining unregistered. There is not a single Orthodox among them. Orthodoxy exhibits extreme legalism in this regard. It operates only within the framework outlined by the authorities. Islam, which enjoys discreet support from local authorities in many places, counts forty-four such communities, Lutherans have sixty-two, Baptists—as many as eighty-six, Mennonites—thirty-three, Pentecostals-Subbotniks—twenty-eight, Catholics—twenty-seven, Seventh-day Adventists—nine, and Jehovah's Witnesses—five. In addition, there were isolated communities of

Molokans, Old Believers-Bespopovtsy, and Murashkovtsy ("Evangelical Christians Holy Zionists").[2] Catholics, we should emphasize, do not have a single officially registered community at that time.

It was the subsequent liquidation of the Gulag camp system that would prove to be of crucial importance for the development of Catholicism in Kazakhstan, although, as we can see, it did not yet entail the legalization of religious life. After 1956, a number of priests—chief among them Władysław Bukowiński, Bronisław Drzepecki, and Józef Kuczyński—were freed from the forced labor camps, and this gave an immense impulse to the renewal of Catholic religious life in Kazakhstan. The memory of the itinerant priests, although today somewhat blurred, continues to live among Kazakh Poles, with some of them still remembering certain of the clergymen. In Shortandy, Leonid Ostrowski (born in 1945) recalled when the village was visited by Father Władysław Bukowiński from Karaganda, Father Kaszuba from Taiynsha (Krasnoarmeysk), and also Father Aleksander Bień. He further mentioned a Latvian priest (not remembering his name) who was summoned to give the last rites—as it turned out, this had been a provocation organized by the security service. The cleric was beaten up and no one saw him there ever again. Mr. Ostrowski best remembered the frail Father Kaszuba, whom following each visit to Shortandy, dressed in "civilian" clothes, he would escort back to Tselinograd (Akmolinsk). It was particularly important to retain vigilance at railway stations, where priests were often caught. Father Kaszuba gave Mr. Ostrowski's mother monies (probably collected elsewhere) for the erection of a house of prayer.[3]

We know from other accounts that the faithful in Shortandy purchased an item of real estate for this very purpose in 1957 (a year after they were struck from the register of special settlers), but barely a year later the authorities seized the property and turned it into a library. Again, therefore, people were forced to pray in private homes, taking care to change locations insofar as was possible. In Kamyshenka, for example, this role was served by the large house of an unmarried gentleman (Mr. Kaszperski). Church services held in secret by Father Kaszuba lasted some three to four hours, for in their course the priest also conducted marriages, christened children, and heard confessions. They were participated in only by those who were "in the know," with no more than one or two persons going at a time; this was crucial in order not to arouse any suspicions, since local "activists" (mainly Russians) regularly eavesdropped on such gatherings, sometimes clambering onto rooftops to achieve their goal.[4]

Visits from the local constable (*uchastkovyi*), who could order a search, were not uncommon, and, regrettably, there were also informers (*sekretnye sotrudniki*) within the communities themselves. The people who were informed on would be summoned to the *selsoviet*, where they received various penalties—including terms of imprisonment. Children, on the other hand, could face harassment in schools, for example, if they were reported by colleagues. Ludmila Rebintseva and Raisa Marchevska (at the time aged sixteen) were secretly christened by Father Kaszuba. They later wore their crosses hidden under their red Young Pioneers' scarves. Both remember from their childhood the nighttime masses held in a crowded room with drawn curtains, stuffy from the burning incense. Sometimes the children would be afraid of the priest, while on occasion they fell asleep during the services. Two other women—Bronislava Linok from Krasnodolsk (born in 1948) and Maria Sokovska from the Kellerovka region in Kokchetav Oblast (born in 1951)—were secretly baptized and confirmed by Father Józef Kuczyński. He did not issue any documents in the course of the ceremonies, instead giving out holy pictures to the children who were taking the sacraments. Ms. Linok also remembers how together with her girlfriends she went to Father Kuczyński for her first confession—not openly, of course, but nonetheless dressed in all her finery, with her hair let down. One of her peers, Maria Levkowich (born in 1938), recalled how the clergyman, having received permission from the authorities to hold mass, started coming to Krasnodolsk not at night, but by day. Obviously, there were also a great many people who had no contact with a clergyman for years. When faced with such a lengthy absence, those who, for example, wanted to christen their children would turn to the "old women" or try to have the ceremony performed while on their travels. As regards interethnic relations in Catholic villages with mixed populations, Poles and Germans on the whole prayed separately, unless there were very few German residents—then they would join their Polish coreligionists.[5]

This "underground" Catholic religiosity was noted in the reports of the Soviet security services, particularly during the period of the NKVD's *special command offices* (until 1956). For example, in his memo dated December 10, 1952, the deputy commander of the Ministry of State Security unit stationed in the Tchkalovo region in Kokchetav Oblast made the following observations:

> In the region there are 14 villages inhabited by Polish and German special settlers. Among them there function religious sects which congregate at the homes of various residents and hold religious ceremonies, and these are accompanied by anti-Soviet agitation calculated at drawing the youth away from the social, cultural and educational activities organized in the villages. And thus, for example, in 1951 in the village of Kalinovka there was liquidated a religious group headed by Adolf Shultz and Wilhelm Wolski. They gathered some 30–40 persons at a time for purposes of religious ceremonies, and once even led the kolkhozniki to the cemetery, where nearly 400 people assembled. The organizers were arrested and subjected to criminal prosecution under Article 58 of the Criminal Code of the Russian Soviet Federative Socialist Republic. Presently, religious gatherings are taking place in the village of Beloyarka, in the house of a German woman, one Attylia Rode, and in the village of Podolskie, in the house of 70-year-old Anna Kosowska. Such religious groups are active in each special settlement and exert a considerable influence on the youth, drawing it away from village social life and involving them in religious sects, which also participate in these congregations.[6]

During this period, there was a wave of arrests in Kokchetav Oblast with the specific aim of combating the "anti-Soviet agitation" taking place in the course of "religious gatherings," which—as we learn from a report addressed by the district office of the Ministry of State Security to the Central Committee of the Communist Party of Kazakhstan—took the form of, among others, persuading people that "they should not work on Sundays or holidays, for this is a sin." A special Party Commission that visited the Kellerovka region at the time noted thus:

> A religious fanaticism may be observed amongst the special settlers of all contingents. The youth are influenced by their parents, who hold religious ceremonies, and are therefore not willing to join the Young Pioneers or the Komsomol. ... Religious fanaticism manifests itself in such a way, among others, that even at this very moment the special settlers are observing the Advent post, and therefore do not go to cinemas, clubs or other places of social entertainment.[7]

Pursuing Official Registration

The only chance to get out of this religious "underground" was to officially register a religious community in accordance with Soviet legislation, but this was not an easy matter for Kazakhstani Catholics. The faithful I visited in November 2018 in the Shortandy region, for example, obtained permission for the erection of a church only in 1990, and thus functioned in the religious "underground" practically throughout the entire Soviet period. Catholics in other parts of Kazakhstan, however, undertook efforts—sometimes successful—to register their congregations.

The case discussed in the following is an example of a relatively easy way to obtain official registration. On October 26, 1981, the executive committee of the Rozdolne *sel'sovet* approved the application of a group of Catholic faithful from the village of Lineevka for opening a house of prayer and turned to the regional authorities with a request for approval of its decision. The document contains a brief description of the group, stating that it was established in 1905, at the time was comprised of thirty-two women aged between fifty-two and eighty-seven. It was headed by Elizaveta Maier (a German born in 1910, with no criminal record), who also ministered (*sluzhitel' kul'ta*). The place of worship was to be located in the home of one of the female members of the congregation (with her consent). Acting in its capacity of supervisory body, the committee assured that the assembly of faithful was not infringing the law, "demonstrated a loyal approach to Soviet reality," and "was not engaged in agitation among the youth aimed at attracting them to the group." In 1980, the group was entered into the "temporary register" (*vremennyi uchet*) for a specific "test period," which it successfully passed.

The list with the thirty-two names of its founders—all female pensioners—contains only two that are Polish (the rest were German): Szymanowska and Herlińska (in Russian: Gerlinskaia); interestingly, the prayer meetings were to be held in the house of the former, while the latter became a member of the audit commission. In her résumé, however, Herlińska stated that she was of German ethnic nationality, so she had probably taken her Polish surname from her husband. It could have been the same in the case of Szymanowska. Maier's records indicate that in the years 1929–54 Lineevka's religious leader worked in a kolkhoz, and thereafter (1954–6) in a sovkhoz, retiring in 1965. Szymanovska herself wrote in her résumé that, just like Herlińska, she was born in Lineevka. We may therefore venture the hypothesis that in the case of

Lineevka we are dealing with a Catholic community with pre-Revolutionary roots and not constituted of special settlers deported in 1936 from the Ukrainian Soviet Socialist Republic. This would explain why the village was subjected to collectivization in 1929. In 1954, along with the inauguration of the "virgin lands campaign," the mode of land management was changed from the kolkhoz to the sovkhoz.

Thereafter, the process of registration progressed rather speedily. Already on October 30, 1981, the Executive Committee of the Council of People's Deputies of Kokchetav Oblast turned to the Council for Religions at the Council of Ministers of the USSR with a motion for registration of the community, which was duly effected on November 20. In their substantiation, the oblast authorities employed the term "German religiousness":

> At present, out of the 80,000 Germans living in Kokchetav Oblast, more than 3,100 faithful have been entered in a temporary register. This number accounts for approximately 3% of the entire German population. In recent years, Soviet authorities have registered 6 religious associations of Evangelical Christians-Baptists, and 6 of Lutherans, some 1,500 persons in total, that is more than 46% of the total number of faithful figuring in the temporary register. In consequence, the majority of faithful operate in unregistered congregations, i.e. illegally .... In order to systematise the situation of religious associations comprising persons of German ethnic nationality, and also strengthen control over their activities, the Executive Committee of the Council of Workers' Delegates of Kokchetav Oblast considers it justified to grant the request of the faithful and register an independent religious association of faithful Catholics operating in the village of Lineevka in the Kokchetav region of Kokchetav Oblast.[8]

The case of Taiynsha (Krasnoarmeisk) differs from that of Lineevka in three important aspects: namely, the number of faithful comprising the community was considerably larger, the vast majority were Poles who had been deported to Kazakhstan in 1936, and the registration process took much more time. The party responsible for slowing down the entire procedure was the local administration, not the Council for Religious Affairs. Documented correspondence starts with a letter sent by the local plenipotentiary of the Council for Kokchetav Oblast to the chairman of the Regional Executive Committee in Krasnoarmeisk, dated February 5, 1975. In the letter he demanded a response to his letter of August 15, 1974, concerning the application of the local Catholic community for the registration of a house of prayer (dated May 17, 1974), which had already been submitted to the municipal council. In its reply of March 11, the executive committee informed the plenipotentiary that

> the application of the Catholics had not been processed for 8 months for a specific purpose. During this time, the aforementioned group of faithful had been subjected to surveillance. This disclosed that the Catholic faithful, acting in violation of the Act on Religious Cults, regularly gathered for religious meetings in the homes of individual members of the congregation, thereby infringing Soviet legislation concerning religious cults, against which they have been repeatedly cautioned.[9]

On July 25, 1975, the municipal council received another application, in which the faithful complained that their request had been dismissed by the Krasnoarmeisk *raispolkom*'s chairman, although they were entitled to a place for common prayer, similarly to members of the Orthodox Church and other believers in the USSR. A few days later, the plenipotentiary of the Council for Religious Affairs (CRA) submitted another letter, requesting that the application of the faithful be reconsidered pursuant to the Decree of the Presidium of the Supreme Council of the USSR, dated April 12, 1968, *On the Procedure for Considering Propositions, Motions and Complaints Submitted by Citizens*. In his letter, the plenipotentiary called it "inadmissible" to forbid citizens to satisfy their religious needs. In the meantime, the faithful intervened at a higher level, with the plenipotentiary of the Council for the Kazakh Soviet Socialist Republic. When asked to take up the matter, the oblast plenipotentiary intervened once again with the local authorities of Krasnoarmeisk. However, registration was once again refused. He duly informed the republican bodies of the council and responded to the chairman of the executive committee that regular prayer gatherings did not constitute an infringement of Soviet law. At the same time, he requested that the oblast executive committee enter the community in the temporary register for the purpose of supervision. Meanwhile, the community submitted fresh complaints to the plenipotentiary and the oblast authorities, citing Article 124 of the Constitution of the USSR on freedom of religion. But all this made no impression on the Krasnoarmeisk Executive Committee, which in November 1976 refused to register the congregation again.[10]

As it turned out, the next year—when the matter reached the central authorities of the Council for Religions in Moscow—proved decisive. Toward the end of January 1977, the plenipotentiary of the Council for Kokchetav Oblast wrote to the headquarters in Moscow, motioning for a positive consideration of the case:

> The Catholic faithful in Krasnoarmeisk have been applying for the registration of their assembly for some 6–7 years. Their activity particularly intensified after 1974, when an application was submitted by 248 citizens of Catholic faith .... The Catholic faithful are loyal people, have a positive stance towards the legislation on religious cults, and do not infringe the law through their activities. The composition of their community is as follows. Three faithful aged between 30 and 40, 30 persons aged between 40 and 50, and 215 people aged over 50. Of these 248 Catholics, 38 are employed, while the rest are aged pensioners or elderly housewives.[11]

When appearing in the same registration case, the deputy chairman of the Executive Committee of Kokchetav Oblast added:

> Presently there are 27,000 Catholics in Kokchetav *Oblest*, of whom some 400–500, that is approximately 2% of the total Polish population, are believers. Until 1970, the Catholics had never applied for registration of their community. From April to July 1970, a few applications were received for the opening of Catholic churches in certain townships in the Chkalovo and Kellerovka regions. Due to the small

numerical strength of these congregations, the matter was not taken up at the time. Lately, the Catholic faithful from Krasnoarmeisk have started to act with greater vigor. This is a sizable community, numbering 248 persons, of whom some 30 are Germans who adopted Catholicism … . In order to regulate the situation concerning religious assemblies comprising citizens of the USSR of Polish ethnic nationality, we consider it justified to register the Catholic congregation in the city of Krasnoarmeisk in the Krasnoarmeisk region of Kokchetav *Oblest*.[12]

A month later, on February 24, 1977, the council adopted both recommendations and issued a decision approving registration of the community. Three months later, the plenipotentiary applied for approval for the congregation to convert an item of real estate belonging to one of the faithful into a prayer house, stressing that it was located on the outskirts of the city, away from schools, nurseries, and other public utility buildings. From May 1981 onward, the position of priest in Krasnoarmeisk was held by Father Jan Paweł Lenga, who was born in Khmelnytskyi Oblast in the Ukrainian Soviet Socialist Republic in 1950 and who would go on to become the Apostolic Administrator of Kazakhstan. Documents show that he had taken holy orders only in 1980 and that his first parish was Qurghonteppa in the Tajik Soviet Socialist Republic. The new appointee promised the municipal council that he would "hold all religious ceremonies in accordance with the canons of the Catholic Church and the provisions governing religious cults." Conversely, when they hired the clergyman, the executive committee of the community simultaneously undertook to exercise control over him in this regard. Extant documents contain handwritten memos authorizing Father Lenga to minister in Krasnoarmeisk and also present arguments in favor of the decision, such as "otherwise extremists may come in from Poland or other places and the situation could get even worse" [*sic*].[13]

Father Lenga's predecessor had been Karol Kisielewski (Karlis Kiselevskis, 1906–1979) from Liepāja, a Latvian with Polish roots who had graduated from the seminary in Riga as a doctor of theology and taken holy orders in 1937. In 1949, he was deported to Karaganda, where he remained in exile until 1956. After his return, he ministered in the Daugavpils region of the Latvian Soviet Socialist Republic. Father Kisielewski does not figure in the list of collaborators of the KGB of the Latvian Soviet Socialist Republic, unlike the man who had recommended him for the position, Iulianis Vaivods, the apostolic administrator of the Archdiocese of Riga and the Diocese of Liepāja (a cardinal from 1983), who had been registered by the secret services in 1948 under the pseudonym "Omega."[14]

The "German" example of Lineevka in Kokchetav Oblast would appear to confirm a certain tendency, namely that the pre-Revolutionary traditions of self-organization of religious communities also played a role in the Soviet era. This rural and not very numerous congregation petitioned for registration rather late, but succeeded relatively quickly. It may be that this was due in some part to the "German factor"—perhaps the efforts of many different communities exceeded the "critical mass," or maybe the outcome was influenced by the failed project of German autonomy in Kazakhstan.[15] In Krasnoarmeisk, a larger city, albeit devoid of pre-Revolutionary traditions and mainly inhabited by former special settlers, the considerably larger Polish community started applying at an earlier date, but the whole process took considerably more time. As we can see, the "Polish ethnic factor," demographically a much lesser problem for the authorities, proved to play a much less effective role. On the other hand, the faithful initiated their efforts rather quickly, perhaps due to the influence of Father Kuczyński.

In both cases, however, we are dealing with a similar age structure, with the activists being pensioners and the elderly. In Lineevka, the group was strongly feminine. The Soviet authorities were happy with such a state of affairs: pensioners and elderly women could "devote themselves to matters of religion in their old age" in a building located on the outskirts of the city and safely distant from schools, thus having little impact on the public and professional spheres and on youth. At the same time, these groups would actually find it easier to engage in the organization of religious practices, as they had more time and were free of the "pressure of the workplace." Further, this would be an extension of the situation that existed during the period of the "religious underground," that is, with the "old women" functioning as quasi priests of the community.

For Catholics in the Kazakh Soviet Socialist Republic, this state of affairs lasted for a very long time when compared with the other, officially recognized" denominations. Until 1956, Polish and German Catholics were special settlers with limited rights and were considered "agents of the Vatican" although they did not rank at the bottom of the hierarchy in this regard. Therefore, they could not take part in the religious rebirth engendered by the Great Patriotic War and were thus deprived of a unique opportunity of achieving legalization of their communities. They were forced to function underground for many years, away from the Soviet public sphere, which they tried to reintegrate after the liberalization of the special settler's status.

Legalization, the "pass" to reintegration into the official sphere, was granted relatively late. For Krasnoarmeisk, in 1977, for Lineevka, in 1981. When we project these dates onto the timeline of the Kazakh Soviet Socialist Republic, we see just how delayed these "successes" were in relation to the religious revival that occurred in the republic toward the end of the war and immediately after its conclusion. Importantly, we should keep in mind that shortly after these registrations, some other local denominations—and in particular Islam—came to the end of a cycle of postwar "prosperity," which reached its zenith in the Brezhnev era. This relative affluence, which was felt particularly strongly in the Muslim regions of the USSR, resulted in the introduction of ostentatious consumption at religious and family ceremonies—a phenomenon that was criticized by the new general secretary of the Communist Party of the USSR, the "puritanical" Iurii Andropov.

When discussing the conclusions of the June 1983 Plenary Assembly of the Central Committee of the CPSU and the "tasks" that these implied for ethnography, Iurii Bromlei, the long-standing director of the Institute of Ethnology and Anthropology of the Academy of Sciences of the USSR, recommended that the paradigm of "lenient" treatment of religious ceremonies as "national traditions" be rejected:

> Important tasks have been set for the science of ethnography as regards combating the anachronism of religion. This has special significance today, when many religious phenomena take the form of religious rituals and customs ... .Rituals have become an inherent element of the Soviet style of life, and play an ever greater

role in the social awareness of people .... In this context, the improvement of the standard of living, which should lead to the expansion of manifestations of the socialist way of life, actually results in a deformation of socialist principles and customs. Conspicuous weddings, monuments, anniversaries, etc. have flooded the southern regions—the republics of trans-Caucasia and Central Asia, while at present—and this is borne out by the observations of ethnographers—they are boldly making headway in the northern areas, including in regions inhabited mainly by the Russian nation.[16]

Conclusions

First of all, it should be emphasized that Kazakhstani Catholics were allowed to legally exist in the Soviet public sphere at all so late compared to other denominations, although they did not rank at the bottom of the hierarchy in this regard. They could not benefit from the religious revival sparked by the "Great Patriotic War" social mobilization.

As a result after the de-Stalinization moves of 1956 and the liberalization of regulations applicable to the so-called "special settlers," Kazakh Poles and Germans functioned in two parallel and mutually contradictory realities: the Soviet public sphere, represented first and foremost by the school and the workplace, which was hostile toward religion, and the private sphere, where Catholic religious traditions—ridiculed at school—were cultivated, mainly through the involvement of women. This situation was in many ways similar to that of other religions in the Soviet Union.

Some Kazakhstani Catholics tried to change their circumstances and made efforts to officially register their religious communities. While certain of them succeeded—albeit quite late, only in the 1980s—others had to wait for the collapse of the USSR. The cases I analyzed indicate that the factors facilitating this process were dominance of ethnic Germans in the community (the authorities felt some "demographic pressure" from this group) and pre-Revolutionary traditions of religious self-organization. The long years spent in the "religious underground" endowed Kazakh Catholicism with very specific features and unique attributes when compared, for example, with the system, faith, and practice of the Catholic Church in Poland or Germany.

Notes

1. Tselinnyi Krai is an administrative unit that existed from December 1960 to October 1965, formed from the regions of North Kazakhstan, Kustanay, Kokchetav, Pavlodar, and part of Tselinograd (formerly Akmola).
2. A. Musagaliyeva, R. Musabekova, and U. Sandybaeva, *Severnyi Kazakhstan kak region politicheskikh repressii i deportatsii narodov SSSR* (Astana: Eurasiatic National University Press, 2017), 211–13.
3. Leonid Ostrowski, born in 1945, interviewed on November 4, 2018; Mieczysław Kuczyński, born in 1957, interviewed on November 3, 2018; Ludmiła Rebincewa,

born in 1968, interviewed on November 3, 2018; Walenty Kaszubski, born in 1945, interviewed on November 3, 2018; Ludmiła Żewłakowa, interviewed on November 3, 2018; Raisa Marczewska, born in 1938, interviewed on November 4, 2018; Anna Stawska, born in 1930 (all recordings—Shortandy); Franciszka Olejnik, born in 1935, and Anna Niewęgłowska, born in 1933, interviewed in Piotrowka on November 4, 2018; Maria Lewkowicz, born in 1938, Bronisława Linok, born in 1948, Maria Sokowska, born in 1951, Halina Habowska, born in 1964, Stanisława Wołyńska, born in 1954—interviewed on December 5–6, 2019, June 28, 2020, and September 30, 2020, in Środa Wielkopolska; an account similar in vein: M. Murawicka, *Mimo wszystko*," in *Z ziemi kazachskiej do Polski. Wspomnienia repatriantów z Kazachstanu, wysiedlonych w latach 30. XX w. w głąb ZSRR*, vol. 2, ed. W. Kudela (Kraków: KNHS UJ 2007), 112 and subsequent.
4. Ibid.
5. Ibid.
6. L. D. Degitaeva, ed., *Iz istorii poliakov v Kazakhstanie v Kazakhstanie (1936–1956 gg.). Sbornik dokumentov* (Almaty: "Kazakstan" Publishing House, 2000), 79.
7. Ibid., 79–83 and subsequent; concerning secret church services in Beloyarka, the home village of the painter Feliks Mostowicz—cf. A. Milewska-Młynik, *Feliks Mostowicz i jego droga do polskości*, "Zesłaniec" 30 (2007), 197–9; the very use of the term "religious fanaticism" to describe the stance of the Catholic clergy and faithful is by no means a Soviet innovation—for example, it had already been applied in the middle of the nineteenth century by Governor General Ilarion Vassiltchikov to portray the Polish clergy and gentry in the Ukraine: "the spirit of religious fanaticism has not disappeared altogether. It sometimes takes the form of a concealed and at once impotent hatred of the Orthodox faith and Russians"; quoted from D. Beavois, *Trójkąt ukraiński. Szlachta, carat i lud na Wołyniu, Podolu i Kijowszczyźnie 1793–1914* (Lublin: Wydawnictwo UMCS, 2011), 423.
8. "Zaregistrirovannoe obshchestvo katolikov s. Letovochnoe," GAAO (State Archive of Akmola Region), Fond 730, Finding Aid1, File 51, sheets 10, 4–9, 16, 20, 24–28. The dossier has been erroneously titled, for the documents concern the village of Lineevka, which was founded in 1901 and inhabited by German Catholics, and not Letovochnoe, a colony established in 1936 for Polish and German special settlers, cf. the heading *Lineevka, Letovochnoe* in V. F. Diesendorf, *Die Deutschen Russlands: Siedlungen und Siedlungsgebieten: Lexikon* (Moscow: MSNK-Press, 2006); Maria Karpińska née Kwiatkowska, who was born in Lietowocznoje (1937), recalled that in addition to the Polish and German deportees of 1936, the village was also inhabited by Ingushes (interview by Adam Kaczyński and Kamila Zacharuk, Dołbysz, February 19, 2019).
9. Katoliki g. Krasnoarmeyska 1975–1979, GAAO, folio 730, series 1, dossier 23, sheets 77, 79.
10. GAAO, folio 730, series 1, dossier 23, sheets 68–75, 81–7, 89, 90.
11. Zaregistrirovannoe obshchestvo katolikov v g. Krasnoarmeyske 1977–1982 gg., GAAO, folio 730, series 1, dossier 30, sheet 62.
12. GAAO, folio 730, series 1, dossier 30, sheet 64.
13. GAAO, folio 730, series 1, dossier 30, sheets 41, 42, 44, 46, 57, 58, 59, 60; Amerlia Homycz, born in 1942, remembered traveling with her mother from Iasna Polana to the district of Taiynsha/Krasnoarmeisk to confess and that "there was a small prayer house there." Interview by author, Środa Wielkopolska, June 27, 2020.
14. Katoliki g. Krasnoarmeyska 1975–1979, GAAO, folio 730, series 1, dossier 23, sheets 54–60; card-index of collaborators of the KGB of the Latvian Soviet Socialist Republic,

available on the website of the KGB of the Latvian SSR https://kgb.arhivi.lv/ (accessed May 17, 2020).
15. In 1972, over 3,500 German Russians sent a petition to Moscow again requesting an autonomous republic in the Volga regions. The government responded with an ad hoc committee to study this request. In 1976, the commission finally agreed to create an autonomous oblast (county) in Northern Kazakhstan, centered in Ereymentau. See Siro Khan'ya, "Tselinograd, iiun' 1979 g.: k voprosu o nesostoiavsheisia nemetskoi avtonomii v Kazakhstane," *Acta Slavica Iaponica* 20 (2003): 230–6.
16. Yurii Bromlei, "O niekotorykh aktualnykh zadachakh etnograficheskogo izuchenia sovremiennosti," *Sovetskaya etnografia* 6 (1983): 22.

Bibliography

Archival Documents

GAAO, State Archive of Akmola Region, Kokshetav, Kazakhstan
Katoliki g. Krasnoarmeyska 1975–1979, GAAO folio 730, series 1, dossier 23
Zaregistrirovannoe obshchestvo katolikov s. Letovochnoe, GAAO folio 730, series 1, dossier 51

Research Literature

Beavois, D. *Trójkąt ukraiński. Szlachta, carat i lud na Wołyniu, Podolu i Kijowszczyźnie 1793–1914*. Lublin: Wydawnictwo UMCS, 2011.
Bromlei, Yurii. "O nekotorykh aktual'nykh zadachakh etnograficheskogo izuchenia sovremennosti." *Sovetskaia etnografiia* 6 (1983): 10–23.
Diesendorf, V. F. *Die Deutschen Russlands. Siedlungen und Siedlungsgebieten. Lexikon*. Moscow: MSNK-Press, 2006.
Degitaeva, L. D., ed., *Iz istorii poliakov v Kazakhstanie (1936–1956 gg.). Sbornik dokumentov*. Almaty: "Kazakstan" Publishing House, 2000.
Khan'ya, Siro, "Tselinograd, iyun' 1979: k voprosu o nesosostaiavsheisya nemetskoi avtonomii v Kazakstane." *Acta Slavica Iaponica* 20 (2003): 230–6.
Kudela, Wiktoria, ed. *Z ziemi kazachskiej do Polski. Wspomnienia repatriantów z Kazachstanu, wysiedlonych w latach 30. XX w. w głąb ZSRR*, vol. 2. Kraków: KNHS UJ, 2007.
Milewska-Młynik, Anna. "Feliks Mostowicz i jego droga do polskości." *Zesłaniec* 30 (2007): 197–9.
Murawicka, M. "Mimo wszystko." In *Z ziemi kazachskiej do Polski. Wspomnienia repatriantów z Kazachstanu, wysiedlonych w latach 30. XX w. w głąb ZSRR*, vol. 2, edited by W. Kudela. Kraków: KNHS UJ 2007.
Musagalieva, Arailym S., Roza M. Musabekova, and Ulbolsyn M. Sandybaeva, *Severnyi Kazakhstan kak region politicheskikh repressii i deportatsii narodov SSSR*. Astana: Eurasian National University Press, 2017.

10

A Forest Sámi Reindeer Herder's Diary during the Covid-19 Pandemic, Swedish Side of Sábme

May-Britt Öhman and Henrik Andersson

This chapter explores the management of the Covid-19 pandemic and it effects focusing on Norrbotten County, the largest county in Sweden, which occupies a quarter of the country, with 98,245 square kilometers and a population of 250,000. Norrbotten has two international borders, Finland and Norway, crossing Indigenous Sámi territories and reindeer grazing and herding lands. The effects are linked to geography, cold climate, natural resource exploitation, industries, multicultural population, and sparsely populated areas with long journey times to access healthcare. The county has a large Sami population and the largest number of reindeer and reindeer herders on the Swedish side of Sábme.

The research project "Pandemic in the (sub) Arctic North: A supra and cross-disciplinary data collection on experiences, resilience and social mobilization during the COVID-19 pandemic focusing on Norrbotten county," was initiated in March 2020 and ended by April 2022. The project was led by the author of this chapter, Dr. May-Britt Öhman, Associate Professor of Environmental History, Lule and Forest Sámi of the Lule River valley.

Within the project, an important part was the participants' own documentation of their everyday life, including reflections on the events and developments during the crisis management period. One of the project participants was Henrik Andersson, a reindeer herder in the Gällivare Forest Sámi community, Flakaberg group, and also a coauthor of this chapter. Gällivare Forest Sámi village is one of fifty-one reindeer herding Sámi villages on the Swedish side of Sábme. The reindeers' land stretches from the inland around Gällivare city and out into the archipelago of Luleå city. In wintertime the reindeer are in the area of the archipelago in the Gulf of Bothnia, and during the summer they move to the grazing lands in the inland.

Andersson started documenting his everyday life in March 2020, when he first heard of the pandemic. He uses a first-person perspective bringing together situated knowledge[1] and ego-histoire.[2] The diary contains written entries and photographs and thereby documents the experiences from Sámi reindeer herding throughout almost two years of the Covid-19 pandemic. In this chapter, May-Britt Öhman has made a selection of entries, starting from day one, covering from the first day when Henrik

Andersson heard about Covid-19 in March 2020 to the end of August 2020. The entries thus follow half of the reindeer herding year, including winter season when the grazing is often hard to find, spring migration from the coastal areas toward the inland, the calving season and the calf marking season, and the short time of rest that follows in August before the herders' work begins again.

Öhman and Andersson elaborated on some of the entries, where clarification was needed. The entries are followed by a concluding analysis and discussion, mainly written by Öhman, although still in close collaboration with Andersson. Öhman however assumes the main responsibility for the entire chapter.

Documenting and Analyzing Sámi Livelihood with Indigenous, Sámi, and Decolonizing Methodologies

The Sámi territories, known as Sábme in Lule Sámi, or Sápmi in North Sámi, encompass the Fennoscandia Peninsula in areas of the modern-day nation-states of Norway, Sweden, Finland, and the northeastern part of Russia. The Sámi have lived in this region since the time of the last ice age, about ten thousand years. There are written records of Sámi as a distinct people, separate from the Nordic/Germanic peoples dating back two thousand years, the first known being the Roman historian Tacitus who mentions two northern peoples, the *suiones*, the Swedes, and the *fenni*, the Sámi.[3]

While the Nordic peoples and Sámi shared territory and had extensive trade and cultural exchange, relationships began to deteriorate in the sixteenth century with the establishment of the modern nation-states. The nation-states expanded, taking over more and more Sámi territories. Sámi residing in central Sweden were by force deported northward, starting from the seventeenth century.[4] In the nineteenth century, with industrialization and the demand for more natural resources, racism and discrimination became an increasing part of the picture. Sámi were pushed more and more aside. Sámi also became subject to both erasure and land theft by the nation-states.[5] However, through Sámi mobilization, which has included international collaborations, the Sámi have been able to achieve a certain influence and recognition.

In 1977, the Sámi were recognized as an Indigenous people and an ethnic minority by the Swedish Parliament, with specific rights. In 2011, the status as a People was confirmed within the Swedish Constitution, as well as our rights to preserve and develop our cultural and social life:

> The opportunities of the **Sami people** and ethnic, linguistic and religious minorities to preserve and develop a cultural and social life of their own shall be promoted. (emphasis added)[6]

Documenting and analyzing Sámi livelihood today is both a contribution to history writing and a challenge to the way the history of the Fenno-Scandinavian region is commonly discussed. It responds to the exclusion of Sámi experiences and perspectives in colonial and settler historiography.

As an Indigenous people, there is an aspect that concerns the Sámi in particular; Sámi livelihood is intimately linked to lands and waters and thereby to the rights linked to lands and waters. As expressed within the Sámi Parliament Environmental program, the Sámi relationships to lands, waters, and nonhuman companions differ from what Sámi perceive as a Western view:

> The Sami view of nature as an animated, living being stands in strong contrast to the Western view of nature. Our view of nature has characterized our values, customs, social structures and relationships. Our view of life builds our common core value that is reflected in the Sami language. Sápmi is our home. If we—or someone else—destroy its nature, our culture is destroyed as well.[7]

The Swedish state has signed international conventions and agreements with regard to minorities and Indigenous peoples that firmly support Sámi rights. Yet, the actions of individuals, state representatives, and authorities continuously obstruct Sámi livelihood in general, and reindeer herding in particular. This comes through in Andersson's corona diary entries.

The research project and this article were guided and inspired by Indigenous methodologies, with the ambition of providing research from Sámi perspectives. Indigenous methodologies aim to contribute to change, as proposed by international Indigenous scholars like Linda Tuhiwai Smith[8] and in earlier works by Sámi forerunners Elsa Laula Renberg and Karin Stenberg.

South Sámi woman Elsa Laula Renberg's book of 1904, *In Face of Life or Death*,[9] is, on the one hand, a call to Swedish politicians to end the theft of Sámi territories, and on the other, a call to Sámi to educate ourselves and mobilize—to influence important political decision-making influencing Sámi lives and livelihood.

In 1920, Forest Sámi woman Karin Stenberg produced an important challenge to non-Sámi outsiders' false and exotifying depictions of Sámi. She collaborated with the Forest Sámi in Arvidsjaur and author Valdemar Lindholm to call attention to such accounts written by fiction authors and scientists traveling around in Sábme. The title of their book, translated into English, is *It Is Our Wish: An Appeal to the Swedish Nation from the Sámi People*.[10] This manifesto presents Sámi views and insights to the 1919 established governmental "lap committee" that was set in place to review Swedish legislation adopted in the late nineteenth century, and which controlled the Sámi and their rights to reindeer herding and livelihood.[11] Stenberg writes:

> The worst of all is that the Swedish authorities, when developing legislation often take these literary and scientific "truths about the lap" as point of departure, and thereby work, surely in good will, but at the same time biased, while inaccurate, thereby leading to wrong conclusions.[12]

Over the last few decades, the field of Indigenous Studies has evolved, advancing the development and uptake of Indigenous research methodologies. While Indigenous Studies has not yet become strong in the FennoScandinavian nation-states, it has strongholds in the United States, Canada, Australia, and Aotearoa—New Zealand.

In 1999, Linda Tuhiwai Smith, Ngāti Awa, and Ngāti Porou, *Māori*, published the influential Indigenous methodology book *Decolonizing Methodologies: Research and Indigenous Peoples*, in which she both challenges the Western outside perspective and study of Indigenous peoples, and proposes a number of projects to decolonize, acknowledge, and support Indigenous peoples' own perspectives. Smith writes:

> Indigenous peoples across the world have other stories to tell which … serve to tell an alternative story: the history of Western research through the eyes of the colonized. These counter-stories are powerful forms of resistance.[13]

This article is inspired by Laula Renberg's and Stenberg's calls to Sámi to mobilize and counter false and biased stories about Sámi livelihood. It is also inspired by Smith's proposal to work on decolonizing, which in this context means honoring the expertise of Sámi, recognizing the expertise of their nonhuman companions, as well as to develop appropriate methods of assembling data and stressing the importance of writing in collaboration.

Sámi Reindeer Herding on the Swedish Side of Sábme

Reindeer herding in the Arctic region has been practiced for millennia by several different Indigenous peoples in Europe, including the Sámi. There are currently more than twenty-four different Indigenous reindeer herding peoples within the settler colonial states of Norway, Sweden, Finland, Russia, Mongolia, China, Alaska, Canada, and Greenland.[14] Reindeer herding is essential to a way of life and encompasses expertise about reindeer, social relationships, and nature. The reindeer and their herders follow an annual cyclical pattern where the seasons, weather, and ecological conditions are the foundation. The herders follow the reindeer and their natural instinct to migrate between grazing lands, as well as the reindeer's expertise in finding food and to avoid danger. Expertise on the reindeer, nature, and ecology is passed on from generation to generation, and children in reindeer herding families participate from a very young age.[15]

In Sábme, the Sámi territories, reindeer herding has been part of Sámi tradition since at least a millennium, starting from the early Iron Age.[16] With regard to rights to land and waters, individual Sámi are known to have paid taxes for a specific area since the sixteenth century. These so-called tax lands, or "lap tax lands," were attached to rights that are similar to farming lands. They included hunting and fishing rights, and until the nineteenth century there were Sámi rights holders in Norrbotten County. With the increased state colonial expansion and the drive to access natural resources in Sámi territories, Sámi have lost many rights to lands and waters. This has impacted their ability to protect lands and waters against industrial intrusions and environmental destruction.[17]

Traditionally, reindeer herding was pursued by individuals of the same family within a particular geographic area known as the Siida. The settler colonial states have, however, interfered with the Sámi way of organizing reindeer herding through legislation and different policies, beginning in the nineteenth century.[18] On the Swedish side of Sábme, reindeer herding is pursued today within a state defined administrative organization. Sámi villages, "Sameby," are economic organizations within specific geographic areas. There are fifty-one such Sámi villages located from the county of Dalarna and northward.[19] The number of reindeer varies between 220,000 and 260,000 in the winter herd, with the total number allowed for each Sámi village regulated by the Swedish state through legislation that was first introduced in 1886.[20] The majority of reindeer and reindeer herders are located in Norrbotten. While the ways of managing differ between geographical areas and correspond to the landscapes, waterscapes, and traditions, there are three main different types of reindeer herding on the Swedish side of Sábme: mountain reindeer herding (thirty-three villages), forest reindeer herding (ten villages), and concession herding (eight villages).[21] The current way of organizing reindeer herding on the Swedish side of Sábme is a Swedish state invention; notably, this is not well suited to Sámi traditions and mode of organization.[22]

While holding expertise built on millennia of knowledge, reindeer herding has changed with the rest of the society, both through adaption to technical machinery and also due to the fragmentation of grazing lands. Until the 1960s, reindeer herding was mainly done by skiing and walking. Since the introduction of the snowmobile, and later the quad bike, vehicles have become of major importance but there are still herders who use skis in winter as their territories are still well preserved. In other reindeer herding territories, however, like the Gällivare Forest Sámi village, the grazing lands have become severely fragmented due to industrial intrusions, road, railroads, and highways with fences. This inhibits the reindeers' ability to migrate without being exposed to extreme dangers. Thereby some Sámi villages have to move the reindeer by trucks between certain spots. The conditions have thus changed radically over the last century, but even more so over the last three decades. Settlements and traffic have expanded, as has wind power, mining, and tourism, causing disruption particularly in the Forest Sámi reindeer herding area. Forest Sámi are throughout the year sharing territories with others, unlike mountain reindeer herders. Mountain reindeer herders, at least in those areas where there is so far no wind power, mining, or high presence of tourism, may withdraw to more undisturbed grazing lands during the summer.[23]

Henrik Andersson—Forest Sámi Reindeer Herder

Henrik Andersson, born in 1980, is of the Forest Sámi reindeer herding community, Gällivare Forest Sámi village, and the Flakaberg group. Growing up with reindeer herding, he has a lifelong education and expertise gained from working with earlier generations. Andersson started full time as a reindeer herder at the age of fifteen. Apart from his full-time work with the reindeer, he also works actively to protect the reindeer and the grazing and calving lands for future generations. He started posting in social media in 2012, documenting many aspects of his life and using the platforms to tell about the life as a reindeer herder, Sámi culture.[24]

Corona Diary of Henrik Andersson

Day one, March 1, 2020

I collected my reindeer out on the Island of Smultronskär so they won't stay behind when the ice is melting. This was also the day when I heard about Covid-19 for the first time.

March 13

My son's surviving skills in the wild may be useful now.[25] Because of the Covid-19 situation the borders are going to be closed. We do not know yet if the grocery trucks can pass the borders and can refill our stores with food. I bought some salt and coffee and all the other people at the store bought toilet paper. I found it funny, that this was so important for them in that situation.

March 14

Today I prepared some more stuff to be safe if the Covid-19 situation is going to be worse. I salted some reindeer meat so I can make dry meat out of it. If the borders will really be closed, we will have enough food for us to survive.

March 15

I taught my son and some volunteers how to take care of the reindeer hide. I think that this is important for them to know because of the current situation. Reindeer hide can be used, for example, to make tents and clothes, and you can use it for sitting and sleeping on. It is a good insulation material and it does not let any cold go through. The reindeer hair has a hollow space where there is air inside, which makes it light and gives it that good insulation ability.

Today and also thinking about the next days was very stressful for us. No one knew what is coming next and everyone was nervous about what to do.

March 16

Today I taught my son and my volunteers how to take care of the reindeer meat. Due the Covid-19 situation my volunteers were scared and they checked the news all the time. They were scared that they would get stuck here in the middle of nowhere for a long time. One of them ordered a ticket to go home and later on I drove her to the Finnish border. It was too risky for her to stay at my home because no one knew what was going to happen next.

March 17

Once per year I take my slicing machine out of the garage for making *renskav*.[26] Due to this machine being so hard to clean, I just do it all in one day. I freeze the reindeer meat until that day and I take it out again. Today I had 80 kilograms of meet to slice up, which will last 'til the next year.

March 18

Last tourist guiding for today. Everyone else canceled because of the Covid-19 situation. I guided fifty-six people this winter. Usually I guide around forty more, but sadly all of them had to cancel.

March 19

Today I am taking the last reindeer, which were used for the tourist guiding, to my home. Covid-19 is making me unemployed and the reindeer herd cost a lot of money to feed. I need to try to find some other work to earn enough money for feeding my herd through the winter.

March 20

I found a few reindeer out on the frozen sea.

March 21

Today I opened an Internet page that is called "adopt a reindeer." I need to open this page because feeding my herd is too expensive without my job as a tourist guide. I am out of income at the moment, which is why I had no other choice. The idea is that people can adopt a reindeer and give them names and pay for their food for the rest of the winter.

March 24

We are moving the reindeer to a place where the forest company cut all the trees down. The reindeer are eating from the branches there. An old forest—when at least 100 years old—has a lot of reindeer food—lichen—on the branches. It is good for a short window of time, but then it is of no use. It will be the last time that the reindeer can find some food in this area for the next 100 years, until the forest is fully grown again.

March 25

My son and I are testing some survivor skills. It is 15 degrees below zero and we slept in the *goahte* (like a tipi), which does not have any insulation. The cover is made of birch bark.

March 26

On the way home from our outstaying we drove the snowmobile and checked for wolverine and lynx tracks. We are not even noticing Corona up here.

March 28

Every day when we are feeding the reindeer we also have some time to fish a little. We dry the pikes for dog food.

March 29

Every second day a truck fully loaded with reindeer food is coming and even if it is in the morning evening or night when it's coming we need to load it up, no matter what time it is. My website is also starting to work. My first ten reindeer have been "adopted." This will give me a little extra income to pay for the food.

March 30

Every day we make some new holes in the ice to fish. Some of them we eat by ourselves and some of them are the dogs' food. Tonight we will also start to smoke some of them.

March 31

My son and I have fished now a hundred kilos of pike for our dog Tjubbo. It is really fun to teach my son our history and how important fishing was in our history as Sámi people.

April 1

While we are feeding the reindeer we are hearing the news over the radio about the current Covid-19 situation. If you look at the reindeer herd here it feels so far away from the real world.

Today my father helped to feed. He is a member of the risk group for Covid-19 but he refuses to stay away from the reindeer.

April 2

Today I should have been booked for guiding a big tourist group. Sadly they canceled because of the current situation. Maybe there will not be any tourist guiding for this spring any more.

April 3

My brother and his reindeer herd are on the way, moving by foot and he will arrive at my place probably tomorrow. It is about four months ago since we separated the herd. My cousin and his herd are also on the way to my place.

April 7

Six to seven thousand Swedish crowns, about six to seven hundred euros, is the cost of the reindeer food we are feeding, per day, and none of us have any big income since last fall. We do not have any chance to make any money because of the current situation. We will now need to start to borrow some money from family and friends.

April 8

I started to plant some flowers to get some summer feelings. I also planted some vegetables so I have something to eat, if the current situation gets worse because of Covid-19.

April 11

Today I had a phone conversation with the Sami Parliament to ask them where the promised money for the reindeer food is. That is the disaster support available when the winter grazing is not available. They promised to help us with half of the feeding cost, but we still did not get any money. The situation is starting to get harder and harder. At the moment we do not know if we have enough money to order the amount of reindeer food we need.

April 12

Today we tracked a bear that has been approaching the reindeer herd. It is very early for them to wake up from their winter hibernation. Now he is walking inside our herd of pregnant females. I already started to write to the county administration board to get the permission to shoot him.

April 13

After a sleepless night with a lot of writing and calls I drove out and found a dead reindeer. I called the county administrative board again and explained the situation. After this call I finally got the written permission to shoot the bear. To avoid any risks of being charged for a faulty way of hunting—something that has happened to several reindeer herders, causing severe problems and also causing hatred and verbal attacks—we use a helicopter for the protective hunting. It is terribly expensive, but we prefer this to ending up in a court process, and possibly prison. That way we can make sure to follow the detailed instructions from the county administrative board and also have a witness who can verify that we have done exactly as stated in the permission. However, during this time, because of the Corona restrictions we can be just two persons inside of the helicopter. So the pilot and another herder took off and 16 minutes later they landed again with the coordinates of where to get the bear. After we found him we loaded him in the car for the further transportation. It was a fully grown male.

April 15

Today when we met up I found many happy faces but there is also a lot to do with gathering the herd again after the bear attack. And my cousin is coming up today with his herd too.

April 16

Every day we drive around the herd twice a day to watch out to make sure no more bears are coming into the herd. The police helicopter is watching us so we are not doing anything stupid in their eyes, for example, killing another bear without any permissions. Yet, whenever I report to the police that my reindeer have been hurt or killed by poachers or haters, or that people let their dog chase reindeer—all prohibited by law—there is no available police who can follow up. Nothing happens. Is this how the system should be?

20th April

Today is my grandfather's birthday. My family and I could not celebrate his birthday because of the Covid-19 situation. So we just called him to congratulate but nothing more.

April 21

Today I did some machine service on the snowmobile. Because of the current situation it is not the easiest to get some new spare parts, so I ordered a spare snowmobile for the next season so I will not be dependent on those parts any more.

April 23

The hard snow makes the reindeer spread out to bigger areas to search for food. They are walking toward the calving grounds. In a few days they will arrive. Now we are putting our hands together and pray that the bears will spare us.

April 24

On this picture (see Figure 10.1) you can see how big a female's stomach is right before calving. In there is the next generation of reindeer. Whatever the current Covid-19 situation looks like, a new generation of reindeer will be born soon.

April 25

Everything went wrong today. My snowmobile broke, a tree hit me in my face, and the sun tried to make me blind. But I am still managing to drive around the herd two times a day. One good thing today: no predators in our way!

April 26

Some days there are still some reindeer left and it is great to see them, but today we stopped giving them food because we are bankrupt and they can find something to eat in the forest by now. It is finally springtime.

Figure 10.1 Female reindeer right before calving.
Photo by Henrik Andersson, April 24, 2020.

April 27

I saw the first reindeer calf of the season. For a few seconds all the problems we had in the winter were forgotten. All problems are only happiness in this moment. A new reindeer year started today.

April 28

Today I took a nice trip to the city and bought some flowers. The Covid-19 situation in the city was bad, which you do not notice while being in the forest herding the reindeer.

May 7

The calving is going on and we let the herd be until this time is finished. The calving season takes about one month.

May 14

While the calving is going on I am having some more free time for doing other things than reindeer herding. I've been living in this house for already five years and I never got the time to do renovations. Now I have some time, so I take the opportunity to build my veranda.

June 18

Today we repaired the corral and the bridge so we have a connection over the river. We have already put the herd together and we will start marking the calves after we fix this.

June 25

Today was finally the day when we marked all the calves. The Covid-19 situation made us build several fireplaces for protecting the old people. Usually we are all sitting together at one big fire within the breaks but now we split up into smaller groups.

July 2

This year's calf marking is going very well. Soon all calves will be marked. It usually takes us several days. Feeding the reindeer and hunting the predators resulted in the calving being the best in ten years. Now we are hoping that they will survive and that the herd will get the chance to recover from all the years that were very hard for the reindeer and us.

July 9

Today we were at the neighbor's calf marking. Our own calves are already finished but there are still a few calves that need to be marked at our neighbors' place in the Sami community. The Covid-19 situation is more noticeable by now because only one reindeer herder from every family is allowed go to other corrals.

July 16

I was fishing today and refilled my freezers. The lakes around here are full with such kind of fish. I have loved to fish since I was small and I used to do it every year.

August 6

At the moment I am picking a lot of cloudberries, day by day. There are big nice berries growing in the swamps and because of the Covid-19 situation, no other berry pickers are coming to collect them. So it's more to pick for myself.

September 6

Because of the Covid-19 situation, the company will buy less moose and reindeer meat from us and the prices are going down a lot compared to the past few years. This is happening because the restaurants are not having as many clients as they had before, and they are the ones who buy the most meat. Today's moose hunt went well and I shot a big bull.

Summary and Discussion

There are several themes showing up in Henrik Andersson's diary during the first months of Covid-19. News of the pandemic is causing concern and there are questions of what will it lead to, in terms of not only personal health, but also for the reindeer herding and associated income-generating activities such as tourism. Henrik Andersson discusses his responses in terms of preparation, noting the significance of access to food and learning how to live in traditional ways. He writes about how this knowledge may be necessary in the event of a major crisis and about how access to the natural resources in the lands and waters are of major importance for fishing and picking berries. In addition to this, Andersson writes about his own cultivation of vegetables and access to traditional medicine. Knowledge of how to conserve food, including drying and salting meat, is a part of Henrik Andersson's expertise. He and the people around him seem likely to do well in case of a major crisis.

The diaries show, however, that concerns are piling up. Grazing for the reindeer is bad in that particular year. The causes for it are mentioned in this selection of entries—the weather in fall, in combination with the contemporary industrial forestry practices destroying the grazing lands and the access to lichen. Infrastructural expansion has also made lands unavailable. During the fall 2019, the snow fell, melted, and then froze, causing the lichen to be locked in under ice and thus unavailable to the reindeer. While reindeer can dig through a thick cover of snow, they cannot dig through ice layers. Because of this, Henrik and many others had to feed the reindeer with pellets for a large part of the 2019–20 winter, as noted in the corona diary. He also notes that there is a specific kind of support that can be applied for from the Sámi Parliament, but that it covers at best up to 50 percent of the costs for the feeding. The winter of 2019–20 was thus very hard, and several of the Sámi reindeer herding villages had to apply for disaster support to feed their reindeer. Henrik Andersson describes how he uses the income from tourism to pay for such costs, but with the tourists canceling this becomes impossible. This was a major issue during the Covid-19 pandemic, as noted by the Sámi Parliament; support packages that were provided for Swedish companies did not help reindeer herders who lost income both from loss of sales and from loss of income from tourism.[27] To manage the income loss and get support with the feeding, Andersson set up a website for people to "adopt" a reindeer.

An aspect that shows up in the entries is the presence of volunteers, who were there when the pandemic restrictions started, as noted on March 15. In recent years, while still having to rely on farm hands for more complicated tasks, Henrik Andersson has started to accept volunteers. Today, as the internet makes it possible to get in touch over larger geographical distances, there are volunteers that come from Sweden and beyond. In exchange for a possibility to experience reindeer herding, a place to sleep, and food, they can assist with simpler tasks.

Another issue showing up in the diary is the annual concern around protecting the reindeer and newborn calves against predators. This is not a pandemic-related issue, but the predator policies of Sweden are causing the loss of a lot of calves and adult reindeer alike, while further disturbing the reindeer in their grazing.[28] Andersson describes an attack by a bear and how they have to work to get the authorization to kill the particular bear that has been killing their reindeer.

Once approved by the authorities to kill the bear, Andersson still has to make sure that he will not get in trouble and ultimately end up in prison. Everything must be done by the book, and there needs to be a witness to the authorized hunt. It is a common problem that reindeer herders might end up being prosecuted after having performed protective hunting. This is the reason for using a helicopter, as noted on April 13. Typically there would be two people in the helicopter, plus the pilot, but due to the restrictions, it was not possible on this day. The days after the hunt, he writes about how the herders work to protect the reindeer herd by driving around the herd twice per day, to make sure there are no other bears around. While they do this, they are monitored by the police from helicopters, indicating that rather than collaborating with the Sámi reindeer herders, the authorities treat them in a repressive way.

Another theme coming involves the recommendations for older people and people within risk groups to avoid social contacts to decrease the risk for being contaminated with Covid-19. Andersson's father is within the risk group, and according to the recommendations, he should have stayed away. Andersson's diary shows that it is of major importance for his father to come to work with the reindeer. Reindeer herding is a way of life; the whole family is valued, and to be left out of the work due to the restriction was very hard for the elders.

In this article, we have only entered the first few months of Henrik Andersson's corona diary, showing the initial thoughts, responses, and difficulties that emerged. As most are aware, the situation continued for very long. When this article was being finalized, in early 2023, the Covid-19 situation was far better, but still not completely over. The reindeer herding year continues its cycle, this last winter—2022–3—has been far better in terms of grazing due to weather conditions than described in the diary. It is soon time for the new calves to be born.

There has been very little study on the situation of the reindeer herders during the Covid-19 pandemic, at least not on the Swedish side of Sábme. Our research project, which was mainly data collection, has contributed to highlight a few of the issues at stake and will hopefully result in more research and writing on this subject.

Acknowledgments

The data collection was funded by FORMAS Dnr 2020-02706. An application for ethical review was submitted and approved (Dnr 2021-04114). The work with the article was funded by FORMAS Dnr 2016-01039, and FORMAS Dnr 2019-01975 within the Swedish National Research Program on Climate.

Notes

1. Donna Haraway, "Situated Knowledges: The Science Question in Feminism and the Privilege of Partial Perspective," *Feminist Studies* 14, no. 3 (1988): 575–99.
2. Pierre Nora, "Between Memory and History: Les Lieux De Mémoire," *Representations* 26 (1989): 7–24.
3. Inger Zachrisson, "The Sámi and Their Interaction with the Nordic Peoples," in *The Viking World*, ed. Stefan Brink and Neil S. Price (London: Routledge, 2012), 32–9.
4. Gunilla Larsson, "Forest Saami Heritage and History," in *Currents of Saami Pasts: Recent Advances in Saami Archaeology*, ed. Markus Fjellström, Anna-Kaisa Salmi, Marte Spangen, and Tiina Äikäs (Helsinki: Archaeological Society of Finland, 2020), 121–48, 135.
5. May-Britt Öhman, "Subttsasa Biehtsevuomátjistema: Recalling the Memories and Stories from Our Little Pine Forest," in *The Routledge Companion to Global Indigenous History*, ed. Ann McGrath and Lynette Russell (London: Routledge, 2022), 524–49, 539.
6. Sweden, *Constitutional Documents of Sweden: The Instrument of Government, the Riksdag Act, the Riksdag Regulations* (Stockholm: Swedish Riksdag, 1972), Ch. 1, Art.2, accessed March 1, 2023, https://www.riksdagen.se/globalassets/07.-dokument--lagar/the-instrument-of-government-2015.pdf.
7. Sametinget, "The Sami Parliament's Living Environment Program EALLINBIRAS," Sami Environmental Program, 2021, 4, accessed March 1, 2023, https://www.sametinget.se/158400?file_id=1.
8. Linda Tuhiwai Smith, *Decolonizing Methodologies: Research and Indigenous Peoples* (London: Zed Books, 1999).
9. Elsa Laula, *Inför lif eller död?: Sanningsord i de lappska förhållandena* (Stockholm: Wilhelmssons Boktryckeri, 1904).
10. Karin Stenberg, Valdemar Lindholm, and Arvidsjaursameh, *Dat läh mijen situd!: Det är vår vilja; En vädjan till den svenska nationen från samefolket* (Örnsköldsvik: Ågrens boktryckeri, 1920).

11. Patrik Lantto, *Tiden börjar på nytt: En analys av samernas etnopolitiska mobilisering i Sverige 1900–1950* (Umeå: Department of Historical Studies, Umeå University, 2000), 90–2.
12. Stenberg, Lindholm, and Arvidsjaursameh, *Dat läh mijen situd!*, 8. Translation from Swedish by the author.
13. Smith, *Decolonizing Methodologies*, 2.
14. Svein Disch Mathiesen, "Reindeer Husbandry in the Circumpolar North," in *Reindeer Husbandry: Adaptation to the Changing Arctic*, vol. 1, ed. Svein Disch Mathiesen, Inger Marie Gaup Eira, Ellen Inga Turi, Anders Oskal, Mikhail Pogodaev, and Marina Tonkopeeva (Cham: Springer, 2023), 1–14.
15. See, for example, Weronika Axelsson Linkowski, Kajsa Kuoljok, and Ann-Catrin Blind, *Ájddo—reflektioner kring biologisk mångfald i renarnas spår: en kunskapssammanställning om renar och renbete*, ed. Håkan Tunón and Brita Stina Sjaggo (Uppsala: Naptek, 2012).
16. Sven-Donald Hedman, "Boplatser och offerplatser: Ekonomisk strategi och boplatsmönster bland skogssamer 700–1600 AD," Doctoral Thesis, Umeå Universitet, Umeå, 2003, 225–7.
17. Gudrun Nordstedt, "A Land of One's Own: Sami Resource Use in Sweden's Boreal Landscape under Autonomous Governance," Doctoral Thesis, Swedish University of Agricultural Sciences, Umeå, 2018, 53–5.
18. Kristina Labba, "The Legal Organization of Sami Reindeer Herding and the Role of the Siida," in *Indigenous Rights in Scandinavia: Autonomous Sami Law*, ed. Christina Allard and Susann Funderud Skogvang (London: Routledge, 2016), 141–53.
19. The villages are identified and GIS-mapped at Sametinget, "Kartor som underlag för planer," Sametinget, 2022, accessed March 1, 2023, https://www.sametinget.se/underlag.
20. Labba, "The Legal Organization," 141 and subsequent.
21. Sametinget, "Rennäringens tillstånd 2020—Sametinget," Sametinget, 2020, accessed March 1, 2023, https://www.sametinget.se/158400?file_id=1.
22. Labba, "The Legal Organization," 141.
23. Henrik Andersson, personal communication, November 10, 2022.
24. Henrik Andersson, Facebook, accessed March 20, 2023, https://www.facebook.com/henrik.andersson.982.
25. Andersson's son, at that time 16 years old, spent an entire month on his own in the forest in the summer 2019. Hampus Andersson, May-Britt Öhman, and Petri Storlöpare, *When the Climate Apocalypse Comes I'll Make It: 16 Year Old Hampus Andersson's Survival Month Living off the Lands and Waters in the Forests of Norrbotten, Sweden* (Dálkke: Indigenous Climate Change Studies Research Group, 2020), accessed March 1, 2023, https://www.youtube.com/watch?v=AoQ79anZ0VA.
26. *Renskav* is thinly sliced reindeer meat, which is sautéed with butter when it is prepared for a meal. It needs to be sliced when the meat is frozen.
27. Sametinget, "Så påverkas renköttsbranschen av coronapandemin," Sametinget, June 7, 2020, accessed March 1, 2023, https://www.sametinget.se/150167.
28. See also, for instance Inger Maren Rivrud, Therese Ramberg Sivertsen, Atle Mysterud, Birgitta Åhman, Ole-Gunnar Støen, and Anna Skarin, "Reindeer Green-wave Surfing Constrained by Predators," *Ecosphere* 9, no. 5 (2018), https://doi.org/10.1002/ecs2.2210.

Bibliography

Andersson, Hampus, May-Britt Öhman, and Petri Storlöpare. "When the Climate Apocalypse Comes I'll Make It: 16 Year Old Hampus Andersson's Survival Month Living off the Lands and Waters in the Forests of Norrbotten, Sweden." Dálkke: Indigenous Climate Change Studies Research Group, 2020. Accessed March 1, 2023. https://www.youtube.com/watch?v=AoQ79anZ0VA.

Haraway, Donna. "Situated Knowledges: The Science Question in Feminism and the Privilege of Partial Perspective." *Feminist Studies* 14, no. 3 (1988): 575–99.

Hedman, Sven-Donald. "Boplatser och offerplatser: Ekonomisk strategi och boplatsmönster bland skogssamer 700–1600 AD." Doctoral Thesis, Umeå Universitet, Umeå, 2003.

Labba, Kristina. "The Legal Organization of Sami Reindeer Herding and the Role of the Siida." In *Indigenous Rights in Scandinavia: Autonomous Sami Law*, edited by Christina Allard and Susann Funderud Skogvang, 141–53. London; New York: Routledge, 2016.

Lantto, Patrik. *Tiden börjar på nytt: En analys av samernas etnopolitiska mobilisering i Sverige 1900–1950*. Umeå: Department of Historical Studies, Umeå University, 2000.

Larsson, Gunilla. "Forest Saami Heritage and History." In *Currents of Saami Pasts: Recent Advances in Saami Archaeology*, edited by Markus Fjellström, Anna-Kaisa Salmi, Marte Spangen, and Tiina Äikäs, 121–48. Helsinki: Archaeological Society of Finland, 2020.

Laula, Elsa. *Inför lif eller död?: Sanningsord i de lappska förhållandena*. Stockholm: Wilhelmssons Boktryckeri, 1904.

Linkowski, Weronika Axelsson, Kajsa Kuoljok, and Ann-Catrin Blind. *Ájddo—reflektioner kring biologisk mångfald i renarnas spår: en kunskapssammanställning om renar och renbete*, edited by Håkan Tunón and Brita Stina Sjaggo. Uppsala: Naptek, 2012.

Mathiesen, Svein Disch. "Reindeer Husbandry in the Circumpolar North." In *Reindeer Husbandry: Adaptation to the Changing Arctic*, vol. 1, edited by Svein Disch Mathiesen, Inger Marie Gaup Eira, Ellen Inga Turi, Anders Oskal, Mikhail Pogodaev, and Marina Tonkopeeva, 1–14. Cham: Springer, 2023.

Nora, Pierre. "Between Memory and History: Les Lieux De Mémoire." *Representations* 26 (1989): 7–24.

Nordstedt, Gudrun. "A Land of One's Own: Sami Resource Use in Sweden's Boreal Landscape under Autonomous Governance." Doctoral Thesis, Swedish University of Agricultural Sciences, Umeå, 2018.

Öhman, May-Britt. "Subttsasa Biehtsevuomátjistema: Recalling the Memories and Stories from Our Little Pine Forest." In *The Routledge Companion to Global Indigenous History*, edited by Ann McGrath and Lynette Russell, 524–49. London: Routledge, Taylor & Francis Group, 2022.

Rivrud, Inger Maren, Therese Ramberg Sivertsen, Atle Mysterud, Birgitta Åhman, Ole-Gunnar Støen, and Anna Skarin. "Reindeer Green-Wave Surfing Constrained by Predators." *Ecosphere* 9, no. 5 (2018). https://doi.org/10.1002/ecs2.2210.

Sametinget. "Kartor som underlag för planer." Sametinget, 2022. Accessed March 1, 2023. https://www.sametinget.se/underlag.

Sametinget. "Rennäringens tillstånd 2020—Sametinget." Sametinget, 2020. Accessed March 1, 2023. https://www.sametinget.se/158400?file_id=1.

Sametinget. "Så påverkas renköttsbranschen av coronapandemin." Sametinget, June 7, 2020. Accessed March 1, 2023. https://www.sametinget.se/150167.

Sametinget. "The Sami Parliament's Living Environment Program EALLINBIRAS." Sami Environmental Program, 2021. Accessed March 1, 2023. https://www.sametinget.se/158400?file_id=1.

Smith, Linda Tuhiwai. *Decolonizing Methodologies: Research and Indigenous Peoples.* London: Zed Books, 1999.

Stenberg, Karin, Valdemar Lindholm, and Arvidsjaursameh. *Dat läh mijen situd!: Det är vår vilja; En vädjan till den svenska nationen från samefolket.* Örnsköldsvik: Ågrens boktryckeri, 1920.

Sweden. *Constitutional Documents of Sweden: The Instrument of Government, the Riksdag Act, the Riksdag Regulations.* Stockholm: Swedish Riksdag, 1972. Accessed March 1, 2023. https://www.riksdagen.se/globalassets/07.-dokument--lagar/the-instrument-of-government-2015.pdf.

"When the Climate Apocalypse Comes I'll Make It: 16 Year Old Hampus Andersson's Survival Month Living off the Lands and Waters in the Forests of Norrbotten, Sweden." Dálkke: Indigenous Climate Change Studies Research Group, 2020. Accessed March 1, 2023. https://www.youtube.com/watch?v=AoQ79anZ0VA.

Zachrisson, Inger. "The Sámi and Their Interaction with the Nordic Peoples." In *The Viking World*, edited by Stefan Brink and Neil S. Price. London: Routledge, 2012.

Part III

Minority Rights and Their Politization

11

Staying in Contact: The Role of Minorities in Diplomatic Contacts between Western Europe and Southeast Asia after Decolonization

Andreas Weiß

This chapter examines how the question of human rights, with a focus on minorities, structured the relations between the European Communities (ECs) and its partners, here ASEAN, the Association of Southeast Asian Nations. For doing so, I investigate how the institutions of the ECs used human right issues in their interactions with their partner. I also trace how different institutions, especially the European Commission and the European Parliament, and also the member states used the human rights discourse and how debates between the ECs and ASEAN developed over time. Some of these questions have been discussed in political science publications with a focus on the 1990s, when the Asian financial crisis delegitimized the "Asian Value" debate. The topic, however, still misses a comprehensive historical analysis.[1]

I develop my argument in three steps. First, I briefly explain the common European stand on human rights keeping in mind the long entangled history between several ECs member states and ASEAN countries. In 1973, with France, the Netherlands, and the United Kingdom, three out of nine members had a not so distant colonial past in Southeast Asia. Later, this number even rose with Portugal and Spain. All former colonial powers had used minorities as auxiliaries and collaborators during their rule. In a second step, I sketch out the relations between the ECs and ASEAN, regarding the question of minority human rights. Finally, I turn to one concrete example that exemplifies the complicated Gordian knot of propagating human rights, making Realpolitik and confronting one's own colonial past: the question of Indonesia's colonialism toward West Papua and East Timor.[2]

The European Communities and Human Rights

The issue of human rights in the European integration history is a complicated one. The early documents of the institutions, such as the Treaty of Rome, did not mention human rights. Yet, all member states of the ECs were signatories of the European

Convention on Human Rights (formally "Convention for the Protection of Human Rights and Fundamental Freedoms," 1950), based on the Universal Declaration of Human Rights.[3] Likewise, they were members of the institution behind the declaration, the Council of Europe. In the 1990s, minority rights emerged as an important issue during the Eastern Enlargement of the Union. This process proved to be significant for the development of international law, as the European Union included the question of minority and human rights into the accession treaties in an attempt to assign new responsibilities for minority groups, like Sinti and Roma, to the new member states.[4]

To understand the arguments of the ECs in favor of human rights, we have to keep two things in mind. One, the European Economic Community, the core of the Communities was created against the experiences of the Second World War. That left the Communities with the idea that everything should be undertaken to save lives, protect minorities, and defend the rule of law. Nonetheless, that thinking was initially state-centered and implied the existence of an (ill-defined) state population equalized with the majority population. During the 1970s, the process to codify these questions gained momentum. The 1973 adopted "Declaration on Europe's Identity," which stated that the "respect for human rights" is a "fundamental element[s] of the European identity"; the summit itself was convinced that "this will enable them [the ECs, AW] to achieve a better definition of their relations with other countries and of their responsibilities and the place which they occupy in world affairs."[5] The ensuing Helsinki Process made the question of human rights not only an internationally important one, but also significant for the commission.[6] With the intention to influence the further direction of the political path of the European integration process, the body felt it had to support topics that spoke to a wider audience.[7]

However, there were more reasons to shift the attention to human rights and to clarify the standpoint of the ECs regarding the rights of minorities. One reason for this was the membership application of Franco's Spain. Most member states held the opinion that an authoritarian state should not be allowed to enter the Communities. Another reason was the widespread conviction among the members to the necessity to further adjust the Communities' foreign policies and common positions abroad "in accordance with the purposes and principles of the United Nations Charter."[8] Against this background, more references to human rights were included in European legislations, for instance, in the 1986 Single European Act. But only with the Copenhagen Criteria of 1993, human rights were written into the *acquis communautaire* (the body of European Union law) of the then European Union. This process only found its conclusion with the Charter of Fundamental Rights of the European Union, proclaimed at the end of the year 2000, but entering full legal status only in 2009 with the Treaty of Lisbon. The question what counts as a protected minority, however, was and still is defined by the single member state.

The other issue to keep in mind is the question of executive power of the ECs concerning the use of military force, as this tool of foreign policy is the prerogative of the member states. This makes the Communities' proclamations and demands to keep the standards of human rights and minority issues not only assailable. The larger problem is that these demands cannot be enforced, as the only international power the Community has is economic sanctions, a tool it only rarely uses—and if it does, often not to its full extent, being an economic unity containing diverse interests. Economic sanctions also can conflict with the proclaimed interest to protect minorities. The questions remain of how far you defend human rights when that might complicate your relationship with trading partners? And, how do you protect minorities, even under a UN umbrella, if you are not ready to use force?

The European Communities, ASEAN, and the Question of Cold War Refugees

Regarding the question of human rights, European intervention, and ASEAN, we find a complex picture when looking into the secondary literature, which emphasizes changing viewpoints and perspectives on the behavior of the ECs/European Union. While some authors stated that ASEAN respected human rights, for example, Jürgen Dauth in 1979, others, like Bernhard Stahl, wrote that human rights only really became an issue after the Tiananmen massacre, but especially the question of Timor-Leste (Portuguese for East Timor) put it on the agenda, a point questioned in the latter part of this chapter.[9]

Dauth's article is of interest here not only as it was part of a special issue on China after the death of Mao for the bulletin *Aus Politik und Zeitgeschichte*, the supplement of the periodical *Das Parlament*, edited by the German Bundestag, but also as it gives a contemporary impression differing from the later analyses. The interesting point of Dauth's intervention is his mentioning of the human rights question in the context of debates on ZOPFAN, the Zone of Peace, Freedom and Neutrality, a Malayan proposal signed by the other ASEAN members in 1971 with the intention to reduce East–West tensions in the region. Dauth held the opinion that Vietnam regarded this concept as directed against it, as the ASEAN definition of freedom would include human rights.[10]

The question of the Vietnamese "boat people" was a hotly debated one in the late 1970s and early 1980s, as Southeast Asia was a hotbed of the proxy wars of the "Cold War," something that by itself created many problems.[11] The issue was in such a way present that it influenced the Bali declaration of 1979: "With regard to the refugees, the President said that ASEAN had exerted great efforts in tackling the problems in providing temporary accommodation, and had arranged processing centers for the refugees, based on humanitarian considerations in cooperation with UNHCR."[12] The background to this statement by the then President of Indonesia, Suharto, was the refugee crisis initiated by the Indochina wars, both the Vietnam War and the Vietnamese occupation of Cambodia. Like the ECs, ASEAN member states hardly acted in one voice regarding minorities and human rights, but referred to the UN as sole arbiter. Furthermore, Suharto explained that he "regretted that the influx of refugees had increased in immense proportions lately, which had forced ASEAN countries to reconsider further assistance. This was done for the sake of preserving peace and stability of the region, necessitated by the need to expedite the implementation of development." He stated therefore that ASEAN regarded help granted to refugees not as a human right but as an additional surplus. This interpretation is supported by a later statement made by the ASEAN Foreign Ministers, saying, "The unrestricted flow of Indochinese displaced persons and illegal immigrants (refugees) has further exacerbated the situation in the region."[13] Unclear here is how much the notion of the Indochinese refugees as illegal was coined by the ethnic ascription as Chinese.

The European Parliament used the publicity of the Vietnamese refugee crisis to expand its power by involving itself in debates about future cooperation between the ECs and ASEAN. For doing so, it also put the issue of human rights on the table before the 1990s, the period regarded by some authors as "dominated by controversy over human rights violations in Southeast Asia."[14] This becomes clear from political statements issued in the 1970s. As the question of "human rights" was on the political agenda of the ECs from 1973 onward, a process started in which "the self-definition of the EC's external role shifted from 'civilian' ... to 'normative' power, seeing itself more and more as a promoter of human rights in Europe and abroad."[15] This development also allowed the weakest political institution, the European Parliament, to engage more actively in politics. Its solely verbal interventions in Third World affairs were politically a low-risk maneuver for Europe, as the ASEAN states could ignore European parliamentary demands as long as its legitimate base, and power, was rather low. In 1975, the French communist Member of the European Parliament (MEP), Marie-Thérèse Goutmann, had directed an official question to the commission, regarding the role of human rights and its defense in the relations with Southeast Asia. Her question had concerned the existence of concentration camps in Indonesia. The commission, however, had answered unspecific stating that it would always condemn any violation of human rights. And a "report drawn up on behalf of the Committee on External Economic Relations on the outcome of the visit by a delegation from the European Parliament to the countries of the Association of South-East Asian Nations (ASEAN)" by James Scott-Hopkins from June 29, 1976, stated,

> In the political sphere, while recognizing the differences in situation and history as well as the principles of non-interference which must be respected it would be wrong to overlook a priori the indirect influence of the Community on its partners in such sensitive but vital areas as the defence and restoration of civil liberties, representative democracy or basic human rights.[16]

The report especially mentioned Indonesia and that the delegation raised the issue of human rights during the meetings. But Scott-Hopkins saw the weakness of the European position by speaking of "indirect influence." His view was in line with the thinking of the commission, which strove to offer legal aid and institutional assistance to develop the newly independent countries.

Discussions regarding human rights between the two partners could also turn conflictual. A high point in this regard was the conference in Manila 1992, which was strained by European insistence to respect human rights.[17] The importance attached to the question of human rights further showed in 1996 when the EU developed a common standpoint on Eastern Timor (see later) with the African, Caribbean and Pacific Group of States (ACP)[18] and condemned Myanmar for its "absence of progress towards democratization and at the continuing violation of human rights."[19] The Economic and Social Committee went even further that year and stated:

Dialogue on human rights is a delicate matter. The Committee reiterates its earlier calls for inclusion of a social clause in the work programme of the World Trade Organization, based on ILO Conventions. On the specific question of East Timor, the Committee considers that a Council "troika" should hammer out a diplomatic solution based on the UN General Assembly resolutions.[20]

Thorny Issues: Minorities as Proxies in Political Debates?

A conflict that became an issue for the Communities was the Indonesian occupation of "Irian Jaya" (West Papua), the former Netherlands New Guinea, and Eastern Timor after the Dutch and Portuguese withdrawals. The European founding treaties of 1957, for both EURATOM and the EEC, regarded Netherlands New Guinea as integral part of the Kingdom of the Netherlands.[21] What was more, the Papua and the East Timor question were intertwined for Indonesia as the country feared already in 1977 that its earlier occupation of East Timor would again influence its relations with the Netherlands.[22]

The bloody occupation of East Timor became again a hotly debated topic in the public spheres after the killing of five Western journalists in 1977, so much that members of the British Parliament felt it important to enquire the Foreign and Commonwealth Offices (FCO) about the situation on the ground in public sessions.[23] Despite the voiced concerns, the British government did not discuss stopping aid to Indonesia against the background of general cuts in foreign aid.[24] At this time, the United Kingdom had the Presidency of the European Council. Yet, it seems that the British apolitical stance did not find common ground among all members states as the next Copenhagen resolution emphasized again the importance of human rights. Here the main thrust were the member states themselves who pointed to the external dimension in the "aims of the Communities," which was understood as an indirect hint on the European Political Co-operation.[25]

The East Timor question was likewise a hot topic in the UN meetings in the 1970s and 1980s and its mentioning became such a "nuisance" that the Indonesian ambassador to West Germany intervened in Bonn, for example, in 1981.[26] Since 1975, Portugal had started petitions against Indonesia based on its function as the "administering power" in the United Nations.[27] With the Indonesian occupation of East Timor in late 1975 and the ensuing fighting, Portugal also became a safe haven for Timorese refugees, not only for former white settlers who left the colonies after the new Portugal declared its retreat after the "Carnation Revolution." The Indonesian interventions seemed to be successful for a while, as West Germany abstained always in the period between 1975 and 1982.[28]

The German restrain, however, has seemingly also other reasons: one might have been the US government's acceptance of Indonesia incorporating East Timor during the 1970s, another one that the German government hoped to sell weapons and military ships to Indonesia.[29] The British, too, felt in 1984, that the "Indonesians ... have been quite successful in steadily eroding the Portuguese position at the United Nations."[30] The division of the Community on this issue shows in the preparatory paper for a meeting between the British prime minister Margaret Thatcher and the Portuguese government in 1984. It states that the community abstained from the voting in the UN General Assembly on this issue except Ireland and Greece voting with Portugal.[31] A confidential paper prepared for the thirty-ninth session of the United Nations General Assembly, written on September 6, 1984, made this point more explicit:

> 9. But we try to avoid antagonising the Indonesians over an issue which they feel deeply and on which they are not susceptible to argument. Indonesia occupies a key strategic position in South East Asia. It is a member of ASEAN, which we regard as an important stabilising factor in the region. The European Community have been steadily developing their relations with ASEAN since 1972. The process culminated in 1977 in the establishment of a formal "dialogue." The Nine abstained on the General Assembly resolution of December 1976 and do so on similar resolutions from 1978 to 1982. The exceptions are the Greeks and the Irish. Greece has consistently voted against Indonesia because of the implications of the East Timor issue for Cyprus; Ireland also voted against Indonesia at the 1982 General Assembly we believe on human rights grounds.[32]

Things seemed to become more complicated with the Portuguese accession ahead, as the same document indicates, but does not state directly. Portugal had applied for accession already in 1977. That it would enter the Community was clear from 1980 onward, at the latest, when Greece got its go. However, only with the finalization of the negotiations in 1985 it became a fact. Despite the existence of the East Timor Question, the commission held until 1985 the opinion that

> the subject of Timor has not been on the agenda of the meetings held by the Commission within the framework of EEC-Asean [sic] cooperation, which deal essentially with commercial and economic matters. It should also be noted that the subject does not appear to have been raised at the regular meetings which Parliament's Asean delegation has held with the Asean Inter-Parliamentary Organization. 4. The problem of Timor has not been discussed in talks with Portugal.[33]

Shortly afterward this restraint was given up:

> The Ten are carefully monitoring the confidential negotiations taking place between Portugal and Indonesia on the East Timor problem. The situation in this territory and reports of human rights violations have been discussed in European political cooperation. Certain Member States have expressed their concern to the Indonesian authorities on this matter.[34]

Nonetheless, the Indonesians clearly tried to continue influencing the common voting decision of the European Community (EC), as they contacted all the embassies in Jakarta in connection with the postponement of the debate on East Timor in 1984, as it happened in the year(s) before.[35]

But the main reason for the British abstaining in the UN votes seemed not only that they wanted to be on friendly terms with both sides, but also that the British government disliked the "wording in the resolutions which has equated self-determination with independence."[36] Another preparatory paper implied mundane reasons:

> 2. Invasion was condemned in two UN Security Council resolutions (1975, 1976). Since 1976 UK has abstained on Annual General Assembly resolutions calling for self-determination (wording has implied independence which is unacceptable to Indonesia, with whom we wish to maintain good relations and our increasingly valuable export market). There was no resolution last year as the Secretary-General decided to present his report on East Timor at the next session. In 1982, a modified and less confrontational resolution drew from us an abstention with the rest of EC (except Greece and Ireland) and an explanation of vote. SETTLEMENT [sic] 3 There are recent signs of a Portuguese search for a face-saving compromise. We consider matter is primarily bilateral problem—involvement of international bodies might be counter-productive (difficult to see Indonesia accepting UN role). We have stated our readiness to help if asked to. Integration into Indonesia is probably the only viable solution.[37]

But the statement delivered to the UN read as follows:

> "In abstaining on the resolution on East Timor contained in document L8, I should like to stress that the United Kingdom is conscious of the fact that the co-sponsors have made substantial effort this year to table a more constructive text than we have seen at past sessions. The United Kingdom continues to believe that the people of East Timor deserve the opportunity to determine their own future in accordance with their own political aspirations unaffected by pressures of one kind or another. Our earnest hope is that following this debate, a more favorable atmosphere can be created for a dialogue between the two countries who alone have it in their power to resolve this issue: Portugal and Indonesia. As a friend of both, we urge them to make every effort to do so because we firmly believe that a solution fair and acceptable to all concerned can be found by diplomatic means. In particular we appeal to them both to do all in their power to find a settlement which will be in accordance with the wishes and interests of the people of East Timor.[38]

The situation had gained further tension in 1983 when Indonesia increased its military activity in East Timor that showed to be successful. At the same time, the Southeast Asian state intensified propagating its standpoint on the East Timor Question. As a consequence, the European Parliament discussed again the question of refugees from West Papua in 1985. With Portugal being a European Union member state since 1986, the question of East Timor was used to put pressure on ASEAN and especially Indonesia to respect the will of the Timorese people. In 1991, Portugal sued Australia in the International Court of Justice, because Australia signed the Timor Gap Treaty to exploit maritime oil resources in the area, thereby accepting Indonesia's claim on East Timor, while Portugal regarded itself still as the administering power, defending the Timorese right to self-determination.[39]

The conflict between Portugal and Indonesia, and the involvement of Australia in it, followed similar lines as an earlier, similar conflict, the abovementioned between the Netherlands and Indonesia on West Papua. There, and in difference, Australia stood with the Netherlands and West Germany supported the later position in the NATO.[40] That they were regarded as combined is demonstrated in the documents. In 1988, the European Parliament stated that the immigration of hundreds of thousands of Indonesians to Irian Jaya "is seriously undermining the ethnic identity of the indigenous Papuans."[41] The same document declared that there are many human right issues in Indonesia, "especially serious in the territory of East Timor, subject since 1975 to forcible occupation by Indonesian troops, which prevents the people of East Timor from exercising their right to self-determination and from having their fundamental rights – especially, in many cases, the right to life – respected."

Conclusion

The chapter has demonstrated that the question of human rights in the cooperation between the ECs and ASEAN was discussed not only against a real humanitarian interest, but was also used as a political argument. The same seems to be true for the question of minorities: as it was often not clear at all if their rights became a topic as they were considered in danger—like nowadays the Rohingya—or the interest in them was connected to larger issues, such as deforestation or border conflicts.

The analyzed debates have to be seen in their specific time frames and contexts, nonetheless, human rights and the protection of minorities was an issue for the ECs, especially for the parliament. The concern for human rights was closely tied to the question of "norms" that constituted the heart of the foundation of the ECs, who turned self-confident to the self-description as "civil-normative superpower" in the 1990s, when the commission itself took up the issue.

What the chapter has shown is that the debate on human rights gave weak institutions, such as the European Parliament, and smaller member states, for instance, the Netherlands and Portugal, the opportunity to exert a stronger influence on the foreign policy of the ECs then could be expected from the political power small states normally hold in international affairs.

In the case of East Timor, it seems very likely that the Indonesian state saw European interventions as undermining its sovereignty, interfering in its internal affairs and as a neo-colonial maneuver. For the EC, taking a standpoint regarding the boat people and East Timor, however, became a question of universal human rights. While there has been and continues to be voiced criticism that this position is a Eurocentric one, the European institutions are convinced that human rights are an important political issue. Hence, being part of the EC could assist smaller countries in their geopolitical claims as highlighted in Portugal's case.[42] This is especially obvious when compared to the situation of the Netherlands around 1960, when the question of the transfer of West Papua was discussed and Amsterdam had to concede to American pressure. Now, in the 1970s, the Community had really began to coordinate and strengthen its foreign policy, a process culminating in the initiatives of the early 1990s.

Furthermore, the different outcome in both these two cases (Irian Jaya and East Timor) demonstrate the increased importance of human rights since the 1970s. In the early 1960s, it was still possible to ignore this question politically. In the 1970s, human rights began to dominate the media, and in the 1990s, they could stop negotiations. This was perhaps also a lesson learned, as the newly decolonized states rarely stopped their own human rights abuses when not pressured by others. Minority rights seemed secondary to the creation of the new nation(s)—and the new nationalism that came with it.

Notes

1. Maria-Gabriela Manea, "The Constitution of Collective Identities and Interregional Human Rights Norms Diffusion: Analyzing Human Rights Interactions and Discourses in the EU-ASEAN Relations and the ASEM Process." Doctoral Thesis, Freiburg im Breisgau, Universität, 2021, esp. 136-273, accessed November 5, 2023, https://d-nb.info/1236550250/34. See for the connection between the Asian crisis and the delegitimization of the "Asian Values" debate, Amitav Acharya, *The Making of Southeast Asia: International Relations of a Region* (Singapore: ISEAS, Institute of Southeast Asian Studies, 2012), 242-3.
2. José Ramos-Horta, UN representative of Fretilin, used the term "third-world colonialism" in regard to new expansionist policies of decolonized states and used it in UN debates.
3. The European Communities were established in 1967 after the fusion of European Economic Community (EEC), European Atomic Energy Community (Euratom), and the European Coal and Steel Community (ECSC) under one Commission and with one Parliament.
4. Bernd Rechel, *Minority Rights in Central and Eastern Europe* (London: Routledge, 2009); James Hughes and Gwendolyn Sasse, "Monitoring the Monitors: EU Enlargement Conditionality and Minority Protection in the CEECs," *Journal on Ethnopolitics and Minority Issues in Europe* 4, no. 1 (2003): 1-37.
5. European Communities, "Declaration on European Identity," *Bulletin of the European Communities* 6 (1973), 12, 118-22, here 119 §I.1.
6. The Helsinki Process, also known after its most important conference, the Conference on Security and Co-operation in Europe (CSCE), was a series of East-West conferences during the early 1970s, originally to de-escalate the Cold War. In the end, the documents guaranteed minority rights especially in the Communist bloc.
7. One example is the support of the Commission for "Southern" positions in the North–South relations; see Andreas Weiß, "Auf der Suche nach dem Süden: Die Europäischen Gemeinschaften und ihr Blick nach Süden in den 1970er und 1980er Jahren," in *Nord/Süd. Perspektiven auf eine Globale Konstellation*, ed. Jürgen Dinkel, Steffen Fiebrig, and Frank Reichherzer (Berlin: De Gruyter Oldenburg, 2020), 65-84.
8. Declaration on European Identity, 120 §II.9. The United Nations were an important frame of reference for both the EC and ASEAN in the 1960s and 1970s, even if their real influence was rather limited.

9. Jürgen Dauth, "ASEAN—Die Gemeinschaft der südostasiatischen Nationen," *Aus Politik und Zeitgeschichte* 8 (1979): 31–43; Bernhard Stahl, "Die Beziehungen der Europäischen Union zur ASEAN: Zwischen ökonomischen Interessen und schlechtem Gewissen," in *Die Europäische Union als Akteur der Weltpolitik*, ed. Klaus Schubert and Gisela Müller-Brandeck-Bocquet (Opladen: Leske+Budrich, 2000), 157–72. On the positions of ASEAN regarding human rights and the establishment of the Regional Working Group for the Establishment of Regional Human Rights Mechanisms (RWGHR), see Maria-Gabriela Manea, "The Claims of the ASEAN to Human Rights and Democracy: What Role for Regional Civil Society?," *ASIEN* 136 (July 2015): 73–97. More critical, Jimmy Masilamani and Logan Peterson, "The 'ASEAN Way': The Structural Underpinnings of Constructive Engagement," *Foreign Policy Journal*, October 15, 2014.
10. Dauth, "ASEAN," 35. The declaration itself does not contain the words "human rights" and speaks only of "equal rights" (https://www.pmo.gov.my/wp-content/uploads/2019/07/ZOPFAN.pdf), accessed November 5, 2023.
11. As the topic of the Vietnamese refugees is widely analyzed in the literature, especially the institutionalization of humanitarian aid, I will not use it here, for the sake of space; see, for example, Bertrand Taithe, "Reinventing (French) Universalism: Religion, Humanitarianism and the 'French Doctors,'" *Modern & Contemporary France* 12, no. 2 (2004): 147–58 and in Peter Gatrell, "'Villages of Discipline' Revolutionary Change and Refugees in South-East Asia," in *The Making of the Modern Refugee* (Oxford: Oxford University Press, 2013), 203–22 (chapter 7); Michael Vössing, *Humanitäre Hilfe und Interessenpolitik. Westdeutsches Engagement für Vietnam in den 1960er und 1970er Jahren* (Göttingen: Vandenhoeck & Ruprecht, 2018).
12. Joint Communique of the Twelfth ASEAN Ministerial Meeting Bali, June 28–30, 1979, 2 (https://www.nas.gov.sg/archivesonline/data/pdfdoc/1404-1979-06-30.pdf); accessed November 5, 2023. As the convener of this conference, Indonesia had a special role in the ASEAN ceremonial; additionally, Indonesia is the biggest member state, both by area and by population, also being the largest Islamic democracy in the world.
13. Ibid., 3. On general positions of Southeast Asian states toward refugees, see Sebastien Moretti, "Keeping up Appearances. State Sovereignty and the Protection of Refugees in Southeast Asia," *European Journal of East Asian Studies* 17 (2018): 3–30.
14. Even if the regular dialogue between the European Parliament and the ASEAN Inter-Parliamentarian Organization (AIPO) started in 1975, Manea sees the tensions mainly in the EC–ASEAN interregional dialogue; see Manea, "Constitution of Collective Identities," 157, 160. Also Kenneth Christie and Denny Roy emphasize the importance of the 1990s when it comes to Indonesia; see Kenneth Christie and Roy Denny, eds., *The Politics of Human Rights in East Asia* (London: Pluto Press, 2001).
15. Manea, "Constitution of Collective Identities," 144.
16. James Scott-Hopkins, "Report Drawn Up on Behalf of the Committee on External Economic Relations on the Outcome of the Visit by a Delegation from the European Parliament to the Countries of the Association of South-East Asian Nations (ASEAN) and on Future Relations between the European Community and ASEAN," *European Parliament Working Documents 1976–1977*, Document 181/76, June 29, 1976, 15. James Scott-Hopkins was a British MEP and the rapporteur for this report.

17. "Joint Answer to Written Questions Nos. 1834/91, 1835/91, 1838/91, 1839/91, 1842/91, and 1843/91 Given by Mr. Marin on behalf of the commission (July 2, 1993)," *Official Journal of the European Communities*, no. C283, October 20, 1993, 4–5.
18. "Joint Assembly of the Convention Concluded between the African, Caribbean and Pacific States and the European Community (ACP-EU): Resolution on the Occupation of East Timor by Indonesia," *Official Journal of the European Commission C 062*, February 27, 1997, 53.
19. "Common Position of 28 October 1996 Defined by the Council on the Basis of Article J.2 of the Treaty on European Union, on Burma/Myanmar," *Official Journal of the European Commission* L287, November 8, 1996, 1–2.
20. Carlos Ferrer, "Opinion on Relations between the European Union and ASEAN," *Official Journal of the European Communities*, no. C97, April 1, 1996, 31–45, here 32. Human rights are mentioned another twelve times in this text.
21. Treaty establishing the European Economic Community, Protocol on the Application of the Treaty establishing the European Economic Community to the non-European parts of the Kingdom of the Netherlands:

    > THE HIGH CONTRACTING PARTIES [sic!], ANXIOUS [sic!], at the time of signature of the Treaty establishing the European Economic Community, to define the scope of the provisions of Article 227 of this Treaty in respect of the Kingdom of the Netherlands, HAVE AGREED [sic!] upon the following provisions, which shall be annexed to this Treaty: The Government of the Kingdom of the Netherlands, by reason of the constitutional structure of the Kingdom resulting from the Statute of 29 December 1954, shall, by way of derogation from Article 227, be entitled to ratify the Treaty on behalf of the Kingdom in Europe and Netherlands New Guinea only."

22. Foreign and Commonwealth Offices FCO 15/2252/4, press article. The Netherlands requested also a copy from the Dunn report, see ibid., 2.
23. FCO 15/2255 (1977), Atrocities in East Timor, for example, 86–90, 95–8. The British files clearly demonstrate that some members of the FCO tried to delegitimize the Dunn report. The public interest was also demonstrated by requests by the public to have a look into the British ministerial archives, a request denied by reference to the 30-year rule. The request was for a master thesis on "British Attitudes to the Annexation of East Timor"; see FCO 15/4003 (1984), Indonesian occupation of East Timor: UK foreign policy; Commonwealth views, 4.
24. FCO 15/2255, 86/E. The protocol between the Labour Minister of State for Foreign and Commonwealth Affairs, Lord Goronwy-Roberts, and the Indonesian Ambassador to the United Kingdom, Admiral Subano, mentions on various occasions the question of human rights, but Lord Goronwy-Roberts also stressed the political objective of noninterference. He became, however, at one point more explicit:

    > Lord Goronwy-Roberts said Cambodia seemed to be going mad. They needed aid from outside, but reports of atrocities would not help them. There was a message in this for Indonesia: do everything possible on human rights. The new President, Carter, was concerned about this issue, and he was a friend worth having. (Ibid.: 5)

25. Conclusions of the sessions of the European Council, Copenhagen, April 7–8, 1978, 99, accessed November 5, 2023, http://aei.pitt.edu/1440/1/Copenhagen_1978.pdf.

26. PA AA 323.42-22978, Archivliste der Botschaft Kuala Lumpur 1974–1982, Telex, November 9, 1981, Kuala Lumpur.
27. One can deduct from the online archive of the United Nations that the number of resolutions and debates around the "East Timor Question" clearly rises after 1979, a time frame that also coincides with accession negotiations with the ECs.
28. Some historians regard the mid-1970s as a turning point in Southeast Asian-European relations; see Till Florian Tömmel, *Bonn, Jakarta und der Kalte Krieg. Die Außenpolitik der Bundesrepublik Deutschland gegenüber Indonesien von 1952 Bis 1973* (Berlin: De Gruyter Oldenburg, 2018), 298. For the voting behavior, see https://etan.org/etun/Unvotes.htm, accessed January 20, 2023.
29. For the US acceptance see FCO 15/2252, 43. For the arms deals, see Tömmel, *Bonn, Jakarta und der Kalte Krieg*, 319–20. The German Embassy suspected since 1965 that Indonesia wanted to occupy East Timor; Tömmel, *Bonn, Jakarta und der Kalte Krieg*, 202, fn. 360.
30. FCO 15/4002 (1984), Relations between Portugal and East Timor, 7. It is interesting that the FCO collected a file on this issue in the year that accession agreements on the joining of Spain and Portugal to the ECs were finalized.
31. Ibid., 5, 1. The paper states that Great Britain not only did not support Timorese independence, but also abstained from voting because of "avoiding offence to Portugal or Indonesia, both friendly countries." The UK did not regard human rights as an issue important enough to alienate Indonesia over it; ibid., 2. This seems to be in contrast with the handwritten remarks on a later item in the same file, that the prime minister had a "ready sympathy for the Portuguese point of view"; ibid., 3. There are other hints to a coordination of voting habits in this question; see FCO 15/4004 (1984), Relations between East Timor and the United Nations, 21.
32. FCO 15/4004/18.
33. "Written Question No. 914/84 by Mr. Klaus Hansch (S–D) to the Commission of the European Communities (24 October 1984) (85/C 39/22): Subject: East Timor, Answer given by Mr Haferkamp on behalf of the Commission (14 December 1984)," *Official Journal of the European Communities*, no. C39, February 11, 1985, 14. Wilhelm Haferkamp was the commissioner for external relations at that time.
34. "Written Question No 392/85 by Mr Ernest Glinne (S–B) to the Foreign Ministers of the 10 Member States of the European Community meeting in political cooperation (8 May 1985) (85/C 233/55): Subject: Self-determination for the people of East Timor, Answer (15 July 1985)," *Official Journal of the European Communities*, no. C233, September 12, 1985, 29–30, here 29.
35. FCO 15/4004/19. See also FCO 15/4004/18, "EAST TIMOR UK AIMS: 1. To avoid taking a position which risks giving offence to either Portugal or Indonesia. 2. To act, as far as possible, in concert with our EC colleagues."
36. Ibid., 17. This position was nonetheless problematic, as the abovementioned classified document stated that Great Britain faced a similar position at the Falklands, Gibraltar and, among others, Belize; reason, why they voted in 1975 and 1976 against the occupation.
37. FCO 15/4003/1, 1.
38. Ibid., Annex A.
39. Roger S. Clark, "Some International Law Aspects of the East Timor Affair," *Leiden Journal of International Law* 5, no. 2 (1992): 265–71. Clark argued that Indonesia

has no claim and legal right to East Timor whatsoever and that the question of human rights in criticizing Indonesia was secondary to East Timorese rights to self-determination. In 1992, Portugal even blocked a cooperation treaty between ASEAN and the EC and got the Netherlands, West Germany, Belgium, and Luxembourg on its side to criticize Indonesian human rights violation at the abovementioned conference in Manila.

40. Christiaan Penders, *The West New Guinea Debacle: Dutch Decolonisation and Indonesia, 1945–62* (Honolulu: University of Hawaii Press, 2002); on West Germany, 364; on the change of mind of Australia after this experience, 441. On the mixed Australian—and British—attitudes toward East Timor, the Indonesian occupation and the resistance, as early as 1977, see, for example, FCO 15/2252, "Australian Attitude over East Timor."
41. "Texts Adopted by the European Parliament: RESOLUTION [sic!] on Human Rights in Indonesia," *Official Journal of the European Communities*, no. C94, April 11, 1988, 191–2, here 191.
42. This point is also in line of the argument, that the European Parliament wanted to use the Southern Enlargement (Greece, Spain, Portugal) to democratize the ECs themselves; see Christian Salm, "Diffusing Democracy in Europe: The European Parliament and European Community Enlargement Policy 1974–79," *JEIH Journal of European Integration History* 27, no. 1 (2021): 99–120.

Bibliography

Archival Sources

The National Archives, Kew: Foreign and Commonwealth Offices (FCO) FCO 15/2252; 15/2255; 15/4002–4004
Political Archive of the Federal Foreign Office (PA AA): PA AA 323.42-22978

Printed Sources

Conclusions of the Session oft he European Council, Copenhagen, April 7–8, 1978, 99, http://aei.pitt.edu/1440/1/Copenhagen_1978.pdf.
Declaration "Zone of Peace, Freedom and Neutrality Declaration"; https://www.pmo.gov.my/wp-content/uploads/2019/07/ZOPFAN.pdf.
European Communities. "Declaration on European Identity." *Bulletin of the European Communities* 6, no. 12 (1973): 118–22.
Joint Communique of the Twelfth ASEAN Ministerial Meeting Bali, June 28–30, 1979; https://www.nas.gov.sg/archivesonline/data/pdf doc/1404-1979-06-30.pdf.
Official Journal of the European Communities C39, C233 (1985), C94 (1988), C283 (1993), C97 (1996), L287 (1996), C062 (1997).
Scott-Hopkins, James. "Report Drawn Up on Behalf oft he Committee on External Economic Relations on the Outcome oft he Visit by a Delegation from the European Parliament tot he Countries oft he Association of South-East Asian Nations (ASEAN) and on Future Relations between the European Community and ASEAN." *European Parliament Working Documents 1976–1977*, Document 181/76, June 26, 1976, 15.

Treaty Establishing the European Economic Community; https://eur-lex.europa.eu/legal-content/EN/ALL/?uri=CELEX:11957E/TXT

Research Literature

Acharya, Amitav. *The Making of Southeast Asia: International Relations of a Region*. Singapore: ISEAS, Institute of Southeast Asian Studies, 2012.

Christie, Kenneth, and Roy Denny, eds. *The Politics of Human Rights in East Asia*. London: Pluto Press, 2001.

Clark, Roger S. "Some International Law Aspects of the East Timor Affair." *Leiden Journal of International Law* 5, no. 2 (1992): 265–71.

Dauth, Jürgen. "ASEAN—Die Gemeinschaft der Südostasiatischen Nationen." *Aus Politik und Zeitgeschichte* 8 (1979): 31–43.

Gatrell, Peter. *The Making of the Modern Refugee*. Oxford: Oxford University Press, 2013.

Hughes, James, and Gwendolyn Sasse. "Monitoring the Monitors: EU Enlargement Conditionality and Minority Protection in the CEECs." *Journal on Ethnopolitics and Minority Issues in Europe* 4, no. 1 (2003): 1–37.

Manea, Maria-Gabriela. "The Claims of the ASEAN to Human Rights and Democracy: What Role for Regional Civil Society?" *ASIEN* 136 (July 2015): 73–97.

Manea, Maria-Gabriela. "The Constitution of Collective Identities and Interregional Human Rights Norms Diffusion: Analyzing Human Rights Interactions and Discourses in the EU-ASEAN Relations and the ASEM Process." Doctoral Thesis, Albert-Ludwigs Universität Freiburg i Br., 2021.

Masilamani, Jimmy and Logan Peterson. "The 'ASEAN Way': The Structural Underpinnings of Constructive Engagement." *Foreign Policy Journal*, October 15, 2014.

Moretti, Sebastien. "Keeping up Appearances. State Sovereignty and the Protection of Refugees in Southeast Asia." *European Journal of East Asian Studies* 17 (2018): 3–30.

Penders, Christiaan. *The West New Guinea Debacle: Dutch Decolonisation and Indonesia, 1945–62*. Honolulu: University of Hawaii Press, 2002.

Rechel, Bernd. *Minority Rights in Central and Eastern Europe*. London: Routledge, 2009.

Salm, Christian. "Diffusing Democracy in Europe: The European Parliament and European Community Enlargement Policy 1974–79." *JEIH Journal of European Integration History* 27, no. 1 (2021): 99–120.

Stahl, Bernhard. "Die Beziehungen der Europäischen Union zur ASEAN: Zwischen ökonomischen Interessen und schlechtem Gewissen." In *Die Europäische Union als Akteur der Weltpolitik*, edited by Klaus Schubert and Gisela Müller-Brandeck-Bocquet, 157–72. Opladen: Leske+Budrich, 2000.

Taithe, Bertrand. "Reinventing (French) Universalism: Religion, Humanitarianism and the 'French Doctors.'" *Modern & Contemporary France* 12, no. 2 (2004): 147–58.

Tömmel, Till Florian. *Bonn, Jakarta und der Kalte Krieg. Die Außenpolitik der Bundesrepublik Deutschland gegenüber Indonesien von 1952 bis 1973*. Berlin: De Gruyter Oldenburg, 2018.

Vössing, Michael. *Humanitäre Hilfe und Interessenpolitik. Westdeutsches Engagement für Vietnam in den 1960er und 1970er Jahren*. Göttingen: Vandenhoeck & Ruprecht, 2018.

Weiß, Andreas. "Auf Der Suche Nach Dem Süden: Die Europäischen Gemeinschaften Und Ihr Blick Nach Süden in Den 1970er Und 1980er Jahren." In *Nord/Süd. Perspektiven auf eine globale Konstellation*, edited by Jürgen Dinkel, Steffen Fiebrig, and Frank Reichherzer, 65–84. Berlin: De Gruyter Oldenburg, 2020.

12

Universal Basic Income as a Tool against Minority Marginalization

David P. Schweikard and Craig Willis

Introduction

National minorities in Europe, despite being a very diverse array of communities, are deeply affected by socioeconomic developments and are in many cases likely to face more difficult situations than majority populations.[1] Such issues relate to material deprivation in terms of high poverty and unemployment rates, but can also relate to cultural and linguistic exclusion——creating a vicious, perpetual cycle that existing policy has failed to curb. One particular case is the Roma communities across Europe, who continue to be the most marginalized group across the continent.[2] Thus, the question of how to mitigate or redress the marginalization of those national minorities who continue to face socioeconomic exclusion warrants a reevaluation and consideration of progressive policy measures that have not yet been applied to combat this historic injustice.

Using Iris Marion Young's influential work on injustice and marginalization as a theoretical framework,[3] we aim to inquire whether a universal basic income (UBI) could function as a tool against the marginalization of national minorities. As such, we first unpack various definitions of the term "national minority," allowing us to demonstrate the types of groups we are primarily focusing on (see the section "National Minorities"). Then we clarify in reference to Young's work what we understand by marginalization and in how far it constitutes an injustice (see the section "Marginalization as Injustice"), before we turn to the empirical situation of national minorities' marginalization in material deprivation and other forms as well as how this is typically addressed and the shortcomings of such attempts (see the section "How Are National Minorities Marginalized and How Is This Typically Addressed?"). In the section "Universal Basic Income: Definition and Summary of Intended Benefits," we introduce the concept of UBI and outline the main aspects of the theory relating to reducing deprivation and effects on particularly marginalized communities, allowing us to analyze in the section "UBI as a Tool against Minority Marginalization" how this applies to the situation of national minorities.

National Minorities

Turning first to the concept of national minorities, it is important to highlight that the term holds no broadly accepted legal, societal, or academic definition.[4] The terminology can be overlapping or interchangeable; "ethnic," "autochthonous," and "indigenous" are all terms in use to refer to the minorities in question, and there are also no agreed international definitions.[5] The Council of Europe's most prominent legislation, the *Framework Convention for the Protection of National Minorities* (FCNM)[6] and the *European Charter for Minority and Regional Languages* (ECRML)[7] both avoid a definition, as does the Organization for Security and Co-operation in Europe (OSCE)'s High Commissioner on National Minorities.. However, the United Nations' special rapporteur on minority issues suggests a numerical criterion that considers an ethnic, religious, or linguistic minority community to constitute "less than half of the population in the entire territory of a State" and goes on to add that "a person can freely belong to an ethnic, religious or linguistic minority without any requirement of citizenship, residence, official recognition or any other status."[8] A similar academic definition is offered by Jackson Preece who requires that a minority community should "show, if only implicitly, a sense of solidarity, directed towards preserving their culture, traditions, religion or language."[9] Brubaker adds that a national minority is not determined by "static" facts relating to ethnic demography but rather a "dynamic" political stance that claims a different ethnocultural nation to the majority and for state recognition and consequent rights.[10]

These definitions point to a minoritized position in terms of size and dominance, but this also can be applied to refugees or economic migrants and it is therefore the notion of historical legitimacy that grounds a major differentiation between "old" and "new" minorities.[11] This is emphasized by Kymlicka, who suggests that national minorities are "groups who formed functioning societies on their historical homelands prior to being incorporated into a larger state."[12] A recent debate has emerged on whether "new" minorities should be handed protection by states under such international treaties as the FCNM.[13]

However, for purposes of scope we shall here work with existing recognized national minorities for two main reasons. Firstly, recognition deals with one aspect of corrective justice in that the group in question has been given legitimacy by the state in which it resides. Secondly, focusing on recognized national minorities allows us to concentrate on the literature and monitoring reports that highlight the issues these groups are facing. Within this classification of recognized national minorities, two relevant factors of differentiation are kin-state and geographical concentration. There are national minority communities with and without a so-called kin-state—an external state whereby the ethnic kin of the minority "compose a titular majority,"[14] also referred to as an "external national homeland."[15] And by consequence, there are national minority communities who do not have a kin-state. Another key differentiation between minority communities regards geographical concentration, which leads to distinguishing between concentrated (or non-dispersed) and dispersed minorities.[16] These aspects can obviously influence the ability for minority communities to self-organize politically as well as economically, affecting also how national minorities are marginalized.

Regarding specific examples of such groups, across the Council of Europe area there are hundreds of recognized minority communities and it is hard to determine the actual number, given that many member states do not specifically list recognized minority communities. At the broad end, the United Kingdom is an example of a member state that defines an ethnic group through case precedent and thus includes a wide range of minority communities, blurring so-called new and old minorities.[17] An example of a narrower recognition is Germany, which recognizes just four minority communities, namely, Danish, Frisian, Sinti and Roma, and Sorbian.[18] The levels to which these minority communities are marginalized vary considerably, elaborated upon in the section "How Are National Minorities Marginalized and How Is This Typically Addressed?." First, we locate the concept of marginalization within Young's philosophical approach to injustice.

Marginalization as Injustice

A central tenet of Young's theorizing about injustice is to address its varieties and specific aspects as *structural* phenomena. This involves, as a *first pillar* of her approach, that she does not see the scope of a philosophical theory of justice as limited to understanding problems regarding the distribution of goods. Distributive justice is the main if not the sole concern of most work on justice following John Rawls' seminal contributions.[19] The "distributive paradigm," as Young terms it, subsumes all questions of justice under the question as to how a given set of goods, that is, "material goods such as things, resources, income, and wealth" and "social positions, especially jobs,"[20] is to be distributed among individuals. Young notes that the model employed by such theories of distribution features a form of social atomism, since individuals' relations to the goods in question are external, and that its orientation toward the results of distributive patterns reveals an underlying commitment to a static conception of society.[21] Though these two features may also attract criticism along the lines of a holistic and (more) dynamic conception of society, Young's own critique highlights that accounts reducing justice to the results of distributive patterns tend to (1) downplay or even ignore the institutional context within which distribution occurs and (2) misrepresent what is at stake regarding nonmaterial goods and resources, such as rights, opportunities, and self-respect.[22]

Young's key idea here is not to say that how the distribution of material goods in a society turns out is irrelevant to considerations of justice. It is rather to acknowledge that the institutional context as well as its history matter at least as much and that the logic by which the situation of individuals and groups in society is evaluated would be implausibly constrained by looking only at who has how much of which good at a certain time, as nonmaterial goods specifically aren't adequately captured by this logic. The upshot of this critique is that "the concept of distribution [should explicitly be limited] to material goods, like things, natural resources, or money" and that the "scope of justice is wider that distributive issues."[23]

More specifically, and this is a *second pillar* of Young's approach, theorizing about justice should incorporate understandings of domination and oppression as definitive of injustice. This still acknowledges that a patterned distribution of material goods can produce injustices, as when individuals belonging to certain groups in society are systematically disadvantaged in terms of how much they can possess or gain. But if the scope of social justice is recognized to be broader, then its provision needs to rely on principles wider in range and different in character. Young here takes her cue from Agnes Heller[24] who "suggests that justice is primarily the virtue of citizenship, of persons deliberating about problems and issues that confront them collectively in their institutions and actions, under conditions without domination or oppression, with reciprocity and mutual tolerance of difference."[25] The corresponding wider, political idea of justice thus involves looking beyond schemes of distribution and to procedural questions regarding political participation and inclusion in public deliberation.[26] On this approach, norms are just only insofar as those subject to them have an effective voice in their institution and can assent to or dissent from them without coercion. And a social condition is just only insofar as it enables "all to meet their needs and exercise their freedom."[27] Young thus regards considerations of justice as pertinent with regard to all aspects of an encompassing concept of the political, where inclusion entails that no one living under shared institutions and within shared practices may be systematically excluded from the fruits of collaboration and any processes of regulating political life.

Young does not conceive of this idea of political justice as grounded in a conception of human nature or an otherwise ambitious axiology regarding the good life. Some foundation of general values is needed, however, in order to guide both an understanding of how exactly political institutions, practices, and actions are to be shaped and any critical stance toward constellations diverging from the ideal. On her view, justice and the values constituting the good life are not identical, rather "social justice concerns the degree to which a society contains and supports the institutional conditions necessary for the realization of these values."[28] Two very general values shape the good life according to this account: (1) the value of the development and exercise of one's capacities as well as the expression of one's experience and (2) the value of shaping one's own action as well as the conditions in which they are performed.[29] It is at the same time a cornerstone of this philosophical account and a continuing political challenge that these values are universal and thus their pursuit should be open to every individual. According to Young, individuals find themselves in conditions of injustice if they are subject to "oppression, the institutional constraint on self-development, and domination, the institutional constraint on self-determination."[30]

For present purposes, it is important to note that while individuals may be the ultimate victims of oppression and domination, they often suffer injustice by virtue of belonging to particular groups in society.[31] Especially where discrimination and exclusion are systemic or structural, as evidenced by unequal treatment of migrant workers or wherever rights of political participation are tied to elaborate requirements, individuals suffer the concomitant harms *qua* members of particular groups. In terms of oppression, this occurs within systematic institutional processes that prevent the members of some groups from "from learning and using satisfying and expansive skills in socially recognized settings" or within "institutionalized social processes which inhibit people's ability to play and communicate with others or to express their feelings and perspective on social life in contexts where others can listen."[32] Members of certain groups are dominated within institutional settings insofar as these "inhibit or prevent" them "from participating in determining their actions or the conditions of their actions. Persons live within structures of domination if other persons or groups can determine without reciprocation the conditions of the action, either directly or by virtue of the structural consequences of their actions."[33]

Young regards marginalization as one of five faces of oppression, and specifically as "perhaps the most dangerous form,"[34] the others are exploitation, powerlessness, cultural imperialism, and violence. It consists in entire groups being excluded or even expelled from societal life. Such marginalizing exclusion, to which we will turn in view of national minorities in the next section, may be explicit and intentional, but it can also result from more implicit structural features of a given society. It can bring forth sometimes severe material deprivation concomitant to a low social and moral status for the members of the marginalized groups.

Whereas material deprivation, as Young details,[35] can be and is in some states addressed by the provision of welfare payments, this does not suffice to address the injustices connected with marginality. First off, recipients of welfare payments are at risk of being made permanently dependent on the provision of benefits, which is regularly tied to specific preconditions and combined with constraints on basic rights to privacy, respect, and individual choice. The latter consequences are by no means necessarily connected with dependency; the challenge is rather to provide material support without invasive monitoring of eligibility and without lowering recipients' social, moral, or legal status. Moreover, Young argues that even when welfare payments are sufficient to cover basic needs such as food and shelter of the marginalized, their oppression does not end there. As long as they are not integrated as productive and recognized participants in societal cooperation, they are bound to experience low self-esteem and lack meaningful occupation. Young's example here is that many old people are thus marginalized and kept external from much of life in society,[36] but the observation holds equally for other marginalized groups.

In view of oppression and domination generally, but regarding marginalization in particular, we concur with Young's two-pronged analysis: "marginalization definitely entails serious issues of distributive justice, it also involves the depreciation of cultural, practical, and institutionalized conditions for exercising capacities in a context of recognition and interaction."[37] Although she does point to the idea of a "social wage" in that same passage, Young does not expound ways of addressing the injustices marginalization engenders. In taking up this challenge, we explore how a UBI could function as a tool against specific forms of marginalization. We argue that whereas a UBI would serve to mitigate material deprivation directly, it would also support improvement regarding nonmaterial aspects of marginalization, although the latter would also need to be addressed by other means.

How Are National Minorities Marginalized and How Is This Typically Addressed?

As outlined earlier, national minorities are often marginalized on an individual and community scale. At the extreme end, this marginalization can manifest itself in the form of material deprivation but, as Young suggests, marginalization can also take other forms, including cultural and linguistic marginalization. We now take up these issues in turn and outline how they are typically addressed, to then demonstrate how familiar responses have failed to eradicate or sufficiently reduce such marginalization.

Material Deprivation

The Advisory Committee to the FCNM (ACFC) states that persons belonging to national minorities "can be confronted with more difficult socio-economic situations than the majority population."[38] It also states that certain national minorities, specifically Roma, face "more significant difficulties than others in accessing the labor market, education and training, housing, health care and social protection" and suggests that these areas are mutually reinforcing, lead to a spiral of exclusion, and leave women particularly vulnerable.[39] Similarly, the UN has stated that ethnic minorities and Indigenous peoples "tend more often than other population groups to live in poverty," providing specific statistics on Roma in this regard.[40] In the context of central and eastern Europe, it is suggested that national minorities are among those who "have lost the most as a result of conflict and transition" since 1989, while "Roma remain the most socially and economically marginalized minority group across the whole region."[41]

Indeed, Roma are the one specifically named group routinely mentioned as particularly vulnerable who are often living in poverty and conditions of material deprivation. The Council of Europe's specific Roma body, ADI-ROM, and the Roma and Travellers Team highlight the barriers and exclusion Roma persons face in labor markets across Europe.[42] On the EU level, the Framework for National Roma Integration Strategies (operational between 2011 and 2020) monitored issues across the bloc relating to a number of foci including education, employment, healthcare, and housing. Its most recent report demonstrates that serious issues still remain and the percentage of Roma in employment is much lower than national averages and worse still for Roma women.[43] On the individual state level, the most recent ACFC Opinions frequently feature recommendations for states to aim for economic equality through reducing unemployment rates, combating marginalization and increasing socioeconomic participation of Roma persons and communities.[44] Further, high unemployment rates and overreliance of informal work are mentioned in Bulgaria[45], Czech Republic[46], Slovak Republic,[47] and Serbia[48]. Examples of such conditions were also exacerbated during the Covid-19 pandemic and consequent societal lockdowns for many national minorities, with a "real risk that they may fall into poverty and social exclusion."[49] Research showed that Roma communities faced particularly acute economic issues and were often not eligible for income replacement support schemes during the pandemic.[50]

Other Forms of Marginalization

Whereas issues of material deprivation have a considerable impact on the marginalization of many minority communities, it is not unanimously the case. Indeed, there are many examples of economically prosperous national minorities or at least no worse off than the majority population. However, there are important other forms of marginalization that can have detrimental effects or act as barriers to socioeconomic participation for such populations, particularly relating to culture and language. For example, limitations to mother-tongue education or access to state institutions in a minority language, such as in the fields of employment or healthcare.[51] These issues can be due to direct discrimination but are more often now indirect: for example, mother-tongue education in a minority language may be available but only provided at inconvenient times or locations, or state offices for employment may offer services in minority language but in a limited form.

Similar issues have been raised through pan-European activism, a prominent example being the Federal Union of European Nationalities (FUEN), which represents over 100 member organizations of autochthonous minority communities across thirty-five European countries. The organization aims to "work for the preservation and promotion of the identity, language, culture, rights and traditions of the European minorities."[52] Its most substantial focus of recent has been its sponsorship of the Minority SafePack Initiative (MSPI), a EU Citizens' Initiative that called for stronger rights at the EU level.[53] Much of the MSPI was tied to specific EU treaty articles but analysis suggests that its core goals are living in one's homeland, learning in one's mother tongue, preservation of linguistic and cultural diversity, and aiming for equality.[54] The MSPI also contains elements related to minorities with a kin-state, calling for a reduction in barriers between states but also draws attention to the situation of stateless minorities such as Roma who are in extra need of supranational level support. It is clear that such aims relate to broader aspects of marginalization but are ultimately linked to material deprivation as a core issue when aiming for equality with the majority population.

How Is Marginalization Typically Addressed?

The official recognition of national minorities has slowly led to an improvement in efforts to address the issues such groups and individuals face, to a varying degree across Europe. This includes issues of material deprivation and nonmaterial marginalization but progress is for the most part very incremental. The monitoring bodies of these two instruments offer cyclical updates on the situation of national minorities and, while they show general improvements in many situations such as legal representation, they are not enforceable in court and remain soft law—with all the shortcomings this can entail. This is another reason why the MSPI campaign sought to increase protection at the EU level, with its greater legal substance and enforceability. Furthermore, the focus was mostly on securitization and political representation, rather than on socioeconomic aspects. In the realm of socioeconomic participation, there have been targeted strategies for Roma across Europe such as the Roma Decade for Inclusion,

2005–15. However, this was reported to have limited impact and consequent reports stated that Roma remain isolated from public policies and the socioeconomic gap between Roma and non-Roma remains significant.[55] Thus, socioeconomic participation for national minorities remains both underexplored[56] and insufficiently treated even when considered.

Therefore, despite all of these strategies and incremental improvements for the situation of minorities in Europe, inequality is still high and material deprivation certainly still exists—leaving many minorities economically, culturally, and linguistically marginalized. This is echoed by the continuing calls for improvement in the ACFC monitoring cycles, as well as the recognition that the Roma Decade had a limited impact. Moreover, the Covid-19 pandemic and subsequent lockdowns demonstrated this starkly, particularly in the case of those already in marginalized positions, such as Roma.

Universal Basic Income: Definition and Summary of Intended Benefits

The concept of a UBI is not a modern idea, despite its increasing political salience post-2008. Under various different names,[57] the core concept of providing a minimum income to all people has existed in various forms for a couple of centuries and is suggested to stem from Thomas More and then Thomas Paine in the sixteenth and eighteenth centuries.[58] Following an initial wave of interest in the United States and Canada during the 1960s and 1970s, scholarly work began to accelerate from the 1990s and political activists and parties began increasingly to take notice in the twenty-first century. Such scholarly work approached the concept from varying disciplines but predominantly economics, philosophy, and sociology. Based on the writing of key scholars,[59] we use the following working definition of a UBI:

> A UBI is a universal payment made periodically to all members of a given society, that should be unconditional and of a financial amount high enough to cover the basic needs of an individual.[60]

Let us briefly elaborate on the key aspects of this definition. The term "periodically" is usually taken to suggest that UBI be paid on a monthly basis—in line with income from labor or state welfare policies, yet some proposals do suggest an annual basis.[61] Moreover, most scholars suggest that the monthly format would be most suitable for realizing the intended benefits of a guaranteed income. Moreover, we suggest that "all members of a given society" would receive a basic income, thus it would not be limited to citizenship but rather to territorial political boundaries, although in an ideal scenario a truly UBI would be global. This also points to the element that there should be no means-testing, with a UBI paid regardless of income levels, wealth, or demographics such as age; in this sense a UBI would likely replace certain existing benefits such as unemployment, universal basic pensions, and universal child allowance. Finally, the phrase that it should be of a "high enough" amount points to the fact that UBI should be sufficient to live on alone in order to achieve the intended benefits, typically this should be at least as high as existing minimum wage levels for full-time employment or income replacements.

Regarding the intended benefits of a UBI, scholars and activists approach this from a number of angles, which often overlap but can be in tension with one another. From an economic perspective, UBI is seen as a tool not only to eradicate poverty but also to reduce economic inequalities through redistribution. Relatedly, UBI is seen as facilitating an increased freedom of choice in terms of how to spend one's time both in the labor market (including part-time and voluntary work) and regarding education and retraining.[62] Finally, UBI is also seen by some as a way to streamline government spending.[63] Much of this overlaps with the philosophical angle that sees UBI not only as a tool of redistributive and social justice but also has support from a libertarian standpoint due to the increased freedom and lower levels of government intrusion and institutional discrimination that often accompanies means-tested welfare.[64]

Furthermore, some scholarship has explicitly linked the benefits of UBI to various minoritized groups, along ethnic and gender lines. From a feminist standpoint, arguments are made in both directions with suggestions that UBI could increase gender equality by providing an independent income for the individual rather than the couple or family and also recognize unpaid labor such as caring for relatives (old and young) or housework.[65] However, counterarguments suggest that UBI could reinforce existing gender roles and sidestep the larger issues.[66] Regarding minority ethnic groups, UBI has been explored in the context of African Americans as a tool of compensatory justice as well as recognizing that it could have an exponential positive effect on so-called nonwhite groups given their overall lower levels of income.[67] Similarly, previous work has also considered UBI in the context of national minorities in Europe—from the angles of empowerment[68] as well as meeting minorities' demands on the EU level.[69] This link to ethnic minorities takes priority in the next section, where we intend to demonstrate how the specific challenges faced by marginalized minorities can be addressed by a broad policy such as UBI.

UBI as a Tool against Minority Marginalization

The introduction of a UBI across societal levels would be a more encompassing scheme than any existing targeted intervention, with the broad intention of reducing poverty and inequality by providing an income floor. Thus, insofar as members of marginalized groups suffer disadvantages in this regard, they will share in the general benefits of a UBI. However, despite being an individual intervention, when a large number of a community suffers from material deprivation there will clearly be a community level effect from such a scheme. UBI is therefore not specifically targeted at national minorities, yet if it is true that marginalization means that marginalized groups are particularly affected by material and nonmaterial deprivation (and exclusion) then there will be specific benefits from a UBI for these groups.

In terms of material deprivation, if introduced at a level high enough to sustain basic needs, a UBI will directly prevent extreme forms of poverty as well as taking away the risk posed by the so-called poverty trap of existing benefits systems—thus making the decision to take on a job less of a risk. By achieving this, UBI helps disadvantaged groups in general and marginalized groups (including national minorities) in particular to engage in self-development and self-determination and offers subsequent indirect effects once the material deprivation is adequately reduced. These indirect effects relate to the other forms of deprivation discussed by Young, chiefly cultural and linguistic in the case of national minorities. Through its very nature, UBI would eradicate the chance for discrimination in welfare claims by removing the discretionary aspect as everyone in society automatically qualifies for a UBI. This can be particularly relevant for minorities who do not know how to navigate the existing bureaucratic systems or face a language barrier to the majority society.

Furthermore, a UBI would also allow individuals the freedom to remove themselves from discriminatory workplace situations, offering an exit option with the income support to fall back on—similarly with regard to taking the first steps in self-employment. The freedom of a secured regular income also relates to the ability to invest time into (re)education, the possibility to fund one's life during full-time studies or to only work part-time and study the rest of the time. This is a particularly salient element in the case of national minorities who suffer from high rates of high-school dropouts due to economic pressure to join the workforce as soon as possible, or faced difficulties due to discrimination while in school. Finally, as Standing[70] suggests, freedom also entails the possibility to spend one's time in voluntary activities, which is of particular relevance for minority communities who often rely heavily on volunteers for cultural activities, own language teaching, but also political activism and engagement. Again, it is particularly relevant for minorities without a kin-state to provide such services and support. Thus, a UBI could allow individuals to acquire resources to invest in cultivating important skills and in participating in political discourse.

In sum, we suggest that a UBI could be an effective tool to mitigate minority marginalization. It encapsulates what we would call a *sufficientarian intervention*[71] by lifting every member of a given political community to (or above) a threshold of decent material standing. Though distributively indiscriminate, a UBI as specified here would benefit marginalized minorities specifically by addressing material deprivation directly and by promoting cultural and political inclusion indirectly. Notwithstanding its character as a redistributive scheme, UBI is arguably also apt to support forms of addressing nonmaterial exclusion, thus complementing efforts that regard the legal and political status of marginalized groups in society.

Conclusion

In this chapter, we have sought to highlight how national minorities are subject to specific forms of injustice by being materially and nonmaterially marginalized in affluent democratic states. Our suggestion that a UBI could function as a tool to eradicate material and political inequalities engendered by such marginalization relies on working out understandings of who these minorities are, of the particular injustices of marginalization, and of the precise character of their marginalization. Accordingly, we brought together the situation of national minorities—in particular Roma—with the theory posited by Young of marginalization as injustice, in terms of both material and nonmaterial forms of deprivation, and suggested that the introduction of a UBI would significantly reduce the material deprivation and offer opportunities to address the cultural- and linguistic-related issues that affect national minorities' ability to participate socioeconomically.

However, it is also important to state that this will only be the case if a UBI is truly unconditional and of a high enough amount to meet basic needs, for example, at the same monthly level as a national minimum wage given full-time employment. In addition, an introduction of a UBI will only be a progressive step if it does not strip back other forms of state support. Whereas it is clear that existing welfare schemes such as unemployment benefits, child allowance, and basic state pensions would be replaced by a UBI, additional support may be necessary for certain groups and public institutions. Free healthcare and education would remain a vital part of the ability to reduce marginalization and enhance socioeconomic participation. Simplification and universality should not therefore imply an erosion of the status quo.

Although our focus here is on national minorities in Europe, it should be apparent that such a policy would have similar benefits for other marginalized groups in a given society, for example, migrant communities that also face discrimination and poverty conditions. Investigating this in detail as well as elaborating on the proposal outlined here will be tasks for future research.

Notes

1. ACFC, *Commentary on the Effective Participation of Persons Belonging to National Minorities in Cultural, Social and Economic Life and in Public Affairs* (Strasbourg: Council of Europe, 2008), accessed November 1, 2023, https://rm.coe.int/CoERMPublicCommonSearchServices/DisplayDCTMContent?documentId=09000016800bc7e8.
2. European Commission, *Report on the Implementation of National Roma Integration Strategies—2019* (Brussels: European Commission, 2019), accessed November 1, 2023, https://eur-lex.europa.eu/legal-content/EN/TXT/PDF/?uri=CELEX:52019DC0406&from=FR; United Nations Development Programme, *Marginalised Minorities in Development Programming* (New York: United Nations Development Programme, 2010), accessed November 1, 2023, https://www.ohchr.org/Documents/Issues/Minorities/UNDPMarginalisedMinorities.pdf.
3. See especially, Iris Marion Young, "Five Faces of Oppression," in *Justice and the Politics of Difference, REV-Revised* (Princeton, NJ: Princeton University Press, 1990), 39–65.
4. Jennifer Jackson Preece, *Minority Rights* (Cambridge: Polity Press, 2005); Tove Malloy, "Introduction," in *Minority Issues in Europe: Rights, Concepts, Policy*, ed. Tove Malloy, vol. 1 (Berlin: Frank & Timme, 2013), 13–26.
5. United Nations, "Chapter VII—Indigenous Peoples and Ethnic Minorities: Marginalization Is the Norm," *Promoting Inclusion through Social Protection*, Report on the World Social Situation 2018 (New York: United Nations, 2018), 91–101.

6. *Framework Convention for the Protection of National Minorities 1995* (Strasbourg: Council of Europe, 1995).
7. *European Charter for Regional and Minority Languages 1992* (Strasbourg: Council of Europe, 1992).
8. OHCHR, "Concept of a Minority: Mandate Definition. Special Rapporteur on Minority Issues," n.d.
9. Preece, *Minority Rights*, 28.
10. Rogers Brubaker, "National Minorities, Nationalizing States, and External National Homelands in the New Europe," *Daedalus* 124, no. 2 (1995): 112.
11. Malloy, "Introduction," 13–26.
12. Will Kymlicka, *Politics in the Vernacular. Nationalism, Multiculturalism, and Citizenship* (Oxford: Oxford University Press, 2001), 54.
13. Roberta Medda-Windischer, Caitlin Boulter, and Tove H. Malloy, eds., *Extending Protection to Migrant Populations in Europe: Old and New Minorities* (London: Routledge, 2019).
14. Natalie Sabanadze, "Minorities and Kin-States," *Helsinki Monitor* 17, no. 3 (2006): 244–56.
15. Brubaker, "National Minorities, Nationalizing States, and External National Homelands in the New Europe," 112.
16. John Coakley, "Introduction: Dispersed Minorities and Non-Territorial Autonomy," *Ethnopolitics* 15, no. 1 (January 2016): 1–23.
17. Timothy Jacob-Owens, "Immigration and Multicultural Citizenship in Europe: Insights from the Framework Convention for the Protection of National Minorities," *International Journal on Minority and Group Rights* 29, no. 1 (2022): 167–97; Craig Willis, "An Overview of the UK's Approach to Ethnic Data Collection in the Context of the Framework Convention on the Protection of National Minorities," *Journal on Minority Issues Ethnopolitics and Minority Issues* 19, no. 2 (2020): 47–75.
18. Federal Ministry of the Interior and Community, "National Minorities," Federal Ministry of the Interior and Community, n.d.
19. Beginning with John Rawls, *A Theory of Justice* (Cambridge, MA: Harvard University Press, 2020).
20. Young, "Five Faces of Oppression," 15.
21. Ibid., 18.
22. Ibid., 18–30.
23. Ibid., 33.
24. Agnes Heller, *Beyond Justice* (New York: Basic Books, 1987).
25. Young, "Five Faces of Oppression," 33–4.
26. Cf. Iris Marion Young, *Inclusion and Democracy* (Oxford: Oxford University Press, 2000).
27. Young, "Five Faces of Oppression," 34.
28. Ibid., 37.
29. Ibid.
30. Ibid.
31. Iris Marion Young, "Equality of Whom? Social Groups and Judgments of Injustice," *Journal of Political Philosophy* 9, no. 1 (2001): 1–18.
32. Young, "Five Faces of Oppression," 38.
33. Ibid., cf. also Claudia Card, "Injustice, Evil, and Oppression," in *Dancing with Iris—The Philosophy of Iris Marion Young*, ed. Ann Ferguson and Nagel Mechthild (Oxford: Oxford University Press, 2009), 147–59.

34. Young, "Five Faces of Oppression," 53.
35. Ibid., 53–4.
36. Ibid., 55.
37. Ibid.
38. ACFC, *Commentary on the Effective Participation of Persons Belonging to National Minorities in Cultural, Social and Economic Life and in Public Affairs*, 17.
39. Ibid., 17–18.
40. United Nations, "Chapter VII—Indigenous Peoples and Ethnic Minorities: Marginalization Is the Norm," 95.
41. United Nations Development Programme, *Marginalised Minorities in Development Programming*, 171.
42. Council of Europe, "Roma and Travellers. About Us," n.d., accessed November 1, 2023, https://www.coe.int/en/web/roma-and-travellers/about-us.
43. European Commission, *Report on the Implementation of National Roma Integration Strategies—2019*.
44. ACFC, "Fourth Opinion on the Slovak Republic Adopted on 3 December 2014." ACFC/OP/IV(2014)004 (Strasbourg: Council of Europe, 2014), accessed November 1, 2023, https://rm.coe.int/CoERMPublicCommonSearchServices/DisplayDCTMContent?documentId=0900001680303190; ACFC, "Fourth Opinion on Germany Adopted on 19 March 2015." ACFC/OP/IV(2015)003 (Strasbourg: Council of Europe, 2015a), accessed November 1, 2023, https://rm.coe.int/CoERMPublicCommonSearchServices/DisplayDCTMContent?documentId=09000016805946c6; ACFC, "Fourth Opinion on the Czech Republic Adopted on 16 November 2015." ACFC/OP/IV(2015)004 (Strasbourg: Council of Europe, 2015b), accessed November 1, 2023, https://rm.coe.int/CoERMPublicCommonSearchServices/DisplayDCTMContent?documentId=0900001680684ff9; ACFC, "Fourth Opinion on Romania—Adopted on 22 June 2017." ACFC/OP/IV(2017)005 (Strasbourg: Council of Europe, 2017), accessed November 1, 2023, https://rm.coe.int/fourth-opinion-on-romania-adopted-on-22-june-2017/168078af76; ACFC, "Fourth Opinion on Bulgaria—Adopted on 26 May 2020." ACFC/OP/IV(2020)001Final (Strasbourg: Council of Europe, 2020), accessed November 1, 2023, https://rm.coe.int/4th-op-bulgaria-en/16809eb483.
45. ACFC, "Fourth Opinion on Bulgaria," 47.
46. ACFC, "Fourth Opinion on the Czech Republic," 6.
47. ACFC, "Fourth Opinion on the Slovak Republic," 28.
48. ACFC, "Fourth Opinion on Serbia Adopted on 26 June 2019." ACFC/OP/IV(2019)001 (Strasbourg: Council of Europe, 2019), 39, https://rm.coe.int/4th-op-serbia-en/16809943b6.
49. OSCE, "OSCE High Commissioner on National Minorities Offers Recommendations on Short-Term Responses to COVID-19 That Support Social Cohesion," OSCE High Commissioner on National Minorities, March 26, 2020, accessed November 1, 2023, https://www.osce.org/hcnm/449170.
50. Fundación Secretariado Gitano, "The Fundación Secretariado Gitano Carries out a Telephone Survey to 11,000 Roma People That Reveals the Serious Social Impact of the Covid-19 Crisis," Fundación Secretariado Gitano Newsroom, April 27, 2020, accessed November 1, 2023, https://www.gitanos.org/actualidad/archivo/131067.html; Neda Korunovska and Zeljko Jovanovic, "Roma in the COVID-19 Crisis. An Early Warning from Six EU Member States," Open Society Roma Initiatives Office, 2020, accessed November 1, 2023, https://www.opensocietyfoundations.org/publications/roma-in-the-covid-19-crisis; Craig Willis, "Roma and the First Wave of the

Covid-19 Pandemic: Income Loss and Its Effects across Roma Communities in Seven Non-EU Countries," *Journal on Minority Issues Ethnopolitics and in Europe* 21, no. 2 (2022): 10–34, https://doi.org/10.53779/AQQL3201.
51. ACFC, *Commentary on the Effective Participation of Persons Belonging to National Minorities in Cultural, Social and Economic Life and in Public Affairs*; OSCE, "Thematic Recommendations and Guidelines," n.d., accessed November 1, 2023, https://www.osce.org/hcnm/thematic-recommendations-and-guidelines.
52. FUEN, "About Us," accessed March 28, 2023, https://www.fuen.org/en/article/The-Federal-Union-of-European-Nationalities-FUEN.
53. European Citizen's Initiative, "Minority SafePack—One Million Signatures for Diversity in Europe," accessed March 28, 2023, https://europa.eu/citizens-initiative/initiatives/details/2017/000004/minority-safepack-one-million-signatures-diversity-europe_en; Katharina Crepaz, "The Minority Safepack Initiative: A European Participatory Process Supporting Cultural Diversity," *European Yearbook of Minority Issues* 17 (2020): 23–47.
54. Craig Willis, "The Minority SafePack Initiative and Universal Basic Income: A Combination to Address Minority Issues in the European Union?," *International Journal on Minority and Group Rights* 28, no. 4 (2021): 575–604, https://doi.org/10.1163/15718115-BJA10012.
55. Regional Cooperation Council, "Roma Integration 2020. Project Overview," n.d., accessed November 1, 2023, https://www.rcc.int/romaintegration2020/pages/1/overview; Bernard Rorke and Margaret Matache, "The End of a Decade: What Happened to Roma Inclusion?," openDemocracy, September 29, 2015, accessed November 1, 2023, https://www.opendemocracy.net/en/can-europe-make-it/end-of-decade-what-happened-to-roma-inclusion/.
56. Andreea Cârstocea and Craig Willis, "Less Equal than Others: National Minorities and the Overlooked Challenge of Socio-economic Inequalities," *ECMI Minorities Blog* (blog), September 30, 2021, accessed November 1, 2023, https://doi.org/10.53779/AACB5478.
57. cf. Guy Standing, *Basic Income: And How We Can Make It Happen* (London: Penguin Random House, 2017), 3–21.
58. cf. Philippe van Parijs and Yannick Vanderborght, *Basic Income: A Radical Proposal for a Free Society and a Sane Economy* (Cambridge, MA: Harvard University Press, 2017), 71.
59. Standing, *Basic Income: And How We Can Make It Happen*, 54; Malcolm Torry, *Money For Everyone. Why We Need a Citizen's Income* (Bristol: Polity Press, 2013); Parijs and Vanderborght, *Basic Income*, 55.
60. See also Willis, "The Minority SafePack Initiative and Universal Basic Income," 51.
61. Standing, *Basic Income: And How We Can Make It Happen*, 8.
62. Ibid., 60–1.
63. Charles Murray, "Guaranteed Income as a Replacement for the Welfare State," *Basic Income Studies* 3, no. 2 (2008): 1–12, https://doi.org/10.2202/1932-0183.1115.
64. Parijs and Vanderborght, *Basic Income*, 71; Torry, *Money For Everyone. Why We Need a Citizen's Income*; Matt Zwolinski, "Classical Liberalism and the Basic Income," *Basic Income Studies* 6, no. 2 (2012), https://doi.org/10.1515/1932-0183.1221.
65. Ingrid Robeyns, "Hush Money or Emancipation Fee? A Gender Analysis of Basic Income," in *Basic Income on the Agenda: Policy Objectives and Political Chances*, ed. Robbert-Jan van der Veen and Loek Groot (Amsterdam: Amsterdam University Press, 2000), 121–36; Caitlin McLean and Ailsa McKay, "Beyond Care: Expanding

the Feminist Debate on Universal Basic Income," in *WiSE Working Paper Series*, #1 (Glasgow: Glasgow Caledonian University, 2015), accessed November 1, 2023, https://www.gcu.ac.uk/wise/media/gcalwebv2/theuniversity/centresprojects/wise/90324WiSE_BriefingSheet.pdf.
66. Parijs and Vanderborght, *Basic Income*, 187.
67. Dorian Warren, "A Universal Basic Income +," Economic Security Project, October 10, 2017, accessed November 1, 2023, https://economicsecurityproject.org/news/a-universal-basic-income/; Max Ghenis, "How Universal Basic Income Would Affect the Black-White Poverty and Wealth Gaps," UBI Center, June 20, 2020, accessed November 1, 2023, https://medium.com/ubicenter/how-universal-basic-income-would-affect-the-black-white-poverty-and-wealth-gaps-452e2af1497b.
68. Sonja Wolf and Craig Willis, "Universal Basic Income as a Tool of Empowerment for Minorities," *ECMI Working Paper* #109, 2018, accessed March 29, 2023, https://www.ecmi.de/publications/ecmi-research-papers/109-universal-basic-income-as-a-tool-of-empowerment-for-minorities.
69. Willis, "The Minority SafePack Initiative and Universal Basic Income."
70. Standing, *Basic Income*, 60–1.
71. For a general discussion, cf. Liam Shields, *Just Enough: Sufficiency as a Demand of Justice* (Edinburgh: Edinburgh University Press, 2016).

Bibliography

Printed Sources

ACFC. *Commentary on the Effective Participation of Persons Belonging to National Minorities in Cultural, Social and Economic Life and in Public Affairs*. Strasbourg: Council of Europe, 2008. Accessed November 1, 2023. https://rm.coe.int/CoERMPublicCommonSearchServices/DisplayDCTMContent?documentId=09000016800bc7e8.

ACFC. "Fourth Opinion on the Slovak Republic Adopted on 3 December 2014." ACFC/OP/IV(2014)004. Strasbourg: Council of Europe, 2014. Accessed November 1, 2023. https://rm.coe.int/CoERMPublicCommonSearchServices/DisplayDCTMContent?documentId=0900001680303190.

ACFC. "Fourth Opinion on Germany Adopted on 19 March 2015." ACFC/OP/IV(2015)003. Strasbourg: Council of Europe, 2015a. Accessed November 1, 2023. https://rm.coe.int/CoERMPublicCommonSearchServices/DisplayDCTMContent?documentId=09000016805946c6.

ACFC. "Fourth Opinion on the Czech Republic Adopted on 16 November 2015." ACFC/OP/IV(2015)004. Strasbourg: Council of Europe, 2015b. Accessed November 1, 2023. https://rm.coe.int/CoERMPublicCommonSearchServices/DisplayDCTMContent?documentId=09000016806884ff9.

ACFC. "Fourth Opinion on Romania—Adopted on 22 June 2017." ACFC/OP/IV(2017)005. Strasbourg: Council of Europe, 2017. Accessed November 1, 2023. https://rm.coe.int/fourth-opinion-on-romania-adopted-on-22-june-2017/168078af76.

ACFC. "Fourth Opinion on Serbia Adopted on 26 June 2019." ACFC/OP/IV(2019)001. Strasbourg: Council of Europe, 2019. Accessed November 1, 2023. https://rm.coe.int/4th-op-serbia-en/16809943b6.

ACFC. "Fourth Opinion on Bulgaria—Adopted on 26 May 2020." ACFC/OP/IV(2020)001Final. Strasbourg: Council of Europe, 2020. Accessed November 1, 2023. https://rm.coe.int/4th-op-bulgaria-en/16809eb483.

Council of Europe. "Roma and Travellers. About Us," n.d. Accessed November 1, 2023. https://www.coe.int/en/web/roma-and-travellers/about-us.

European Charter for Regional and Minority Languages 1992. Strasbourg: Council of Europe, 1992.

European Commission. *Report on the Implementation of National Roma Integration Strategies—2019.* Brussels: European Commission, 2019. Accessed November 1, 2023. https://eur-lex.europa.eu/legal-content/EN/TXT/PDF/?uri=CELEX:52019DC0406&from=FR.

Federal Ministry of the Interior and Community. "National Minorities." Federal Ministry of the Interior and Community, n.d. Accessed November 1, 2023. https://www.bmi.bund.de/EN/topics/community-and-integration/national-minorities/national-minorities-node.html.

Framework Convention for the Protection of National Minorities 1995. Strasbourg: Council of Europe, 1995. Accessed November 1, 2023. https://rm.coe.int/16800c10cf.

OHCHR. "Concept of a Minority: Mandate Definition. Special Rapporteur on Minority Issues," n.d. Accessed November 1, 2023. https://www.ohchr.org/en/special-procedures/sr-minority-issues.

OSCE. "OSCE High Commissioner on National Minorities Offers Recommendations on Short-Term Responses to COVID-19 That Support Social Cohesion." OSCE High Commissioner on National Minorities, March 26, 2020. Accessed November 1, 2023. https://www.osce.org/hcnm/449170.

OSCE. "Thematic Recommendations and Guidelines," n.d. Accessed November 1, 2023. https://www.osce.org/hcnm/thematic-recommendations-and-guidelines.

Regional Cooperation Council. "Roma Integration 2020. Project Overview," n.d. Accessed November 1, 2023. https://www.rcc.int/romaintegration2020/pages/1/overview.

United Nations. "Chapter VII—Indigenous Peoples and Ethnic Minorities: Marginalization Is the Norm." *Promoting Inclusion through Social Protection*, 91–101. Report on the World Social Situation 2018. New York, NY: United Nations, 2018.

United Nations Development Programme. *Marginalised Minorities in Development Programming.* New York: United Nations Development Programme, 2010. Accessed November 1, 2023. https://www.ohchr.org/Documents/Issues/Minorities/UNDPMarginalisedMinorities.pdf.

Research Literature

Brubaker, Rogers. "National Minorities, Nationalizing States, and External National Homelands in the New Europe." *Daedalus* 124, no. 2 (1995): 107–32.

Card, Claudia. "Injustice, Evil, and Oppression." In *Dancing with Iris—The Philosophy of Iris Marion Young,* edited by Ann Ferguson and Nagel Mechthild, 147–59. Oxford: Oxford University Press, 2009.

Cârstocea, Andreea, and Craig Willis. "Less Equal than Others: National Minorities and the Overlooked Challenge of Socio-economic Inequalities." *ECMI Minorities Blog* (blog), September 30, 2021. https://doi.org/10.53779/AACB5478.

Coakley, John. "Introduction: Dispersed Minorities and Non-Territorial Autonomy." *Ethnopolitics* 15, no. 1 (January 2016): 1–23.

Crepaz, Katharina. "The Minority Safepack Initiative: A European Participatory Process Supporting Cultural Diversity." *European Yearbook of Minority Issues* 17 (2020): 23–47.

European Citizen's Initiative. "Minority SafePack—One Million Signatures for Diversity in Europe." Accessed March 28, 2023. https://europa.eu/citizens-initiative/initiatives/details/2017/000004/minority-safepack-one-million-signatures-diversity-europe_en.

Feinberg, Melissa. *Elusive Equality: Gender, Citizenship, and the Limits of Democracy in Czechoslovakia, 1918–1950*. Pittsburgh: University of Pittsburgh Press, 2006.

FUEN. "About Us." Accessed March 28, 2023. https://www.fuen.org/en/article/The-Federal-Union-of-European-Nationalities-FUEN.

Fundación Secretariado Gitano. "The Fundación Secretariado Gitano Carries Out a Telephone Survey to 11,000 Roma People That Reveals the Serious Social Impact of the Covid-19 Crisis." Fundación Secretariado Gitano Newsroom, April 27, 2020. Accessed November 1, 2023. https://www.gitanos.org/actualidad/archivo/131067.html.

Ghenis, Max. "How Universal Basic Income Would Affect the Black-White Poverty and Wealth Gaps." UBI Center, June 20, 2020. Accessed November 1, 2023. https://medium.com/ubicenter/how-universal-basic-income-would-affect-the-black-white-poverty-and-wealth-gaps-452e2af1497b.

Heller, Agnes. *Beyond Justice*. New York: Basic Books, 1987.

Jackson Preece, Jennifer. *Minority Rights*. Cambridge: Polity Press, 2005.

Jackson Preece, Jennifer. *National Minorities and the European Nation-States System*. Oxford: Clarendon Press, 1998.

Jacob-Owens, Timothy. "Immigration and Multicultural Citizenship in Europe: Insights from the Framework Convention for the Protection of National Minorities." *International Journal on Minority and Group Rights* 29, no. 1 (2022): 167–97.

Justice and the Politics of Difference. Princeton, NJ: Princeton University Press, 2011. https://doi.org/10.2307/j.ctvcm4g4q.

Korunovska, Neda, and Zeljko Jovanovic. "Roma in the COVID-19 Crisis. An Early Warning from Six EU Member States." Open Society Roma Initiatives Office, 2020. Accessed November 1, 2023. https://www.opensocietyfoundations.org/publications/roma-in-the-covid-19-crisis.

Kymlicka, Will. *Politics in the Vernacular. Nationalism, Multiculturalism, and Citizenship*. Oxford: Oxford University Press, 2001.

Malloy, Tove. "Introduction." In *Minority Issues in Europe: Rights, Concepts, Policy*, edited by Tove Malloy, vol. 1, 13–26. Berlin: Frank & Timme, 2013.

McLean, Caitlin, and Ailsa McKay. "Beyond Care: Expanding the Feminist Debate on Universal Basic Income." *WiSE Working Paper Series*, #1. Glasgow: Glasgow Caledonian University, 2015. Accessed November 1, 2023. https://www.gcu.ac.uk/wise/media/gcalwebv2/theuniversity/centresprojects/wise/90324WiSE_BriefingSheet.pdf.

Medda-Windischer, Roberta, Caitlin Boulter, and Tove H. Malloy, eds. *Extending Protection to Migrant Populations in Europe: Old and New Minorities*. London: Routledge, 2019.

Müller-Sprenger, Ludwig. *Die Staatsangehörigkeit der verheirateten Frau*. Berlin: Funk, 1930.

Murray, Charles. "Guaranteed Income as a Replacement for the Welfare State." *Basic Income Studies* 3, no. 2 (2008): 1–12. https://doi.org/10.2202/1932-0183.1115.

Parijs, Philippe van, and Yannick Vanderborght. *Basic Income: A Radical Proposal for a Free Society and a Sane Economy*. Cambridge, MA: Harvard University Press, 2017.

Rawls, John. *A Theory of Justice*. Cambridge, MA: Harvard University Press, 2020.

Robeyns, Ingrid. "Hush Money or Emancipation Fee? A Gender Analysis of Basic Income." In *Basic Income on the Agenda: Policy Objectives and Political Chances*, edited by Robbert-Jan van der Veen and Loek Groot, 121–36. Amsterdam: Amsterdam University Press, 2000.

Rorke, Bernard, and Margaret Matache. "The End of a Decade: What Happened to Roma Inclusion?" openDemocracy, September 29, 2015. Accessed November 1, 2023. https://www.opendemocracy.net/en/can-europe-make-it/end-of-decade-what-happened-to-roma-inclusion/.

Sabanadze, Natalie. "Minorities and Kin-States." *Helsinki Monitor* 17, no. 3 (2006): 244–56.

Seckler-Hudson, Catheryn. *Statelessness: With Special Reference to the United States: (A Study in Nationality and Conflict of Laws)*. Washington, DC: Digest Press, 1934.

Shields, Liam. *Just Enough: Sufficiency as a Demand of Justice*. Edinburgh: Edinburgh University Press, 2016.

Standing, Guy. *Basic Income: And How We Can Make It Happen*. London: Penguin Random House, 2017.

Torry, Malcolm. *Money for Everyone. Why We Need a Citizen's Income*. Bristol: Polity Press, 2013.

Warren, Dorian. "A Universal Basic Income +." Economic Security Project, October 10, 2017. Accessed November 1, 2023. https://economicsecurityproject.org/news/a-universal-basic-income/.

Willis, Craig. "An Overview of the UK's Approach to Ethnic Data Collection in the Context of the Framework Convention on the Protection of National Minorities." *Journal on Ethnopolitics and Minority Issues in Europe* 19, no. 2 (2020): 47–75.

Willis, Craig. "The Minority SafePack Initiative and Universal Basic Income: A Combination to Address Minority Issues in the European Union?" *International Journal on Minority and Group Rights* 28, no. 4 (2021): 575–604. https://doi.org/10.1163/15718115-BJA10012.

Willis, Craig. "Roma and the First Wave of the Covid-19 Pandemic: Income Loss and Its Effects across Roma Communities in Seven Non-EU Countries." *Journal on Ethnopolitics and Minority Issues in Europe* 21, no. 2 (2022): 10–34. https://doi.org/10.53779/AQQL3201.

Wolf, Sonja, and Craig Willis. "Universal Basic Income as a Tool of Empowerment for Minorities." *ECMI Working Paper*, #109, 2018. Accessed March 29, 2023. https://www.ecmi.de/publications/ecmi-research-papers/109-universal-basic-income-as-a-tool-of-empowerment-for-minorities.

Young, Iris Marion. "Five Faces of Oppression." In *Justice and the Politics of Difference, REV-Revised*, 39–65. Princeton, NJ: Princeton University Press, 1990.

Young, Iris Marion. *Inclusion and Democracy*. Oxford: Oxford University Press, 2000.

Young, Iris Marion. "Equality of Whom? Social Groups and Judgments of Injustice." *Journal of Political Philosophy* 9, no. 1 (2001): 1–18.

Zwolinski, Matt. "Classical Liberalism and the Basic Income." *Basic Income Studies* 6, no. 2 (2012). https://doi.org/10.1515/1932-0183.1221.

13

"A Woman without a Country"—Marriage, Derivative Citizenship, and the Consequences of Conflicting Nationality Laws in the Interwar Period

Laura Frey

Introduction

The United States was among the first countries worldwide to introduce the principle of the "equality of the sexes" in their nationality law with the adoption of the Cable Act, also known as the Married Women's Independent Nationality Act, in 1922.[1] The act ruled that women should not be treated differently from men in the naturalization process. This meant that any foreign woman who married an American citizen would not become a citizen of the United States by the simple fact of marrying a citizen. Instead, she would have to apply for citizenship following the regular naturalization process.[2] Additionally, the act stipulated that any female citizen of the United States would not cease to be a citizen on the grounds of marrying a foreign man.[3] The Cable Act thus abolished the principle of derivative citizenship, which had connected the citizenship status of a married women to that of their husbands.[4]

With the introduction of the Cable Act, female American citizens did not face the threat of becoming stateless through marriage or of undergoing an unwanted change in citizenship without agreeing to it.[5] But it also led to an increase of cases of statelessness among foreign women who married American men[6] and were citizens of countries, such as the German Weimar Republic, where the principle of derivative citizenship remained in place. In the 1920s in Germany alone, at least 1,000–2,000 German women married American soldiers in the occupied Rhineland according to contemporary estimates, and at least 200–500 of these marriages took place after the introduction of the Cable Act.[7]

These women automatically became stateless because the German nationality act ruled that they were no longer German citizens and had to follow their husband's nationality, while new US nationality act prevented them from becoming US citizens simply through marriage. German women were not the only women experiencing statelessness since the nationality acts of most countries still upheld the principle of derivative citizenship.[8] The rise of cases of statelessness among foreign women married to American men due to conflicting nationality acts led to an increased interest of different national governments to find an international solution for the problem.[9]

While there is excellent work on the derivative citizenship of women[10] and on the fight for equal nationality rights in the international women's movement,[11] there is a lack of research on the transnational dimension of statelessness and on marital denaturalization caused by conflicting nationality laws in the interwar period.[12]

Women becoming stateless through marriage faced similar problems in their daily life than those faced by the masses of people left stateless after the dissolution of different European Empires in the interwar period.[13] However, these women's position was also fundamentally different as them losing their citizenship status was not intended by national governments but came into existence through a gap in international law. These similarities as well as the dissimilarities shaped the fight of women's rights groups against the "process of legal minoritization"–namely the fight for equal nationality rights. Women's rights groups were able to claim their right to nationality in the context of rising nationalisms and a changed setting of gender relations in the interwar period. Although not often successful with their claims, at least the demands of women's rights groups were mostly well received by different national governments as well as the League of Nations.

This chapter looks at the introduction of the Cable Act in the United States with a focus on the difficulties that it caused for German women marrying American men, the arguments that were used by supporters of independent nationality rights of women, and the reactions of the German government, German members of parliament, and women's rights activists toward the change in the United States. The chapter will show that the situation caused by diverging citizenship laws was used as a window of opportunity by actors engaged in the fight for an "independent nationality of married women" and that it finally led to the adoption of the international "Convention on Certain Questions Relating to the Conflict of Nationality Laws" in 1930. Although the convention did not recommend abolishing the principle of derivative citizenship as such, it did bind the signing parties to tie the marital denaturalization of female citizens to the condition that they would automatically be naturalized in their husband's home country. Germany is an interesting case study for this period, because the opportunities for German women to meet and marry American men rose shortly after the First World War through the presence of American occupation soldiers stationed in the German Rhineland. The chapter is based on archival engagement with personal letters by women affected by marital denaturalization as well as with correspondence between actors of different German and international women's organizations, the German government, and the League of Nations.

Diverging Legal Dogmas: Family Unity versus Equality of the Sexes

Since the introduction of the Civil Code in France in 1804, the principle of derivative citizenship had been laid down in the nationality acts of several countries. Up through the early twentieth century, derivative citizenship was a worldwide dogma with exceptions in some countries in Latin American and Japan.[14] The dogma was based on the idea that men, through military service and political rights, had a direct connection to the state, whereas women in general, and married women in particular, only had a mediated connection to the state via their husbands.[15] Internationally, thirteen different European states reaffirmed this dogma during the Hague Conference on Private International Law, and the conventions adopted between 1902 and 1905 were based on this principle.[16] Like many other countries, the UK and the United States were not part of these conferences and did not sign the convention,[17] but they both still had introduced the principle in 1870 and 1907, respectively.[18]

However, the dogma of the "unity of the family" had been contested since the time of its introduction. Beginning in the early twentieth century, national and international women's organizations such as the International Council of Women started investigating and protesting the dogma.[19] Statelessness or not possessing the same citizenship rights as men was an experience shared by women worldwide and across political lines. In a 1909 article entitled "A Women without a Country," the Russian-American anarchist Emma Goldman talks about her own experience of losing her nationality through marriage.[20] In Germany, women's rights activists published a number of articles with more or less the same title, such as the politician and women's rights activist Helene Lange's 1913 article "Women Have No Fatherland," which appeared in *Die Frau*, the magazine of the Federation of German Women's Associations (Bund Deutscher Frauenvereine, BDF).[21]

Before the First World War, the issue was mostly addressed by women's rights organizations as part of a broader struggle to improve the legal position of women in family law.[22] In Germany, different women's rights organizations such as the Federation for the Legal Protection of Women, the Prussian Union for Women's Suffrage, and the more conservative BDF used the general revision of the German nationality law in 1912-13 to petition for an end to the principle of marital naturalization and denaturalization.[23] By the time their demand was supported by the Social Democratic Party (SDP) in the German Reichstag, the opposition by the other parties and the government was too strong.[24]

The outbreak of the First World War made many people aware of their nationality, as men were drafted for military service and aliens were often interned when they lived in a so-called enemy country. After the war, political and social rights became increasingly connected with the institution of citizenship, so that the distinction between holding and not holding citizenship became fundamental in the daily life of many people. Additionally, passport controls were reinstalled during the war, so the First World War can be considered a turning point with regard to the centrality of nationality in the experience of the majority of the population in Europe and the United States.[25]

The Introduction of the Cable Act in the United States

The introduction of the Cable Act marked a departure from older assumptions about the interconnection between nationality and marriage in the United States. Prior to the adoption of this law, marriages of American women to aliens were perceived as "un-American" acts, so it was believed that these women "deserved" to lose their citizenship.[26] At the same time, in the case of marriages of an American man to a foreign woman, it was assumed that the foreign woman would be loyal to her husband and "lose" her connection to her former nation. These assumptions served as legitimization for the practice of derivative citizenship not only in the United States but also in Germany.[27]

In 1920, the according to the Nineteenth Amendment to the United States Constitution, voting rights were granted to women with American citizenship. This changed the situation fundamentally for women's rights organizations, which turned to the issue of equal nationality rights, as well as for members of Congress and the government. Before then, most of the latter had opposed a change to the nationality act.

In the discussions that led to the introduction of the Cable Act, foreign women married to American men were often targeted as undeservingly privileged by marital naturalization. For example, the author Mary Sumner Boyd, who had published the book *The Woman Citizen* in 1918, argued that it would not be acceptable to grant foreign women who had married American men the right to vote, while American women married to foreign men would be deprived of that right.[28] This was a general sentiment among suffragists, who questioned the fitness of foreign wives to be good American citizens.[29] The National League of Women Voters (NLWV) argued a bit more diplomatically as they tried to emphasize the disadvantages of marital naturalization for foreign women. They argued that seeking their own naturalization would enhance foreign women's status as citizens.[30]

The introduction of voting rights for women also had an effect on the position of many members of the Congress, not only because some members were convinced of the picture drawn by women's rights advocates about the lack of loyalty of automatically naturalized foreign women, but also because they now had to consider a large group of female voters as a new electorate who, so it was assumed, would be in favor of equal nationality rights.[31]

Support for the fight for equal nationality rights came from public officials arguing for a restrictive immigration policy. Especially immigration officers had long advocated abolishing the marital naturalization of foreign women. In the so-called Dillingham Report, which was published in 1909, immigration officers described scandalous, often-invented "fraudulent marriages" between foreign prostitutes and American men. Allegedly, these women married to prevent their deportation from the United States because of their "immoral sexual behavior."[32] So the officers feared that by automatically naturalizing migrant women, "undesired elements" would become American citizens.[33] Regarding the debate in the US Congress that led to the adoption of the Cable Act in 1922, Helen Irving notes that many delegates used the anti-German sentiment present in the United States immediately after the First World War to problematize marriages between German women and American men.[34]

In summary, a general change of perspective regarding female citizens—which was expressed through, among other things, the Nineteenth Amendment—in combination with an anti-immigration sentiment that targeted foreign wives of American men led to the introduction of the Cable Act in 1922.

Reactions to the Cable Act in Germany

The introduction of the Cable Act resonated with the German press and the German government. Already in October 1922, shortly after the introduction of the Cable Act, a civil official of the German Consulate in New York sent a report to the German Foreign Ministry, about the change to American nationality law and warned of the severe consequences that this change could have for German women.[35] The officer of the consulate emphasized that German women who married American citizens would no longer be issued passports by American officers and would consequently become stateless due to their marriages to American citizens.

In December 1922, different deputies from the liberal German Democratic Party (DDP)[36] filed a petition in the German Reichstag, requesting the government to change the German nationality act in the face of changes in the United States and elsewhere so that German women could keep their citizenship upon marriage with foreign men.[37] Among them were Marie Elisabeth Lüders,[38] who was one of the first female representatives of the DDP in the national parliament and was also actively engaged in different women's rights organizations such as the BDF and the International Women Suffrage Alliance (IWSA), and Walther Schücking, an expert in international law. In response, a senior civil servant from the German Ministry of Interior[39] stated that they could not change the law unilaterally, as the government was internationally bound by the Hague Conventions on Private International Law, which were based on the principle of the derivative citizenship of women.[40]

In December 1921, Lüders, Schücking, and other deputies had already filed a petition in the Reichstag with a similar demand and received the same answer,[41] despite the fact that the petition was well received by the German government, which was a coalition between the Catholic Center Party, the DDP, and the SPD at the time. During a consultation with the petitioners in the German Ministry of Interior, representatives from different ministries argued that international solutions were needed.[42] It was suggested that the Ministry for Justice would conduct an internal examination to clarify which international rules would need to be changed and then the Ministry of Interior would request the Institut de Droit International to examine the possibility of introducing a convention granting women independent nationality rights.[43]

Nevertheless, the problems faced by German women did not come to a halt with the prospect of a future international conference on the topic. In another letter dated February 1923, a civil official of the German Consulate in Washington asked the Foreign Office in Berlin for legal solutions for stateless German women as they were confronted with a growing number of women in need of support.[44] The officer in charge at the German Foreign Ministry responded by repeating the position of the German government that they were not able to offer any solutions to this problem and that international agreements were needed.[45]

Even with this rather firm position of the German government, Lüders did not stop her attempts to broaden public awareness of the topic. She published numerous articles in which she argued for the need to change the German nationality act. During the First World War, Lüders had been the head of a newly established women's department in the War Ministry. Her task was to establish a central office for employment for female workers to place women in different factories and enterprises.[46] Due to her work, she was well aware of the situation of women married to foreigners. During the war, they had to report to the police regularly, were not able to obtain a job, and were ineligible for poor relief.[47] This might be one of the reasons why she was especially eager to grant women independent nationality rights.

In a 1922 article by Lüders in the daily newspaper *Berliner Tagesblatt*, she used the existing fear about population decline as well as the general sentiment regarding the superiority of the German nation to demand independent nationality rights for women.[48] In the article, she stated that no nation had as urgent an interest in the proposed reform as Germany, "because its national existence has been grossly injured by the forced loss of vast tracts of land."[49] Lüders went on to emphasize that the German people could not allow themselves "the luxury of banishing many thousands of German-minded, German-feeling, German-educated sisters from our national community for the sake of beautiful theories."[50] There was a strong fear of a decline of the mere numerical size of the population after the end of the First World War, as the treaty of Versailles had led to a perceived "loss" of population and territory.[51]

However, similarly to the debates in the United States, support for independent nationality rights in Germany also came from immigration hardliners such as the German jurist Ernst Isay. In an article published in 1929, Isay argued that although in general he supported derivative citizenship, he would favor granting women independent citizenship rights in the face of the declining German population.[52] He also targeted foreign spouses of German men, stating that it would be a "disadvantage to have to admit foreign women who marry a national indiscriminately to all civil rights, including the right to vote and to stand for election, whereas otherwise a foreigner is granted national status and these rights only after very careful examination and only in exceptional cases."[53] Nevertheless, the argument seemingly did not develop the same impact as it did in the United States, as it did not lead to a change in the nationality act.

The Case of Aloisia Johnson, née Adams, and the Hague Conference in 1930

Especially the situation of German women who had married American occupation soldiers and thereby become stateless seemed to concern politicians and the public. An article titled "The destiny of the American military spouse," which was published in the *Kölnische Zeitung* in January 1923, scandalized the increasing number of stateless German women who had married American occupation soldiers.[54] The author claimed that the Cable Act was introduced to fight German immigration to the United States. Although this was probably an exaggeration, it is crucial to note that German reporters were aware of the anti-German and anti-immigration arguments used by delegates during the debates for the introduction of the Cable Act in the US Congress.

In early 1923, the German Ministry of Interior started an inquiry together with the Reich commissioner for the occupied territories in Germany on the observed increase in marriages between German women and American soldiers.[55] One of the women who became stateless due to the conflicting nationality laws in Germany and the United States was Aloisia Johnson, née Adams. Her case became nationally and internationally known because her father, Aloys Adams, had contacted Marie Elisabeth Lüders in the 1920s asking for help for his daughter.[56] He was far from the only person to contact Lüders. In the 1920s, she was publicly known for her attempts to change the German nationality act. In 1927, a writer in the *Vossische Zeitung* even called the proposition of a new nationality act based on the principle of the equality of the sexes the "Lex Lüders."[57] As a consequence of her public visibility regarding the cause, she received many letters from German women who had married foreign men or from their relatives describing their desperate situations and the problems caused by internationally conflicting nationality acts.[58]

From them all, Lüders chose the case of Aloisia Johnson, née Adams, to scandalize the practice of marital denaturalization and the problems of the diverging legal dogmas.[59] The case seemed to be well suited for public usage, because Aloisia Adams had held a respectable occupation as a language teacher, which she had lost due to her statelessness since German citizenship was a prerequisite to work as a teacher. She had lived and met her future husband, the American soldier Benjamin Johnson, in the occupied Rhineland, also a topic that could be easily scandalized, as the occupation and the presence of occupation soldiers was perceived as a major injustice by the German public.

Additionally, the soldier who had married Aloisa Adams, on January 20, 1923, was a white man, so her case did not touch on the whole subject of relationships between black occupation soldiers and white women. Lüders would not have defended such a case: like many other women's rights activists, she used racialized arguments against the presence of black American or French soldiers. She was even involved in a campaign that accused black occupation soldiers of raping German women.[60]

Five days after their marriage, Johnson had been relocated with his unit to the United States, leaving his newly wed wife, Aloisia Adams, behind.[61] After his departure, she had tried to contact him privately as well as through official channels but could not reach him. Besides the assumed disappointment about the disappearance of her husband, she faced harsh material consequences, as she became unemployed and was ineligible for poor relief due to her statelessness. To add to this, Adams could not get a divorce because the German code of civil procedure ruled that the residence of the husband was decisive for which court was in charge of the divorce. Lüders was able to help Adams. They first managed to regain Adams's permission to work and with the support of the Prussian minister for interior, she was able to regain her nationality on August 30, 1927.[62] Finally, Adams was able to obtain a divorce because the responsible judge in Koblenz interpreted the law for an annulation of a marriage in her favor.[63]

The case of Aloisia Adams became internationally known when Walther Schücking brought it in front of the League of Nations's Commission on Nationality.[64] The commission was established in September 1924 to deal with questions of international private law, including the nationality of married women.[65] The aim of the commission was to prepare an international conference to sign a convention on international private law.[66] Walther Schücking was part of the commission, not as a representative of the German state, which was only allowed to join the league in September 1926, but as an expert in international law.⁶⁷ In a note dated 1927, Schücking informed Lüders that they had discussed the case of Aloisia Adams in the commission and that it planned to suggest to the league that although the coming international conference would not set independent nationality rights for women as an achievable aim, the league should try to find a way to avoid the "worst cases of statelessness," such as when a wife loses her citizenship through marriage but does not automatically acquire that of her husband.⁶⁸

The League of Nations started investigating the topic not only on account of the desperate situations many women were faced with due to conflicting nationality acts but also because international women's rights organizations such as the Women's International League for Peace and Freedom (WILPF) and the IWSA⁶⁹ had been pressuring the league secretary to adopt an international convention on the issue for several years. Already during the First World War, Chrystal Macmillan, a lawyer and a leading British and international women's rights activist, wrote in *Jus Suffragii*, the magazine of the IWSA, that "the war ha[d] brought home to all women ... the need for some drastic alteration in those laws on nationality."⁷⁰

The 1919 Congress of the WILPF in Zurich decided to petition the newly established League of Nations to establish a committee to deal with the consequences of marriages between partners with different nationalities for women. In 1920, Emily S. Balch, the secretary of the WILPF at the time, described the situation of women married to foreigners in a letter to the secretary-general of the League of Nations, Eric Drummond. She stated that "the cases of persons who, as a result of the lack of harmony in the legislation of different countries ... have no claim to citizenship in any country ... is very considerable." Balch continued her letter to say that "even more tragic [would] have been the innumerable cases during the war of women who have become by marriage citizens of a country with which their own was at war and who thereby became liable to expatriation, internment and other measures directed at enemy aliens."⁷¹

In 1923, the IWSA introduced a committee to deal with the question of the nationality of married women. It suggested the ratification of an international convention on the nationality of married women to the League of Nations.⁷² This proposal was recognized and discussed by the league's Commission on Nationality, but it was not perceived as suitable for an international convention. Instead, the league developed a separate convention in correspondence with the representatives of different member states of the league.

The conference demanded by the league's Commission on Nationality and international women's rights organizations took place in The Hague in March 1930. As a result of the conference, the Convention on Certain Questions Relating to the Conflicts of Nationality Laws was signed by the representatives of forty states.⁷³ Marie Elisabeth Lüders was among the very few female delegates who participated in the conference, because the Federation of German Women's Associations pressured the German government to include her.⁷⁴ As might have already been predictable at the beginning of the convention, it did not demand that states grant married women the right to retain their original citizenship, but it did make acquiring the nationality of the husband a prerequisite for marital denaturalization.⁷⁵ The United States was the only country that refused to sign the convention. Different women's rights organizations also protested the results and tried to lobby national governments and the League of

Nations not to ratify the convention but rather to hold another conference to adopt a convention granting women the right to keep their nationality after marriage.

Conclusion

This chapter has analyzed the interwar period as a period of transition for the legal dogmas underlying the nationality acts of Germany and the United States. In some countries, such as the United States, the principle of the "equality of the sexes" was already introduced in the nationality act in the 1920s, while in other countries, such as Germany, the principle of derivative citizenship was still upheld. This specific situation caused an increase in cases of statelessness among women with spouses of a different nationality.

Equality in nationality laws was not fought for merely on the basis of humanistic arguments but also on the basis of nationalistic argumentations regarding the qualification of foreign women to become citizens, especially in the face of increasing political rights for women. Additionally, pronatalist arguments—which in Germany reflected the fear of a population loss after the First World War—served as a tool to argue for equality in nationality rights. This was also true for the United States with a slightly different emphasis. While in the case of the German state, one can observe a reflection of these general sentiments in the choice of case studies to scandalize the practice of marital denaturalization, even these arguments did not lead to the introduction of equal rights in the nationality law until 1957.

The German government, contrary to the government in the United States, felt bound by the Hague Convention of 1902 and 1905 to the principle of derivative citizenship and obliged to seek international solutions for the problem of statelessness among married women due to conflicting international laws. The Hague Convention of 1930 offered such a solution, although it was perceived as a failure by international women's organizations because it did not reject the principle of derivative citizenship.

Notes

1. See Candice Lewis Bredbenner, *A Nationality of Her Own: Women, Marriage, and the Law of Citizenship* (Berkeley: University of California Press, 1998), 3.
2. The only facilitation was that a foreign woman married to a citizen needed to prove a one-year period of residence in the country instead of the regular five-year period before filing the petition for naturalization. See An Act Relative to the Naturalization and Citizenship of Married Women, Bundesarchiv (BArch) R1501/108059, 125.
3. Ibid. This rule stipulated, however, that the husband was theoretically eligible for US citizenship and that the couple did not live for more than two years in his home country. The addition that her husband needed to be eligible for citizenship represented a continuation of racial marriage policy in the United States. For example, American women who married Chinese men were not allowed to keep their citizenship upon marriage. See Martha Gardner, *The Qualities of a Citizen: Women, Immigration, and Citizenship, 1870–1965* (Princeton, NJ: Princeton University Press, 2009), 124.

4. Derivative citizenship meant that a married woman did not possess citizenship independent of the citizenship of her husband and that her citizenship status depended on that of her husband. Consequently, when a woman married a man of another nationality, she would automatically adopt his citizenship, a process that is known as "marital naturalization" or "martial denaturalization." In case the husband's citizenship changed during the marriage, the woman was assumed to automatically acquire his new legal status, too.
5. Helen Irving, *Citizenship, Alienage, and the Modern Constitutional State: A Gendered History* (Cambridge: Cambridge University Press, 2016), 206.
6. Linda K. Kerber, "Toward a History of Statelessness in America," *American Quarterly* 57, no. 3 (2005): 735.
7. The American social scientist Catheryn Seckler-Hudson speaks of 1,000 cases of marriages between American occupation soldiers and German women, while Ludwig Müller-Sprenger gives an estimate of 2,000 cases. See Catheryn Seckler-Hudson, *Statelessness: With Special Reference to the United States: (A Study in Nationality and Conflict of Laws)* (Washington, DC: Digest Press, 1934), 95; Ludwig Müller-Sprenger, *Die Staatsangehörigkeit der verheirateten Frau* (Berlin: Funk, 1930).
8. Melissa Feinberg speaks of the "tremendous impact" that the Cable Act had on Czech women in Melissa Feinberg, *Elusive Equality: Gender, Citizenship, and the Limits of Democracy in Czechoslovokia 1918-1950* (Pittsburgh: University of Pittsburgh Press, 2006), 77.
9. Irving, *Citizenship, Alienage, and the Modern Constitutional State: A Gendered History*, 161.
10. Bredbenner, *A Nationality of Her Own*, 1440–74; Anne Marie Nicolosi, "We Do Not Want Our Girls to Marry Foreigners: Gender, Race, and American Citizenship," *National Women's Studies Association Journal* 13, no. 3 (2001): 1–21; Gardner, *The Qualities of a Citizen: Women, Immigration, and Citizenship, 1870–1965*, 622–54; Ida Blom, "From Communal Family Rights to Individual Rights in Women's National Citizenship in Norway, 1888–1950," in *Women's Rights and Human Rights: International Historical Perspectives*, ed. Patricia Grimshaw, Katie Holmes, and Marilyn Lake (Basingstoke: Palgrave Macmillan UK, 2001), 1984–98; Betty de Hart, "The Morality of Maria Toet: Gender Citizenship and the Construction of the Nation-State," *Journal of Ethnic and Migration Studies* 32, no. 1 (2006): 49–68; Philip Girard, "If Two Ride a Horse, One Must Ride in Front: Married Women's Nationality and the Law in Can-Ada 1880---1950," *Canadian Historical Review* 94 (2013): 28–54; Regina Wecker, "'Ehe ist Schicksal, Vaterland ist auch Schicksal und dagegen ist kein Kraut gewachsen.' Ge-Meindebürgerrecht und Staatsangehörigkeitsrecht von Frauen in der Schweiz 1798–1998," *L'homme* 10, no. 1 (1999): 14–32.
11. Ellen Carol Dubois, "Internationalizing Married Women's Nationality: The Hague Campaign of 1930," in *Globalizing Feminisms, 1789 – 1945*, ed. Karen M. Offen (London: Routledge, 2010), 204–16; Linda Guerry, "Married Women's Nationality in the International Context 1918–1935," *Clio. Women, Gender, History* 43 (2016): 73–93; Leila J. Rupp, *Worlds of Women: The Making of an International Women's Movement* (Princeton, NJ: Princeton University Press, 1997).
12. Miriam Rürup, "Das Geschlecht der Staatenlosen. Staatenlosigkeit in der Bundesrepublik nach 1945," *Journal of Modern European History* 14, no. 3 (2016): 411–29.
13. Mira Siegelberg, *Statelessness: A Modern History* (Cambridge: Harvard University Press, 2020).

14. Irving, *Citizenship, Alienage, and the Modern Constitutional State: A Gendered History*, viiii.
15. Carole Pateman, *The Sexual Contract* (Stanford: Stanford University Press, 1988); Gerhard Ute and Valentine Maunier, "Civil Law and Gender in Nineteenth-Century Europe," *Clio. Women, Gender, History* 43 (2016): 250–75; Dieter Gosewinkel, *Einbürgern und Ausschließen. Die Nationalisierung der Staatsangehörigkeit vom Deutschen Bund bis zur Bundesrepublik Deutschland* (Göttingen: Vandenhoeck & Ruprecht, 2001), 296.
16. Christian von Bar, "Die Eherechtlichen Konventionen der Haager Konferenz(En)," *Rabels Zeitschrift Für Ausländisches Und Internationales Privatrecht* 57, no. 1/2 (1993): 63–119.
17. Gustav A. E. Bogeng, *Die Haager Abkommen über internationales Privat- und Zivilprozeß-Recht: Textausgabe mit Einleitung, Anmerkungen und Sachregister* (Berlin: De Gruyter, [1908]2018).
18. Irving, *Citizenship, Alienage, and the Modern Constitutional State: A Gendered History*, 54–66.
19. Guerry, "Married Women's Nationality in the International Context 1918–1935," 75.
20. Emma Goldman, "A Women without a Country," *Mother Earth*, 1909.
21. Helene Lange, "Die Frauen haben kein Vaterland," *Die Frau*, vol. 20, no.11, August 1913.
22. Marion Röwekamp, "Gerechtigkeit für Frauen im Sozialstaat? Weibliche Staatsangehörige im Kaiserreich und in der Weimarer Republik," in *Gerechtigkeit im Sozialstaat: Analysen und Vorschläge*, ed. Ulrike Haerendel (Baden-Baden: Nomos Verlagsgesellschaft, 2012), 76.
23. Petition of different women's rights organizations, February 1912, BArch R1501/108014, 165–75.
24. Second Reading of the Nationality Act in the Reichstag, May 1913, 153. Session, 5272–5275.
25. John Torpey, "Passports and the Development of Immigration Controls in the North Atlantic World during the Long Nineteenth Century," in *Migration Control in the North Atlantic World. The Evolution of State Practices in Europe and the United States from the French Revolution to the Inter-War Period*, ed. Andreas Fahrmeir, Oliver Faron, and Patrick Weil (New York: Berghahn Books, 2003), 83–6.
26. Bredbenner, *A Nationality of Her Own*, 6.
27. Christoph Lorke, *Liebe Verwalten: "Ausländerehen" in Deutschland 1870–1945* (Paderborn: Ferdinand Schöningh, 2020).
28. Bredbenner, *A Nationality of Her Own*, 74.
29. Ibid., 52.
30. Ibid., 92–3.
31. Ibid., 81.
32. William Paul Dillingham, *Importing Women for Immoral Purposes: A Partial Report from the Immigration Commission on the Importation and Harboring of Women for Immoral Purposes*, Senate Document 61st Congress, No. 196 (Washington, DC: Government Printing Office, 1909).
33. Bredbenner, *A Nationality of Her Own*, 29.
34. Irving, *Citizenship, Alienage, and the Modern Constitutional State: A Gendered History*, 159.
35. Letter of the German Consulate General in New York, October 24, 1922, BArch R1501/108059.

36. The DDP was a liberal party in the Weimar Republic. Politicians such as Friedrich Naumann, Walther Rathenau, and Gustav Stresemann were part of it. The DDP was, with a very short interruption in 1927–8, part of every government during the Weimar Republic, including in December 1922. See Werner Schneider, *Die Deutsche Demokratische Partei in Der Weimarer Republik 1924–1930* (München: Wilhelm Fink Verlag, 1978).
37. Petition no. 1928, no. 5342 Reichstag, electoral period 1920–2, December 7, 1922, BArch N1151/245.
38. Lüders was born in 1878 to a bourgeois family. She was among the first women in Germany to be enrolled at the University of Berlin in 1909 and one of the first women to acquire a doctoral degree, with a thesis on the legal and economic foundations of wage labor among women. During the rule of the German National Socialist Party, Lüders had to stop her political engagement. However, she remained one of the leading activists in the quest for equal nationality rights in the early Federal Republic of Germany, then as a member of the national parliament for the Free Democratic Party of Germany (FDP).
39. The government at the time of the petition was a coalition between the Catholic Center Party, the DDP, and two smaller parties.
40. Answer to the petition by Lüders and others concerning the nationality of married women, December 15, 1922, BArch N1151/245.
41. Petition by Lüders, Schücking, and others in the Reichstag, electoral period 1920–1, BArch N1151/245.
42. Report about a provisional consultation in the Ministry of Interior, March 18, 1922, BArch R1501/108059, 11–19.
43. Ibid.
44. German Ministry of Interior to the German Foreign Ministry, March 24, 1923, BArch R1501/108059, 129.
45. German Foreign Ministry to the German Consulate in Washington, February 28, 1923, BArch R1501/108059.
46. Wolther von Kieseritzky, *Marie-Elisabeth Lüders. Vorkämpferin für Menschenrechte* (Potsdam-Babelsberg: Friedrich-Naumann-Stiftung für die Freiheit, 2021), 9.
47. Material of the center for support and information about the consequences of the Nationality Law, July 22, 1913, BArch N1136/13.
48. Marie Elisabeth Lüders, "Vaterlandslose Frauen," *Berliner Tagesblatt*, September 8, 1922.
49. Ibid.
50. Ibid.
51. On this topic, see, among others, Mark Mazower, *Dark Continent: Europe's Twentieth Century* (London: Penguin, 1999).
52. Ernst Haymann Isay, "Die Staatsangehörigkeit der Ehefrau," *Zeitschrift für Standesamtswesen* 9 (1929): 348–50.
53. Ibid.
54. Unknown, "Das Schicksal der amerikanischen Soldatenfrauen," *Kölnische Zeitung*, January 17, 1923.
55. German Ministry of Interior to the Reich Commissioner for the Occupied Territories, June 7, 1923, BArch R1501/108059.
56. This is based on correspondence between Aloys Adams, Aloisia Adams, Dr. Marie Elisabeth Lüders, an official of the Prussian Ministry of Justice, and the barrister Dr. Hugo Kaufmann I, February 1927–March 1928, BArch N1151/246.

57. Unknown, "Lex Lüders," *Vossische Zeitung*, March 3, 1927.
58. Letters from the audience, 1928–31, BArch N1151/246.
59. Correspondence between Aloys Adams, Aloisia Adams, Dr. Marie Elisabeth Lüders, and Dr. Hugo Kaufmann I, February 1927–March 1928, BArch N1151/246.
60. Letter of Marie Elisabeth Lüders to Margery Corbett Ashby, December 30, 1927, Barch N1151/246.
61. Correspondence between Aloys Adams, Aloisia Adams, Dr. Marie Elisabeth Lüders, and Dr. Hugo Kaufmann I, February 1927–March 1928, BArch N1151/246.
62. Letter from Lüders to the Prussian Ministry of Interior, April 7, 1927, Geheimes Staatsarchiv Preußischer Kulturbesitz (GSta PK) I HA Rep. 77, Tit. 2770, No. 3 J Bd.3, p. 216.
63. Correspondence between Aloys Adams, Aloisia née Adams, Dr. Marie Elisabeth Lüders, and Dr. Hugo Kaufmann I, February 1927–March 1928, BArch, N1151/246.
64. Correspondence between Walther Schücking and the German Foreign Ministry, Mai 1927, BArch, N1051-F/90.
65. League of Nations Archive (LON) R1275/19/42199/10950.
66. Szymon Rundstein's comments—expert in international law and another member of the commission—on Schücking's observations, June 7, 1926, BArch N1051-F/90.
67. Foreign Ministry to the Ministry of Justice, November 9, 1925, BArch R1501/108060.
68. Note from Schücking to Lüders, 1927, BArch N1151/245.
69. The IWSA was founded in 1904 and consisted mostly of elitist white Christian women from Europe or the United States. For more, see Rupp, *Worlds of Women*, 22.
70. Chrystal Macmillan, "The Nationality of Married Women," *Jus Suffragii* 11 no. 10 (October 1916): 2–3.
71. Emily S. Balch to Eric Drummond, December 9, 1920, LON, R1273/19/9443.
72. Provisional draft of the international convention on the nationality of married women, May 24, 1923, LON R1273/19/9443.
73. Irving, *Citizenship, Alienage, and the Modern Constitutional State: A Gendered History*, 51.
74. Camilla Jellinek, "Internationale Frauen-Solidarität/Frauenkundgebung im Haag," *Nachrichtenblatt*, April 1930.
75. Convention on Certain Questions Relating to the Conflict of Nationality Laws, The Hague, April 12, 1930.

Bibliography

Archival Sources

Bundesarchiv (Arch), Berlin
 N1051-F/90
 N1136/13
 N1151/245
 N1151/246
 R1001/108014
 R1501/108059
 R1501/108060
Geheimes Staatsarchiv Preußischer Kulturbesitz (GSta PK), Berlin
 I HA Rep.77, Tit. 2770

League of Nations Archive (LON), Geneva
R1273/19/9443
R1275/19/42199/10950

Printed Sources

Bogeng, Gustav A. E. *Die Haager Abkommen über internationales Privat- und Zivilprozeß-Recht: Textausgabe mit Einleitung, Anmerkungen und Sachregister*. Berlin: De Gruyter, 1908.
Convention on Certain Questions Relating to the Conflict of Nationality Laws, The Hague, April 12, 1930.
Dillingham, William Paul. *Importing Women for Immoral Purposes: A Partial Report From the Immigration Commission on the Importation and Harboring of Women for Immoral Purposes*. Senate Document 61st Congress, No. 196. Washington, DC: Government Printing Office, 1909.
Goldman, Emma. "A Women without a Country." *Mother Earth*, 1909.
Haymann Isay, Ernst. "Die Staatsangehörigkeit der Ehefrau." *Zeitschrift für Standesamtswesen* 9 (1929): 348–50.
Jellinek, Camilla, "Internationale Frauen-Solidarität/Frauenkundgebung in Haag." *Nachrichtenblatt*, April 1930.
Lange, Helene. "Die Frauen haben kein Vaterland." *Die Frau*, vol. 20, no. 11, August 1913.
Lüders, Marie Elisabeth. "Vaterlandslose Frauen." *Berliner Tagesblatt*, September 8, 1922.
Macmillan, Chrystal. "The Nationality of Married Women." *Jus Suffragii*, vol. 11, no. 10, October 1916, 2–3.
Unknown. "Das Schicksal der amerikanischen Soldatenfrauen." *Kölnische Zeitung*, January 17, 1923.
Unknown. "Lex Lüders." *Vossische Zeitung*, March 3, 1927.

Research Literature

Bar, Christian von. "Die Eherechtlichen Konventionen der Haager Konferenz(En)." *Rabels Zeitschrift für ausländisches und internationales Privatrecht* 57, no. 1/2 (1993): 63–123.
Blom, Ida. "From Communal Family Rights to Individual Rights in Women's National Citizenship in Norway, 1888–1950." In *Women's Rights and Human Rights: International Historical Perspectives*, edited by Patricia Grimshaw, Katie Holmes, and Marilyn Lake, 184–98. Basingstoke: Palgrave Macmillan UK, 2001.
Bredbenner, Candice Lewis. *A Nationality of Her Own: Women, Marriage, and the Law of Citizenship*. Berkeley: University of California Press, 1998.
Cott, Nancy F. "Marriage and Women's Citizenship in the United States 1830–1934." *American Historical Review* 103, no. 5 (1998): 1440–74.
Dubois, Ellen Carol. "Internationalizing Married Women's Nationality: The Hague Campaign of 1930." In *Globalizing Feminisms, 1789–1945*, edited by Karen M. Offen, 204–16. London: Routledge, 2010.
Feinberg, Melissa. *Elusive Equality: Gender, Citizenship, and the Limits of Democracy in Czechoslovakia 1918–1950*. Pittsburgh: University of Pittsburgh Press, 2006.
Gardner, Martha. *The Qualities of a Citizen: Women, Immigration, and Citizenship, 1870–1965*. Princeton, NJ: Princeton University Press, 2009.

Girard, Philip. "If Two Ride a Horse, One Must Ride in Front: Married Women's Nationality and the Law in Canada 1880–1950." *Canadian Historical Review* 94 (2013): 28–54.

Gosewinkel, Dieter. *Einbürgern und Ausschließen. Die Nationalisierung der Staatsangehörigkeit vom Deutschen Bund bis zur Bundesrepublik Deutschland.* Göttingen: Vandenhoeck & Ruprecht, 2001.

Guerry, Linda. "Married Women's Nationality in the International Context 1918–1935." *Clio. Women, Gender, History* 43 (2016): 73–93.

Hart, Betty de. "The Morality of Maria Toet: Gender Citizenship and the Construction of the Nation-State." *Journal of Ethnic and Migration Studies* 32, no. 1 (2006): 49–68.

Irving, Helen. *Citizenship, Alienage, and the Modern Constitutional State: A Gendered History.* Cambridge: Cambridge University Press, 2016.

Kerber, Linda K. "Toward a History of Statelessness in America." *American Quarterly* 57, no. 3 (2005): 727–49.

Kieseritzky, Wolther von. *Marie-Elisabeth Lüders. Vorkämpferin für Menschenrechte.* Potsdam-Babelsberg: Friedrich-Naumann-Stiftung für die Freiheit, 2021.

Lorke, Christoph. *Liebe Verwalten: "Ausländerehen" in Deutschland 1870–1945.* Paderborn: Ferdinand Schöningh, 2020.

Mazower, Mark. *Dark Continent: Europe's Twentieth Century.* London: Penguin, 1999.

Nicolosi, Anne Marie. "We Do Not Want Our Girls to Marry Foreigners: Gender, Race, and American Citizenship." *National Women's Studies Association Journal* 13, no. 3 (2001): 1–21.

Pateman, Carole. *The Sexual Contract.* Stanford: Stanford University Press, 1988.

Röwekamp, Marion. "Gerechtigkeit für Frauen im Sozialstaat? Weibliche Staatsangehörige im Kaiserreich und in der Weimarer Republik." In *Gerechtigkeit im Sozialstaat: Analysen und Vorschläge*, edited by Ulrike Haerendel, 71–87. Baden-Baden: Nomos Verlagsgesellschaft, 2012.

Rupp, Leila J. *Worlds of Women: The Making of an International Women's Movement.* Princeton, NJ: Princeton University Press, 1997.

Rürup, Miriam. "Das Geschlecht der Staatenlosen. Staatenlosigkeit in der Bundesrepublik nach 1945." *Journal of Modern European History* 14, no. 3 (2016): 411–29.

Schneider, Werner. *Die Deutsche Demokratische Partei in der Weimarer Republik 1924–1930.* München: Wilhelm Fink Verlag, 1978.

Siegelberg, Mira. *Statelessness: A Modern History.* Cambridge: Harvard University Press, 2020.

Studer, Brigitte. "Citizenship as Contingent Belonging: Married Women and Foreigners in Twentieth-Century Switzerland." *Gender and History* 13, no. 3 (2001): 622–54.

Torpey, John. "Passports and the Development of Immigration Controls in the North Atlantic World during the Long Nineteenth Century." In *Migration Control in the North Atlantic World. The Evolution of State Practices in Europe and the United States from the French Revolution to the Inter-War Period*, edited by Andreas Fahrmeir, Oliver Faron, and Patrick Weil, 73–91. New York: Berghahn Books, 2003.

Ute, Gerhard, and Valentine Maunier. "Civil Law and Gender in Nineteenth-Century Europe." *Clio. Women, Gender, History* 43 (2016): 250–75.

Wecker, Regina. "'Ehe ist Schicksal, Vaterland ist auch Schicksal und dagegen ist kein Kraut gewachsen.' Ge-Meindebürgerrecht und Staatsangehörigkeitsrecht von Frauen in der Schweiz 1798–1998." *L'homme* 10, no. 1 (1999): 14–32.

14

Defending the Rights of Women as "Mothers, Workers, and Citizens." WIDF's Practices of Cooperating with Female Activists in Latin America (1960s–70s)

Yulia Gradskova

The Women's International Democratic Federation (WIDF) was founded in Paris in 1945. The federation declared that its main goal was uniting women of the "whole world" around issues like the defense of peace, women's rights, and protection of mothers and children.[1] In contrast to many other transnational women's organizations working for women's rights during the same historical period,[2] from its first days, WIDF regarded the rights of women to work outside of the home and state protection of motherhood to be important for its program. Indeed, WIDF saw women's roles as those of "mothers, workers, and citizens" at the same time. The importance of all three elements in this interpretation could be found, for example, in the keynote speech by one of WIDF's vice presidents, Sweden's Andrea Andreen, at the Women's World Congress organized by WIDF in Copenhagen in 1953. According to Andreen, women's participation in economic life together with men is one of the conditions for true equality between men and women.[3] At the same time, said Andreen, women give birth to children and need the right to participate in social life in order to ensure that their children will have a happy life.[4] WIDF continued to refer to this interpretation of women's social roles later as well, and at the WIDF Congress in Helsinki in 1969, Cecile Hugel, WIDF's general secretary, spoke about importance of the triple role of women: mother, worker, and citizen.[5] Thus, it is possible to say that the idea of woman as a mother, worker, and citizen continued to be in the center of the federation's work during the whole Cold War period.

In spite of the federation presenting itself as speaking in the name of "women of the whole world,"[6] in the West, WIDF was looked upon rather as a "Soviet front" organization. Indeed, in the Cold War context, WIDF mainly supported the Soviet Union and the Soviet bloc, and a significant number of its leaders were members of communist parties.[7] However, recent scholarship has questioned the federation's full dependency on Moscow. In particular, it has showed the complexity of internal relationships in the federation, conflicts between women's organizations from different countries around decision-making, and a growing diversity of WIDF leadership and inclusion of many demands of women from non-European countries into WIDF's agenda.[8] Several researchers have also shown that the federation played an important role in organizing solidarity of women fighting against colonialism and apartheid.[9] Finally, Francisca de Haan showed that WIDF was crucial for establishing the International Women's Year (1975) and adoption of the Convention on Elimination of All Discrimination Against Women (CEDAW) convention in 1979.[10]

WIDF was one of several women's organizations active in Latin American countries.[11] Moreover, it was the Cuban Revolution of 1959 that made women's activism on the continent and role that Latin American woman played in the WIDF to be particularly visible. However, most research on Latin American women's participation in WIDF has focused on the early Cold War.[12] In contrast, Latin American women's participation in WIDF after the Cuban Revolution of 1959 has been explored less. Furthermore, Latin American women in WIDF have been studied mainly from the perspective of particular countries (the exception is Ramirez Chicharro, who explored Mexican and Cuban chapters in WIDF). Research in a comparative perspective has paid less attention to WIDF strategies in general and to the dynamics of the influence of Latin American women in the federation's programs and everyday work.[13] Finally, the role of the Soviet Union and of the countries of Soviet bloc in the defense of women's rights in Latin America is also under-researched.

The main aim of this chapter is to analyze WIDF's work in Latin American countries in the 1960s and 1970s, when the WIDF actively worked for increasing Latin American women presence in the WIDF. I am focusing on the federation's centralized efforts for spreading its message among Latin American women and for the efforts of sharing power and tasks inside WIDF in the process of cooperation with non-European women, initially minority in the WIDF's leadership. In this context I am particularly interested in the place of Cuba and Cuban chapter of WIDF, the Federation of Cuban Women (Federación de Mujeres Cubanas in Spanish, hereafter FMC), in realization of WIDF's goals in Latin America.

In order to answer to these questions, I analyze WIDF's official publications, first of all its own journal Women of the Whole World (WWW), which began publication in 1951 in several languages (in Russian, the name is *Zhenshiny mira*, or ZM). I also look at a journal published by FMC named Mujeres[14] and analyze archival materials preserved in the State Archive of the Russian Federation (GARF) in Moscow, collection of the Committee of Soviet Women (CSW, the Soviet chapter of WIDF, fond 7928). This collection partly preserves classified correspondence among Soviet employees about various aspects of the work of WIDF's leadership. Finally, I used published memories of one of WIDF's prominent leaders, Fanny Edelman, an Argentinian communist who served as WIDF's general secretary between 1972 and 1978.

I start with a short overview of the contemporary problems of women in Latin America and WIDF's work there as presented in WIDF's official publications. In the second part of this chapter, I explore personal and classified documents on the internal life of the WIDF. Finally, the last part of this chapter is dedicated to the role of Cuba in the work of the federation.

WIDF's Work in Latin America—Main Directions and Events as Presented in Its Periodical Publications

Latin America was where national women's organizations got involved in trans-American liberal and reformist organizations in the 1940s and 1950s.[15] However, left-oriented women's groups and organizations were in many cases created by or in close cooperation with local communist parties, often as broad coalitions of socialist, communist, and nonparty members,[16] in difference to liberal women's organizations they were less involved into transnational cooperation. Further, it is possible to suppose that the size of the communist party in the various countries influenced popularity of leftist organizations among women. In 1959, the biggest communist parties in Latin America were (in decreasing order) in Argentina, Brazil, Venezuela, and Chile,[17] thus, visibility of Latin American women from particular countries in the WIDF to some extent could be traced through the size, position, and developments in the communist parties and their women's sections in these countries. Indeed, it was Argentina, Brazil, Chile, Uruguay, and Cuba who sent representatives to WIDF's founding congress in Paris,[18] and women from these countries were more visible in WIDF publications.[19]

In the second half of the 1950s, WIDF expanded its activities and on November 19–22, 1959, the first congress for Latin American women was organized and held in Santiago de Chile. Another historical event in the same year—namely the Cuban Revolution—seems to have contributed even more to the increasing visibility and influence of Latin American women in WIDF. WIDF's journal reported on the congress in Santiago de Chile and observed that the meeting included 503 delegates from thirteen countries, and that WIDF's president, Eugenie Cotton, attended this congress.[20]

Margarita de Ponce, WIDF's vice president from Argentina, presented a detailed report about the 1959 congress at the first WIDF bureau meeting outside of Europe (Jakarta, Indonesia, in 1960).[21] She noted that Latin American and African countries had a similar need to overcome legacies of colonialism and problems associated with underdevelopment: according to de Ponce, 70 percent of Latin American men and women were illiterate and 60 percent were agricultural workers.[22] The first congress of Latin American women has been dedicated to three main themes, the first of which explicitly referred to the main slogan of the federation: "For the dignity of Latin American women as mothers, workers and citizens."[23] Thus, it is possible to see that WIDF's first Latin American congress partly followed the agenda elaborated in Europe. However, as in the case of other events organized by WIDF,[24] it is easy to suppose that delegates of this congress discussed much broader number issues and approaches to women's rights that might be visible in the official reports.

In the 1960s, WIDF's journal continued publishing materials on various aspects of women's lives and activism in Latin America and paid more attention to individual female leaders and organizations (e.g., there were articles on Lidia Gouverneur from Venezuela[25] and Olga Poblete from Chile[26]). Much attention was paid to Cuba and especially to the leader, Vilma Espín, of the new women's organization (i.e., FMC) created in Cuba in 1960. Indeed, the journal published Espín's speech at the congress in Santiago de Chile, where she described transformation of women's lives in Cuba focusing on housing programs, eradication of illiteracy, and transformation of the health centers.[27] Another article dedicated to Espín[28] described the Cuban leader's early years and participation in the partisan struggle. However, it is interesting to note that, near the end of the article, the journal showed her to be an involved mother, as if suggesting that she also corresponded to the WIDF ideal of woman as a mother, worker, and citizen.[29]

The next big event organized by WIDF in Latin America consisted of two seminars in 1968 held separately for women from northern and southern Latin America, namely in Santiago de Chile and Mexico City.[30] Both seminars concluded that outdated systems of land use, lack of state involvement in building affordable housing and childcare facilities, and not enough attention to the problems of illiteracy and food shortages meant that many women were suffering discrimination. These, in turn, were key areas for women's activism.[31] Five years later, in October 1974, the third Latin American seminar was organized in Lima, Peru, and was specifically dedicated to women's education. In contrast to the WIDF-sponsored events in the 1950s and 1960s, the third seminar had more perspective on "development" and used the rhetoric of "human rights."[32]

All these events and reports obviously contributed to better communication among Latin American women and made it possible for them to engage in common actions. However, as I show in the next part of this chapter, in practice the cooperation of women in the context of WIDF activities was characterized by many contradictions and complexities, including more conflicts and misunderstandings than had been presented in the official documents.

Memoires and Classified Soviet Reports on Latin American Women about the WIDF's Apparatus

As it is possible to understand from the description earlier, over the years, many Latin American women participated in the work of the federation. Two Argentinian women, Rosa Jasovich Pantaleón and Fanny Edelman, occupied the important position of the federation's general secretary in 1963–8 and 1972–8, respectively,[33] during which time they lived and worked in East Berlin. Several other women from Argentina, Chile, and Brazil and, later, Cuba were WIDF vice presidents.[34] These women frequently visited WIDF headquarters in East Berlin and took part in internal discussions and decision-making. Many other women, including some regular members of women's organizations in Latin America, attended congresses, seminars, and study trips organized by WIDF in state socialist countries. The Latin American dimensions of the work of WIDF cannot be fully understood without paying attention to the processes of selection of participants for various events and to the role of these processes in WIDF's decision-making as a short article cannot adequately discuss all the less visible aspects of WIDF's work. However, I would like to explore some of the possible directions of such an investigation and review the diversity of reactions and results of communication between women from Latin America and WIDF's leadership, and state socialist reality.

I will start with the memoires of one of the most prominent WIDF participants from Latin America, Fanny Edelman,[35] which were published in 1996. About half Edelman's book covers her time as general secretary, and this time is presented as encounters with many brilliant, well-looking, and courageous women. The reader gets the impression that women from different continents mainly supported each other and did not have conflicts or disagreements among them, or at least, these disagreements were not worth of remembering. It also gives the impression that the federation was mainly unanimous with respect to its understanding of the rights of women. Edelman presented herself as a strong believer in the achievements of women's rights in the countries of state socialism, exemplified in the book primarily by gender equity in the Soviet Union and East Germany. For example, Edelman wrote about her pleasure in working with Valentina Tereshkova, the first female cosmonaut, and several other women from the CSW, all "women of extreme modesty."[36] Edelman stated that she participated in all the congresses of the FMC after 1975[37] and was also glad to write about Cuban women and visit Cuba. The leader of FMC, Vilma Espín, is described by Edelman as a beautiful and modest woman.[38] The memoires suggest that it was Vilma Espín with whom Edelman had established a closer and more personal relationship, noting, for example, that it was nice to spend time with Raul (Castro)[39] and Vilma and their children and grandchildren.[40] Edelman's memoires can contribute to the understanding of how she was positioning herself as a Latin American communist woman representing the WIDF internationally, but at the same time, it seems that Edelman wrote these memoires in order to defend the federation (and state socialist gender equality politics) from its Western critics.

Some of Edelman's published narratives express ideas similar to those that can be found in official speeches. For example, in 1970, a commemoration of the twenty-fifth anniversary of WIDF's founding took place in Moscow and included presentations by several guests from Latin America. One of them, Argelia Laya, representative of the Venezuelan women's organization, spoke about the solidarity of the women of Venezuela with women in Vietnam and Cambodia and said that her organization worked for changing the consciousness of Venezuelan women. She also explained that transformation of capitalist society was an important condition for solving the problem of women's rights.[41] The representative from the Democratic Union of Columbian Women, Elena de Moreno, in her turn, stated that while most of the women's organizations in the country were dealing with unimportant (from de Moreno's perspective) topics like mandatory social service or family planning, only the Democratic Union of Columbian Women (a WIDF member), acted for supporting children and women in practice.[42] Thus, it is possible to infer that the representatives of Latin American organizations were expected to describe WIDF as the only transnational women's organization truly defending women's interests.

In contrast to the notion of harmony within WIDF, classified archival documents from Moscow suggest that conflicts and disagreements within WIDF leadership and between member organizations from different countries concerning the WIDF's goals, slogans, and work practices were constantly present and, in some periods, became heated. One such time was the period around the Moscow Congress in 1963. This congress became a place for discussing imperialism, détente, and internal democracy in the context of growing disagreements between Moscow and Beijing. The discussions were also heated due to the position of some European organizations, like Italy's, which aspired to increase internal democracy in the WIDF.[43] Some women's organizations from the Global South demonstrated their support for the Chinese rather than Soviet position with respect to anti-imperialism. For example, according to a Soviet classified report, representatives from Zanzibar, Mozambique, Venezuela, Brazil, the Comoro Islands, Indonesia, Nepal, and South Vietnam took part in a meeting in Beijing in July 1963, which had been organized after the Moscow Congress; these participants complained not least about the lack of effectiveness of the Moscow congress.[44] It was at just about this time that another Argentinian communist, Rosa Jasovich, became WIDF's general secretary. The documents show that she was very preoccupied with this situation and suggested that the Secretariat should take actions "very carefully" while thinking about response to the accusations aimed at the Moscow Congress.[45] Thus, it is possible to see open discrepancy in opinions between WIDF's leadership and representatives of several Latin American women's organizations.

My study of the archival documents shows a constant preoccupation with the political and ideological positions of particular women's organizations or individual activists among WIDF's leaders.[46] In most of the cases, the leaders were concerned not only that a "correct" vision of women's social roles was being maintained (as a combination of a mother, worker, and citizen), but also that a "friendly" position toward the Soviet bloc in the context of the Cold War confrontation was being put forth. For example, the selection of the prospective participants for the Moscow Congress of 1963 was influenced by considerations of political "friendliness" and only those women considered "friendly" were supposed to receive a financial support for their travel.[47] It was not rare the opinions to come from the leaders of the communist parties of various countries, as it was in the case of Bolivia, for example.[48]

The classified documents also indicate that when prominent female activists expressed doubts in the balance of the narrative around rights of "worker, mother, and citizen," it could lead to conflict between these leaders and WIDF's international leadership. Indeed, Argelia Laya is a good example of this conflict. While for a long period Laya was considered a "good friend" of the Soviet Union, having a "correct" ideological position,[49] the situation changed around 1972.[50] At that time, there was conflict inside Venezuela's communist party, and Laya became a leader of another leftist political party that focused more on protection of women and minorities, especially Black women.[51] This change was not tolerated by the Soviet Union or (later) by WIDF's leadership. Indeed, a letter from Xenia Proskurnikova, vice president of CSW from January 18, 1972, informed the Soviet representative in Berlin that Laya's participation in the next session of the WIDF council would not be desirable.[52]

From this short overview, it is possible to say that Latin American activists, similarly to activists from African and Asian countries, were not always in unanimous agreement with the WIDF leadership and did not always praise the federation's achievements, as might be read from WIDF's official documents. Several leaders changed their views on WIDF's agenda and on politics of the state socialist countries and the achievement of women's rights there. At the same time, power in the federation was not given exclusively to the Soviet representatives and experienced many changes over time.

Due to the special role that Cuba and Cuban women's organizations (FMC) took in both the WIDF official publications and Edelman's memoires about the 1970s, in the next section I will look more closely at the role of Cuba in WIDF and Latin America.

The Cuban Chapter of WIDF and Role of Cuba in the Federation's Work with Latin American Women

The Democratic Union of Cuban Women was WIDF's Cuban chapter from the early days of the federation.[53] In particular, the representatives of this organization were active in the campaign against the war in Korea[54] and organizing celebrations of Children's Day (June 1) that had been established by the federation in 1951.[55] However, after the Cuban Revolution of 1959, the then existing women's organization was replaced by a new one, the FMC, in 1960.[56] Scholars already have shown that, in the years immediately after the Cuban Revolution, the female activists participating in the armed revolutionary struggle were particularly visible even if they were a minority of women contributing to the revolutionary change in the country.[57] For example, the participants of the WIDF congress of Latin American women in Santiago de Chile in 1959 were particularly impressed by the Cuban women arriving to the congress in military uniform.[58]

The archival documents I studied suggest the WIDF leadership saw Cuban female revolutionaries as important actors who, like African female activists,[59] should be recruited to WIDF. The Soviet Union's member organization, the CSW, must have played an important role here, not least because Soviet women were expected to show the achievements of Soviet emancipation to the Cuban female leaders, and CSW members used every opportunity for doing it. For example, in 1961, one of the CSW's secretaries, Zinaida Fedorova, informed the central committee of the Communist Party of the Soviet Union (CPSU) that the mother of Che Guevara and other Cuban women were returning to Havana from an event in Beijing and making a flight transfer in Moscow. CSW members offered the highly positioned Cuban guests special gifts and invited them to spend several days in the USSR. The stay, fully paid for by the Soviets, included a trip to Leningrad.[60]

While Cuban archival documents were not accessible to me, the documents preserved in Moscow suggest that the new Cuban women's organization seemed to be very interested in the Soviet experience of politics for women's rights and for protection of motherhood.[61] At the same time, it wanted to show Cuban achievements to Soviet women and establish closer contacts. Indeed, in a classified letter sent to Moscow in March 1961 by the Soviet representative in WIDF's Secretariat, Zinaida Lebedeva, several representatives of the Secretariat and the WIDF leadership received an invitation from FMC to visit Cuba and to make a three-week journey around the country. According to a personal request by Vilma Espín, Lebedeva herself was invited to join the delegation (together with Maria Magdalena Rossi, Margarita de Ponce, and representatives from Algeria, Venezuela, and the United States).[62] After coming back from the trip, Lebedeva published an official report about her visit to Cuba in the Federation's journal[63] and sent the CSW an eight-page classified report about the trip.[64]

While the official report showed how Cuban women participated in production work, voluntary services, and educational campaigns, in her classified report for the CSW leadership, Lebedeva paid special attention to the attitudes of Cubans to the Soviet Union. Lebedeva's report was mainly positive: she noted that the staff in hospitals and childcare centers showed her condensed milk sent from the USSR and expressed gratitude, while textile factory workers stressed that most of their cotton came from Uzbekistan.[65]

It is probable that these positive observations made by Lebedeva helped strengthen the integration of the new Cuban women's organization and its leaders with WIDF, with Vilma Espín becoming one of WIDF's vice presidents at the end of the 1960s.[66] In its turn, establishing better contacts with Cuban women gave WIDF further opportunities of cooperating with women in Latin America. The documents show that Cuban female leaders also considered their contacts with the Soviet women and WIDF to be important. Indeed, in her letter from March 1961, Zinaida Lebedeva informed CSW that the WIDF leadership had decided that some of the members of the WIDF delegation should use the invitation by the Cuban women for travel further around Latin America, for example, to Mexico, Venezuela, and Brazil.[67]

At the same time, as we know from research on Cuba's role in Latin America and Africa, Cuban revolutionary leaders had their own vision of their country's place in Latin American and anticolonial "Tricontinental"[68] solidarities.[69] Indeed, Cuba attempted to have a relatively independent (from the Soviet Union and WIDF) position among women in Latin America. For example, in the context of multiple discrepancies in WIDF around 1963 and the deterioration of the Cuban/Soviet relationship after the missile crises of 1961, Havana hosted the Congress of American Women in January 1963. The Havana Congress was attended by many delegations from Latin American countries, with Mexico alone sending ninety-six women.[70] At the same time, it counted only two representatives of WIDF, namely General Secretary Rosa Jasovich and Elena Vilcosi, a member of the Secretariat. The congress was addressed by the leader of the Cuban Revolution, Fidel Castro. According to him, American women had to become revolutionary altogether.[71]

Analysis of the publications in FMC's journal *Mujeres* in the 1970s through the early 1980s suggests that, by this time, Cuba had lower expectations for worldwide anti-imperialist struggle, while at the same time it also became more authoritarian and dependent on the Soviet Union ideationally and economically.[72] Despite these setbacks, *Mujeres* continued to present Cuba as an important actor in women's rights activism in Latin America and the Global South. While analysis of the journal shows that it regularly published articles on the Soviet Union and other European countries under state socialism,[73] *Mujeres* also gave a significant amount of space to women from countries in the Global South, suggesting that relationships with women from African and Asian countries were at least similarly important (it differed from how Western Europe was represented: articles about women in these regions were practically nonexistent). Through the 1970s and 1980s, each issue of the journal usually published one or two articles dedicated to the participation of women in anticolonial and revolutionary activities in Latin America, Africa, and Asia or in the fight against racism.[74]

The journal also reported about events organized by WIDF, although mainly concentrating on events connected to Latin America or highlighted Cuban participants and leaders. For example, in 1973, an article in *Mujeres* described a WIDF bureau meeting in Havana, and Fidel Castro's address to the delegates took up most of this report. Issue 4 from March 1979 told readers about a regional seminar of WIDF that discussed preparation for the second UN women's conference in Copenhagen (1980). Again, Fidel Castro's address to the participants of the seminar was an important part of the report.

Based on WIDF's official publications and archival files, it is possible to see that in spite of some initial mistrust and competition, the Cuban leadership and FMC seemed to see their participation in WIDF as an opportunity to broaden the contacts of Cuban women with women in Africa and Asia. WIDF documents also suggest the growing visibility of Cuban women in WIDF, as I have shown earlier. Furthermore, WIDF materials show that cooperation with WIDF partly contributed to Cuban aspirations of establishing its leadership for women in the "Third World." For example, a conference in Khartoum in 1970 on women's education in Africa had Cordelia Navarro Garcia from FMC sharing her experiences of a literacy campaign in Cuba.[75] It is possible to say also that WIDF itself started a slow process of decentralization in the late 1970s, as a result of which Cuba found itself in the position of being one of the central WIDF actors in Latin America (and beyond) at the end of the Cold War.

The archival materials from Moscow confirm that in the 1970s, Cuba had an ever more important role in WIDF activities aimed at Latin American women. Indeed, in 1973, a WIDF bureau meeting was convened in Havana, one of few meetings outside of Europe (the two others in Indonesia and Mali in the 1960s). In 1978, Havana hosted a meeting of the leaders of women's organizations from the socialist countries. Together with East European countries, the meeting was attended by representatives from Korea, Vietnam, and Laos.[76] The archival documents also show that in 1978, WIDF attempted to create several regional centers, one in Mongolia (for women from Asia) and one in Havana (for women in Latin America). These centers would have been local resource centers for gathering information and organizing short courses and other educational programs for female activists. The center in Mongolia seems to have met a lot of difficulties,[77] but the center in Havana successfully capitalized on previous experiences and aspirations of the FMC. For example, in 1980, *Mujeres* published an article about FMC's school for female cadres from Cuba and other Latin American countries, the program of which included courses in Marxism and Leninism and other political systems.[78] In its journal, WIDF also wrote about this training center, prizing its achievements in preparing female activists.[79] Finally, the archival documents show that in the context of the UN's Decade for Women (1975–85), Cuba hosted an NGO forum for Latin America and the Caribbean in 1984, which seems to have been prepared rather independently from WIDF's or Moscow's leadership, and discussing among other things the importance of women's NGOs, sexual education, and birth control programs that would benefit women.[80] These organizational efforts of the Cuban women's organization, together with trust from WIDF and the Soviet Union, seem to have helped preserve Cuba's important role in women's rights activism after the fall of the Eastern bloc. Indeed, in 1990, the Cuban office created by WIDF for work among women of Latin America was transformed into an independent regional center for women in Latin America (*Oficina regional*) led by Dora Carcaño, a leading member of FMC.[81] Until the 2020 Covid-19 pandemic, the center continued to organize courses for female activists from the region.

Conclusion

Analyses of WIDF's archival materials and official publications show that Latin American women were seen as an important object of WIDF's work for the rights of women as "mothers, workers, and citizens." The earlier years of the federation's work were focused on women who lived in cities (and were therefore seen as similar to European working women and housewives), but as time went on, WIDF started to be more attentive to the diversity of Latin American women and their needs and demands. In particular, the problems of peasant and Indigenous women from various parts of Latin America were written about in WIDF's periodical publications and addressed during congresses and other events. Developmentalism and the anticolonial movements in Asia and Africa contributed to the inclusion of the problems of Latin American women into the broader work addressing "developing countries."

As it was shown in the previous research, the Cold War confrontation was particularly strong in the women's movement in the Americas (see the work by Marino in 2019). In order to improve its position the WIDF attempted first using tactic of creating broader women's organizations around female communist leaders, but it showed itself to be only partly successful. The Cuban Revolution of 1959 contributed to a change of tactics and a slow, partial transfer of the leadership role in organizing women's movements to Cuban women's organization. However, based on FMC's official publications, and some archival documents preserved in Moscow, it seems that the Cuban leadership of the FMC did not always have similar priorities as women's activists in Moscow. Of course, the actual role of the FMC should be investigated further.

An analysis of WIDF's work in Latin America suggests that it followed a common pattern comparable to other regions of the world. The similarities included slogans and broad solidarity campaigns as well as attempts to control the ideological positions of female leaders and activists.

Notes

1. Francisca de Haan, "The Women's International Democratic Federation (WIDF): History, Main Agenda and Contributions (1945–1991)," in *Women and Social Movements (WASI) Online Archive*, ed. Thomas Dublin and Kathryn Kish Sklar, 2012, http://alexanderstreet.com/products/women-and-social-movements-international; Jadwiga E. Pieper Mooney, "El antifascismo como fuerza movilizadora: Fanny Edelman y la 'Federación Democrática Internacional de Mujeres," *Anuario IEHS: Instituto de Estudios histórico sociales* 28 (2013): 207–26.

2. See Katherine M. Marino, *Feminism for the Americas: The Making of an International Human Rights Movement*, Gender and American Culture (Chapel Hill: University of North Carolina Press, 2019); Leila J. Rupp, *Worlds of Women: The Making of an International Women's Movement* (Princeton, NJ: Princeton University Press, 1997).
3. *Za Ravnopravie, Schastie i Mir* (Berlin: WIDF, 1953), 11.
4. Ibid., 31.
5. *Zenschiny Mira (ZM)* no. 3 (1969), Kristina Vrohno, Vsemirnyi Kongress Zhenshchin, 5.
6. *Women of the Whole World* was the title of the WIDF journal.
7. Roger E. Kanet, ed., *The Soviet Union, Eastern Europe and the Third World* (Cambridge: Cambridge University Press, 1988), 84–114.
8. de Haan, "The Women's"; Yulia Gradskova, *The Women's International Democratic Federation, the Global South and the Cold War: Defending the Rights of Women of the "Whole World"?* (London: Routledge, 2021); Manuel Ramirez Chicharro, "Radicalizing Feminism: The Mexican and Cuban Associations within the Women's International Democratic Federation in the Early Cold War," *International Review for Social History* 67, no. 30 (2022): 76.
9. Katharine McGregor, "Opposing Colonialism: The Women's International Democratic Federation and Decolonisation Struggles in Vietnam and Algeria 1945–1965," *Women's History Review* 25, no. 6 (2016): 925–44; Elisabeth Armstrong, "Before Bandung: The Anti-Imperialist Women's Movement in Asia and the Women's International Democratic Federation," *Signs* 41, no. 2 (2016): 305–31; Allison Drew, "A Gendered Approach to the Yu Chi Chan Club and National Liberation Front during South Africa's Transition to Armed Struggle," *International Review of Social History* 67, no. 30 (2022): 179–207.
10. Francisca de Haan, "The Global Left-Feminist 1960s. From Copenhagen to Moscow and New York," in *The Routledge Handbook of the Global Sixties: Between Protest and Nation-Building*, ed. Jian Chen, Martin Klimke, Masha Kirasirova, Mary Nolan, Marilyn Blatt Young, and Joanna Waley-Cohen (London: Routledge, 2018), 230–42.
11. Pieper Mooney, "El antifascismo"; Michelle Chase, *Revolution within the Revolution. Women and Gender Politics in Cuba, 1952–1962* (Chapel Hill: University of North Carolina Press, 2015); Ramirez Chicharro, "Radicalizing Feminism"; María Fernanda Lanfranco González, "Between National and International: Women's Transnational Activism in Twentieth-Century Chile," *International Review of Social History* 67, no. 30 (2022): 49–74.
12. Chase, *Revolution*; Adriana María Valobra and Mercedes Yusta Rodrigo, *Queridas Camaradas: Historias iberoamericanas de mujeres comunistas* (Buenos Aires: Miño y Dávila editores, 2017); González, "Between National and International."
13. However, see Francisca de Haan, "La Federación Democratica Internacional de Mujeres (FDIM) y America Latina, de 1945 a Los Años Setenta," in *Queridas Camaradas: Historias iberoamericanas de mujeres comunistas* ed. Adriana María Valobra and Mercedes Yusta Rodrigo (Buenos Aires: Miño y Dávila Editores, 2017), 17–44.
14. I am very grateful to the Cuban Heritage Collection, University of Miami, for possibility of reading journal.
15. See Marino, *Feminism for the Americas*; Lanfranco Gonzàles, "Between National and International."
16. Valobra et al., *Queridas camaradas*; Chase, *Revolution*; Lanfranco Gonzàles, "Between National and International."

17. Communist Political Propaganda and Use of U.S. Mails: Hearings, part. 1–2, 1959 https://lawcat.berkeley.edu/record/303708, 34.
18. de Haan, "La Federación," 42. The archive in Moscow—State Archive of the Russian Federation (further GARF) indicates that representatives of Mexico also planned their participation (GARF f. 7928, o. 1, d. 4, p. 16). On the other hand, Lanfranco Gonzàles has shown that two Chilean representatives at the constituting congress of WIDF came to it from Europe and not directly from Chile—Lanfranco Gonzàles, "Between National and International."
19. Yulia Gradskova, "La FDIM y Los Derechos de Las Mujeres En América Latina: Expectativas y Alianzas Durante La Guerra Fría, 1950–1970," *Descentrada* 5, no. 2 (2021a): 1–15, https://doi.org/10.24215/25457284e150.
20. *ZM*, 1960, no. 2, p. 3 (no title)
21. GARF f. 7928, o. 1, d. 4, p. 410.
22. Ibid., 48.
23. Ibid., 49.
24. See Gradskova, *The Women's*.
25. *ZM*, 1962, no. 9, pp. 15–16. Carmen Clemente Travieso, Vechno zhivaia v serdtse venesuelskogo Naroda. Lidia Governeur.
26. *ZM*, 1962, no. 10, pp. 15–16. Maria-Luisa Vicentini, Olga Poblete -laureat mezhdunarodnoi leninskoi premii.
27. *ZM*, 1960, no. 6, pp. 10–12. Vilma Espín Castro, Kuba—svobodnaia zemlia.
28. *ZM*, 1963, no. 1, pp. 6–8. Onelia Oguilar, Ot Sierry-Maestry k Federatsii kubibskikh zhenshchin. Vilma Espin.
29. Ibid., 8.
30. *ZM*, 1969, no. 1. The first issue of a WIDF journal especially dedicated to Latin America.
31. *ZM*, 1969, no. 1, pp. 12–13.
32. *WWW*, 1975, no. 2, pp. 9–13. Third Latin American Seminar (no author)
33. For more on Edelman, see Peiper Mooney, "El antifascismo."
34. de Haan, "La Federación," 43.
35. See Pieper Mooney, "El antifascismo."
36. Fanny J. Edelman, *Banderas, Pasiones, Camaradas* (Buenos Aires: Ediciones Dirple, 1996), 105.
37. Ibid., 155.
38. Ibid., 153.
39. Raul Castro was Espín's partner.
40. Edelman, *Banderas, Pasiones, Camaradas*, 163.
41. GARF, f. 7928, o. 3, d. 2434, p. 75.
42. Ibid., 86.
43. Chiara Bonfiglioli, "Revolutionary Networks: Women's Political and Social Activism in Cold War Italy and Yugoslavia (1945–1957)," Doctoral Thesis, Utrecht University, 2012; Gradskova, *The Women's*.
44. GARF f. 7928, o. 4, d. 169, p. 110.
45. Ibid., 111.
46. More see Gradskova, *The Women's*.
47. GARF, f. 7928, o. 4, d. 169, p. 91.
48. Ibid., 99. The Bolivian Communist party directly advised to invite one organization—Union of Housewives—in place of another one—Union of Women of Bolivia.

49. GARF f. 7928, o. 4, d. 147, p. 125, 128, 130.
50. Laya (1926–1997) was a Black leftist feminist (capiremov.org/en/experience/argelia-laya-a-black-communist-woman-against-the-tide/). The current regime in Venezuela identifies her as an important historical personality and has named a university in Merinda after her.
51. A biography of Laya published on the internet suggests that Laya decided to deal with women's issues in a more direct way, focusing on women's rights specifically (peoplepill.com/people/argelia-laya).
52. GARF 7928, o. 3, d. 2941, p. 6.
53. Chase, *Revolution*.
54. Michelle Chase, "'Hands Off Korea!': Women's Internationalist Solidarity and Peace Activism in Early Cold War Cuba," *Journal of Women's History* 32, no. 3 (2020): 64–88.
55. See Gradskova, *The Women's*.
56. Vilma Espín, "Entrevista Concedida a Mirta Rodriguez Calderón, El Periodico Granma," in *Mujer de Cuba. Vilma Espin* (La Habana: Federacion de Mujeres Cubanas, 1985), 37–50.
57. Ramirez Chicharro, "Radicalizing Feminism."
58. Adriana María Valobra, "Mujeres-sombra" y 'Barbudas': Género y política en el Primer Congreso Latinoamericano de Mujeres, Chile-1959," *Anuario del Instituto de Historia Argentina*, no. 14 (2014).
59. See Gradskova, *The Women's*.
60. GARF, f. 7928, o. 4, d. 147, pp. 224–5.
61. Espín, "Entrevista."
62. GARF, f. 7928, o. 4, d. 147, p. 30
63. ZM, 1961, no. 8, pp. 11–14. Z.Lebedeva. Vse budet khorosho—skazal nam Fidel Castro.
64. GARF, f. 7928, o. 4, d. 147, pp. 46–53.
65. GARF, f. 7928, o. 4, d. 149, p. 49.
66. *WWW*, 1969, no. 2, p. 5. Cecile Hugel, A New Stage.
67. GARF, f. 7928, o. 4, d. 147, p. 28.
68. The Tricontinental Conference in Havana in 1966 is one of the important attempts of Cuban leadership to establish itself as an important actor in African, Asian, and Latin American cooperation and solidarity.
69. Fernando Camacho Padilla and Eugenia Palieraki, "¡Hasta Siempre, OSPAAAL!," NACLA, January 16, 2020, https://nacla.org/news/2020/01/16/hasta-siempre-ospaaal-habana-cuba.
70. Ana Victoria Jimenes Alvarez and Francisca Reyes Castellanos, *Sembradoras de Futuro. Memoria de La Union Nacional de Mujeres Mexicanas* (Mexico: UNMM, 2000), 101.
71. www.marxists.org/history/cuba/archive/castro/1963/01/16.htm.
72. Jacqueline Loss and José Manuel Prieto González, eds., *Caviar with Rum: Cuba-USSR and the Post-Soviet Experience*, New Concepts in Latino American Cultures (Basingstoke: Palgrave Macmillan, 2012); Rebecca Gordon-Nesbitt, *To Defend the Revolution Is to Defend Culture: The Cultural Policy of the Cuban Revolution* (Oakland, CA: PM Press, 2015), 275, 378.
73. For example, issue 2 from 1973 had an article on the female Komsomol member Nadezhda Popova (p. 10); issue 3 from 1973 had an article on GDR preparations for a youth festival (p. 58) and on women's councils in Hungary (p. 88); issue 3 from 1979 had articles on Nadezhda Krupskaia (pp. 12–13).

74. Issue 2 (1973) published an article on women in Guinea and about visit of Angela Davis to Cuba (*Mujeres*, 1973, 2, p. 87). Issue 3 from 1973 had an interview with Puerto-Rican activist Flavia Rivera (pp. 84–5) and a report about a visit to Cuba by Consuelo Gonzales de Velasco (the spouse of Peru's leader) and a Chilean delegation (pp. 85, 87). The first issue in 1979 had article on women in Guinea-Bissau (pp. 42–3); issue 3 had an article on Vietnam (pp. 4–5).
75. *WWW*, 1970, no. 3–4, pp. 51–60. Cordelia Navarro Garcia, The Literacy Campaign and Adult Education in Cuba.
76. GARF, f. 7928, o. 3, d. 4488, p. 87.
77. Gradskova, *The Women's*.
78. *Mujeres*, 1980, no. 4, pp. 60–1.
79. ZM, 1983, no. 1, p. 28; Fanny Edelman, Nancy Ruiz, 5 let regionalnomy tsentru MDFZh v Gavane ; *WWW*, 1985, no. 3, p. 35. Nancy Ruiz, The good work done by the WIDF regional center in Havana.
80. GARF, f. 7928, o. 3, d. 6121.
81. Jimenes Alvarez and Reyes Castellanos, *Sembradoras de Futuro. Memoria de La Union Nacional de Mujeres Mexicanas*, 318.

Bibliography

Archival Sources

Communist Political Propaganda and Use of U.S. Mails: Hearings, part. 1–2 1959, https://lawcat.berkeley.edu/record/303708.
State archive of the Russian Federation (GARF), Moscow, Fond 7928, Antifascist Committee of Soviet Woman.

Printed Sources

Mujeres, 1973, 1978–83.
Women of the Whole World—1969, 1970, 1975–83.
Zhenshchiny mira, 1953, 1958–75.

Research Literature

Armstrong, E. "Before Bandung: The Anti-Imperialist Women's Movement in Asia and the Women's International Democratic Federation." *Signs* 41, no. 2 (2016): 305–31.
Banks, E. "Sewing Machines for Socialism?" *Comparative Studies of South Asia, Africa and the Middle East* 41 (2021): 27–40.
Bonfiglioli, Chiara. "Revolutionary Networks: Women's Political and Social Activism in Cold War Italy and Yugoslavia (1945–1957)." Doctoral Thesis, Utrecht University, 2012.
Camacho Padilla, Fernando, and Eugenia Palieraki. "¡Hasta Siempre, OSPAAAL!" NACLA, January 16, 2020. https://nacla.org/news/2020/01/16/hasta-siempre-ospaaal-habana-cuba.
Chase, Michelle. " 'Hands Off Korea!': Women's Internationalist Solidarity and Peace Activism in Early Cold War Cuba." *Journal of Women's History* 32, no. 3 (2020): 64–88.

Chase, Michelle. *Revolution within the Revolution. Women and Gender Politics in Cuba, 1952–1962*. Chapel Hill: University of North Carolina Press, 2015.
Donert, Celia. "Whose Utopia? Gender, Ideology, and Human Rights at the 1975 World Congress of Women in East Berlin." In *The Breakthrough: Human Rights in the 1970s*, edited by Jan Eckel and Samuel Moyn, 68–87. Philadelphia: University of Pennsylvania Press, 2014.
Drew, Allison. "A Gendered Approach to the Yu Chi Chan Club and National Liberation Front during South Africa's Transition to Armed Struggle." *International Review of Social History* 67, no. 30 (2022): 179–207.
Edelman, Fanny J. *Banderas, Pasiones, Camaradas*. Buenos Aires: Ediciones Dirple, 1996.
Espín, Vilma. "Entrevista Concedida a Mirta Rodriguez Calderón, El Periodico Granma." In *Mujer de Cuba. Vilma Espin*, 37–50. La Habana: Federacion de Mujeres Cubanas, 1985.
Gordon-Nesbitt, Rebecca, . *To Defend the Revolution Is to Defend Culture: The Cultural Policy of the Cuban Revolution*. Oakland, CA: PM Press, 2015.
Gradskova, Yulia. "La FDIM y Los Derechos de Las Mujeres En América Latina: Expectativas y Alianzas Durante La Guerra Fría, 1950–1970." *Descentrada* 5, no. 2 (2021a): e150. https://doi.org/10.24215/25457284e150.
Gradskova, Yulia. *The Women's International Democratic Federation, the Global South and the Cold War: Defending the Rights of Women of the "Whole World"?* London: Routledge, 2021b.
Haan, Francisca de. "La Federación Democratica Internacional de Mujeres (FDIM) y America Latina, de 1945 a Los Años Setenta." In *Queridas Camaradas: Historias Iberoamericanas de Mujeres Comunistas*, edited by Adriana María Valobra and Mercedes Yusta Rodrigo, 17–44. Buenos Aires: Miño y Dávila Editores, 2017.
Haan, Francisca de. "The Global Left-Feminist 1960s. From Copenhagen to Moscow and New York." In *The Routledge Handbook of the Global Sixties: Between Protest and Nation-Building*, edited by Jian Chen, Martin Klimke, Masha Kirasirova, Mary Nolan, Marilyn Blatt Young, and Joanna Waley-Cohen, 230–42. London: Routledge, 2018.
Haan, Francisca de. "The Women's International Democratic Federation (WIDF): History, Main Agenda and Contributions (1945–1991)." In *Women and Social Movements (WASI) Online Archive*, edited by Thomas Dublin and Kathryn Kish Sklar, 2012. http://alexanderstreet.com/products/women-and-social-movements-international.
Jimenes Alvarez, Ana Victoria, and Francisca Reyes Castellanos. *Sembradoras de Futuro. Memoria de La Union Nacional de Mujeres Mexicanas*. Mexico: UNMM, 2000.
Kanet, Roger E., ed. *The Soviet Union, Eastern Europe and the Third World*. Cambridge: Cambridge University Press, 1988.
Lanfranco Gonzàles, María Fernanda. "Between National and International: Women's Transnational Activism in Twentieth-Century Chile." *International Review of Social History* 67, no. 30 (2022): 49–74.
Loss, Jacqueline, and José Manuel Prieto González, eds. *Caviar with Rum: Cuba-USSR and the Post-Soviet Experience*. New Concepts in Latino American Cultures series. Basingstoke: Palgrave Macmillan, 2012.
Marino, Katherine M. *Feminism for the Americas: The Making of an International Human Rights Movement*. Gender and American Culture series. Chapel Hill: University of North Carolina Press, 2019.
McGregor, Katharine. "Opposing Colonialism: The Women's International Democratic Federation and Decolonisation Struggles in Vietnam and Algeria 1945–1965." *Women's History Review* 25, no. 6 (2016): 925–44.

Pieper Mooney, Jadwiga E. "El antifascismo como fuerza movilizadora: Fanny Edelman y la 'Federación Democrática Internacional de Mujeres.'" *Anuario IEHS: Instituto de Estudios histórico sociales*, no. 28 (2013): 207–26.

Ramirez Chicharro, Manuel. "Radicalizing Feminism: The Mexican and Cuban Associations within the Women's International Democratic Federation in the Early Cold War." *International Review for Social History* 67, no. 30 (2022): 75–102.

Rupp, Leila J. *Worlds of Women: The Making of an International Women's Movement*. Princeton, NJ: Princeton University Press, 1997.

Valobra, Adriana María. "'Mujeres-sombra' y 'Barbudas': Género y política en el Primer Congreso Latinoamericano de Mujeres, Chile-1959." *Anuario del Instituto de Historia Argentina*, no. 14 (2014). http://www.anuarioiha.fahce.unlp.edu.ar/article/view/IHAn14a0.

Valobra, Adriana María and Mercedes Yusta Rodrigo. *Queridas camaradas: Historias iberoamericanas de mujeres comunistas*. Buenos Aires: Miño y Dávila editores, 2017.

Za Ravnopravie. Schastie i Mir. Berlin: WIDF, 1953.

Part IV

Representations of Minorities in National History Curriculums

15

Reversal of Exclusion? Education and National Narratives amid Changing Majority/Minority Power Dynamics in Rwanda and Burundi

Denise Bentrovato

Introduction

Various researchers have pointed to the capacity of schools, and specifically history and social sciences education, to act as "tool[s] for the subjugation, assimilation or, conversely, emancipation of minorities."[1] Across the globe, scholarship has detailed cases of the "acculturation, discrimination or invisibilization" of minoritized groups through national homogenization processes whose central narratives have been in the control of dominant groups.[2] Among other issues, this work has noted how the discursive construction of internal "others" has, time and again, served to justify the "repression and assimilation of national minorities."[3] The codification of narratives and discourses around sameness and otherness in state-approved school curricula and textbooks has been a crucial component of such processes, reproducing inequality and perpetuating social stratification.[4] Recently, practices of minoritization have increasingly come under fire[5] as globalized norms such as multiculturalism, human rights, and social justice have risen to prominence in the discursive landscape, setting the stage for "the growing legitimacy of minority narratives in the canon of history teaching."[6]

This chapter seeks to retrace manifestations, in the educational sphere, of discourses and practices of inclusion, exclusion, and alienation in contrasting scenarios of state control exerted by elite members of an "ethnic" group that is either a numerical majority or a numerical minority. It examines how these dynamics have played out in Rwanda and Burundi, two of Africa's most culturally and linguistically homogenous countries, infamous for their history of sectarianized conflict and genocidal violence that has involved their respective Hutu majorities and Tutsi minorities. The historical, socio-demographic, and cultural features the two neighbors share in common stand in contrast to postindependence paths that have seen these "false twins of Africa" each become the reverse image of the other, notably with respect to majority/minority power relations and politics of identity and memory.[7] The comparative, diachronic analysis in this chapter explores how configurations and reconfigurations of power in systems of ethnically based majoritarianism and minoritarianism have impacted the official national narratives taught in schools and their inherent representations of social identities. It further sheds light on how, arguably, these narratives have sustained the power dynamics observable, paying particular attention to two rare instances of postcolonial minoritarian regimes that occur in the period under study. The case study evidences both similarities and differences in the ways in which the formal and hidden school curriculum may act to control and restrict access to power in such contrasting political contexts as they occur in Burundi and Rwanda. It demonstrates the historical complicity of educational institutions in overt or covert exclusion and repression of the subordinate, minoritized "other," while acknowledging that marginalization and disaffection have been part of the experience of many members of both communities in both countries, regardless of the regime in place.

Context of the Study

Burundi and Rwanda are neighboring countries whose populations have a comparable "ethnic" makeup. Most of the literature reproduces estimates from the colonial period that describe the two countries' respective populations of approximately 11 and 12 million as being composed of 85 percent Hutu, 14 percent Tutsi, and 1 percent Twa. These identity labels, and the pertinence of the notion of minority or indigeneity in this context, have been the subject of long-standing controversy and politicization in this region. There is now a broad scholarly consensus on the inapplicability of traditional "ethnic" markers to these three societal groupings, as they share a culture, language, and territory. Current scholarship acknowledges the significant impact and legacy of the manipulation, crystallization—that is, ethnicization or racialization—and antagonization of what had historically been fluid social identities during the two countries' shared colonial era under German and later Belgian administration. Their upshot is that, while the social and political salience of Hutu, Tutsi, and Twa identities varied in precolonial and colonial times, it is irrefutable today in both countries, not least on account of the recurring sectarianized tensions that accompanied their postindependence trajectories and culminated in civil war and mass violence in the 1990s. Until this caesura, the Tutsi minority held power in Burundi and the Hutu majority controlled Rwanda. Civil wars, with rebel movements each dominated by the hitherto oppressed "ethnic" group, broke out in Burundi between 1993 and 2005 and in Rwanda from 1990 to 1994. The process of their resolution differed, as did the nature of the political transition that followed in each case, with a negotiated settlement in Burundi and a violent overturning of the previous dispensation in Rwanda. In parallel, the two countries then reversed the power relations previously in place: a Hutu-led party, the National Council for the Defense of Democracy—Forces for the Defense of Democracy (CNDD-FDD), took power in Burundi, and the Tutsi-dominated Rwandan Patriotic Front (RPF) came to office in Rwanda. Both these organizations, once rebel movements that became all powerful in their respective states, exercise an authoritarian rule evident in the curtailing of freedoms, insidious government surveillance, and effectively hegemonic regimes of representation. Significantly, while both regimes have embraced unity as a key value underlying post-conflict state-building and nation-building and underpinned its status in their constitutions, the identity politics each pursues differ greatly. The Rwandan state has repudiated the notion of "ethnicity" and erased it from the public sphere, while Burundi has recognized it and made constitutional provisions for its, to a degree, proportional political representation.

It is important to note at this point that most discussion of the issue of "ethnicity" in Rwanda and Burundi—and this article is no exception—will generally speak in binary terms, of Hutu and Tutsi. The countries' third community, the Twa, might be describable as a "micro-minority," or as the "insignificant other," "lack[ing ...] demographic weight or political resources."[8] Historically "marginal, in terms of both numbers and status" and "excluded from the realm of public discourse,"[9] this group arguably found itself "resented, if not despised by both Hutus and Tutsis, who considered them as socially inferior."[10]

Methodological and Theoretical Considerations

This chapter sets out a situated analysis of the manifestations within education systems of discursive constructions and renegotiations around communitarian identities against the backdrop of varying majority/minority power dynamics in the cases under review. It traces the occurrence of such discursive constructions in state-imposed curriculum policies as translated via officially sanctioned textbook narratives and representations. Theories of discourse, and specifically critical discourse analysis, will support the investigation by revealing how such texts may work to construct, embody, and sustain normalized or concealed asymmetries of power. Proceeding from the premise that text and discourse are "constructive of social formations, communities, and individuals' social identities,"[11] and referencing Michel Foucault's work on knowledge and power,[12] the analysis illuminates the action of discourse in defining, categorizing, and positioning social subjectivities, and constructing and regulating social relations. Informed by the methodology of critical discourse analysis, it engages with the matter of "who can speak, when, where and with what authority,"[13] a question crucial to educational settings. Examining the Rwandan and Burundian cases via the lens of discourse analysis will help illustrate the differing uses and impacts of discourse by and on minority communities with various statuses in terms of societal power. The particular focus of this study on representations mediated via the school setting reveals education as a site of everyday articulations and manifestations of wider "discursive formations" entangled with power relations. These "discursive formations," occurring as they do within societally circulating texts that co-inform young people's sense-making abilities, act—in Foucauldian terms—as "disciplinary" tools implicated in practices of "governmentality" that operate by configuring beliefs and habits. They serve to introduce and habituate young people to a body of official knowledge that encompasses a specific understanding of "similarity and difference, of normalcy and deviance."[14] We can read them, and the representations they embody, as "linguistic and discursive artifacts ... that often hide or disguise their own status and authority" and attempt to foreclose "the possibility of alternative readings and interpretations" through a tone of "certainty and facticity."[15] The result is the construction of a preferred social reality that is both reflective and reproductive of dominant power relations.

This study will uncover these "discursive formations" and deconstruct the associated "authoritative discourses"[16] via inductive, synchronic, and diachronic content analysis of state-sanctioned textbooks from the two countries, taking a qualitative and comparative approach. The books analyzed were in widespread use in the two countries before and after their recent wars and mass violence.[17] Identifying key recurring rhetorical elements and tropes, the analysis will highlight "nodal points"[18] and silences within their broader narrative "emplotment."[19] As a study of how social identities and social relations between minority and majority communities solidify in educational discourses, this work seeks to note practices that effect the essentialization, homogenization, and dichotomization of particular groups. Further, it will examine the discursive placing of specific groups in a "superordinate" or "subordinate" position—or "propositional referentiality";[20] the attribution of agency or causation to a particular group or, conversely, the erasure of its actorship; and discourses of denigration versus those of elevation. In ascertaining the contribution of educational media to "the formal institutionalization and codification of ethnic [or] national categories,"[21] the analysis takes account of the reinforcing or undermining effects of the hidden and societal curriculum of everyday practices and experiences at work in each context.

"Ethnic" Majority Rule and the Othered Minority in Pre-Genocide Rwanda

Following its independence, Rwanda experienced three decades of Hutu majority rule during which the Tutsi minority suffered systematic discrimination and cycles of mass violence and forced displacement, notably in 1959–61, 1963–4, 1972–3, and, notoriously, in the early 1990s. The culmination of the ensuing tensions, which led to civil war in 1990, occurred in 1994, when a state-orchestrated genocide, mostly executed by "militias," took the lives of an estimated 800,000 Tutsi, alongside Hutu opposed to the government, in the course of one hundred days. It is important to note that, until the 1990s, "the main axis of conflict [in Rwanda] was based on region and class, and for the most part these were conflicts between Hutu factions."[22] In this context, the version of history taught in schools under Hutu rule, and amplified by hate- and fear-mongering extremist media during the civil war and the genocide,[23] sought to mobilize ethnic consciousness among the majority as a regime survival strategy. Education, specifically history textbooks such as the state-produced *Histoire du Rwanda* series, evidenced "practices of reification of ethnicity, operationalized through discourses on the primordiality of ethnic difference and internal conflict which centered Hutu [autochthony,] victimhood and victimization."[24] These textbooks engaged a colonial discourse that had contrasted a supposedly autochthonous majority to a supposedly conquering and domineering foreign minority. Asserting the existence of historically distinct *ethnies*,[25] they described the precolonial "enslavement" and "domination" of the Hutu by Tutsi latecomers[26] and the colonial "reinforcement of the Tutsi hegemony ... over the peasant masses,"[27] with Tutsi authorities acting as "faithful" agents of indirect European colonial rule.[28] In justifying and celebrating the "popular insurrection"[29] of 1959 that brought the Hutu to power shortly before independence from Belgium, causing many deaths among Tutsi and forcing tens of thousands to a life in exile where they were often second-class citizens, the textbooks referenced a "democratic" Hutu cause facing a Tutsi "feudal monarchy."[30] Such terms, in the political context, resonantly allude to the struggle of the masses—"the people," and as such a majority—against a minority lacking legitimacy.[31]

In an additional demarcation of ingroup and outgroup, the rooted and the alien, these discourses legitimated the Hutu leadership as the protectors of "the oeuvre of pacification, reconciliation, and national unity"[32] and condemned foreign-based Tutsi rebels as "terrorists," "invaders," and "enemies," who, "ha[ving] *chosen* [italics added] the path of exile,"[33] were intent on "crush[ing]" the republic.[34] Indeed, the textbooks blamed these exiles for retaliatory acts against Tutsi living in the country who had "more or less accommodated themselves ... to the Hutu hegemony,"[35] thus praising a submissively assimilating minority while demonizing dissent. This discursive distinction faded during the war and genocide, as the assailed government "indiscriminately categorized [Tutsi living inside Rwanda] as potential accomplices of the RPF."[36]

In practices of ethnic essentialization, dichotomization, and explicit propositional referentiality, these textbooks narrated the victorious supersession of illegitimate, minority Tutsi hegemony with a naturally "democratic," and therefore legitimate, hegemony of the Hutu majority, connoted as "the people." On the basis of this discursive marking, echoing the majority/minority opposition inscribed into triumphs of political democracy further afield, the narrative continued, depicting the ongoing righteous struggle against unprovoked and destabilizing Tutsi terrorism intent on reinstating despotic minority rule. Reinforcing formal curricular content and the imposed codification of "ethnic" subjectivities outside school settings, such as the colonial-era requirement to carry ethnic identity cards, education policies and everyday classroom practices further performed and perpetuated these discourses, initiating and inserting young people into "symbolic orders of knowledge and power."[37] These included an ethnic quota system based on an artificial formula intended to favor Hutu education and employment, and routines enacting identification with an ethnicity as a public social act, with students (and teachers) required to explicitly state their ethnicity both on administrative files and in the classroom, often on the first day of school. Such records of ethnicity periodically facilitated targeted violence in schools and expulsions of students and eventually served effectively as death warrants for Tutsi during the genocide.

Minority Dominance and the Self-Undermining Erasure of "Ethnicity" in Post-Genocide Rwanda

In 1994, Rwandan politics experienced a fundamental shift from a majoritarian dispensation to rule by a politically ascendant demographic minority. The Tutsi-dominated RPF attained power following its military victory. It used its unchallenged rule in post-genocide Rwanda to launch a tightly controlled social engineering project that adopted an integrationist model foregrounding a nationalistically defined citizenship and sought, via "narrative canonization,"[38] to build an ethnicity-free Rwanda. This endeavor has entailed educating the population on a "true" history of national unity and passing strict laws prohibiting "divisionism" and "revisionism"—laws that, as indicated by extensive school-based research involving teachers and students, have secured the *de facto* hegemony of this narrative.[39] Both within and outside of schools, the state-perpetuated discourse of unitary nationalism centered on the notion of "Rwandanness" or "Rwandicity" (*ndi umunyarwanda*), which fundamentally erases "ethnic" identities and the associated segmentation of the population, that the new discourse has systematically rejected and criminalized as manifestations of dangerous divisionism. This move to, in effect, abolish "ethnic" categorizations and replace them with a shared national civic identity amounts to the imposition of an "ethnic amnesia," which critics have denounced as masking the re-infliction in reverse of past injustices committed on the basis of ethnicity.[40]

In history classrooms, this ostensible obliteration of the "ethnic" under the supremacy of the national/civic emerges in newly designed curricula and textbooks, which, arriving in schools after a decade-long moratorium on the teaching of national history, have centered a purportedly unifying national narrative of rebirth and progress contingent upon the renunciation of ethnic identification. The campaign of "mass (re)education" working to this end figures ethnically based individual and group subjectivities as a divisive colonial invention that resulted in genocide; it promotes in their place a supposed return to "traditional values of unity"[41] based in a mythical national oneness. Two central tropes evident in history curricula and textbooks structure this narrative. One is the construction of a precolonial utopia via accentuating "elements which prove the existence of social cohesion"[42] of Rwandans as a united "people, who had lived in peace for centuries."[43] The other is an externalization of blame for this unity's disruption, charging colonial agents and (Hutu) collaborators with dividing Rwandan traditional society into "so-called ethnic groups"[44] and thus precipitating the "break-up of an alliance that was as old as Rwanda's hills and history,"[45] and "la[ying] a basis for Genocide."[46] The utopianism of this narrative, asserting the envisaged and realized restoration of an idealized precolonial unity, is accompanied by a threatened dystopia consisting in a resurgence of the "ethnic," that is, of plurality in identity.

The discursive essentialization and homogenization of the Rwandan nation that finds expression in the concept of "Rwandanness" might appear, taken at face value, to dissolve and render obsolete societal distinctions between majority and minority groupings. The approach is compromised and undermined from within, however, by dichotomizing ethnically charged attributions of victimhood and guilt relating to the genocide. Alongside an emphasis on decades of "state terrorism"[47] against the Tutsi, a minority subjected to "deplorable exclusion"[48] and "systematic" and "cold-blood[ed]" "massacres,"[49] stands a largely unnuanced depiction of the Hutu majority—with few exceptions—as perpetrators. The currently ruling party appears as the redeemer of the Rwandan nation and the custodian of its "miraculous"[50] recovery and survival and of "national unity [… and] true democracy";[51] its exculpation from any wrongdoing during or subsequent to the "noble" "Liberation War"[52] contrasts with the subsumption of that war's (Hutu) victims under the categories of "*génocidaires*" or unavoidable collateral damage.

Textbook discourses thus embody a "tension between an official—inclusive—stance that outlaws discussion of ethnicity in the interests of promoting national unity and an official understanding of victimization that—in an exclusive manner—primarily defines victims by ethnicity in order to counter 'revisionism.'"[53] Processes of commemoration and legal redress have principally centered crimes perpetrated against the Tutsi (by Hutu); in 2008, the constitutionally enshrined term "Genocide against the Tutsi" replaced the more general expression "Rwandan genocide," officially inscribing into the events the victimhood of the politically ascendant minority and undermining, again from within, the state-driven erasure of ethnicity as a category of Rwandan societal being. Concomitant to these acts of memorialization is a silencing of historical Hutu suffering, particularly with regard to the victims of the RPF.[54]

Minority Rule, Mythical Unity, and the Violent Alienation of the Majority in Prewar Burundi

Bordering Rwanda, postindependence Burundi experienced four decades of Tutsi minority rule associated with systematic state discrimination and violence against the Hutu majority. Recurring crises have seen assassinations of Hutu leaders followed by Hutu uprisings and killings of Tutsi to which the state responded with violent acts of repression against Hutu. Echoing the later, post-genocide unitarian discourse in neighboring Rwanda, the Burundian state propagated a discourse of unity encapsulated in the notion that "we are all Burundians" and similarly criminalized references to ethnicity. This "protective theme"[55] of the dominant minority amounted to the "aboli[tion] [of] ethnic 'otherness' as a socially relevant frame of reference [thus] remov[ing] the critical issues of ethnic hegemony and discrimination from the realm of legitimate debate."[56]

The official teachers' guide for the country's history classrooms, *Histoire du Burundi*,[57] sought to buttress the aimed-for "sense of overriding oneness"[58] via strategies strikingly reminiscent of those in use during Rwanda's post-1994 minoritarian rule: an erasure of ethnicity and a discursive essentialization and homogenization of the nation. Alongside these, the guide evidences a distinct complicity in a "conspiracy of silence"[59] and disinformation on Burundi's postindependence violence, in which the state used its media monopoly and limits on freedom of expression to blame externally supported "terrorists" and "enemies of the people."[60] As in Rwanda today, the narrative of *Histoire de Burundi* revolved around the celebration of a centuries-old prelapsarian unity as "a true nation-state" and its destruction by alien disunity.[61] This story described the halcyon days dominated by "an ideal of life 'ubuntu ubupfasoni' [humanism-respect for others and for oneself] and agro-pastoral activities across the hills"[62] and the subsequent systematic attack on traditional values unleashed by the colonizers, eventually compromising Burundians' "bonds of mutual aid and solidarity."[63] The passages on the fight for independence took an accordingly celebratory tone, accompanied by the lionization of the "truly nationalist"[64] UPRONA ruling party and its leader, Prince Rwagasore, who "led all the Barundi, without ethnic, social or religious distinction, to independence."[65] Consistent with the official intent to erase ethnicity, the guide's description of Burundi's traditional, colonial, and postindependence society omitted all references to Hutu and Tutsi.

The truncated narrative of *Histoire de Burundi* ended with the departure of the colonizers in 1962 and the resurgence of a "nationalist spirit [that] survived colonial domination,"[66] consigning to silence the rise of "ethnic" friction and the internecine violence that ravaged postindependence Burundi. The guide's encouragement of students to "discover" the ancient roots of Burundian unity and to cite "examples [of this unity] from everyday life"[67] strikes a dissonant note in view of the conflict that in fact permeated Burundian society in this period. A hidden and societal curriculum of everyday violence and discrimination prevailed, insistently undermining and subverting the idyll of an ethnicity-free unity imposed by the hegemonic minority. Schools were a preeminent site of largely covert discriminatory practices, such as the manipulation of examination results, which substantially restricted the political, social, and economic power of Hutu, constituting a key driver of intercommunal conflict.[68] Recurring violence against the schooled Hutu population was especially effective in sustaining power asymmetries. Its most horrific manifestation was the "events" of April 1972, which some consider a state-orchestrated "intellectual genocide" aimed at preventing the emergence of a Hutu elite. During the violence an estimated 100,000–300,000 educated Hutu "disappeared" and 200,000 fled abroad following the army's response to an insurgency and the killing of thousands of Tutsi. Consequently, "for the next fifteen years, only Tutsi were qualified to gain access to power, influence, and wealth."[69] The trauma of the massacres, alongside fear of renewed violence fed by rumors, led many parents to withdraw their children from school,[70] while the silencing of the events on pain of severe punishment left numerous "parents ... even wary of their children and their imprudent language."[71] Educational institutions once again became key sites of atrocities during the 1993 civil war, when political killings targeting Hutu—most notably Melchior Ndadaye, the country's first democratically elected president—led to what some consider a genocide of Tutsi and to reprisals against Hutu carried out by the largely Tutsi army, whose size had reportedly swelled in the mid-1990s following recruitment from secondary and tertiary institutions of learning.[72] Arguably, as Cochet suggests, "in the 1993 pogroms, when tens of primary and secondary Tutsi schoolchildren were killed, there seemed to be a sense of revenge for the killing of [Hutu] secondary students in 1972 and for all the peasant families who never saw a single one of their children ... get into secondary school from that time on."[73] The recurring lived and/or historical experience of violence, specifically in the education context, thus acts as a hidden curriculum that undermines the state-ordained absence of majority/minority "ethnic" conflict and the "illusion ... of bounded groupness"[74] intended to both carry and cover this absence.

Power-Sharing, Institutionalized Ethnicity, and Historical Amnesia in Postwar Burundi

Burundi's path after the armed conflict of the 1990s has diverged from that of Rwanda in several respects. Its civil war ended through a negotiated compromise that led to ethnic, consociational power-sharing and engendered an underlying system of institutionalized societal segmentation. Burundi's approach expressly brings together an idea of national unity and an acknowledgment of the ethnic diversity characterizing its population, and also encompasses a commitment to protecting minorities. The peace process, arguably influenced by international mediators,[75] mandated the establishment of quotas in the allocation of political and military posts and a presidency heading a transitional government alternating between Hutu and Tutsi. The constitution decrees a "corrected" proportionality in political representation, with the country's National Assembly made up of 60 percent Hutu and 40 percent Tutsi and the Senate equally composed of Hutu and Tutsi delegates, alongside three co-opted Twa in each chamber.[76] The principles of ethnic balance and equal representation on which these arrangements rest were among the most significant elements of the settlement in terms of assuaging minority fears of political marginalization or exclusion and of the loss of collective security and rights in the context of unconstrained majoritarian politics.[77] Multiparty elections that followed the transitional period in 2005 eventually saw the victory of the former Hutu rebel movement CNDD, which has faced increasingly intense challenges to its legitimacy in recent years.

While postwar Burundi has seen overt contention among conflicting accounts and memorializations of distinct group suffering, political actors of all sides implicated in the violence have frustrated the possibility of open debate by furthering historical amnesia. One manifestation of this continued conspiracy of silence is the long and arduous road to the establishment of a Truth and Reconciliation Commission (TRC), proposed in the 2000 peace agreement with the task of "rewriting Burundi's history so that all Burundians can interpret it in the same way."[78] Its deferral has hindered progress toward postwar truth-telling, accountability for crimes, and reparations for victims.[79] It is perhaps arguable that its stated remit—to facilitate, or even generate, a homogeneous Burundian interpretation of the country's history—may limit its prospects of success from the outset; there is an evident tension between the proportionality and acknowledgment of "ethnicity" inscribed in the postwar political settlement and the ideal of a reading of history to be subscribed to by "all Burundians," thus superseding the experience of distinct ethnic groups. The difficulties of this approach emerging in Rwanda may prove cause for concern in this context.

A delay analogous to that in setting up the TRC has occurred in reforms to history education in the country. Notwithstanding regime change, Burundian history curricula and textbooks have continued to "truncate history and amputate its troubling, recent, sensitive components" relating to Hutu–Tutsi relations,[80] leaving young people in a state of ongoing susceptibility to the "simplified and subjective reading[s] of the conflict" circulating around them.[81] The introduction of the school subject "Formation Patriotique et Humaine" and accompanying textbooks produced by the state in 2015 is illustrative of this persistent tendency. The subject's aim of instilling values that include unity, solidarity, respect for diversity, patriotism, peace, and human rights stands on unsustainable ground owing to its omission of all discussion on Burundi's violent history of gross human rights violations and brutal war; in effect, it turns the political personal, emphasizing interindividual conflict and its resolution. Historical allusions are generally scarce and fragmented and touch only obliquely on sensitive issues around power relations.[82]

Burundi after 2015: Toward an Exclusive Official History Written by the Majority?

Recent events in Burundi have brought about dramatic change, which is likely to significantly affect the teaching of history in schools. In 2014, following negotiations lasting for more than a decade, a TRC finally came into being, becoming officially operational in 2016 amid tensions not seen since the 1990s. Between these dates, in 2015, fell elections that confirmed the rule of the incumbent officeholders amid renewed violence triggered by president Nkurunziza's stated intention, earlier that year, to run for a constitutionally questionable third term. The political context of the TRC's establishment was thus one of rising authoritarianism and egregious human rights violations committed particularly by the ruling party and affiliated forces. Those opposition and civil society actors who have spoken out despite increasing intolerance and suppression of dissent and widespread surveillance of the population have accused the Burundian government of hijacking the highly controversial TRC process in order to rewrite history and specifically of instrumentalizing the memory of historical atrocities against the Hutu in order to consolidate power. Critics of the TRC have alleged it lacks independence from a fundamentally pro-Hutu government and has pursued selective and "unbalanced" investigations and exhumations, giving precedence to crimes against Hutu while "ignoring the Tutsi victims."[83] Alongside collecting testimonies on the 1972 violence and exhuming Hutu killed in these massacres and buried in mass graves, the TRC has organized large-scale commemorations of the 1972 massacres, broadcasting them on national radio and television. Since 2016 in particular, an openly Manichean rhetoric has resurfaced in public discourse, drawing on the memory of 1972 to justify the violent government crackdown on opposition figures and to mobilize the Hutu electorate. Having strategically labeled the opposition and other dissenting voices as Tutsi, government officials have periodically affirmed a need to protect the Hutu majority from a genocidal Tutsi minority planning to retake power; in this way, they have othered the minority and minoritized the dissident. In 2016, amid local and international concerns about the possibility of impending genocide, the CNDD vice president encouraged "war[iness] of the Tutsi who governed the country for 40 years," adding that "we must not sleep, but wake up and revenge ourselves of those years of colonization."[84] Again, the minority finds itself figured as an essentially non-Burundian, foreign, invading (colonizing) force.

While recognizing instances of crimes against humanity that victimized Tutsi and Twa, a 5,000-page progress report issued by the TRC on December 20, 2021 declared the 1972 "events" a genocide of the Hutu at the hands of the then all-powerful party UPRONA, an accusation the party "reject[ed] entirely" in a tweet.[85] Issued ahead of the fiftieth anniversary of the 1972 massacres and endorsed by Burundi's parliament, the declaration received a mixed public response. Its critics see in it a case of the political, divisive use of history in a context of "monopolized power" and monopolized suffering.[86] The report's findings have yet to make their way into formal documents of history education; given the overall political context, they may represent potential for an exclusive, ethnically based majority historiography that would play a part in undermining the proportionality and coexistence of ethnic majority and minority on which Burundi's post-conflict political system was predicated.

Discussion and Conclusion

The two case studies set out in this chapter provide insights into cycles and patterns of exclusion experienced by both minority communities and minoritized majority groups throughout Rwanda's and Burundi's parallel, interconnected histories of autocratic ethnocracies and sectarianized conflict. The chapter's comparative perspective promotes our understanding of the interplay linking particular sociopolitical contexts to configurations of power between majorities and minorities and the accompanying discourses circulating inside and outside schools.

The differences in the trajectories taken by Rwanda and Burundi, and particularly in the postwar settlements with which the two societies have attempted to move on from the violent past, both belie and highlight the underlying similarities in their responses to historical events and the discourses that carry them. The curricula and educational media of both countries evidence an essentialist approach that frames social identity, be it nationality or ethnicity, as atavistic and its trajectory as seamless. This essentialist thinking appears alongside practices that have included homogenizing, silencing, and/or othering and the creation of a posited "enemy" as typically found in narratives that divide societies into victims, perpetrators, and self-declared saviors and protectors. We observe, across the various regimes that have ruled Burundi and Rwanda since their independence and across their various power retention strategies, the cultivation and manipulation of fears of a return to past victimization, effected by invoking powerful, selective histories of injustice and thus kindling sentiments of distrust and enmity. The analysis points to divergent, yet essentially linked, models of *overtly exclusionary ethno-nationalism* and *covertly exclusionary civic nationalism*, or, in other words, overt or covert sectarianization, that is, the top-down politicization of identity in the context of competition for power. The differences identified in the analysis, in terms of the various regimes' accentuation or silencing of difference or of commonality and solidarity, thus exist within fundamentally exclusionary systems, throughout which the contested theme of majority/minority relationships runs.

The (Hutu) ethnic majoritarianism exemplified in postwar Burundi and, more blatantly, pre-genocide Rwanda has sought to legitimize itself as intrinsically democratic by the invocation of a sectarian and adversarial majority-versus-minority narrative, whose components have included populist representations of ethnic Hutu as "the people" alongside claims to indigeneity, which, in its turn, are read as conferring authenticity. The associated implication is that the minority is excluded from true nationhood; indeed, most strikingly in Rwanda, the minority appears discursively subsumed along with the country's erstwhile colonizers in a predatory alien elite aiming at dispossessing and deracinating the majority and reinstituting a tyranny of the minority. Particularly in Rwanda, this discourse was central to, and effective in, legitimizing and inciting genocidal violence.

Prewar Burundi and post-genocide Rwanda exemplify a contrasting, rarer context of (Tutsi) ethnic minoritarianism, a system characterized by a dominant minority and a minoritized numerical majority consigned to a condition of political, economic, and/or social subordination. The analysis shows these minoritarian states to be states in denial, discursively rejecting that notion of "ethnicity" that in fact permeates their ethnically stratified polity. These minoritarian regimes harnessed a discourse of civic nationalism that imposes homogeneity and regards the social order as contingent upon the suppression of ethnic identification. The inherent contradictoriness of this stance, recognized in Foucault's observations on the assertion of "the rule of homogeneity" alongside the concomitant delineation of "hierarchies, hyponomic relations,"[87] emerges in post-genocide Rwanda's peculiarly paradoxical condition of concurrent affirmation and denial of ethnic subjectivities. A further, related component of the minoritarian narrative has involved employing the discursive device of securitization, which presents a specific issue as an existential threat to society that necessitates emergency measures.[88] Faced with dissident voices, these regimes have repeatedly raised the purported existential threat of "divisionism." The case studies in this chapter evidence the operation of a coercive, yet self-undermining discourse of unity, as ostensibly inclusive, nationally based concepts of identity have failed to generate societal cohesion due to their underlying coerciveness. They might therefore constitute an object lesson in the truth of the premise that "repression increases the very tensions which it is intended to suppress,"[89] demonstrating that a unity based upon coercion, especially when accompanied by overt or covert identity-based discrimination and violence, may ultimately undermine itself and place reconciliation further out of reach.

The material analyzed for this chapter is illustrative of the role education, specifically history education, has played as one of the mechanisms that have served to legitimize and sustain these contrasting majoritarian and minoritarian regimes. More broadly, and in a manner that may point toward similar patterns in other post-conflict settings and elsewhere, the chapter evidences an uninterrupted history of schooling as a vector of institutionally mediated dogmatic and monolithic truths, or "scriptural message[s]," with politically expedient, categorical social representations standing alongside systematic silences, and students and teachers cut off from possibilities of "talking back"[90] in ways that might articulate alternative discourses. What is taught here amounts, in Foucault's terms, to "technologies of the self,"[91] with participants in education internalizing "the permitted and the forbidden."[92] This imposed curriculum remains, however, in tension with the experiential learning that takes place in students' everyday lifeworlds. The case of postindependence Burundi points impactfully to the dissonance between an institutionalized narrative of unity as a fortress for minority power and a divided, alienating, and violent reality and shows how the experiential, particularly the experience of trauma, can destabilize the discursive.

Notes

1. Marie-Claude Larouche and Pierre-Luc Fillion, "Introduction. La Classe d'Histoire et de Sciences Sociales Sous Tension: Vues Transnationales à Propos Des Rapports Minorités et Majorités," in *Tensions Dans l'Enseignement de l'Histoire Nationale et Des Sciences Sociales. Vues Québécoises et Internationales*, ed. Marie-Claude Larouche, Félix Bouvier, and Pierre-Luc Fillion (Québec: Septentrion, 2022), 20.
2. Piero Colla, Bénédicte Girault, and Sébastien Ledoux, "Introduction Générale," in *Histoires Nationales et Narrations Minoritaires. Vers de Nouveaux Paradigmes Scolaires? XXe-XXIe Siècles*, ed. Piero Colla, Bénédicte Girault, and Sébastien Ledoux (Lille: Septentrion, forthcoming, 2024), 2.
3. Stefan Berger, "De-Nationalizing History Teaching and Nationalizing It Differently! Some Reflections on How to Defuse the Negative Potential of National(Ist) History Teaching," in *History Education and the Construction of National Identities*, ed. Mario Carretero, Mikel Asensio, and María Rodriguez-Moneo (Charlotte, NC: IAP, 2012), 12.
4. Michael W. Apple, "Official Knowledge: Democratic Education in a Conservative Age" (New York: Routledge, 2000); Mario Carretero, Mikel Asensio, and María Rodriguez-Moneo, eds., *History Education and the Construction of National Identities* (Charlotte, NC: IAP, 2012).
5. Michael W. Apple and Kristen L. Buras, "The Subaltern Speak: Curriculum, Power, and Educational Struggles" (New York: Routledge, 2006).
6. Colla, Girault, and Ledoux, "Introduction Générale," 2.
7. For a detailed analysis of Rwanda's and Burundi's trajectories, see Jean-Pierre Chrétien, *Le Défi de l'Ethnisme: Rwanda et Burundi, 1990–1996* (Paris: Karthala, 1997); Jean-Pierre Chrétien and Richard Banégas, eds., *The Recurring Great Lakes Crisis: Identity, Violence and Power* (New York: Columbia University Press, 2008); René Lemarchand, *The Dynamics of Violence in Central Africa* (Philadelphia: University of Pennsylvania Press, 2008); Simon Turner, *Mirror Images: Different Paths to Building Peace and Building States in Rwanda and Burundi* (Copenhagen: Danish Institute for International Studies, 2013); Stef Vandeginste, "Governing Ethnicity after Genocide: Ethnic Amnesia in Rwanda versus Ethnic Power-Sharing in Burundi," *Journal of Eastern African Studies* 8, no. 2 (2014): 263–77.
8. Catharine Newbury, "Background to Genocide: Rwanda," *Issue: A Journal of Opinion* 23, no. 2 (1995): 13.
9. René Lemarchand, *Burundi: Ethnocide as Discourse and Practice* (Cambridge: Cambridge University Press, 1994), 15.
10. Felix Mukwiza Ndahinda, *Indigenousness in Africa: A Contested Legal Framework for Empowerment of "Marginalised" Communities* (Groningen: TMC Asser Press, 2011), 227.
11. Allan Luke, "Text and Discourse in Education: An Introduction to Critical Discourse Analysis," *Review of Research in Education* 21, no. 1 (1995): 9.
12. Michel Foucault, *The Archaeology of Knowledge* (New York: Harper & Row, 1972); Michel Foucault, *Language, Counter Memory, Practice* (Oxford: Basil Blackwell, 1977); Michel Foucault, *Discipline and Punish* (New York: Harper, 1979); Michel Foucault, *Power/Knowledge* (New York: Pantheon, 1980).
13. Stephen J. Ball, "Foucault and Education: Disciplines and Knowledge" (London: Routledge, 1990), 17–18.

14. Luke, "Text and Discourse," 35.
15. Ibid., 19, 35.
16. Mikhail Bakhtin, *The Dialogic Imagination* (Austin: University of Texas Press, 1986).
17. With the exception of Rwanda's post-genocide material, all other sampled material was written in French and translated into English by the author of this chapter.
18. Ernesto Laclau and Chantal Mouffe, *Hegemony and Socialist Strategy* (London: Verso, 1985).
19. Donald Polkinghorne, *Narrative Knowing and the Human Sciences* (New York: State University of New York Press, 1988), 54.
20. James V. Wertsch, *Vygotsky and the Social Formation of Mind* (Cambridge, MA: Harvard University Press, 1985).
21. Rogers Brubaker and Frederick Cooper, "Beyond 'Identity,'" *Theory and Society* 29, no. 1 (2000): 26–7.
22. Newbury, "Background to Genocide: Rwanda," 13.
23. Jean-Pierre Chrétien, *Rwanda: Les Médias Du Génocide* (Paris: Karthala, 1995).
24. Denise Bentrovato, "Narrative Templates and Narrative Fissures in Post-Genocide Rwanda: The Susceptible Sur-Face of a Hardwired National Historical Canon," in *Reproducing, Rethinking, Resisting National Narratives. A Sociocultural Approach to Schematic Narrative Templates in Times of Nationalism*, ed. Ignacio Brescó de Luna and Floor van Alphen (Charlotte, NC: Information Age Publishers, 2021), 8.
25. RoR/MINEPRISEC (Ministry of Primary and Secondary Education), *Histoire du Rwanda, I^e partie* (Kigali: Direction des Programmes de l'Enseignement Secondaire, 1987), 18–19.
26. Ibid., 128–9; RoR/MINEPRISEC, *Histoire du Rwanda, IIe partie* (Kigali: Direction des Programmes de l'Enseignement Secondaire, 1989), 68–76.
27. RoR/MINEPRISEC, *Histoire du Rwanda, IIe partie*, 101–2.
28. Ibid., 94.
29. Ibid., 167.
30. Ibid., 137, 154.
31. Ibid., 126–7.
32. Ibid., 161.
33. Ibid., 152.
34. Ibid., 146, 167.
35. Ibid., 152.
36. Newbury, "Background to Genocide: Rwanda," 14.
37. Luke, "Text and Discourse," 22.
38. Bentrovato, "Narrative Templates and Narrative Fissures in Post-Genocide Rwanda," 12.
39. Denise Bentrovato, *Narrating and Teaching the Nation: The Politics of Education in Pre- and Post-Genocide Rwanda* (Göttingen: V&R Unipress, 2015).
40. Vandeginste, "Governing Ethnicity after Genocide," 5–41; Filip Reyntjens, "Rwanda, Ten Years On: From Genocide to Dictatorship," *African Affairs* 103, no. 411 (2004): 177–210.
41. Republic of Rwanda/Office of the President, *The Unity of Rwandans: Before the Colonial Period and under the Colonial Rule, under the First Republic* (Kigali, 1999), 16.
42. RoR (Republic of Rwanda)/NCDC (National Curriculum Development Centre), *History Program for Ordinary Level* (Kigali, 2008), 11.

43. Emmanuel Bamusananire and Dorothy Ntege, *New Junior Secondary History. Book 2* (Kampala: Netmedia Publishers Ltd., 2011), 105.
44. RoR/NCDC, *The History of Rwanda: A Participatory Approach—Teacher's Guide for Secondary Schools* (Kigali, 2010), 51.
45. Emmanuel Bamusananire, *History of Africa for Rwanda Secondary Schools. Advanced Level* (Kampala: Fountain Publishers, 2012), 355–6; Bamusananire and Ntege, *New Junior Secondary History. Book 2*, 92.
46. NCDC, *History Program*, 41.
47. RoR/NCDC, *The History of Rwanda*, 116–17.
48. Ibid., 134.
49. Ibid., 115.
50. Bamusananire, *History of Africa*, 425; Emmanuel Bamusananire and Dorothy Ntege, *New Junior Secondary History. Book 3* (Kampala: Netmedia Publishers Ltd., n.d.), 134.
51. RoR/NCDC, *The History of Rwanda*, 141.
52. Bamusananire, *History of Africa*, 393, 413.
53. Denise Bentrovato, "Accounting for Genocide: Transitional Justice, Mass (Re)Education and the Pedagogy of Truth in Present-Day Rwanda," *Comparative Education* 53, no. 3 (2017): 404.
54. René Lemarchand, "The Politics of Memory in Post-Genocide Rwanda," Occasional Papers(Minneapolis: Center for Holocaust and Genocide Studies, 2007); Jennie Burnet, Alexander L. Hinton, and Kevin L. O'Neill, "Whose Genocide? Whose Truth? Representations of Victim and Perpetrator in Rwanda," in *Genocide: Truth, Memory, and Representation* (Durham, NC: Duke University Press, 2009), 80–110.
55. Barnabé Ndarishikanye, "La Conscience Historique Des Jeunes Burundais," *Cahiers d'Etudes Africaines* 38, no. 149 (1998): 137.
56. Lemarchand, *Burundi*, 32.
57. République du Burundi. Bureau d'Etudes des Programmes d'Enseignement Secondaire (BEPES), *Histoire du Burundi. Livre du Maitre, Classe de 7e*, 2e éd. (Bujumbura: BEPES, 1987–98).
58. Brubaker and Cooper, "Beyond 'Identity,'" 19.
59. René Lemarchand, "Le Génocide de 1972 Au Burundi: Les Silences de l'Histoire," *Cahiers d'Etudes Africaines* 167, no. 3 (2002): 551, 558–9.
60. Jean-Pierre Chrétien and Jean-François Dupaquier, *Burundi 1972. Au Bord Des Génocides* (Paris: Karthala, 2007), 145.
61. BEPES, *Histoire du Burundi*, 56.
62. Ibid., 86.
63. Ibid., 139.
64. Ibid., 29.
65. Ibid., 178.
66. Ibid., 174.
67. Ibid., 94.
68. Tony Jackson, *Equal Access to Education: A Peace Imperative for Burundi* (London: International Alert, 2000); Nicéphore Ndimurukundo, "Scolarisation Des Elites et Renforcement de La Conscience Ethnique," in *Les Crises Politiques Au Burundi et Au Rwanda: 1993–1994*, ed. André Guichaoua (Lille: Université des sciences et technologies de Lille, 1995), 125–35.
69. Lemarchand, *Burundi*, 103.
70. Marc Sommers, *Emergency Education for Children* (Cambridge: MIT, 1999), 12.
71. Chrétien and Dupaquier, *Burundi 1972*, 465.

72. Filip Reyntjens, *The Great African War: Congo and Regional Geopolitics, 1996–2006* (New York: Cambridge University Press, 2009), 171.
73. Hubert Cochet, *Burundi: La Paysannerie Dans La Tourmente. Eléments d'Analyse Sur Les Origines Du Conflit Politico-Ethnique* (Paris: Fondation Charles Leopold Mayer pour le Progrès de l'Homme, 1996), 76.
74. Brubaker and Cooper, "Beyond 'Identity,'" 26.
75. Caroline Bentley and Roger Southall, *An African Peace Process: Mandela, South Africa and Burundi* (Cape Town: HSRC Press, 2005), 75.
76. Stef Vandeginste, "Power-Sharing, Conflict and Transition in Burundi: Twenty Years of Trial and Error," *Africa Spectrum* 44, no. 3 (2009): 63–86.
77. Stef Vandeginste, "Political Representation of Minorities as Collateral Damage or Gain: The Batwa in Burundi and Rwanda," *Africa Spectrum* 49, no. 1 (2014): 7.
78. République du Burundi, *Accord d'Arusha*, art. 8, Protocol 1, chaps. 2, 23.
79. Stef Vandeginste, "Transitional Justice for Burundi: A Long and Winding Road," in *Building a Future on Peace and Justice*, ed. Kai Ambos, Judith Large, and Marieke Wierda (Berlin: Springer, 2009), 393–422; Stef Vandeginste, "Burundi's Truth and Reconciliation Commission: How to Shed Light on the Past While Standing in the Dark Shadow of Politics?" *International Journal of Transitional Justice* 6, no. 2 (2012): 355–65.
80. Denise Bentrovato, "The Everyday Ellipsis in the Edifice: The Truncation of a Unifying National Narrative Covering and Revealing Silenced Realities in History Education in Post-Independence Burundi," *International Journal of Research on History Didactics, History Education and History Culture* 42 (2021): 133.
81. Aloys Batungwanayo and Benjamin Vanderlick, *Les Lieux de Mémoire, Initiatives Commémoratives et Mémorielles Du Conflit Burundais: Souvenirs Invisibles et Permanents* (Utrecht: Impunity Watch, 2012), 14.
82. République du Burundi, *Sciences Humaines, 7e année, Manuel de l'élève* (Belin International, 2015); République du Burundi. *Sciences Humaines, 8e année, Manuel de l'élève* (Belin International, 2015); République du Burundi, *Sciences Humaines, 9e année, Manuel de l'élève* (Belin International, 2015).
83. Maya Elboudrari, "La Commission vérité et réconciliation reconnaît un génocide controversé contre les Hutu en 1972," accessed December 22, 2021, https://info rmation.tv5monde.com/afrique/burundi-la-commission-verite-et-reconciliation-reconnait-un-genocide-controverse-contre-les; Ephrem Rugiririza, "Burundi: The Commission of Divided Truths," accessed November 25, 2019, https://www.justicei nfo.net/en/43042-burundi-the-commission-of-divided-truths.html.
84. Fédération internationale des ligues des droits de l'Homme (FIDH), *BURUNDI Répression aux Dynamiques Génocidaires* (Bujumbura, 2016), 40.
85. RFI, "Burundi: la Commission vérité et réconciliation reconnaît un génocide des Hutus en 1972 et 1973," accessed December 21, 2021, https://www.rfi.fr/fr/afri que/20211220-burundi-la-commission-v%C3%A9rit%C3%A9-et-r%C3%A9conciliat ion-reconna%C3%AEt-un-g%C3%A9nocide-des-hutus-en-1972-et-1973.
86. Elboudrari, "La Commission."
87. Foucault, *Discipline and Punish*, 183.
88. Barry Buzan, Ole Wæver, and Jaap de Wilde, *Security: A New Framework for Analysis* (Boulder, CO: Lynne Rienner, 1998).
89. Andreas Wimmer, "Dominant Ethnicity and Dominant Nationhood," in *Rethinking Ethnicity: Majority Groups and Dominant Minorities*, ed. Eric Kauffman (London: Routledge, 2004), 41.

90. Bell Hooks, *Talking Back: Thinking Feminist, Thinking Black*, 2nd ed. (New York: Routledge, 2015).
91. Foucault, *Power/Knowledge*.
92. Foucault, *Discipline and Punish*, 183.

Bibliography

Sources

Bamusananire, Emmanuel. *History of Africa for Rwanda Secondary Schools. Advanced Level*. Kampala: Fountain Publishers, 2012.

Bamusananire, Emmanuel, and Dorothy Ntege. *New Junior Secondary History. Book* 2. Kampala: Netmedia Publishers Ltd., 2011.

Bamusananire, Emmanuel, and Dorothy Ntege. *New Junior Secondary History. Book* 3. Kampala: Netmedia Publishers Ltd., n.d.

Fédération internationale des ligues des droits de l'Homme (FIDH). BURUNDI Répression aux dynamiques génocidaires. Bujumbura, 2016.

RoR/MINEPRISEC (Ministry of Primary and Secondary Education). *Histoire du Rwanda, I^e partie*. Kigali: Direction des Programmes de l'Enseignement Secondaire, 1987.

RoR/MINEPRISEC. *Histoire du Rwanda, IIe partie*. Kigali: Direction des Programmes de l'Enseignement Secondaire, 1989.

RoR (Republic of Rwanda)/NCDC (National Curriculum Development Centre). *History Program for Ordinary Level*. Kigali, 2008.

RoR/NCDC. *The History of Rwanda: A Participatory Approach—Teacher's Guide for Secondary Schools*. Kigali, 2010.

Republic of Rwanda/Office of the President. *The Unity of Rwandans: Before the Colonial Period and under the Colonial Rule, under the First Republic*. Kigali, 1999.

République du Burundi. "Bureau d'Etudes des Programmes d'Enseignement Secondaire (BEPES)." *Histoire du Burundi. Livre du Maitre, Classe de 7e*, 2e éd. Bujumbura: BEPES, 1987–98.

République du Burundi. *Accord d'Arusha*. Arusha, 2000.

République du Burundi. *Sciences Humaines, 7e année, Manuel de l'élève*. Belin International, 2015a.

République du Burundi. *Sciences Humaines, 8e année, Manuel de l'élève*. Belin International, 2015b.

République du Burundi. *Sciences Humaines, 9e année, Manuel de l'élève*. Belin International, 2015c.

Research Literature

Apple, Michael W. *Official Knowledge: Democratic Education in a Conservative Age*. New York: Routledge, 2000.

Apple, Michael W., and Kristen L. Buras. *The Subaltern Speak: Curriculum, Power, and Educational Struggles*. New York: Routledge, 2006.

Bakhtin, Mikhail. *The Dialogic Imagination*. Austin: University of Texas Press, 1986.

Ball, Stephen J. *Foucault and Education: Disciplines and Knowledge*. London: Routledge, 1990.

Batungwanayo, Aloys, and Benjamin Vanderlick. *Les Lieux de Mémoire, Initiatives Commémoratives et Mémorielles Du Conflit Burundais: Souvenirs Invisibles et Permanents*. Utrecht: Impunity Watch, 2012.

Bentley, Caroline, and Roger Southall. *An African Peace Process: Mandela, South Africa and Burundi*. Cape Town: HSRC Press, 2005.

Bentrovato, Denise. *Narrating and Teaching the Nation: The Politics of Education in Pre- and Post-Genocide Rwanda*. Göttingen: V&R Unipress, 2015.

Bentrovato, Denise. "Accounting for Genocide: Transitional Justice, Mass (Re)Education and the Pedagogy of Truth in Present-Day Rwanda." *Comparative Education* 53, no. 3 (2017): 396–417.

Bentrovato, Denise. "The Everyday Ellipsis in the Edifice: The Truncation of a Unifying National Narrative Covering and Revealing Silenced Realities in History Education in Post-Independence Burundi." *International Journal of Research on History Didactics, History Education and History Culture* 42 (2021a): 3–22.

Bentrovato, Denise. "Narrative Templates and Narrative Fissures in Post-Genocide Rwanda: The Susceptible Sur-Face of a Hardwired National Historical Canon." In *Reproducing, Rethinking, Resisting National Narratives. A Sociocultural Approach to Schematic Narrative Templates in Times of Nationalism*, edited by Ignacio Brescó de Luna and Floor van Alphen, 3–22. Charlotte, NC: Information Age Publishers, 2021b.

Berger, Stefan. "De-Nationalizing History Teaching and Nationalizing It Differently! Some Reflections on How to Defuse the Negative Potential of National(Ist) History Teaching." In *History Education and the Construction of National Identities*, edited by Mario Carretero, Mikel Asensio, and María Rodriguez-Moneo, 33–47. Charlotte, NC: IAP, 2012.

Brubaker, Rogers, and Frederick Cooper. "Beyond 'Identity.'" *Theory and Society* 29, no. 1 (2000): 1–47.

Burnet, Jennie, Alexander L. Hinton, and Kevin L. O'Neill. "Whose Genocide? Whose Truth? Representations of Victim and Perpetrator in Rwanda." In *Genocide: Truth, Memory, and Representation*, 80–110. Durham, NC: Duke University Press, 2009.

Buzan, Barry, Ole Wæver, and Jaap de Wilde. *Security: A New Framework for Analysis*. Boulder, CO: Lynne Rienner, 1998.

Carretero, Mario, Mikel Asensio, and María Rodriguez-Moneo, eds. *History Education and the Construction of National Identities*. Charlotte, NC: IAP, 2012.

Chrétien, Jean-Pierre. *Rwanda: Les Médias Du Génocide*. Paris: Karthala, 1995.

Chrétien, Jean-Pierre. *Le Défi de l'Ethnisme: Rwanda et Burundi, 1990–1996*. Paris: Karthala, 1997.

Chrétien, Jean-Pierre, and Jean-François Dupaquier. *Burundi 1972. Au Bord Des Génocides*. Paris: Karthala, 2007.

Chrétien, Jean-Pierre, and Richard Banégas, eds. *The Recurring Great Lakes Crisis: Identity, Violence and Power*. New York: Columbia University Press, 2008.

Cochet, Hubert. *Burundi: La Paysannerie Dans La Tourmente. Eléments d'Analyse Sur Les Origines Du Conflit Politico-Ethnique*. Paris: Fondation Charles Leopold Mayer pour le Progrès de l'Homme, 1996.

Colla, Piero, Bénédicte Girault, and Sébastien Ledoux. "Introduction Générale." In *Histoires Nationales et Narrations Minoritaires. Vers de Nouveaux Paradigmes Scolaires? XXe-XXIe Siècles*, edited by Piero Colla, Bénédicte Girault, and Sébastien Ledoux, 2–14. Lille: Septentrion, forthcoming 2024.

Fédération internationale des ligues des droits de l'Homme (FIDH). *BURUNDI Répression aux Dynamiques Génocidaires*. Bujumbura, 2016.

Foucault, Michel. *The Archaeology of Knowledge*. New York: Harper & Row, 1972.
Foucault, Michel. *Language, Counter Memory, Practice*. Oxford: Basil Blackwell, 1977.
Foucault, Michel. *Discipline and Punish*. New York: Harper, 1979.
Foucault, Michel. *Power/Knowledge*. New York: Pantheon, 1980.
Hintjens, Helen. "Post-Genocide Identity Politics in Rwanda." *Ethnicities* 8, no. 1 (2008): 5–41.
Hooks, Bell. *Talking Back: Thinking Feminist, Thinking Black*, 2nd ed. New York: Routledge, 2015.
Jackson, Tony. *Equal Access to Education: A Peace Imperative for Burundi*. London: International Alert, 2000.
Laclau, Ernesto, and Chantal Mouffe. *Hegemony and Socialist Strategy*. London: Verso, 1985.
Larouche, Marie-Claude, and Pierre-Luc Fillion. "Introduction. La Classe d'Histoire et de Sciences Sociales Sous Tension: Vues Transnationales à Propos Des Rapports Minorités et Majorités." In *Tensions Dans l'Enseignement De l'Histoire Nationale et Des Sciences Sociales. Vues Québécoises et Internationales*, edited by Marie-Claude Larouche, Félix Bouvier, and Pierre-Luc Fillion, 11–20. Québec: Septentrion, 2022.
Lemarchand, René. *Burundi: Ethnocide as Discourse and Practice*. Cambridge: Cambridge University Press, 1994.
Lemarchand, René. "Le Génocide de 1972 Au Burundi: Les Silences de l'Histoire." *Cahiers d'Etudes Africaines* 167, no. 3 (2002): 551–67.
Lemarchand, René. "The Politics of Memory in Post-Genocide Rwanda." Occasional Papers. Minneapolis: Center for Holocaust and Genocide Studies, 2007.
Lemarchand, René. *The Dynamics of Violence in Central Africa*. Philadelphia: University of Pennsylvania Press, 2008.
Luke, Allan. "Text and Discourse in Education: An Introduction to Critical Discourse Analysis." *Review of Research in Education* 21, no. 1 (1995): 3–48.
Mukwiza Ndahinda, Felix. *Indigenousness in Africa: A Contested Legal Framework for Empowerment of "Marginalised" Communities*. Groningen: TMC Asser Press, 2011.
Ndarishikanye, Barnabé. "La Conscience Historique Des Jeunes Burundais." *Cahiers d'Etudes Africaines* 38, no. 149 (1998): 135–71.
Ndimurukundo, Nicéphore. "Scolarisation Des Elites et Renforcement de La Conscience Ethnique." In *Les Crises Politiques Au Burundi et Au Rwanda: 1993–1994*, edited by André Guichaoua, 125–35. Lille: Université des sciences et technologies de Lille, 1995.
Newbury, Catharine. "Background to Genocide: Rwanda." *Issue: A Journal of Opinion* 23, no. 2 (1995): 12–17.
Polkinghorne, Donald. *Narrative Knowing and the Human Sciences*. New York: State University of New York Press, 1988.
Reyntjens, Filip. "Rwanda, Ten Years On: From Genocide to Dictatorship." *African Affairs* 103, no. 411 (2004): 177–210.
Reyntjens, Filip. *The Great African War: Congo and Regional Geopolitics, 1996–2006*. New York: Cambridge University Press, 2009.
Sommers, Marc. *Emergency Education for Children*. Cambridge: MIT, 1999.
Turner, Simon. *Mirror Images: Different Paths to Building Peace and Building States in Rwanda and Burundi*. Copenhagen: Danish Institute for International Studies, 2013.
Vandeginste, Stef. "Power-Sharing, Conflict and Transition in Burundi: Twenty Years of Trial and Error." *Africa Spectrum* 44, no. 3 (2009a): 63–86.

Vandeginste, Stef. "Transitional Justice for Burundi: A Long and Winding Road." In *Building a Future on Peace and Justice*, edited by Kai Ambos, Judith Large, and Marieke Wierda, 393–422. Berlin: Springer, 2009b.

Vandeginste, Stef. "Burundi's Truth and Reconciliation Commission: How to Shed Light on the Past While Standing in the Dark Shadow of Politics?" *International Journal of Transitional Justice* 6, no. 2 (2012): 355–65.

Vandeginste, Stef. "Governing Ethnicity after Genocide: Ethnic Amnesia in Rwanda versus Ethnic Power-Sharing in Burundi." *Journal of Eastern African Studies* 8, no. 2 (2014a): 263–77.

Vandeginste, Stef. "Political Representation of Minorities as Collateral Damage or Gain: The Batwa in Burundi and Rwanda." *Africa Spectrum* 49, no. 1 (2014b): 3–25.

Wertsch, James V. *Vygotsky and the Social Formation of Mind*. Cambridge, MA: Harvard University Press, 1985.

Wimmer, Andreas. "Dominant Ethnicity and Dominant Nationhood." In *Rethinking Ethnicity: Majority Groups and Dominant Minorities*, edited by Eric Kauffman, 40–58. London: Routledge, 2004.

Internet Sources

Elboudrari, Maya. "La Commission vérité et réconciliation reconnaît un génocide controversé contre les Hutu en 1972." Accessed December 22, 2021. https://information.tv5monde.com/afrique/burundi-la-commission-verite-et-reconciliation-reconnait-un-genocide-controverse-contre-les.

RFI. "Burundi: la Commission vérité et réconciliation reconnaît un génocide des Hutus en 1972 et 1973." Accessed December 21, 2021. https://www.rfi.fr/fr/afrique/20211220-burundi-la-commission-v%C3%A9rit%C3%A9-et-r%C3%A9conciliation-reconna%C3%AEt-un-g%C3%A9nocide-des-hutus-en-1972-et-1973.

Rugiririza, Ephrem. "Burundi: The Commission of Divided Truths." Accessed November 25, 2019. https://www.justiceinfo.net/en/43042-burundi-the-commission-of-divided-truths.html.

Contributors

Jonas Ahlskog is Lecturer in History at Åbo Akademi University, Finland, and PI of the Kone Foundation research project "Doing Justice to Experience: Relations to the Difficult Past in History and Memory" (2022–27). His research focuses on the history of ideas and philosophy of history. In the history of ideas, Ahlskog is primarily interested in conceptions of nation, class, language, and identity in political and ideological movements during the twentieth century. His philosophical research focuses on historical knowledge and method. Ahlskog is the author of *The Primacy of Method in Historical Research* (2021).

Henrik Andersson is a reindeer herder within the Flakaberg group of the Gällivare Forest Sámi village—a reindeer herding economic and geographic association, on the Swedish side of Sámi territories. He has worked full time within reindeer herding for almost thirty years. He took the initiative to and stars in the documentary *The Last Generation?* (2016) in collaboration with filmmaker Petri Storlöpare, Slowlife Film. He also appears in the short documentary *Ungreen Windpower: Sámi Indigenous and Scientific Perspectives on Fossil Dependent and Environmentally Destructive Designs*, produced in collaboration with the Dálkke: Indigenous Climate Change Studies research group.

Denise Bentrovato is a senior researcher and extraordinary Lecturer in the Department of Humanities Education at the University of Pretoria and a research fellow in the History Department at the Catholic University of Leuven. She currently serves as the co-director of the African Association for History Education (AHE-Afrika) and the president of the International Research Association for History and Social Sciences Education (IRAHSSE). Her research combines interests in education, memory politics, and identity and citizenship formation, and focuses on (post-)colonial and (post-)conflict societies in Africa. Her most recent publications include: *Teaching African History in Schools: Experiences and Perspectives from Africa and Beyond* (with J. Wassermann (eds.)) (2021), and *Teaching to Prevent Atrocity Crimes: A Guide for Teachers in Africa* (with D. Wray and J. B. Habyarimana) (2023).

Jane Burbank is Professor Emerita, New York University. Her areas of research are Russian political culture, law, and empire. Her works include: *Intelligentsia and Revolution: Russian Views of Bolshevism, 1917–1922* (1986), *Russian Peasants Go to Court: Legal Culture in the Countryside, 1905–1917* (2004), and, with Frederick Cooper, *Empires in World History: Power and the Politics of Difference* (2010). Forthcoming, also with Frederick Cooper is *Post-Imperial Possibilities: Eurasia, Eurafrica, Afroasia*.

Mohammad Shameem Chitbahal is a sixth-year PhD student in Anglophone Studies at Bordeaux Montaigne University, a member of CLIMAS laboratory, and is presently a temporary teaching and research assistant (ATER) at Aix-Marseille University. Under the supervision of Professor Lionel Larré, his research explores the forced exile of the Chagossians in the Indian Ocean in the context of decolonization and the Cold War. His dissertation examines the role of the UK and the United States as they conquer the Chagos Archipelago for strategic purposes at the expense of the local population.

Francis Daudi is a PhD candidate at the University of Basel, Switzerland, and holds a position as an Assistant Lecturer at Archbishop Mihayo University College (a constituent college of Saint Augustine University of Tanzania). His research centers on Business History of Africa, especially how local and external forces interacted over time and shaped the structure of insurance business in East Africa. Francis is also a member of the research group *Global Cultures of Risk*, which is funded by the Swiss National Science Foundation (SNSF). His recent publication is "Diamonds, Risk, and Insurance Practices in British Africa with Emphasis on the Gold Coast and Tanganyika" (coauthored with E. S. K. Sewordor, 2023) and contributed to the joint publication: Pearson, Robin, and others. "Economic and Environmental Conditions for the Diffusion of Insurance in Three Non-Euro-American Regions during the Nineteenth and Twentieth Centuries." *Asia-Pacific Journal of Risk and Insurance* (2023).

Laura Frey is a PhD candidate at the Basel Graduate School of History. She works on the intersection of gender, race, and citizenship in the German Empire in the late nineteenth to early twentieth century. She holds a BA from the University of Leipzig, and a Joint MA from the University Leipzig and University of Vienna. Currently, she is a scholarship holder of the Gerda Henkel Foundation. Her most recent publication is a coauthored article with Prof. Dr. Robbie Aitken "'Appartenances coloniales.' Les répercussions du traité de Versailles sur le statut juridique des Allemands noirs et de leurs familles entre les deux guerres."

Yulia Gradskova is Associate Professor in History; she is research coordinator at the Center for Baltic and East European Studies and researcher at the Department of Gender Studies, Södertörn University. Her last monograph is *The Women's International Democratic Federation, The Global South and the Cold War. Defending the Rights of Women of the "Whole World"?* (2021). She is also a coeditor of *Gendering Postsocialism* (with Ildiko Asztalos Morell, 2018).

Kwangmin Kim teaches Chinese history at the University of Colorado, Boulder, and specializes in the history of borders and transnational relations in China and East Asia. He is the author of *Borderland Capitalism: Turkestan Produce, Qing Silver, and the Birth of an Eastern Market* (2016). His most recent publications include: "Xinjiang and the Peripheral Pattern of Economic Development in Qing China" in *Borders in East and West* (2022). Currently he is conducting research on rural transformation of Manchuria in the nineteenth century.

Eva Kocher is a PhD candidate at the University of Basel, Switzerland. Her research focuses on global and economic history, decolonization, and particularly the history of international risk management, insurance business, and international cooperation. She is an associated researcher with the project "Global Cultures of Risk," which is funded by the Swiss National Science Foundation (SNSF). She contributed to the recent joint publication: Pearson, Robin, and others. "Economic and Environmental Conditions for the Diffusion of Insurance in Three Non-Euro-American Regions during the Nineteenth and Twentieth Centuries." *Asia-Pacific Journal of Risk and Insurance* (2023).

Helena F. S. Lopes is Lecturer in Modern Asian History at Cardiff University. She previously held a Leverhulme Early Career Research Fellowship at the University of Bristol and lectureships at Oxford and Bristol. Her research focuses on the international, political, and social history of the Second World War and the early postwar period in China. She is the author of *Neutrality and Collaboration in South China: Macau during the Second World War* (2023) and has published articles in *The Historical Journal*, *Twentieth-Century China*, *The Journal of Imperial and Commonwealth History*, and other peer-reviewed journals and edited books.

Jonas Monié Nordin is Associate Professor in Historical Archaeology, Stockholm University. His research focus on early modern colonialism, globalization, and exploitation of human and natural resources. In 2020 he published the monograph *The Scandinavian Early Modern World: A Global Historical Archaeology*. Currently he is researching the processes of eviction and indenture of Sámi in southern and central Sweden during the seventeenth to nineteenth centuries. Jonas is a member of the Swedish Truth committee on the Sámi people that was instigated 2022.

May-Britt Öhman is Associate Professor in Environmental History, researcher at the Centre for Multidisciplinary Studies on Racism, CEMFOR, Uppsala University, Sweden. Öhman is Lule and Forest Sámi of the Lule River valley and has Tornedalian heritage. Öhman leads the research group Dálkke: Indigenous Climate Change Studies, funded by the Swedish National Research Program on Climate Change. Öhman worked extensively with the establishment and development of the research field Indigenous Climate Change Studies, centering Indigenous peoples' expertise, experiences, perspectives, and epistemologies, through publications, filmmaking, the organization of seminars and workshops, and network building.

***Jerzy Rohoziński*,** PhD**,** is a historian, anthropologist of culture, and Lecturer at the Center for Totalitarian Studies (Pilecki Institute, Warsaw). His interests focus on the social and religious history of Tsarist Russia and the USSR. He has authored the following books (all in Polish): *Saints, Flagellants and Red Khans. Developments in the Sphere of Muslim Religiosity in Soviet and Post-Soviet Azerbaijan* (2005); *Cotton, Samovars and Sarts. The Muslim Peripheries of Tsarist Russia 1795–1916* (2014); *Georgia* (series: "Beginnings of States," 2016); *The Birth of Global Jihad* (2017); and *The Most Beautiful Jewel in the Tsar's Crown. Georgia under Russian Rule 1801–1917*

(2018). His latest monograph (in Polish) is: *Pioneers in the Steppe? Kazakhstani Poles as an Element of the Soviet Modernization Project* (2021). He is also the cowriter and codirector of two documentaries: *Three Quarters to Death* (about the deportation of Poles from Soviet Belarus in 1952 to the cotton fields of southern Kazakhstan) and *Soviet Camp No. 0331* (about Polish prisoners of the NKVD filtration and control camp no. 0331 in the Georgian city of Kutaisi).

David P. Schweikard is temporary Professor of Philosophy at Europa-University Flensburg, Germany. His research focus is on political philosophy, normative ethics, social ontology, the philosophy of collective action, and nineteenth-century philosophy. He is the author of *Der Mythos des Singulären – Eine Untersuchung der Struktur kollektiven Handelns* (2011) [*The Myth of the Singular–A Study of the Structure of Collective Action*] and coeditor of *The Journal of Social Ontology*.

Andreas Weiß is an independent scholar, based in Berlin. His research focuses on the history of the European Integration with a special focus on foreign history, transnational history, and contacts between Western Europe and the non-European world. His latest publications are an edited volume, together with Simone Lässig, *The World of Children: Foreign Cultures in Nineteenth-Century German Education and Entertainment* (2019); the special issue "World Knowledge and Non-European Space: Nineteenth-Century Geography Textbooks and Children's Books," *Journal of Educational Media, Memory, and Society*, 10 (2018), 1; and the article "Auf der Suche nach dem Süden: Die Europäischen Gemeinschaften und ihr Blick nach Süden in den 1970er und 1980er Jahren," in Dinkel, Jürgen; Fiebrig, Steffen; Reichherzer, Frank (eds.), *Nord/Süd: Perspektiven auf eine globale Konstellation* (2020), 65–84.

Holger Weiss is Professor of General History at Åbo Akademi University, Finland, and ordinary member of the Finnish Society for Sciences and Letters. His research focuses on global and Atlantic history, West African environmental history, and Islamic studies with a special focus on Islam in Ghana. His latest monographs are: *A Global Radical Waterfront: The International Propaganda Committee of Transport Workers and the International of Seamen and Harbour Workers* (2021); *Zakat in Ghana: A Tool for the Empowerment of the Muslim Community* (2021); and *Moving Mountains: Muslim NGOs in Ghana* (2022).

Mats Wickström is Associate Professor in Nordic History and senior researcher in history and minority studies at Åbo Akademi University. He has published extensively on topics dealing with minorities and ethnopolitics in Finland and Sweden. Currently, he is doing research on nationalism in Finland by exploring the ethno-territoriality of the Swedish-speaking minority within the state of Finland and the responses to this by the Finnish-speaking majority.

Craig Willis is a researcher at the European Centre for Minority Issues as well as a PhD candidate at the Europa-Universität Flensburg, both in Germany. His main focus is on national and linguistic minorities in Europe, from socioeconomic and intercultural perspectives. His MA thesis, titled "Distributing Communal Wealth," focused on the normative challenges of introducing a universal basic income. Moreover, he has also published on the topic of basic income and national minorities in the *International Journal of Minority and Group Rights*. In addition to his studies, Craig has been the assistant editor of the *Journal on Ethnopolitics and Minority Issues in Europe* since 2021.

Index

Africanization/Africanizing 105–7, 110–16
African American entrepreneurs (in Ghana) 107–9
Andreen, Andrea 221
assimilation 2, 41–2, 47, 239
Association of Southeast Asian Nations (ASEAN) 173–6, 178–80

Balch, Emily S. 212
Bhabha, Homi K. 86
British Indian Ocean Territory (BIOT) 70–3, 75–6
Burmese migrants and refugees 6
Burundi 239–41, 245–50
  'events' of April 1972 246
  Histoire de Burundi 245–6
  National Council for the Defence of Democracy – Forces for the Defence of Democracy (CNDD-FDD) 240
  Truth and Reconciliation Commission (TRC) 247–8

Chagos Archipelago 68–73, 75
Chagossians 67–8, 70–6
  Chagos Refugees Group 75
  deportation 73–75
  exile 67–68, 70, 74–76
Charter of Fundamental Rights of the European Union 174
China 37–42, 46–7, 85–8, 90–5
  Da Qing huidian shili [Collected administrative statutes and precedents] 39
  The Great Qing Citizenship Law (*Daqing gouji tiaoli*) 41–2
  Qing government 37–43
citizenship 21, 38, 41–7, 85, 188, 190, 194, 205–14
  derivative citizenship 205–6, 208–10, 213–14
  marital denaturalization 206–7, 211–14

naturalization 39, 41–3, 47, 205–8, 211
Convention on Certain Questions Relating to the Conflict of Nationality Laws 206, 212
Cuba 222–5, 227–30
  Congress of American Women, January 1963 228
  Democratic Union of Cuban Women 227

Dauth, Jürgen 175
decolonizing methodologies 154, 156
  Indigenous methodologies 155
Diego Garcia 68–76
discrimination 2–3, 5, 7, 74, 86–7, 92, 108, 141, 154, 190, 193, 195–7, 239, 242, 245–6, 250
disempowerment 4
Druzhinin, N. 30

East Timor (Timor-Leste) 173, 175–81
Edelman, Fanny 222, 224–5
education systems 241
  authoritative discourses 242
  dichotomization 242–3
  discursive formations 241–2
  essentialization 242–5
  homogenization 239, 242, 244–5
  state-sanctioned textbooks 242
Efimov, V. 28
Espín, Vilma 223–5, 227–8
ethnicity 241–7, 249–50
ethnic minoritarianism 250
European Communities (ECs) 173–6, 180
  European Commission 173
  European Parliament 173, 176, 179–80
European Convention for the Protection of Human Rights and Fundamental Freedoms/ European Convention on Human Rights 3
exclusion 1–2, 4

Federation of Cuban Women (Federación de Mujer Cubana, FMC) 222, 227, 229–30
  Mujeres, 228–9
Federation of German Women's Associations 207, 212
Finland 1–2, 51–3, 55–61
  Communist Party of Finland 56
  Finnish communism/communists 56, 58, 60–1
  Socialist Workers' and Smallholders' Electoral Organization 58
  Social Democratic Party of Finland (SDP) 56–7
Finland-Swedes (Swedish-speakers in Finland) 2, 52, 54–61
  Finland-Swedish communism/communists 54, 56
  Finland-Swedish self-determination 58, 61
  Hurrare-movement 61
  Swedish People's Party (SPP) 55, 57, 61
Fourth World 3
Fourth World Theory 3
Framework Convention for the Protection of National Minorities (FCNM) 5, 188, 192

Germany 189, 205–8, 210–11
  German Weimar Republic 205
Ghana 107–11, 115–16
  Ghana State Insurance Corporation 106
  Gold Coast Insurance Company 110
  Kwame Nkrumah 107–8, 110
  Robert Turner Freeman 107–10
Goldman, Emma 207

Historians without Borders – Finland 1
Hong Kong 85–95
Hutu 239–49

Indigenous people 2–4, 52, 68, 74, 129, 133, 154–6, 188, 192
Indigenous and Tribal Peoples Convention of the ILO 3
Indochinese refugees 175–6
integration 82, 173–4, 192, 244
International Council of Women 207

International Women Suffrage Alliance 209
Isay, Ernst 210

Jasovich Pantaleon, Rosa 224, 226, 228
Johnson, Aloisia 211
Johnson, Kofi 107
jurisdictional sovereignty 38–40

Kazakhstan 141–5, 147, 149
  Catholic communities 145
  German Catholics 148
  Krasnoarmeisk 145–8
  legalization of religious life/communities 142, 148
  Leonid Ostrowski 142
  Lineevka 144–5, 147–8
  Polish Catholics 143–4, 146–8
Korea 37, 41–2, 227, 229
  Choson Kingdom 37, 41–2
  Korean settlers, *Chaoxianzu* 37–43, 45–7
  Korean tenants 41, 45–6
Kuusinen, Otto Ville 58–61
  Kansallisuuskysymyksestä Suomessa (On the National Question in Finland) 58–61

Latin America 222–30
Laya, Argelia 225–6
League of Nations 5, 206, 211–12
  Commission on Nationality 211–12
  League of Nations' Commission on Nationality 211
Lebedeva, Zinaida 227–8
Leont'ev, A. A. 22
Levene, Mark 4
Lüders, Marie Elisabeth 209–12

Macmillan, Chrystal 212
Manchuria 37–43, 45–7
  banner land 39–40
  Chinese people of the Middle Plain (*zhongyuan zhi min*) 39
  civilian land 39–40
  Korean land rights 43–6
  Korean settlers/naturalized 37, 43, 45–6
  Korean settlers/unnaturalized 42–6
  shangzu (rental right) 43, 45
  Southeast Circuit 42–4
Manuel, George 3

Married Women's Independent Nationality
    Act (Cable Act) 205–10
marginalization 2, 7, 76, 187, 189, 191–3,
    195–7, 240, 247
  marginalized communities 7, 187
Mauritius 67–75
  Afro-Mauritians 74
minorities
  age 1
  concentrated 188
  cultural 7
  dispersed 188
  elite 19–20
  entrepreneurial/trading 4
  ethnic 1–3, 37, 154, 188, 192, 195,
    249
  foreign 242
  gender 1
  illegitimate 243
  linguistic 1–2, 7, 55–6, 60, 154, 188
  micro-minority 241
  national 3, 5, 51, 54–5, 58, 60, 187–9,
    191–7, 239
  new/old 1, 6, 189
  numerical 239
  recognized 189
  religious 1–3, 5, 7, 154, 188
  sexual 1
  stateless 193
minoritization 2, 7, 206, 239
  process of legal minoritization 206
minority communities/groups;
    minoritized groups
  acculturation 239
  alienation 239, 245
  assimilation 2, 7, 21, 41–2, 47, 239, 243
  autochthonous 193
  'bordercrossers' 88
  creation 2
  definition 3
  diaspora 7, 67–8, 85, 94
  dichotomization 242–3
  discrimination 2–3, 5, 7, 74, 86–7, 92,
    108, 141, 154, 190, 193, 195–7, 239,
    242, 245–6, 250
  disempowerment 4
  dominant/hegemonic 4, 242–6, 250
  emancipation 239
  essentialization 242–5

exclusion 4, 239, 247
inclusion 239
invisibilization 239
marginalization 2, 187, 192–3, 196, 247
national homogenization processes 239,
    243, 245
otherization 2
power dynamics 239–41, 243–5, 248, 250
protection 5, 174, 247
stigmatization 4, 7
minority
  language 193
  marginalization 187, 192–3, 196
  narratives 239, 249
  nationalism 55–7, 61
  politics 7
  research 1–7
  rights 5–6, 173–4, 181
Minority SafePack Initiative (MSPI) 193
minorized majority groups 249
de Moreno, Elena 225
multiculturalism 239

national homogenization process 239
national question 51–61
  Kansallisuuskysymyksestä Suomessa (On
    the National Question in Finland) 58
  Lenin 52
  Marxism and the National Question
    53, 56, 59
  Otto Bauer 53
  Otto Ville Kuusinen 58–60
  Stalin 52–5, 57
Nyemetei, Henry 107–8

otherization 2
  conceptualization of 'otherness' 4, 239, 245

de Ponce, Margarita 223, 228
Portuguese communities 85, 87–9, 93–4
  Anatole Maher 88
  Eurasian 86–7, 95
  fluid in-betweenness 87
  Hong Kong 85–95
  'in-between' communities 83, 86
  Leonardo d'Almada e Castro 89
  Macau 85–95
  Margaret Gaan 86, 91–2
  non-elite 'bordercrossers' 88

Relief Commission for the Portuguese
  Refugees from Shanghai 88-9
Shanghai 85-95

Rehman, Javaid 5
refugees
  Cold War refugees 175
  Hong Kong refugees 90
  Indochinese 176
  Jewish in Shanghai 88
  Portuguese from Shanghai 88-9
  Timorese 177
  Vietnamese 175-6
  West Papua 179
Roma community/minority group 1, 174, 187, 189, 192-4
  Roma Decade for Inclusion 193-4
Rostovtsev, Ia. I 23
Rwanda 239-45, 249-50
  genocide 242, 245
  Histoire du Rwanda 242
  Rwandan Patriotic Front (RPF) 240, 243
  'Rwandanness' or 'Rwandicity' (*ndi umunyarwanda*) 244
Russian Empire 19-31
  Collected Laws of the Russian Empire 22
  emancipation 20, 22
  inorodtsy (people of other origin) 21
  Justices of Peace 25
  local court (*mestnyi sud*) 19, 26, 28, 30
  peasants, "udel'nye", "gornozavodskie", "gosudarstvennye"/state peasants, reformed courts 24
  reformers and legal experts 20-2, 24, 28-30
  serfdom (*krepostnoe pravo*) 21
  serfdom, abolition of; 1861 Regulation (*General Regulation on Peasants, Emerging from Enserfed Dependence*) 20, 22
  soslovie (estate status) 21
  Statutes on Punishments Applicable by the Justices of the Peace 25-7
  township court 19, 23-31
  unenserfed 22
  zemskii nachal'nik (land captain) 26

Sábme, Sápmi, Sámi people 2, 123-33, 153-7

Abraham Momma Reenstierna 127, 129-30
Arendt Grape 124, 126, 131, 133
Elin Pedersdotter 131
Elsa Laula Renberg 155
Gällivare Forest Sámi community 153, 157
Henrik Andersson 157-66
Jacob Momma Reenstierna 124, 127, 129-31, 133
Jakob Grape 124, 131
Johannes Schefferus 132
Jon Nilsson 131
Karin Stenberg 155
Lappmarksplakatet (the Lappmark law) 130
Lapponia 132
Lars Nilsson 132
Lule lappmark
Olof Larsson 131
Pite lappmark 132
Reindeer/reindeer herding 156-67
Swedish colonialism 126-6
Torne lappmark 125, 130-1
Sámi Parliament Environmental Program 155
school textbooks
  Histoire du Burundi 245-6
  Histoire du Rwanda 242
Schücking, Walter 209, 211-12
Shanghai
  Portuguese Benevolent Association (*Associação de Beneficência de Shanghai*) Committee 89
  Portuguese Residents Association 90
  Relief Commission for the Portuguese Refugees from Shanghai (*Comissão de Socorros aos Portugueses Refugiados de Shanghai*) 88-9
  'White Russians' 92
Sino-Korean borderlands
  naturalization of and tax payment by the unauthorized Korean settlers (1881) 39-40
  Yanbian/Kando (Kantō) 42-4
  Zhongyuan 39
Soviet Union 53, 55, 222, 225
  Committee of Soviet Women (CSW) 222, 225-8

stigmatization 4
Sweden 2, 123, 129, 133, 153–4
   settler colonialism 154, 156
   Swedish crown/state 125–6, 133, 155, 157, 160

Tandy Jr, Vertner 109
Tanzania 106–7, 111–16
   Ali Mtaki 112
   Amon Nsekela 113
   Julius Nyerere 111–13
   National Insurance Corporation of Tanzania (NIC) 106–7, 111–15
   Ujamaa villages 113, 115
territorialization 2, 4, 7, 68
Torne River Valley 123–30, 132
Tutsi 239–48, 250

UN Convention on the Nationality of Married Women 6
UN Declaration on the Rights of Indigenous Peoples 5
UN Declaration on the Rights of Persons Belonging to National of Ethnic, Religious and Linguistic Minorities 5
Universal Basic Income (UBI) 187, 194–7
United States 5, 67–8, 70–3, 205–13
   National League of Women Voters (NLWV) 208
   Nineteenth Amendment to the United States Constitution 208

West Papua (Irian Jaya) 177, 179–80
Wirth, Louis 2
women 3, 88–9, 144, 148, 192, 205–13, 221–30
women's rights 6
Women's International Democratic Federation (WIDF) 221–30
   congress of Latin American women in Santiago de Chile in 1959 223–4, 227
   Moscow Congress of 1963 225–6
Women's International League for Peace and Freedom (WILPF) 212
Woode, Anthony Kobina 107–8
World Council of Indigenous People 3

Yogyakarta Principles 3